PRAISE FOR GRANTLEE KIEZA'S BOOKS

'Engagingly written ... one of the most
nuanced portraits to date'
The Australian

'Vivid, detailed and well written'
Daily Telegraph

'A staggering accomplishment that can't be missed by
history buffs and story lovers alike'
Betterreading.com.au

'A free-flowing biography of a great Australian figure'
John Howard

'Clear and accessible ... well-crafted and
extensively documented'
Weekend Australian

'Kieza has added hugely to the depth of knowledge about
our greatest military general in a book that is timely'
Tim Fischer, *Courier-Mail*

'The author writes with the immediacy of a fine
documentary ... an easy, informative read, bringing
historic personalities to life'
Ballarat Courier

ALSO BY GRANTLEE KIEZA

The Kelly Hunters

Banks

Macquarie

Banjo

The Hornet (with Jeff Horn)

Boxing in Australia

Mrs Kelly: The Astonishing Life of Ned Kelly's Mother

Monash: The Soldier Who Shaped Australia

Sons of the Southern Cross

Bert Hinkler: The Most Daring Man in the World

The Retriever (with Keith Schafferius)

A Year to Remember (with Mark Waugh)

Stopping the Clock: Health and Fitness the George Daldry Way

(with George Daldry)

Fast and Furious: A Celebration of Cricket's Pace Bowlers

Mark My Words: The Mark Graham Story

(with Alan Clarkson and Brian Mossop)

Australian Boxing: The Illustrated History

Fenech: The Official Biography (with Peter Muszkat)

Award-winning journalist Grantlee Kieza OAM held senior editorial positions at *The Daily Telegraph*, *The Sunday Telegraph* and *The Courier-Mail* for many years and was awarded the Medal of the Order of Australia for his writing. He is a Walkley Award finalist and the author of nineteen acclaimed books, including the recent bestsellers *The Kelly Hunters*, *Lawson*, *Banks*, *Macquarie*, *Banjo*, *Mrs Kelly*, *Monash*, *Sons of the Southern Cross* and *Bert Hinkler*.

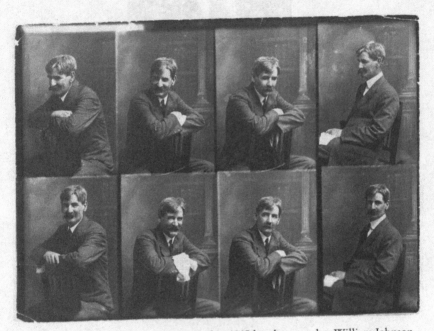

The many faces of Henry Lawson captured in 1915 by photographer William Johnson.
State Library of NSW P1/956, FL3276561

LAWSON

GRANTLEE KIEZA

ABC
BOOKS

For Arthur Stanley, a great journalist
and a great friend for more than forty years

 The ABC 'Wave' device is a trademark of the
Australian Broadcasting Corporation and is used
under licence by HarperCollins*Publishers* Australia.

HarperCollins*Publishers*
Australia • Brazil • Canada • France • Germany • Holland • India
Italy • Japan • Mexico • New Zealand • Poland • Spain • Sweden
Switzerland • United Kingdom • United States of America

HarperCollins acknowledges the Traditional Custodians
of the land upon which we live and work, and pays respect
to Elders past and present.

First published in Australia in 2021
This edition published 2022
by HarperCollins*Publishers* Australia Pty Limited
Gadigal Country
Level 13, 201 Elizabeth Street, Sydney NSW 2000
ABN 36 009 913 517
harpercollins.com.au

A catalogue record for this book is available from the National Library of Australia.

ISBN 978 0 7333 4053 6 (paperback)
ISBN 978 1 4607 1200 9 (ebook)

Cover design by HarperCollins Design Studio
Cover images: Henry Lawson courtesy NAA: A1200, L11408; *View of Arthursleigh*, 1839,
by Conrad Martens courtesy Mitchell Library, State Library of New South Wales [FL1143401]
Typeset in Bembo Std by Kelli Lonergan
Printed and bound in Australia by McPherson's Printing Group

Prologue

Henry Lawson gave us this kingdom for our own, wove it so that we could feel it around us with the comfort of a blanket on fire-warmed nights. The warmth and tenderness of his writing made it vital ...

MILES FRANKLIN, ON THE WRITER WHO INSPIRED HER BRILLIANT CAREER[1]

HE HAD BEEN TRYING TO OUTRUN his personal demons for most of his tumultuous life. Now a brief calm had come over Henry Lawson's often-manic existence, and on the evening of 1 September 1922, at a tiny, rented home in Sydney's inner west, he rested his worn-out body on a soft, welcoming bed. The writer who had defined the Australian character more than anyone before him drew his knees up to his chest to balance some writing paper so that he was half-sitting, half-lying as he began to jot down warm memories for a magazine, appropriately called *Aussie*.

Lawson was recalling a brief period of joy in his life when his mood swings were in the ascent; when he was feted as a writer whose gritty stories of the toiling masses sometimes surpassed even those of the Russians Gorky and Tolstoy with their depth and humanity.

As his pencil scratched out his recollections on the paper, Lawson had been alive for fifty-five years. He had spent most of them capturing the heart and soul of Australia and its people with more clarity and truth than any writer before him.

But hard living, a disastrous marriage, and his constant struggles with alcohol and a self-destructive personality that was most likely bipolar, had taken their toll.

Lawson's deep-brown, sensitive eyes were what people noticed first about him in his younger days; that and a finger-breaking handshake.[2] Most of the strength from his frail, wrecked body was gone now, but his warm, shining eyes remained as the mirror to Australian life.

The reflection was not always pretty. Lawson always wrote from the heart and of his own experiences. The word portraits of Australia, its people and their struggles, were often grim and harsh. He did not spare himself or his family in his tales of hardship and heartbreak either, and readily explored his own dark places, the haunting death of a baby sister, the dissolution of his parents' marriage, and the catastrophe of his own; his brother's criminality and his own agonising fall into an abyss of depression and addiction. It was a time when the bottom of a bottle and the ceiling of a prison cell replaced the vistas of the Australian bush and the waterways around Sydney which he loved.

Though future generations would judge Lawson by the racist and misogynistic climate in which he worked, he was one of the first writers to shine a light on the desperate battles fought by Australia's wives and mothers, and among the first to portray, with sympathy, the despair of Indigenous Australians at the ever-encroaching European tide. Whether it was a gaunt sun-browned bush-woman trying to save the lives of her ragged, dried-up-looking children, or the pale, frail, factory boy being torn apart by the cogs of capitalism and the cruelties of the workplace bully, Lawson had spent his life chronicling the struggles of ordinary Australians, including himself.

Clouds and scattered spring showers loomed over Sydney,[3] but there was a promise of sunshine the next day to warm the small weatherboard cottage that Lawson shared with Mrs Isabel Byers, his housekeeper and long-time companion, who despite being seventy-four still fluttered busily about him like a mother hen, fussing over his many needs and the vagaries of a prickly nature so affected by deafness and discomfort. Lawson propped himself up in his bed and let his mind carry him back through the pages of a turbulent life.

His heroic figures such as the drover's wife; and the fearless unionists in the outback striking for a better deal; and the socialists forming an Australian Labor Party to fight for workers' rights, helped shape Australia's character as did the bonds of love and mateship he created between his central characters. From his earliest days as a poor, lonely, handicapped boy with warring parents on a worthless farm, to his years as a literary lion, then as a hopeless addict cadging for drinks on the streets, and eventually as a prison inmate, locked up in a tiny cell beside murderers, Lawson wrote about life in Australia as it really was.

He became the voice of ordinary Australians as a new nation was being formed at Federation, and he documented the hopes, dreams and struggles of bush battlers and slum dwellers alike; of fiercely independent women, foreign fathers like his own, and larrikin mates.

His friend Tom Mutch,[4] who became the Minister for Education in New South Wales, said Lawson's writing had 'immortalised the people of his time and place ... and left messages of hope and inspiration, richly coloured with the warm glow of passionate love for his native land and faith in its people'.[5]

Lying there in his bed, Lawson cast his mind back to the faces in the street that had stirred his writing, and then to the days when he was king; when he arrived in London as Australia's literary star to launch his career on the world stage.

Lawson was courted by Britain's leading publishers, but his stay ended in calamity, pre-empting a broken marriage and a slide into depression and addiction from which he never truly recovered.

Two decades later as he summoned his thoughts for his *Aussie* article about a curious Cockney in London with a big nose, Lawson had little more in assets to show for his fame except two suits, an overcoat, a tie, a collar-stud, a pipe, a tin matchbox, a walking stick, a pencil, a pair of glasses and two packets of tobacco.[6]

He had his memories, though, and while plagued by a persistent headache, he continued to jot down his recollections for his article.

Lawson had soaked up all the harshness and beauty, all the madness and mayhem of Australian life and infused them into his poetry and prose.

He had been drawn to write by the extraordinary characters surrounding him since his birth into a family of eccentric bush battlers, of drinkers and storytellers, during the 'roaring days' on a teeming goldfield.

Even the stories of his birth were wild …

Chapter 1

And they heard the tent-poles clatter,
And the fly in twain was torn
'Tis the soiled rag of a tatter
Of the tent where I was born.

HENRY LAWSON, FROM HIS POEM 'THE WANDER-LIGHT'[1]

IT WAS A DARK AND STORMY night. At least that's how Henry Lawson's family remembered his birth in the cold winter of the Australian bush, on a rain-drenched goldfield 370 kilometres west of Sydney. According to the Lawson family's dramatic tale, the celebrated writer entered this world as a small, thin, sickly baby in the mining settlement of Grenfell, during a tempest so violent that the nurse rushing to help with the delivery had to be carried over three kilometres of floodwaters.[2] They claimed that a drunken doctor had to be shocked from his stupor at gunpoint into saving the lives of mother and child. Louisa Lawson, then a feisty, headstrong nineteen year old, said she waited anxiously for the birth of her first baby in a flimsy tent near a local cemetery, where hungry miners were tunnelling under coffins searching for their passport out of poverty.[3] She recalled that in the early hours of 17 June 1867 she feared the screaming rain and wind would tear apart the fabric of her humble marital home.

Louisa was a force of nature in her own right, an imposing, stern-faced brunette, whose resolve to rise above rural poverty and assert herself in a male-dominated society would eventually

5

make her a feminist icon. She and her family came to see nature's malevolence that night in Grenfell as a howling portent of the turmoil Lawson would face all his life, an ominous warning about the unforgiving journey that this self-styled 'bush bred mongrel'[4] would make toting his sackful of sadness.

European civilisation was quickly making inroads into the traditional lands of the Wiradjuri people around the mining camps. Though Grenfell now had five churches and a new hospital costing £300,[5] it was still a frontier settlement, a cauldron of hard-drinking prospectors from around the world, in their rough wooden huts and cloth tents, with snarling, savage dogs tied close by to protect their tools and meagre possessions.

The nearby Weddin Mountains had been the hideout for bushranger Ben Hall before his recent demise in a hail of bullets, and the town had just been named in honour of gold commissioner John Grenfell,[6] who had been gunned down refusing to surrender to masked bandits.

By the time of Henry Lawson's birth, the quartz reefs surrounding Grenfell had made it the richest goldfield in New South Wales, producing more than a tonne[7] of the precious metal annually.

Not that Louisa Lawson[8] or her new Norwegian-born husband, Niels,[9] ever saw any of those riches.

Henry Lawson had Nordic ancestry on both sides of his family, once grandiosely calling himself 'a "beery *Bulletin* scribbler" with the blood of Danish kings',[10] but his maternal ancestors arrived in New South Wales as bounty migrants from England. Lawson would remember the English branch of his family as 'a queer tribe, tall and dark and mostly eccentric'. They had been hop pickers in Kent, he said, though they could just as easily have been 'chicken lifters … and the Lord knows what else besides'.[11] He thought they had Romani blood too, but that was most likely only because his great-grandfather John Albury[12] called his tiny dark-eyed wife his little 'gypsy'. John Albury, the son of a farrier, was a shepherd and agricultural labourer from the village of East Farleigh, south of the River Medway, near the town of

John Albury, Lawson's great-grandfather, who
brought his family from Kent to New South
Wales in 1838. State Library of NSW FL9245505

Maidstone. Much of the surrounding land around the fourteenth-
century East Farleigh Bridge was given over to raising sheep and
growing hops but village labourers in the south of England faced
economic calamity in the 1830s.

Parish officials throughout England's south were encouraging
poor families to accept a helping hand from the New South Wales
governor Richard Bourke, whose bounty migrant scheme offered
a new start on the far side of the world.

So it was that in May 1838, after having been evicted from his
land,[13] 43-year-old Albury, his pregnant wife Ann and their eight
offspring[14] left Portsmouth bound for Sydney aboard the emigrant
ship *Woodbridge*,[15] a vessel that the *Sydney Gazette* declared was
'well adapted for conveyance of settler', as unlike so many of the
overcrowded transport vessels carrying human cargo at the time

'her between decks ... [were] more than seven feet and very spacious'.[16] The four-month voyage via the Cape of Good Hope was considered a great success for the *Woodbridge's* commander William Dobson and naval surgeon Alexander Stewart, as 260 'Government Emigrants',[17] mostly agricultural labourers and their families and a few single women, who knew about cleaning houses and milking cows,[18] passed the Macquarie Lighthouse at the southern end of Sydney Heads on 15 September. The voyage resulted in a surprisingly low death toll of only eight children.[19] The Albury family arrived safe and sound in Sydney, a city now fifty years old and which was becoming an ornate colonial outpost, with a spectacular harbour and impressive brick and stone buildings being financed through wool exports.

An immigration official noted that the Alburys were Protestants, that the parents could both read, and their behaviour on the voyage had caused no complaints. Both were marked 'very good' for their 'state of bodily health, strength' and probable usefulness for the colony.[20] The family was taken to the immigrant buildings on Bent Street[21] and offered up as a small workforce for landowners.

The landscape of Australia and the local farming methods were nothing like the Alburys had known in Kent. The sky above New South Wales seemed to stretch forever and Sydney was far hotter and drier than East Farleigh. On the outskirts of the city, they beheld the strangest of creatures – the bounding kangaroos, giant flightless emus, deadly snakes and huge lizards.

John and the now heavily pregnant Ann gathered their children and headed across the Cumberland Plain to toil in the outlying district of Liverpool, thirty kilometres south-west of the harbour.

Much of New South Wales was being given over to huge open sheep runs comprising thousands of hectares and throughout 1838 there was a series of massacres against the first peoples[22] that made horrific reading in the colony's fledgling newspapers.[23]

Ann gave birth to her fifth son, Robert, at Liverpool on 6 December 1838,[24] followed by a fifth daughter and tenth child, Sarah, three years later, though she died in a fire aged six[25] when the family was living at Luddenham. The Alburys buried Sarah's scorched little body at the new St Thomas' Anglican church at Mulgoa, on land that the prominent Cox family had donated.[26]

John Albury leased a farm from the Cox family nearby but he and Ann eventually moved hundreds of kilometres north to Oxley Island in the Manning River district. Ann is said to have worked hard all her life, and when she felt herself going to die aged sixty-six, she climbed out of bed and washed herself, dressed in clean clothes, lay down again, and folded her hands on her breast, 'so as not to give trouble'.[27] The Alburys' older daughters found local husbands around Mulgoa and the boys worked on farms along the Nepean River and South Creek, and as timber-cutters in the foothills of the Blue Mountains.

The second-oldest son, Henry,[28] who was thirteen when the family had arrived in Sydney, found work on the 700-hectare property named 'Clydesdale' on the Richmond Road.[29] It was the grand home of former Warwickshire convict Charles Tompson,[30] a remarkable self-starter who had been transported for stealing two books. Tompson built a two-storey mansion as well as accommodation for his workers.[31] He also promoted the study of literature and his son Charles Jr,[32] the eldest of nine children, was just twenty when he penned what is regarded as the first book of verse by an Australian-born writer to be published in his own country.[33]

In 1845, when Henry Albury was nineteen and a strapping giant with a mane of thick black hair, he married Harriet Winn,[34] one of the servants at George Cox's Mulgoa property, Winbourne.[35] Harriet was a shy, genteel Norfolk girl, newly arrived in the colony following the recent death of both parents,[36] and Henry remarked that she was more like a 'mouse-maid' than a housemaid.[37] Lawson later wrote that his grandfather resembled 'a young god then', and that his grandmother had married Albury pretty much for his looks.[38] The young couple took their vows in St Thomas' Church at Mulgoa. Harriet signed her name on the register and Harry made his mark with an 'X'. They set up home near the area called Saint Marys. Sticking by her husband's side through thick and thin, Harriet would endure more than forty

Henry Albury, Lawson's grandfather and inspiration for some of his best work. State Library of NSW FL9245506

years of what Lawson would call 'a rougher bush life than you could imagine'.[39]

Nine months after the wedding, Henry and Harriet welcomed their first of twelve children, Emma.[40] The family then moved to Bolwarra, a property on the Hunter River near Newcastle, before heading west to a slab hut[41] on the wealthy Rouse family's grazing property, Guntawang, near the township of Gulgong outside Mudgee. The property had once been operated by the Cox family but they were driven out by frequent skirmishes with the Wiradjuri. Henry worked as a shepherd and timber-cutter among the ewes and eucalypts. He was 'six-foot-two in his stockings',[42] a broad-shouldered 'big, strong, dark, handsome man' with olive skin and a Roman profile. His wavy black hair, worn long, was often soaked with sweat.[43] Raised on the stories of England's oppression of the poor, Albury was a free spirit, said what he liked and be damned, and thumbed his nose at authority. He was said to have once risked his own life to save another from drowning in a river but he could be vexatious and quarrelsome as well, and was no stranger to the courtroom as both plaintiff and defendant, at different times charged with a string of offences from unpaid rent to disorderly conduct.[44]

He hid his illiteracy, but he was a loud man with a booming voice who could not conceal his fondness for cheap booze. Though not an alcoholic, he was known to smash all the crockery in the Alburys' sparsely furnished hut when sloshed, and bring home instead 'a string of pint-pots and a pile of tin plates and dump them on the table'.[45] Sometimes he would disappear for days and reappear with two or three of someone else's fowls hidden in his shirt.[46]

Harriet put up with her husband's mischief and while she ached for a life of more refinement, which she had known in England, she was the rock of the family 'in spite of the buffetings of the rough bush life among bark huts, diggers' shanties and bullock drivers' depots'.[47]

It was at Guntawang in 1848 that their second daughter, Louisa Albury, was born.[48] The young family made their home in the middle portion of a split-slab and bark-roofed humpy, a long structure divided into three portions with ex-convicts and their wives at either end.[49] It was always a source of amusement to Henry and Harriet how the bachelors among the pardoned convicts – the ticket-of-leave men – would travel to the Female Factory prison at Parramatta, where women convicts would be paraded before them so they might choose a bride and how a 'man might pick a blessing or an encumbrance; it was simply a matter of luck'.[50]

According to the family's stories, Louisa was a 'lusty infant; she learnt to crawl early, preferred the company of men, and soon established herself as a prime favourite with the bullock drivers', who taught her salty language as soon as she could speak.[51]

A few days before Louisa's third birthday, a burly young Hampshireman, Edward Hargraves, found five specks of gold[52] in a stream between the towns of Bathurst and Orange, at a place he named Ophir, after a region of vast wealth mentioned in the Bible. Soon a Bathurst newspaper declared that a 'complete mental madness' appeared to have seized almost every member of the community with people 'of all trades, callings and pursuits' throwing in their lot to chase their fortune[53] as miners.

News of gold discoveries lured thousands of immigrants to Australia every week, propelled by spectacular reports about the sudden wealth of men once dirt-poor and now filthy rich, filling public troughs with champagne,[54] putting gold shoes on their horses and using £10 notes to light their cigars.

BY THE MID-1850s IT WAS COMMON for sailors arriving in Melbourne to jump ship and rush for the diggings at Ballarat and Bendigo. Sometimes even whole crews and their captains abandoned their vessels.[55] Into this climate of upheaval, the 225-ton Chilean brig *Pedro V,* under the command of skipper Costa Sabina, arrived in Melbourne's Hobsons Bay from the Chilean port of Valparaíso via Tahiti five days before Christmas 1855.[56] The ship carried no passengers, only a small crew and a cargo of flour and bran. On board was Niels Hertzberg Larsen, a short, nuggety[57] 23-year-old Norwegian quartermaster hoping to turn his luck around. He was a quiet, kind and gentle man with blue eyes, reddish-brown hair and the beginnings of a short dark-red beard.[58]

Henry Lawson came to believe that Niels had 'deserted his ship at Melbourne on a voyage from New York or Frisco'[59] though there's no proof that he jumped ship, nor for the claim that all Niels's brothers had been lost at sea.[60] Most likely he signed off with another crew member and friend, the nineteen-year-old German John Slee,[61] after the cargo had been unloaded.

Niels was said to have been a very natty or 'dapper' little fellow in his single days, and a wonderful dancer,[62] but there was little time to celebrate a new life in Australia. Together with Slee, he headed down the hard road of the digger.

Lawson would recall Niels as a soft and quiet man, 'well educated in his own language, could understand and appreciate German poetry, knew French well enough to understand a Frenchman, was a good penman, and wrote good English'.[63]

Niels spoke in a broken English, though, that was never repaired and even though there were 2500 other Scandinavians[64] on the goldfields, his speech often made him feel like an outsider.

One of Niels Larsen's grandfathers was Lars Jensen,[65] a tenant farmer from Fladen, Østre Moland. Lars married when he was a still frisky fifty-five and was sixty-three when he fathered his second son, Peder Larsen,[66] who would become Henry Lawson's grandfather. Peder went to the bishop's teachers' college at Kristiansand and was then appointed to the post of *degn*, or assistant to the priest, at the quaint church at Flademoen on the island of Tromøy, near Arendal, a picturesque port known as the 'Venice of the North'.

The role became vacant after the death of the previous *degn*, Sigvard Diurhuus,[67] another of Lawson's great-grandfathers; a 'good and reasonable man, but very *addicted*' to drink.[68] Sigvard had been the private secretary to a bishop but was banished to the rural outpost of Tromøy with his new wife, Christiane Hertzberg,[69] and their daughter Sophie who was born just two months after the wedding. Christiane was described by the Tromøy curate as 'extremely sober' but 'a capricious female' who found fault in many things, especially her husband who had humiliated her. Her grand-uncle Niels Hertzberg had been a member of the 1814 Norwegian parliament, and her family were forebears of the arctic explorer Fridtjof Nansen. Peder Larsen not only took Sigvard's job and his modest house, but after bestowing a pension on Christiane, he married the couple's eighteen-year-old daughter Martha Margrethe,[70] within a year of moving to Tromøy.

Peder and his new wife started a large family and he kept the church records, led parishioners in singing, and taught the local children scripture. It was said 'he loved women almost as much as he loved alcohol',[71] and he built a lasting reputation as a wit and storyteller. When a school inspector came to visit once, Peder passed the examination splendidly, though the school official noted that Peder sought answers only from children he knew would answer correctly.[72]

Peder also had a reputation for physical courage that grew from his heroics during the *Kanonbåtkrigen*, the 'Gunboat War' between the small, fast gunboats of the Danish and Norwegian forces and the much bigger warships of the British Navy during the Napoleonic Wars. The British had bombarded Copenhagen in 1807 and seized the Danish fleet but four years later Peder did his bit to save a Norwegian schooner that a British frigate was chasing along the coast near Tromøy. The schooner became beached at Spornes, about a kilometre from Peder's church. When a boat put out from the British frigate to board the schooner, Peder marshalled a phantom army on shore, gathering as many of the local women as he could, placing them behind boulders and telling them to hold sticks above the rocks so that from a distance they would look like a forest of muskets. He then ran from one boulder to the next, firing his own musket to create the illusion that the coastline was heavily fortified. The British raiding party withdrew and King Charles XIII of Norway made Peder a member of the Order of Dannebrog for his bravery.[73]

Living by the sea encouraged Peder's offspring to follow maritime careers and his first four sons[74] all became masters of navigation. Two of their sisters[75] also married masters of navigation.

Peder's last child, his fifth son, was born on 12 September 1832 in the church house at Flademoen. He was baptised eleven days later as Niels Hertzberg Larsen. Niels began his education under his father but when the boy was just six, Peder's three decades as *degn* ended ignobly when he was sacked because of his drinking.

Niels and his brother Eilert, three years his senior, finished their schooling under Peder's successor until they were fourteen and Niels took third place in his confirmation class of twenty. Niels then followed his brothers into a career on the sea, learning everything about all manner of vessels by working in wood on their construction at a local shipyard. His passport gave Niels's standing as 'master of navigation'.[76]

Family tradition has it that Niels had a sweetheart at the time,[77] but he had only just begun his career as a ship's junior officer when he returned from a voyage to find that his brother Eilert had stolen her. Broken-hearted, Niels saw Tromøy and his people for the last time on February 1854 as he sailed for Quebec and then New York on the bark *Henriette,* under the command of a cousin.[78] Soon he would be on the cargo ship *Pedro V* in Chile on his way to the Victorian goldfields.

WHILE NIELS LARSEN FOUND GOLD and then lost it 'speculating in puddling-machines, crushing mills and "duffers"',[79] Henry Albury toiled as a farm labourer and timber-cutter, carving out a life for his growing family. In 1854 he bought a half-acre (2000-square-metre) block in Lewis Street, Mudgee, for £26 5s and built a cottage on it. Three years later he paid £86 at an auction of Crown lands for an adjoining block of the same size,[80] expanding the home for his wife and their five girls – Emma, Louisa, Phoebe,[81] Elizabeth[82] and Peace.[83] While he safely established his large, young family of girls in the township, he pitched his camp and built a yard for his bullock team anywhere in the gullies of the adjacent ranges where he could find decent timber.

Louisa was a bright and serious girl and the favourite pupil[84] of the headmaster at the District Model National School in Mudgee, J.W. Allpass,[85] who encouraged her love for literature and loaned her books. She would say that her days at the Mudgee school were the happiest of her whole life, though her father told her he 'never had no eddication, [and] didn't see what his children wanted with it'.[86] Allpass suggested making Louisa a pupil-teacher but Harriet Albury wouldn't tolerate such foolery. Harriet had just buried her daughter Elizabeth, delivered two more girls, Annie and Susannah,[87] and was about to give birth to her first son, Joe.[88] Louisa had so much work to do at home helping her mother, and she resented the missed opportunity at school, writing that there was absolutely no employment except housework for young women in those days 'and the last thing likely for me was domestic service [as] I was neither strong enough or humble enough for either'.[89] Her shattered ambitions made her the 'odd one' of the family who came to view her as 'eccentric' and 'antagonistic always'.[90]

She was fourteen when her family moved a few kilometres north along the Mudgee-to-Maitland bullock track to a selection of sixteen hectares on the Black Spring Flat in the shadow of the 700-metre Lowes Peak. Henry cut down box and stringybark trees and once even worked his bullock team through the night to build a causeway[91] during a heavy flood so that the Mudgee races could take place. Time among the cracking whips and straining teams of huge, grunting beasts – sometimes twenty of them tethered together – was not the intellectual life Louisa imagined for herself.

She was raised as a strict Methodist, but shocked her mother and 'scandalised the congregation' in Mudgee by walking out of church while the Reverend J.G. Turner was preaching what she recalled as 'the beauties of eternal damnation'.[92] She refused to apologise or to return to church, and only her father's intercession prevented Harriet from turning their volatile daughter out of the family nest. Louisa yearned for her father's affection even though at times his aloofness made her feel that he did not care for her. He sometimes threatened to thrash her for insolence, but never once raised a hand.[93] Louisa took after him, tall and broad-shouldered with dark eyes and an assertive manner. Often she spent weeks with him in the mountains timber-getting and amused him by imitating the speech of the Irish and German settlers.[94]

Family legend has it that some of the miners, impressed by her singing of hymns, wanted to take up a collection to send Louisa to England for formal training but Harriet would have none of that either. Instead, Louisa sought comfort from the natural world, marvelling at the red sunsets above her home, riding up Lowes Peak 'to watch the awful storms that so often visited the locality' or riding through the bush alone in teeming rain, all the while singing new songs she had memorised.

'I loved the vivid forked lightning more than anything else,' she recalled, 'and was always sorry when my journey was done.'[95]

In a deep ravine, she found a natural altar on a bank of moss and maidenhair and would rest there in silence, her hands clasped around her knees, meditating. She found a water-worn crystal the size of an egg and clear as glass, and would contemplate it as she listened to the wind whipping through a deep, narrow gully, straining her ears in vain to catch any whispered messages. Sometimes, deep in the bush, she would recite poetry for hours, and write her own verses about beauty and pain. One day, as she fancied her spirit joining that of the trees and the stones, a large black snake slithered close to her shrine. She called the snake 'Judas' because she suspected it was pretending to sleep in order to deceive her. It was a fascinating creature, beautiful in a sinister way. Louisa killed it and set it on fire.

IN FEBRUARY 1863, not long after the arrival of the Alburys in their new bush home, George and John Wurth, the sons of a German vintner, were riding through the area after driving a mob of fat cattle from Tonderburine Station in the Warrumbungle Ranges to the slaughterhouses in Sydney. They stopped on the return journey at the home of their father Frederick Wurth on Pipeclay Creek, about ten kilometres west of the Albury shack. The Wurths went out stripping bark for their old man and during a break to smoke their pipes, they amused themselves by throwing their knives into the dirt. Specks of yellow appeared in the upturned clay.

The brothers hoped to keep their find quiet until they could stake a formal claim[96] but Henry Albury was cutting timber in the adjacent hills and came across fresh dray tracks leading to their camp. The discovery was a secret no more.

Within two weeks 300 miners were carving up Golden Gully and the adjacent Sapling Gully. A week later there were even more diggers. Two general stores and a butcher's shop were established.[97] There were no big nuggets – the biggest being ten to twelve ounces[98] – but men were making good money from their alluvial finds and by making shallow sinks into the quartz under the topsoil.

Henry Albury saw the gold rush in his backyard as his road to riches. He never sank a shaft in his life[99] but he knew every tree worth cutting within miles and for a year he supplied miners and shopkeepers with wood. In February 1864 he sold the home in Mudgee for £130, and bought the goodwill of a grog shanty sitting in Sapling Gully, eight kilometres away. He left his wife and eldest daughters in charge of the makeshift pub – and to nurse two more daughters[100] – while he cut timber. Louisa became 'wretchedly unhappy in the rough surroundings of a bark shanty on the diggings, and the crude company that congregated there'.[101] She could not bear the lewd singalongs nor the fact her father received a conviction for 'causing idle and disorderly persons to frequent a gaming house'.[102]

NIELS LARSEN AND JOHN SLEE had left the Victorian diggings in the hopes of more success on the goldfields at Lambing Flat, outside what is now the New South Wales town of Young. By 1865 they had moved to the New Pipeclay diggings, near the Alburys. Niels built a hut at Wilbetree[103] near his gold claim, the only home on the diggings with a built-in fireplace. Louisa told a story of a 'big, blustering bully who started playing up in Albury's bar' and of a little Norwegian, to whom she had appealed for assistance, stepping in as the hero,[104] and how she later gave him a dish of water to wash the blood from his knuckles.[105]

Louisa thought that Niels was keen on her older sister Emma, when he took her completely by surprise. Louisa was sitting on the end of a low log near her father's house one evening looking at the stars when Niels came up, wanting to return a book he had borrowed from Emma. He told Louisa that he was sorry her mother was not kinder to her, and that everyone on the diggings felt her unhappiness and frustration.

'After a moment's silence,' Louisa continued, 'he asked me, if in the event of him having a home to take me to, say in three months, would I marry him, and I, at eighteen, who was the last one to be a judge of such matters, said yes.'[106]

Perhaps the stern and detached Louisa reminded Niels of his own mother back on Tromøy, and the way she had soldiered on stoically despite Peder's drinking. One of Louisa's nephews would later write that Niels was smitten with her and 'worshipped the ground she walked on'.[107]

Niels was almost twice Louisa's age and a straight talker, neat and sober. She hated sentimentality or romance and called it 'bosh'.[108]

She said that she married Niels 'to relieve father of at least one of the large family'.[109] Louisa's mother was angry at what she called a 'dissolution' of the Albury family partnership but Henry gave his consent to the union and the couple were married at the Wesleyan church in Mudgee on 7 July 1866.[110] Niels used the name Peter Larsen for the marriage register. He was nearly thirty-four and gave his father's occupation as farmer and schoolmaster.[111] Niels believed that he had struck it rich with Louisa and within six weeks he dug up £200 worth of gold. But he soon realised the 'mistake of the marriage'.[112] Louisa had developed a merciless tongue and he was often its victim.

Pipeclay Creek gave up most of its gold, and before long John Slee moved on to Grenfell, hoping to replicate the luck of Cornelius O'Brien,[113] a shepherd there who had sparked the colony's latest gold rush a few months earlier when he uncovered a quartz reef on a hilly outpost of the Brundah sheep run.[114]

Slee wrote to Niels, suggesting that he and his new bride pack up their dray for the 300-kilometre journey across rough, unmade roads and bush tracks to join him. Louisa's sister Emma decided to go too, but not before marrying a German miner named Johann Christian Frederick Rotenberg at Mudgee's Wesleyan church. The witnesses were Henry Albury and Peter Larsen.[115]

At Grenfell, Niels and Slee worked a claim on the One Mile Lead called 'The Result' with two partners, John Lawrence and Charles Jansen, as a thousand or so holes appeared along the quartz reef. 'The Result' produced slim pickings but Niels earned extra money by carting water for the diggers. Louisa, pregnant with her first child, made the most of life in their tent pitched nearby. Henry Albury sent his twelve-year-old daughter Gertrude, 'a neat sewer who made all her own clothes', to Grenfell for six months 'to do the housekeeping and attend to the baby during her sister's illness'.[116]

Gertrude remembered her sister's tent as 'far and away, the best house on Grenfell' with the cloth walls built up high and stretched over a slab frame. The calico roof[117] was protected from the weather by a break of boughs.[118]

Niels doted on his wife and in his heavily accented English always referred to her as 'my Louisa'.[119] He told her he would do anything to make her happy, even change his surname to make it sound less 'foreign'.

Two days before Louisa gave birth, Grenfell's fledging weekly newspaper ran with the story that sixty-five horses had been entered for that year's Melbourne Cup,[120] and that within 'the short space of half a year', 'a wild and unfrequented part of the bush' had been transformed into a thriving town and district'.[121] There was a twice-weekly coach service to Forbes, two pharmacists and three doctors, one of whom offered daily vaccinations for children.[122] Slee was on the committee for a new 'substantial' hospital complete with iron bed-stands from Sydney.[123]

IN THE LATE NINETEENTH CENTURY the Scottish romantic poet Robert Burns[124] had become a cult figure in the Australian colonies and it seems the Lawsons were influenced by the gripping tales of his birth in Ayrshire – during a storm in which the wind and sleet howled so hard that a cottage wall crumbled, leaving mother and child exposed to the savage weather. So it was that Lawson's family related that 'winds, rain and bitter cold' heralded their own bard into a 'troublesome world'.[125]

A large goanna was said to have watched the birth as well.

Over time Louisa's memories merged with fantasy so that in her later recollections she claimed to be the only woman on the Grenfell goldfields 'among 7000 men' at the time of Henry Lawson's birth. Mastitis – or 'milk fever' as the family called it – had made her 'too delirious to mother the new-born poet'.[126] The family's epic concoction around the birth included diggers supposedly finding a broken-down, drunk doctor, 'Woe Whiley', in a distant cave, pressing him into service at revolver-point and forcing him to ride through the mud and rain under 'a tearful moon' to Louisa's tent, where he applied two 'bull–pups' to the young mother's breasts to break the fever and keep 'a light burning that someday would flush out the blue flame of genius'.[127]

But the reality is that the Grenfell newspaper reported no storms or floods in the district until three months after Lawson's birth.[128] Also, John Slee was unlikely to see the wife of his best mate stuck in a tent and hovering close to death when he was on the local hospital committee and when Grenfell had three highly regarded doctors. The fact that Louisa was able to travel to Forbes to register the birth a month later,[129] giving the name of the nurse 'Mrs Dean' as the only other person present at the birth, suggests that the dangerous fever was an invention.

Louisa's sister Emma remembered that the birth actually took place while drunks in the local lock-up could be heard yahooing and that when she saw little Henry just an hour after the birth, he was a 'poor thin wee baby' no one expected to live.[130]

Chapter 2

*His view of life as he found it was based on the experiences of his
boyhood ... And, if there may be regret that he did not always paint
his pictures in bright colours, it is because he did not make
green grass grow on cold stones.*

T.D. MUTCH, LAWSON'S FRIEND AND NSW
MINISTER FOR EDUCATION[1]

NIELS HERTZBERG LARSEN became 'Peter Archibald
Lawson' on a draft registration in Grenfell marking the
birth of his son Henry Archibald Lawson.[2] Louisa had always
had a fond regard for the unrelated pioneering Lawson family
of Mudgee so 'Larsen' to 'Lawson' was an easy Anglicised fit,
though Henry Lawson never forgot his Norse heritage. Louisa
never forgot her husband's origins either, and while 'Lawson' was
used for all official documents, the names of her children were
recorded in the family Bible always as 'Larsen'.[3]

Henry would later claim that at his baptism a deaf clergyman
mistook the intended middle name 'Hertzberg' for Archibald.
When Lawson told the story, he added the rider 'you see bad luck
came to me early and was stuck close by me ever since'.[4]

In his lifetime Lawson learnt little of his father's background,
though, mistakenly imagining that he had 'descended from a
race of poets and pirates under the frozen stars' and believing his
grandfather's name was Lars instead of Peder.[5]

Most of the thousands prospecting at Grenfell did so in a sea of disappointment.[6] Extracting the precious metal from quartz reefs required heavy machinery and was far more expensive and labour intensive than collecting alluvial gold close to the surface or panning for it in streams.

Niels extracted little of value from the Grenfell rock, but inside his tent he had a national treasure whose life would be coloured by a rough start, writing later that he had been born on a 'Grenfell goldfield, and you can't get over that'.[7]

Baby Lawson spent just six months or so[8] in Grenfell before his parents decided to pack everything back on the dray and return to Louisa's family at Sapling Gully, where Niels knew that he could find timber-cutting and building work with his father-in-law, after whom the new child was named. Lawson's father and grandfather got on famously. They were only seven years apart in age, but Lawson never met two characters more opposite in every way: Niels the teetotaller, Henry Albury anything but.

John Slee stayed in Grenfell and married,[9] became a mine manager and before long the first Inspector of Mines for New South Wales.[10]

Henry Albury and his family were still living in their shanty, but it was falling into disrepair after the New Pipeclay gold rush had come and quickly gone. Albury staked a claim on a two-acre (8000-square-metre) block surrounding the building with an eye to purchasing,[11] in an effort to thwart a neighbour[12] who was looking to take the land for himself, including the falling-down shanty that was still valued at £40.

Back from Grenfell, the Lawsons pitched their tent about 100 metres[13] from the shanty, and the tent became Henry Lawson's home for the next three years. From infancy he had a talent for observation, and from the depths of his earliest memories he had 'a dreamy recollection' of the tent as a hut but 'some of my people said it was a tent, on a good frame … There was a tree in front … a blue-gum I think, and I know it had a forked trunk.'[14]

Lawson had a childish dread that the tree would fall on the tent, and when he looked up at the white clouds flying above him, they seemed to make the top of the tree move. He used to also see the impression of a big goanna's toes on the calico ceiling when it crept along overhead and from then on, he always had a horror of reptiles, fuelled no doubt by stories that one had haunted the tent he was born in. As an infant he took screaming fits and would lie down and roll out of the tent and across the flat until he fell asleep exhausted.[15]

He remembered the surrounding bush as 'a stoney barren ridge, two little gullies full of digger holes caving in, a little brown flat, a few tumble down haunted huts, an old farm or two on the outskirts, blue grey scrub, scotch thistles, prickly pears, Bathurst-burrs, rank weeds, goats, and utter dreariness and desolation. But the hills were still blue in the distance.'[16]

The Lawsons were not back from Grenfell long when they welcomed a brother for Henry, Charles William Lawson,[17] who like his older sibling would also have a troubled journey through life. Louisa's mother acted as midwife but young Henry was no help, suggesting his parents throw 'the baby down a diggers hole, or [drown] him, like a surplus kitten'.[18] The tent became too small to hold the family, and Niels moved their home 100 metres north-west, fenced two acres and built a two-roomed slab-and-bark hut 'on the flat on the other side of the gully', which was the other side of young Henry Lawson's whole world as it was then. Niels sunk a well and Henry Albury came over with a dray load of stringybark slabs and poles for a kitchen. Niels valued the whole property at £30 and formally applied to purchase the land on 24 February 1870.[19] Lawson had memories, or imagined memories coloured by time, of happy days living in Sapling Gully; of being covered head to toe with jam after raiding a pot, of his grandfather's bullock teams and sawpit. He remembered that Louisa taught him to sing a song about her sister Phoebe, and said that if he sang it well Aunty Phoebe would come to visit, and sure enough every time he sang it Phoebe would arrive, rush into the hut and kiss him and baby Charlie. 'We thought it very wonderful,' Lawson wrote.[20]

Niels put a pine floor in the room where they ate and on the mantlepiece there were two china dogs, a sentry and a little model church with a double tower. The Lawsons had a sofa with a covering of 'Holland' linen, though Henry and Charles weren't allowed to climb onto it.

Lawson often visited his 'Granny' Harriet Albury at the old shanty, where she introduced Henry to the delights of coffee and he 'was extremely fond of her until the day she died'. He remembered, too, being butted and upended by her billy goat, which left a scar on his head.[21]

That incident was a minor upheaval, though, compared to the commotion that occurred in Lawson's world not long before his third birthday, when Tom Saunders, a shepherd working for Richard Rouse, found gold on 14 April 1870 at Gulgong's Red Hill, twenty kilometres north of the Lawson hut. The ensuing stampede became known as the 'last of the small man's gold rushes', because large amounts of gold were close enough to the surface to be mined with hand tools, rather than heavy crushing machinery.[22]

Further major finds were made at nearby Canadian Lead and Home Rule. Together with shafts at the Caledonian and Black Leads, Happy Valley and others, the area around Gulgong was soon supporting a population of 20,000 and within four years had yielded eight tonnes of gold. The British novelist Anthony Trollope visited Gulgong during the rush, staying in an inn made from slabs, and said the town was a 'rough place' that looked more like a travelling 'fair' with every home and shop appearing to have been erected within a few days.[23] For weeks Niels watched in frustration as prospectors tramped past his front door until he finally could no longer bear the itching in his feet.

In late 1871, when Lawson was four, Niels decided to try his luck as a miner again.

Moving from the tent to the hut in Sapling Gully had been 'a tremendous thing', Lawson said, '[but] we didn't seem to live in the new house anytime before a more tremendous thing happened. We were in a cart with bedding and a goat and a cat in a basket and fowls in a box, and there were great trees all along, and teams with loads of bark and rafters, and tables upside down with bedding and things between the legs, and buckets and pots hanging round, and gold cradles, gold dishes, [windlasses] and picks and shovels; and there were more drays and carts and children and women and goats – some tied behind the carts; and men on horses and men walking. All the world was shifting as fast as ever it could.'[24]

He had a vague memory of being stowed among the bedding for the journey and he remembered the bullock teams, the horse drays, spring carts … 'horsemen, footmen and a circus!' all travelling along 'bad roads, or rather rough tracks, through stringy-bark bush', all heading for Gulgong, a 'hot, dry, barren, hopeless little pastoral town, with patches of gravel and funnel-shaped holes where the shafts were'.[25]

Already Lawson was being inspired by the characters around him in his bush home, among them an old convict named Joe Swallow, who lived in a stone hut on the track from Pipeclay to Happy Valley. Lawson created a dashing persona:

Old Joe Swallow, in the days gone by,
When his form was as straight as a lance –
He'd bring bright sparkles to each bush girl's eye
When he came to the gay bush dance.[26]

In reality, Joe Swallow was close to seventy when young Lawson met him; a tiny, hazel-eyed, red-whiskered Yorkshireman just over 150 centimetres tall. Joe was 'nearly bald'[27] save for a few wisps of brown hair and he had a pock-pitted ruddy face, a scar in the middle of his forehead,[28] scars on his nose and left cheekbone as well as a tattooed image of his dead wife and both their initials on his lower left arm. He had been transported to Van Diemen's Land in 1823 for theft and returned to England a free man six years later only to then receive a fourteen-year sentence in 1832 for shop-breaking. He arrived in Sydney on the *Parmelia* and was put to work for settler David Smith in the Illawarra region as a 'knife cutler',[29] finally joining the charge to Golden Gully three decades later in 1866. Lawson family lore was that little Henry wrote verses for the old man and showed them to him for appraisal and correction[30] but in truth Lawson was just five when Joe was found dead in his hut. Henry Albury, whose many jobs included bush undertaker, is said to have buried him. Albury's timber and building business had also been killed by the rush of miners away from Pipeclay to Gulgong, and Lawson's grandfather left the district for a new base near the railway line at Wallerawang, about 130 kilometres to the south-west. For a time, he ran the National Hotel on Mudgee Road at nearby Lidsdale.[31]

At Gulgong, Louisa Lawson and two of her sisters opened a dressmaking shop as Niels went off to stake his claim at Happy Valley, which despite the optimistic name was regarded by his son as a dismal 'hole of a gully'.[32]

Niels was always working, 'or going somewhere with an axe or a pick and shovel on his shoulder, and coming home late' and every evening Lawson was 'watching for the glint of his white [moleskins] in the dusk, and sometimes following him out again after tea, when it was moonlight, and he went a little way with the axe on his shoulder to split firewood from a log'.[33] Niels had not been turning the earth at Happy Valley for long when he

Lawson's mother Louisa (left), his younger brother Charlie, and Lawson's aunt Phoebe Albury, outside Phoebe's dressmaking shop in Gulgong in 1872. State Library of NSW, FL1235155

found a little gold and was able to send Louisa and his two boys on a trip to Sydney with some of Louisa's sisters.

The horse-coach south stopped at Mudgee where the travellers found Henry Albury, singing his heart out in a pub. Albury had a bullock team with him and it was always thirsty work, but at forty-six he had become a father for the twelfth time and a dozen children was a good enough reason as any to celebrate.[34] Lawson remembered the 'jolly' adventure of the coach ride as they called in to see 'Granny' at Wallerawang. The two boys fell asleep on chairs in the waiting room at the railway station there, and when the little freckled Henry Lawson woke from his deep sleep across the Blue Mountains someone said it was Sydney. There was a lot of smoke from the locomotive and it was raining.[35]

They stayed with 'a Mrs Kelly' in Castlereagh Street and picnicked at Manly Beach. Mrs Kelly had a swing in her backyard, and one day Lawson was swinging high and told Mrs Kelly's little girl that he was going to swing right up to heaven, and she said he was a very wicked little boy to say such a thing. Lawson had a new suit of velveteen knickerbockers and remembered spilling something on it. One day when his mother was away, he and Charlie went out in the street and the door shut behind them; they became frightened and lost, and knocked and hammered at the wrong door, and they went into the wrong house. Some older girls lived there and they took him and Charlie in their arms and kissed them and gave them cake, and one of them took the boys home. Mrs Kelly was very angry and said the boys had gone into 'a bad house' but Lawson, full of cake and fondness for the girls, didn't think that it was so bad. Mrs Kelly's boy taught Lawson the first rhyme he could remember:

Ally-looyer!
I hardly knew yer![36]

It was a line Lawson kept repeating when they went home to Gulgong where Niels celebrated their return by killing a pig.

Niels worked his claim in Happy Valley, and again on the Canadian Lead, with diminishing results. Sometimes Louisa would take Lawson for a drive around the goldfields in a cart, along with one or two of the other diggers' wives. They would stop at a claim where one of the husbands worked and watch him emerge from a hole in the ground 'all covered with yellow mullock'.[37]

Aunt Phoebe was living at Gulgong too, and Lawson amused himself for hours talking to her parrot or watching her work her sewing machine. At the age of six, Lawson fell in love with an elderly married lady who kept a lolly shop next door to Aunt Phoebe's.

> Her husband was away and she seemed lonly. She was fourty or fifty and had [moles] and a moustarsh. I remember I went into her shop one day to buy lollies, she was busy sewing and she was worried, and she said 'Oh Bother!' and it hurt me so much that I cried ... She seemed greatly affected and comforted me, and gave me a lot of lollies – and she wouldn't take the penny ... I kept big things like that locked up tight in my heart ... I was a very sensitive child.[38]

Such hypersensitivity would not bode well for a happy life, though Lawson's ability for observation, and to tap his heart for deep emotion, coloured his finest writing. The growing friction between Lawson's quiet, hard-working father 'whose strong limbs never rested' and his ambitious, often cold, mother 'whose deep mind was never still', made his hypersensitivity worse.[39]

In a world surrounded by hard-toiling men of the land, Lawson's feminine side manifested itself in a fondness for wooden dolls and later in a weakness for cats, which clung to him all his life. His aunts told Louisa he should have been a girl.[40] Sometimes the circus would come to town and 'one night, in a place they called a theatre' Lawson heard a 'most beautiful woman sing'. There was another pretty woman, living in a hut near his, who used to sing 'Love amongst the Rowses (sic)'. She had a black eye. Lawson wanted to fight her husband but decided that perhaps she loved the man who hit her.[41]

BY JULY 1873 MOST of the alluvial gold from the new diggings had been extracted and from his bed, with straining ears, Lawson listened through the cracks in the slabs to his parents talking around their little wooden table.

'They said that Gulgong was done,' Lawson recalled, 'and, one day Mother and Father packed up all the things. Next morning we were waked early; there was a dray at the door and we heard a great scraping overhead. Suddenly we saw the sky and, next moment were nearly blinded by a shower of pungent stringy-bark dust. Father was taking off the roof of the hut – for we carried the house with us in those days.'[42]

They returned to Sapling Gully to find the people who had occupied their hut were refusing to move because there was a dispute over whether the Lawsons actually owned the land or whether it was on a proclaimed goldfield. The Lawsons stayed with the neighbouring Spencer family until the dispute was settled. After Louisa wrote to the Minister for Lands on behalf of her husband, a shy man whose English was not only broken but somehow getting worse, they were finally officially granted the two acres around their hut for £6 under the Free Selection Act of 1861. In August 1873, Niels and Louisa applied for an adjoining forty acres and Niels set about filling in twenty-four abandoned mine shafts, between seven and fourteen metres deep. The family would eventually acquire another 200 acres, mostly because it was poor quality land; heavy sticky clay with lumps of quartz and no permanent water. Nobody else wanted it.

Louisa gave birth to her third son, Peter, on 18 September 1873.[43] She told Lawson she used the £2 10s he had in a money box to buy the baby from a Chinese hawker who came around the settlements carting drapery slung on a pole across his shoulders. The neighbouring Spencer children told Lawson that they hadn't been bought from Chinese hawkers at all, but that their parents had instead found them inside wombat holes. Lawson was dubious about this.

On his holiday to Sydney, he had heard that babies were made on Pinchgut Island in the harbour, but a Chinese hawker had

Lawson's father, Norwegian sailor Niels Larsen, who changed his name to Peter Lawson and became an Australian bush carpenter. State Library of NSW FL9245512

indeed called at the Lawson hut on the morning his new baby brother arrived, so as far as six-year-old Lawson was concerned, that settled the mystery of where babies came from. He didn't think that his new brother was worth so much money though.

The Lawson selection lay round 'a little, rocky, stoney, scrubby, useless ridge',[44] eight kilometres from Mudgee, facing the Home Rule and Gulgong Roads. Jimmy Howlett and Billy Grimshaw, who became characters in Lawson's writing, used to camp near the Lawson hut in bad weather or to spell their bullocks. Lawson would watch the bullocks pulling huge wagon-loads of wool bales packed high, rolling along the rough road like ships in a gale; or bogged with two or three teams of bullocks yoked to one load and trying in vain to move. 'It was cruel for the bullocks,' he wrote. 'I've seen them go down on their knees and bellow under the blows from the heavy handles of the bullock whips.'[45] When Jimmy or his mates were in trouble with their teams the Lawson boys would be called in and shut up out of hearing.

Great flocks of sheep went by the house too.

Once Jimmy Howlett ground up some charcoal and mixed it with axle grease and rubbed it on Charlie Lawson's little face; he rubbed it well into his chin and cheeks with an extra layer under his nose and assured him that it was the very best whisker seed, the only genuine article, and told him to be careful not to rub it off till the whiskers sprouted. Charlie was a sight, but he screamed and wriggled and wouldn't be washed, and had to be put to bed with the whisker seed still on.[46]

LAWSON NEVER KNEW WHETHER his father took up the selection because he had a liking for farming and believed in the chances of success, or because the ground was on an old goldfield and he was a digger at heart. Niels was always putting down a shaft whenever he had spare time. Now in his early forties, he was clever at anything where tools were concerned and he had always had a fancy for a vegetable garden and a few fruit trees, but the land was about the poorest around Pipeclay. The gullies were full of waste heaps of clay from the diggers' holes and in addition to clearing the scrub Lawson had to help his father in what seemed a never-ending task of trying to reclaim land for ploughing by filling up the diggers' holes. There had been a bullock camp on the level part of the Lawson property and several acres were so hard that Niels had to use blasting powder to break up the land for the plough.

The cattle were a 'few weedy stunted cows one of them barren – and, some steers, and [they] were always straying'. A cow, and sometimes a horse, would be cropping the grass round the edge of a mineshaft, and sometimes in wet weather the shaft would fall in. 'Then the cry of "cow in a hole" (it was "man in a hole" once or twice) and we'd run in all directions and scare up the male population of Pipeclay; and, provided the beast hadn't fallen head first and broken its neck or smothered, they'd rig a windlass and get it out.'

Often at daybreak, Louisa would cry 'Get up quick, the cows

are getting away' and one of the Lawson boys, usually Henry, would have to run barefoot across the hard baked sods, or the frosty flats in winter. Lawson remembered how on bitter cold frosty mornings, he would have to rouse a camping cow and then squat with his 'bare perishing feet' on the warm spot where she'd been lying to stay warm.[47]

Lawson saw farming there as hopeless, but Niels, 'domestic, methodical and practical', stuck to it between building contracts. He used to walk 'from five to seven miles to work, at first, work twelve hours and walk home again'. He'd insult anyone who offered him the loan of a riding horse and Lawson never knew a man so 'obstinately independent'.

Niels planted grapevines behind the house, and in front a rose bush and a slip of an ivy plant that the Alburys had brought from England. Louisa talked of naming the farm 'Arundel' (sic) after 'Fathers berthplace in Norway'.

The Lawson hut sat on a road that followed north along the eastern boundary of a land grant of 2000 acres (800 hectares) issued to Robert Lowe in 1825. It had been enclosed by a log fence, and the Wilbetree property of the Lowes was locally called the 'Log Paddock'.

After the small but rich leads in Golden and Sapling Gullies had been worked out, prospecting continued in Log Paddock and gold was found there in Snakes Creek and Newton's paddock about four kilometres north of the Lawsons' slab-and-bark hut. All the traffic from Mudgee to the new diggings passed the Lawsons' front door.

With baby Peter to nurse and two small sons, and with Niels often away working, Louisa began operating a general store from their little home. But the idea backfired, as the shop drew miners to the property who would not otherwise have paid it any attention. Before long all the miners who could not claim ground in Log Paddock started exploring the Lawson selection for possibilities.

Niels and his oldest son had been breaking their backs filling in old mineshafts, but now the invaders started sinking new ones and cutting down the Lawson timber.

Louisa wrote a despairing letter on her husband's behalf to the Lands Department. She wrote again, five days later, and enclosed 2 shillings in stamps for a telegraphic reply. It never came.[48]

One of the miners decided that a frontage to the road was a prime site for a pub, and he cut a deal with Niels, who allowed him to build a bark shanty, but as soon as it was complete the man double-crossed Niels and convinced other miners that the Lawsons had no right to their forty-acre selection, as Niels had not fulfilled an essential condition by residing upon it. This was true, as Niels lived with his family in the slab-and-bark hut on the original two-acre purchase adjoining.

The miners sent a petition to Sydney to have the selection forfeited and described the stressed Niels as 'P. H. [Peter Hertzberg] Lawson – a German'!

Niels fought back by building a hut for himself on the forty acres, and he lived in it, while Louisa and the three boys remained in the house on the other side of the fence, a few metres away.

Then the original shanty-keeper sold out to a new tenant, who would not pay Niels any rent. It took twelve months and a court case, plus an 'inquiry', to resolve the dispute. Niels and Louisa eventually triumphed, but the expensive and traumatic incident was ended by Niels having to buy the bark shanty that had been built on his land.[49]

IT WAS AT THE LAWSON STORE on 24 October 1874 that a meeting was held to draw up a petition for the opening of a local post office. Among the nineteen locals present were names that would feature in Lawson stories – men such as Henry Spencer, Frederick Buchholtz, Thomas Middleton, Joe Southwick JP and John Tierney. The petition recommended that Niels be appointed the first postmaster and he started in the role on New Year's Day 1875 on a salary of £11 a year.

Louisa did most of the work until eight months later, when Niels was forced to resign due to what Louisa wrote, for him, as 'the illness of my wife'. The Lawsons proposed John's brother, Dan Tierney, as his replacement. When the postmaster at Budgee Budgee pointed out the confusion caused by letters being addressed to Pipeclay instead of New Pipeclay, Tierney suggested that New Pipeclay be called by its Aboriginal name 'Eurunderee'.[50] The Lawsons rented their hut to Tierney to use as his home and post office, and moved for a time into the abandoned shanty Niels had just acquired.

They now turned their attention to the education of their eldest son.

Until the beginning of 1875, Lawson had been schooled at home. Louisa found a copy of *Robinson Crusoe* and read it to the children in the evenings.[51] If she stopped at a thrilling place, the children would take the book later and try to spell out the words to discover what happened next. The local youngsters also taught each other about the mysteries of the world; the ghost of Old Joe Swallow in his stone hut at the foot of Sapling Gully, the Chinaman's grave in Golden Gully and the Hairy Man in Long Gully. The children wouldn't go through any of these places after dark; instead, they would go out on the flat in the moonlight and sit in a circle and talk about 'these spookes [sic]' until they frightened each other. Then one would start to run home and the rest would follow screaming.[52]

Long hours of hard work, milking cows in mud and slush or heat and dust, riding with the mail, helping his father clear and plough that cold, hard ground, and minding the young baby, abbreviated Lawson's boyhood and made him feel he was growing up too fast.

Lawson slept in a cot beside his parents' bed and told his father that as he approached the age of seven, he was scared of growing old. He would hold his father's rough workman's hand whenever he grew afraid and his father would talk quietly to him until he fell asleep.

There was a public school about five kilometres away through Sapling Gully, at Pipeclay Creek, but the track between the gap in the hills was lined with unprotected mineshafts, and it was too dangerous to allow the children to go there. It could be fatal for teachers, too. Frederick White, the schoolmaster at Pipeclay Creek, was going home from Log Paddock one weekend when he fell fifteen metres down a shaft in Spencer's paddock and died with a broken neck. His body wasn't found for a fortnight.[53]

The rush at Log Paddock brought many families with children to the district. Most lived where the best gold finds had been made about four kilometres from the Lawsons. A few years earlier some of the local selectors, headed by Joe Southwick, had built a slab-and-bark schoolhouse on a bullock track there near the junction of Snakes and Woonambula Creeks. On Sundays they held a church service and on weekdays a school.

Lawson's first day of formal schooling came there when he was seven at Wilbetree's Woonambula Creek school, which he later used as a setting for his short story 'Shall We Gather at the River?'[54] The school had been furnished with a rough table and a wooden chair for the teacher, and with a few rickety desks and stools cadged from an old school in Mudgee when a new public school was built there. The desks and stools had been fastened to the floor to strengthen them but Lawson recalled they had been made for 'infant' classes, and 'youth out our way ran to length'.[55]

It cost sixpence a week for each child to attend class, and Henry and Charlie Lawson were enrolled in the local school system on 25 January 1875.[56] Lawson's denomination was given as 'Wesleyan' and his father was listed as an innkeeper. Their teacher was 35-year-old Englishman Henry George Hanks,[57] who had failed to find his fortune as a miner but was now endeavouring 'to become useful to society'[58] by wrangling the wild local children. He had been in the colony for ten years and as a sweetener for the position, was allowed to camp at the schoolhouse.

For the first time in his life, Lawson was given a copy book and pen and ink and there was also 'great spitting and hard rubbing on slates'. He told Hanks 'that my name was Henery Lawson, and they say he spelled it that way ...'[59]

Lawson complained that while Hanks talked about 'improving our moral minds', he taught the children about injustice – by example.

At the Southwick farm across the road, there was a hedge of roses – 'a most uncommon thing – round a [lucerne] paddock on the bank of the creek,' Lawson wrote. 'One day, in lunch hour, some of us went to the farm and asked permission to pick some roses and were told to take as many as we liked. We came late back to school each child with a big bunch of the flowers. Hanks was waiting for us, and, as we came up, he took the roses, bunch by bunch, tore them to pieces and scattered them on the ground.' He marshalled the children inside.

'Stand up! You are guilty – of the crime of stealing,' he thundered, 'stealing flowers from a neighbour.' Then in a meek voice, little Bertha Lambert said, 'Pleas[e] Sir, Mrs Southwick said we could take them.'

'Serve out slates,' Hanks mumbled, and he turned to the blackboard.[60]

There was another incident which left a painful impression on Lawson's mind. His family had a quince tree and the children were strictly forbidden to touch the fruit, which was not ripe at the time. One day Charlie pulled a quince, and like Eve with Adam in the Garden of Eden, tempted Lawson to have a bite.

But the theft was detected, and Charlie blurted out in terror that his brother had taken a bite too. Lawson reckoned that Charlie had only persuaded him to try the fruit for fear he might tell on him – or that he wanted him to share the punishment in case of detection. Bursting 'with indignation, and a perverted sense of injustice', Lawson denied that he had touched the quince. Charlie stuck to his story but Lawson was believed because he had always been truthful. Charlie begged his big brother to confess and save him, but instead the younger boy was severely thrashed.

'I don't know what devil possessed me,' Lawson later wrote, 'save that I was horrified that I had told such a lie and in terror lest it should be found out and I be branded as a liar – but I stuck to the lie and he to the truth and he got a second dose and was sent supperless to bed. It was a miserable night and a miserable week for me. I don't think a boy was ever so conscious stricken or a little soul so self-tortured.'[61]

Charlie forgave his brother the next morning but, racked with guilt, Lawson finally told the truth to his parents months later. He went unpunished but for years beat himself up over his cowardice and deceit.

Louisa began making requests for a school to be established nearer the Lawson home. With her calling the shots behind the scenes, Niels officially organised a meeting that produced an application for the establishment of the Eurunderee school dated 29 December 1875. John Tierney,[62] a tall, gaunt, 33-year-old Irishman 'six feet something'[63] from Tipperary was their choice as teacher. Tierney had no previous experience as a schoolmaster but Niels and local men George Wurth and John Müller vouched for him as 'a person of good moral character and believing him to be competent to perform the required duties'.[64]

Parents at Pipeclay Creek protested that the status of their school would be diminished while parents at Woonambula Creek wanted the new school built there, but Louisa was hard to toss in a fight and the district school inspector Gerald O'Byrne selected land for resumption that was once owned by Joe Swallow beside Golden Gully, on a spot near where the Wurth brothers had found gold.

At Sapling Gully, Niels now built his family a sawn timber home with a galvanised iron roof and brick chimney, which was the envy of their neighbours, who had only slab-and-clay chimneys. It became the archetype of the bush home for much of Lawson's writing. Lawson recalled, though, that his father, using timber from their old home, built the new Eurunderee schoolhouse in the 'humpy style of architecture – sapling framework covered with stringybark – and standing on a rather steep siding where the earth had been dug away to give the building a chance of holding on'.[65] There was only one room, about twenty-four by sixteen feet (eight metres by five), with a little skillion below the surface at the back where John Tierney could live. He was a bachelor then but would soon marry local girl Elizabeth Rheinberger, the daughter of German immigrants. The school was called a 'provisional school' and Lawson associated 'provision' with 'tucker' because Dan Tierney's wife used to send one of the children every evening with John's dinner.[66]

The Eurunderee Provisional School opened on 2 October 1876 with twenty-seven boys and eighteen girls enrolled, their ages ranging from four to fourteen and including nine-year-old Henry Lawson and seven-year-old Charlie, who were both admitted to the second class.

The school was furnished with 'odds and ends thrown out of the public school in Mudgee when the public school got new desks stools and things'. Niels made blackboards and easels and mended the rickety furniture. The books and slates were all second-hand and old.[67]

Tierney claimed to have been a pupil-teacher in Ireland at age twelve and said he had joined the Irish Fusiliers at sixteen to fight in the Zulu Wars. He was invalided out of the army with malaria in Bombay. His brother Dan had taken their mother to Australia and Tierney decided to follow, with a recommendation from his commanding officer to a brother, John O'Shannessy, then Premier of Victoria. John joined the rush to Pipeclay Creek in 1863 after his brother wrote to him from there. He was said to have dug up £800 worth of gold to finance a general store but became a schoolmaster after the shop failed because he gave too much credit to the local battlers.[68]

'His strong points,' Lawson wrote, were 'penmanship, arithmetic, geography and the brogue; His weak ones were spelling, grammar and singing.' Tierney spent a month training in the public school in Mudgee and once, in a lesson to Lawson and his other pupils on the vastness of the universe, tied a string to the neck of a stone ink bottle and swung it round, to illustrate the power of gravitation and the course of the earth around the sun. The string broke and the bottle went through a window panel.

Lawson was smitten with a pretty classmate named Lucy but she used to go home in a different direction. His other sweetheart was Mary Buchholtz, a tomboy, but one day they quarrelled and she said she wouldn't be his sweetheart anymore and she became Fred Spencer's girl instead. Fred was a dashing, adventurous lad, the 'Tom Sawyer' of the locale. Mary's sister Bertha began to look kindly on Lawson, but going into the fourth class at school, he'd had enough of women for a while.[69]

Lawson had what he called 'the average healthy boy's aversion to school' which developed into dread, yet Tierney called him 'a model pupil'. He was sensitive, conscientious and was never punished. He was often made uneasy by the sight of a large black goanna, which on summer days would 'lay along a beam over the girls' seats, and improve his mind a little, and doze a lot. The drone of the school seemed good for his nerves.'[70]

Each week Lawson attended Sunday school where the children sang Church of England hymns and were served refreshments afterwards. Lawson maintained that while he was no coward, he wouldn't fight under any provocation, because he thought it was wrong. Charlie, though, on the slightest excuse, wanted to fight everyone.

Once Tierney gave Lawson a note to take home to say that Charlie had played truant. Charlie begged his brother to throw the note away, but Lawson did as he was told. 'I suffered a great deal more than he did,' he recalled. Lawson later turned his conflict into a moving sketch.[71]

Not that Lawson was always so obedient. Sometimes he and the other children would ignore their parents' dire warnings and go swimming in treacherous waterholes, full of snags, being careful to smear their faces and necks with dirt and dust after their adventure lest their cleanliness betray them.

BUILDING THE SCHOOLROOM was not Niels's best work and Tierney was always telling the children that, being constructed of old material and standing on an exposed siding, it might be blown down at any moment. He trained the children to dive under the desks at a given signal to escape falling beams and rafters. 'Most of us,' Lawson explained, 'privately resolved to dive for the door at the first crack.'

Any noise, though, even the crack of a snapping beam, was becoming increasingly difficult for Lawson to hear. As a child his hearing was so keen that he could hear his parents arguing when they thought he was well out of earshot, but shortly after he started at the old bark school, Lawson experienced a nightmare that was 'to cloud' his whole life and 'drive me into myself, and to be, perhaps, in a great measure responsible for my writing'.[72]

He was nine, and already beset by sensitivity, self-doubt and loneliness.

'I remember we children were playing in the dust one evening and all that night I had an excruciating ear-ache and was unspeakably sick on my stomach. Father kept giving me butter and sugar, "to bring it up" which it eventually did. It was the first and last time I had the ear-ache. Next day I was [noticeably] deaf.'[73]

Chapter 3

Looking back from those, the dark days of my life, to my boyhood and childhood, I can find many things that were bright and happy and good, and kind and beautiful and heroic – and sad and beautiful, too.

HENRY LAWSON ON GROWING UP IN THE AUSTRALIAN BUSH[1]

AFTER GIVING BIRTH TO THREE BOYS across the space of almost a decade, Louisa's prayers for a daughter were answered, not once but twice, when twin girls, Annette[2] and Gertrude,[3] were born in Mudgee on 30 April 1877.

Annette, or 'Nettie' as the family called her, 'was the first and last creamy skinned blue-eyed baby'[4] in the Lawson family. Her name was most likely an abbreviation of 'Henriette', the name of the ship that carried Niels from Norway more than a quarter of a century before, and the last point of contact with his homeland and people. Both girls were a source of great joy to their parents, and a source of wonder to nine-year-old Henry.

Annette stayed only a little while, though. When the baby fell ill with a complaint that her family called 'English cholera' eight months later, Louisa took her to Mudgee for treatment, but Nettie died on 20 January 1878 in the room where she was born. Louisa went outside and sat on a log in the yard – sat very still, staring up at the stars. At the time Niels was walking as fast as he could along the lonely eight kilometres of road from home, rushing to see his daughter's beautiful face, but he arrived too late. The death of the baby Henry Lawson called his 'fair-haired, blue-eyed Norwegian sister of mine, buried over there under the darkening Mudgee Hills',[5] hammered another nail into the coffin of the Lawson marriage, too.

Early in the morning after the funeral, Niels took his wood-splitting maul and wedges and his cross-cut saw and went up into the ridges above Sapling Gully to split rails. Lawson heard 'the song of the saw' until dusk. Niels was trying to work the grief out of himself. After tea he 'walked to and fro, to and fro in the starlight',[6] with his arms folded and his head down, occasionally looking up at the stars. Lawson would always be affected by his sister's death and his father's sadness.

There was never much joy at home, and Nettie's death made Louisa even more sombre.

She enforced a strict, almost Puritanical, moral code. Cards were regarded as the Devil's playthings, and horse racing and gambling were unpardonable offences. Following Nettie's death, Louisa turned her back on the Methodists and explored spiritualism, whose followers believed that the living could communicate with the dead. About this time the spiritualist journal *Harbinger of Light*[7] claimed there were 240 adherents of the movement in Gulgong, inspired perhaps by a variety of ghost stories that surrounded the town. Lawson recalled Louisa conducting a seance around their kitchen table with Niels, the children and some sceptical neighbours watching on. Her problem child Charlie, who seemed to have become the family's 'whipping boy', had run away from home again and there was always the fear he could have fallen down a mineshaft, or even worse. But Lawson called the latest escapade merely 'one of his juvenile expeditions ... Incidentally, a horse is missing from a neighbouring squatter's run, but it will turn up alone in a week or so and "no harm done to nobody".'[8]

The 'table-rapping' session ended abruptly when Louisa decried as nonsense one of Niels's ancestors, who could speak no English, apparently using him as a medium to communicate with the bemused gathering. Louisa gave young Lawson a swift backhander for 'allegedly aiding and abetting the Norse spook'.[9]

As another outlet for her pain, Louisa wrote the poem 'My Nettie'.

> With rapture I gaze, for by faith do I see
> The child that my Saviour has taken from me.[10]

The poem appeared in the *Mudgee Independent* in February 1878 and gave Louisa literary ambitions. Lawson copied his mother's verses by hand and, according to Charlie, wrote his own juvenile doggerel about William the Conqueror and some verses about his brother.

WHILE LOUISA NURSED HER GRIEF, Niels worked to forget. Lawson said that his father 'was clever at all sorts of mechanical work, was well educated, the terror, in mathematics, of all the district school-teachers, and I don't believe a kinder man in trouble, or a gentler nurse in sickness, ever breathed'.[9] But he was also one of those bushmen who spoke broken English, whose outlook on life and way of communication was different to many others in the community, even their own children, and who within the ceaseless struggle of farm life became strangers to their families.

Louisa had been worn down by what she saw as a mind-numbing life. Her ambitions to be a teacher had been stifled and now, more than ever, she was sick to hell of being a poor farmer's wife, even though at thirty, and a mother since the age of nineteen, she was the business head of the family.

Lawson's father could express himself clearly but he 'was a shy man, not at all self-assertive, and was quite prepared to allow his wife to become the senior partner'.[11] Louisa took in sewing to help make ends meet and with Niels constantly looking for contracting work, often at a distance from home, the whole of the management of the farm was now in Louisa's hands, including tending and rearing of the stock, such as they were, and the care of what crops they could coax out of the poor soil. Most of the heavy lifting fell upon Lawson's shoulders before he had reached the age of ten.

Niels bought a horse and made a spring cart for himself – all excepting the ironwork – and after working in Mudgee all day in the building trade would bring home a load of manure every night and spread it on the ground. Sometimes he'd burn out stumps by moonlight, all the time trying to make money for his family.

'There was a period of tin plates and pint pots and brown ration sugar, bread and treacle, and bread and dripping,' Lawson wrote. 'Cows, pigs, and fowls came later, and there was milk, butter, eggs, and bacon.'[12]

Louisa wanted to be anywhere but the farm. She told her children that she was descended from gypsy blood[13] and Lawson believed the fiction until his dying day, saying it created a restlessness inside him.

Of his parents' difficulties, he wrote: 'There was hardship and poverty, squalor and misery, hatred and uncharitableness, and ignorance; there were many mistakes, but no one was to blame; it was Fate – it was Fate.'[14]

BY JANUARY 1878 there were sixty-seven children enrolled at the Eurunderee school, with an average daily attendance of forty-eight. Lawson and his classmates studied the National Irish Readers, common books across Australia at the time, designed to provide a non-denominational religious education, with emphasis on literary and moral values, Old Testament history and political economy.[15]

Lawson was taught about the Aboriginal people that 'the inhabitants of New Holland are among the lowest and most degraded to be found on the surface of the earth'.[16] He could not agree with that since he knew many and respected them immensely, writing of them with great fondness later in life. Children were also taught the geography, not so much of their own land, but of Ireland, with a thoroughness gratifying to John Tierney.

And we learnt the world in scraps from some ancient dingy maps
Long discarded by the public-schools in town;
And as nearly every book dated back to Captain Cook
Our geography was somewhat upside-down.[17]

As a child, Lawson was 'fond of grammar' and his composition was always good, but he was 'slow at arithmetic', despite his father's talent in the subject. His spelling was poor and remained so all his life and his handwriting was always wretched, stiff and cramped.[18]

One of his schoolmates, Henry Buchholtz, said that Lawson 'was quiet and shy; and though he played games with the rest, and went swimming in the creek, he did not seem to be a happy boy. He kept to himself a lot. He was very honest.'[19] Gertrude Lawson said other children regarded her big brother as a 'prig'. Charlie called him a tattletale. Another classmate, Charles Wurth, said that as a boy Lawson was 'a very agreeable chap. He always acted as peacemaker in the quarrels and fights between the boys. He always wanted to settle rows before they came to anything.' Wurth once got into a scrap with Lawson and said that 'Henry knocked off first because he thought I had had enough!'[20]

AFTER LITTLE MORE THAN a year in use, the Eurunderee school building was on its last legs too. An architect sent to inspect it reported that the building would not see out the winter.

The New South Wales Council for Education drew up plans for a new school adjacent to the old one, which would serve as Tierney's stable.

Niels, as P.H. (Peter Hertzberg) Lawson, won the contract and undertook to build the school in four months for £497. His estimate was £100 below his principal competitor. Eleven-year-old Lawson helped him during the Christmas holidays and the work was completed on 13 March 1879. But the education council's clerk of works inspected the school a month later, with classes having already commenced and with the third Lawson boy, Peter, sitting at a desk. The clerk reported that 'several of the work' (sic) was unsatisfactory, 'not with any dishonest motive, but from want of practical skill'.[21]

After mortgaging his property to raise funds for the job, Niels now realised he had under-estimated his costs and he asked for the balance of his price to enable him to make the necessary repairs. The council wanted to impose a fine for his failure to honour their arrangement and kept him in a state of anxiety waiting for his money. Five months after the work was finished Louisa penned an appeal.

'I am a poor man,' she wrote for Niels, 'and do not at present no [sic] what to do, I am in such a fix for money.'[22] It still took six months before Niels finally received his payment.[23]

Niels was also given a second stint as postmaster at Eurunderee for eight months from September 1878 at an allowance of £14 per annum before resigning as the payment was woefully inadequate. Again, Louisa did most of the work.

Her moods were often bad.

She fell out with John Tierney, and for a month sent the children on horseback across the range to the Pipeclay Public School, where William Curtis, a more experienced master than Tierney, saw his first duty as being to 'unlearn the Old Bark School' children of all that Tierney had taught them.

Curtis was the first to notice Lawson's solitude. He tried to draw the boy out and asked him whether his schoolmates had been harassing him. Lawson couldn't explain his malady. He was just sad. Sometimes he would run home ahead of the rest, and once or twice Mary Buchholtz came running after him to try to find out what was the matter, but she soon gave up.

Despite the sectarian antagonism between Protestants and Catholics around Eurunderee, Lawson was then sent to a Catholic school in Mudgee. He never knew why Louisa made the decision but suspected she had fallen out with local Protestants. Once the area's coach driver, Pat Tovey, who was taking the mail out on a packhorse because of flooded creeks, gave Lawson a lift home. On the way, he delivered a bag to a post office 'kept by a bigoted Protestant family'[24] with whom the Lawsons were feuding.

'What are they sending that boy to a Catholic school for?' asked the post mistress.

'Sure he's bein educated for a priesht,' said Pat; and a little further on he said, half to himself and half to Lawson: 'Let her put that in her pipe and shmoke it ... It'll be all round the districk be tomorrow morning.'[25]

Lawson was eventually given a weedy horse for the journey to his new school but before riding the eight kilometres there each morning, he usually milked five or six cows.

His new classmates thought he was strange – handicapped, 'painfully sensitive and abnormally conscientious [though] his instincts were clean and straight, and he would tell the truth even if he tortured himself in the process'.[26]

Lawson's deafness was worsening and at the Mudgee school the tall, sad, shambling, dreamy lad was teased and 'tormented by the town boys', who mocked him as 'barmy Harry'.[27]

After school, Lawson would race to the paddock where he left his horse and ride off home as quickly as he could.

His new teacher, another Irishman named Charles Kevin,[28] sensed Lawson's sadness. Knowing of Louisa's love for books and verse, Kevin came and perched himself beside Lawson as the boy sat lonely and unhappy on a stool in a corner of the schoolyard. Kevin encouraged Lawson to read Edgar Allan Poe. Louisa had a book of Poe's poetry and Lawson read 'The Raven', about a weak and weary man's descent into madness. 'Not very healthy reading for a child, was it?' Lawson remarked years later, but the literary world opened before him. Louisa recited the poetry of Henry Kendall[29] and Adam Lindsay Gordon from the *Australian Journal*, which also published the first version of the serialised novel *For the Term of His Natural Life* by Marcus Clarke. Lawson developed a special fondness for Charles Dickens's *A Child's History of England*.

'I read Dickens,' Lawson recalled. 'Got him at the School of Arts in Mudgee and read "The Old Curiosity Shop" first I think. I have read Dickens over and over again and can read him now at any time.' One of his aunts at Wallerawang gave Lawson a volume of Bret Harte short stories and he was fascinated by

'Tennessee's Partner' and 'M'liss'. The stories brought 'a new light, a new world' into his life. He read *Don Quixote* before he was fourteen, and he was 'greatly puzzled and worried about the loss and recovery of Sancho's ass ... And Oh! of course we read *Robbery Under Arms* when it first appeared in the *Sydney Mail*.'[30] A Mudgee doctor loaned Louisa a copy of Mark Twain's *The Adventures of Tom Sawyer* and before long Lawson had read all about Huckleberry Finn and the rest of Twain's books.

Lawson tried playing the fiddle but he became too deaf. Reading became his escape from a home life he described as 'miserably unhappy'.[31] He saw selectors slaving their lives away in dusty holes amongst the barren ridges, saw one or two carried home, in the end, on a sheet of bark; the old men worked till they died like broken-down bullocks. He saw how the selectors' wives lived and toiled, saw the elder sons stoop-shouldered old men at thirty.[32] He also watched old fossickers and farmers earnestly reading *Progress and Poverty*[33] by the American economist Henry George, and then arguing over it on Sunday afternoons. Lawson wished that he could make readers react like that. He was eleven or twelve when he first began to talk about being a writer someday. It exasperated the practical Niels, but Louisa, despite often expressing the notion that her son was 'odd', encouraged his fancy.[25]

THE BREAKDOWN OF HIS PARENTS' marriage was, Lawson surmised, 'the result of one of those utterly impossible matches so common in Australia'. In later life his memories would flood back to 'a violent and painful scene' and of slipping out in the dark and crouching down behind the pigsty and sobbing as if his heart would break. A big black mongrel dog would come round with slobbery sympathy. And the child would put his arms round the dog's neck and bury his wet white face in the shaggy hair.[34]

John Tierney's wife Elizabeth claimed that among the selector families at Eurunderee, Niels was more popular than Louisa, who was 'hated and feared'. Mrs Tierney said 'old Peter' (as Niels was known) was 'a man of some real accomplishments, quite a linguist, excellent company – when the mood was on him'.[35] Lawson remembered that his mother was always ambitious for a literary career. There were nine living daughters in the Albury family, 'most of them big women and all naturally intelligent and refined'. Almost any one of them might have made a mark under other conditions, he wrote, but 'their lots were cast in the rough early days, in big bark humpies where all things were rough and ready and mean and sordid ... The girls used to try to establish little schools, singing classes [etc to] humanise the people but the horizon was altogether too narrow and hopeless, and, as they grew up, they became embittered.'[36]

Niels, meanwhile, impressed Lawson with his quiet, methodical work ethic.

People would say that they never saw Niels rest, and in the semi-autobiographical 'A Foreign Father',[30] Lawson later wrote of a parent who 'had the name of being the hardest working man in the district – and it was a German farming district where [the] old men worked in the fields or vineyards till the last season of their lives; where German women worked [shepherding cows] in the fields up to within a few days of their confinements ...'[37] Niels would seldom wake his boys on a cold winter morning to light the fire; he'd get up himself and light it – 'he never felt the cold; and very often he'd have his breakfast and be away to work while the frosty stars were in the sky'.[38]

Lawson would pen 'A Child in the Dark'[39] about the turbulence in his parents' marriage, and later in his own; of a thin-faced, pale, dark-eyed boy saddled with all the work on the farm while his father is away contracting and his mother, sick of her brood and 'the wretched hole' of a home, battles depression. The house is a mess. The boy lies on a filthy mattress with a bundle of dirty clothes for a pillow. The woman is in bed spitting vitriol, screaming at her husband that the crying baby 'drives me mad'. Lawson wrote of a hard woman's vicious and baseless attacks on her husband; of another younger child quaking in terror, dreading another of 'those cruel and shameful scenes which had made a hell of his childhood'.[33] A childhood friend of the Lawsons, Bridget Lambert,[40] who he sometimes called 'Bertha' in his writings, recalled that Louisa treated the children as nuisances and 'used to have opened and empty tins all over the place, the children dirty, fed as best they could scramble themselves, ragged and uncared for in every way, and the place like a pigsty'.[41] Lawson's sister Gertrude wrote that at times the whole of the responsibility of the farm and family would fall upon Lawson's shoulders when Niels was away, and her mother would take 'strange fits of abstraction in which she would seem to vegetate for days, taking heed of nothing and eating nothing'.[42]

The Lawsons were a strange bunch. Gertrude's recollections of family life at Eurunderee were often coloured by invention, but she recalled once how Charlie's misbehaviour had exasperated his father so badly that for some minor infraction Niels placed a noose around the boy's neck and threatened to hang him. Truth or fiction, it illustrated the turmoil in the home.[43]

Lawson called his mother 'The Chieftainess'[44] and suggested that his parents stayed together only for as long as they did because of Victorian-era mores. He craved Louisa's approval but just as she had seen romance as 'bosh' as a young woman, Lawson believed that 'love, affection, even consideration' towards him was missing. Louisa, tight-lipped and stern, said that if her eldest boy was 'not as mad as his schoolmates said he was', then at the least he was 'very "queer" and idiotic'.[45]

BY THE TIME HE HAD FINISHED his few months at the Mudgee school – and his three years of formal education in total – Lawson was desperate to get away from the chaos at home and Louisa's constant nagging.[46]

At thirteen, and just as he was starting to learn about compound fractions at school,[47] Lawson found his escape route from the 'dreadful and barren gaol' of his boyhood,[48] and all the 'grubbin', clearin', burnin' off, fencin', ploughin', etc'.[49] He left school and went to work as his father's mate.

He summed up his childhood later: 'Rows and scenes and scenes and rows, violent rows that frightened; father and mother separated; home a hell. Boy slavery and freedom.'[50]

Working with his father introduced him to stories of the male bonding that had sustained Niels on the diggings; stories of working men helping each other as they all tried to dig themselves out of tough times. These stories nurtured in Lawson the ideals of Australian mateship that would be the cornerstone of his writing.

THE BUILDING OF THE NEW Eurunderee school, even with its problems, gave Niels the confidence to try again, and in June 1880, with a tender of £811, he won the contract to build a new school at Canadian Lead. Lawson worked alongside Niels there for nine months and then they built additions to the school at Upper Wilbetree. Lawson was always happiest when the older boys were absent from that school when he arrived for work because their taunts and jeers made him withdraw further into himself.

The timber was sawn and planed by hand, which was hard work for a thin young boy. There was stifling heat in summer until part of the building was up, then a rough bunk 'and work from sunrise till dark, and the billy and the frying pan – steak and chops, and bacon – bacon and steak and chops – potatoes sometimes for dinner, milkless tea'. Except on Sunday when they found time to wash their shirts and socks and cook a bit.[51]

Lawson was rewarded with the occasional praise of 'Well, I didn't know it was in you' from his father and finally another trip to Sydney, though it was not so much a holiday as to receive treatment for his deafness, which was now profound.

The skinny teenager travelled down to the train station at Wallerawang on a Cobb and Co coach, and in Sydney stayed with his grandparents who were now running a boarding house in Granville. To enable him to remain in the city for treatment, Lawson took a job house-painting for 30 shillings a week from the company Ritchie Brothers, which made railway carriages and agricultural implements at nearby Auburn.

Lawson did his best to hear the gypsy-themed play *Romany Rye* at Sydney's Princess Theatre, bought a muzzle-loading shotgun for 12 shillings and sixpence,[52] and had his photograph taken for the first time, 'a gem of the while-you-wait variety'.[53]

He visited the 'celebrated surgeon of diseases of the eyes, ear, nose and throat', Prospero Stanich,[54] at his rooms in Wynyard Square. It was on the Croatian-born specialist's 'pauper days', and Lawson said the esteemed doctor 'spoke to me and treated me' like a pauper, 'and did me no good – though, fortunately, no harm'.[55]

Just before he returned home, Lawson's grandparents shifted into a larger cottage in Sydney, and Henry Albury, now fifty-six but as strong as one of his bullocks from the old days, said he could move all the furniture himself.

'It was a great shifting,' Lawson recalled, 'and couldn't have been done quicker if there'd have been a fire.'[56]

Lawson presented his grandmother with a book of poetry and returned home during 'the worst drought the district ever suffered', when all the rocks on the property seemed like 'molten masses turned out on the scrub' and the soil was like ash.[57] He was sent miles through the bush to fetch a starving 'wall-eyed' steer and a barren heifer as a gift for anyone who would take them. The rest of the Lawson cows were riddled with 'th' ploorer' (pleuropneumonia) and Lawson would have to bleed them by cutting their ears and tails in the sickening heat. The bloody, cruel task often made him vomit. Sometimes he would inoculate the cattle 'with a big needle and Berlin-wool dipped in calf-lymph'. He fed them with pumpkin slices from a Chinese market garden that the drought had ruined. Half the cows, including the best milkers, still died.[58]

He resumed building work with his father and they became ever closer.

Niels always professed to be a 'freethinker' but he studied the Bible, and 'was one of the hardest working, kindest hearted men I ever [knew],' Lawson wrote. 'I have known him, after a hard day's work, to sit up all night watching a neighbour's dying child.'[59]

Once, though, among his chums, Lawson had mimicked his father's broken English and for the rest of his life he wished he could forget that. He spent a long time trying to atone in print, starting a decade later with 'The Way I Treated Father'.[60]

Niels used to write long letters home in Norwegian, about once a year. Maybe, Lawson mused, Niels thought in his own language, as he sat quietly by the fire. Gertrude felt that something always stood between Niels and his family. Lawson and his father once went to the dilapidated weatherboard theatre in Gulgong to see *Pirates of Penzance* and Lawson wondered about all the sights his father had seen in his life as a 'dapper little sailor ashore for a run in European ports, in New York, 'Frisco, and the Lord knows where else', and how toiling for years in the Australian bush must have been a world away from his dreams as a young man. He suspected that his father's heart had been irreparably broken when he left Norway and that 'he worked hard so as not to remember'. Lawson never saw his father drink, but he sometimes saw him so worried about his marital woes that he couldn't even smoke his pipe.[61]

Niels worked harder as he grew older, and talked less – but one week, when he and Lawson were camping together on a contract, Niels told Lawson 'a lot about his voyages and adventures in his young days – the first time he ever spoke to me of those things'.[62] Until Lawson was well into his teens, Niels would tuck the blankets around him if he coughed during the night, and say: 'You must keep yourself warm sonny.'[63]

LOUISA OFTEN ASKED LAWSON, and sometimes his young uncle Joe Albury, to give their opinion on her poems before she submitted them to De Courcy Browne,[64] a local politician and editor of the *Mudgee Independent*. Lawson tried his hand at some poetry on his own, and Louisa took his work to the editor without signature. Some of the verses were 'so original in thought and expression' that Browne thought they must have been lifted from other publications and Louisa was filled with indignation.[65]

So it was back to the paintbrush for Lawson, and the saw and the plane; reading Poe by lantern inside his tent in bush camps as he and his father sought building work together. In 1881, Niels won the contract to build the Rylstone railway station on the newly completed line linking Mudgee with Wallerawang, and the following April and May he and Lawson worked on other buildings around there.

Niels and Louisa were happier apart and began planning for separate lives.

On 20 January 1883, Niels made out his will, with the help of Mudgee solicitor Charles Meares, leaving everything to Louisa and appointing her guardian of his four children. Two months later, while Lawson was away working with his father, Louisa packed everything she needed for a permanent move to Sydney, where she believed that her burning desire to take part in literary, political and social activity could be satisfied. She sold her furniture and leased the family's farm to Harry O'Brien, one of Niels's friends. She moved to Sydney in May.

Building work was drying up, and Niels had only enough contracts to keep himself going. For a few weeks Lawson went to stay with his grandfather, who was acting as a caretaker at an empty house in Mount Victoria in the Blue Mountains.[66] But soon Lawson 'was wanted in Sydney'.[67]

LOUISA ARRIVED IN THE BIG CITY with her two younger children, Peter and Gertrude. Lawson would join her soon but Charlie had run away again. At first, Louisa stayed with her parents at Granville before leasing a house in Enmore Road, Marrickville, and taking in boarders to help pay the rent. On 30 August 1883, fourteen-year-old Charlie was remanded in custody at the Sydney Central Police Court, charged with being in possession of a revolver that was thought to be stolen. It was the start of a one-man crime wave that would see Lawson's little brother, using a variety of aliases,[68] spend most of the next decade and a half behind bars.

Just five weeks after his first court appearance, Charlie was at Penrith Police Court being sentenced to three months' hard labour for stealing a rifle, revolver, saddle and bridle. Then, just a week further on, he was brought from prison to the Parramatta

Quarter Sessions to receive twelve months' hard labour for horse stealing and burglary.[69] Lawson worried about a strain of madness running through his family.

In 1884 Louisa moved from Marrickville to a double-fronted cottage at 138 Phillip Street, near present day Martin Place. It had four rooms and a big, detached kitchen. Louisa made a home there for the children – Lawson, now sixteen, Peter Junior, eleven – whom the family nicknamed 'Bert', or 'Birdie'[70] – and Gertrude, seven.

Even for a youth with severely impaired hearing, the sounds of the city were confronting for Lawson, especially the late-night shrieks of alley cats. His mother had to dissuade him from firing a shotgun at them, warning he would be arrested.[71]

Louisa let two of her four rooms to a German inventor and took in sewing from a tailor in Paddy's Market.

While believing Lawson had some potential as a writer, the family's need for money was still dire and Louisa found him a position as an apprentice coach painter with the Hudson Brothers railway carriage works among a 'rough crowd' at Clyde on the Parramatta River, twenty kilometres west of his home. It was a large construction and engineering company with more than a thousand staff and Lawson said they 'imported the best mechanics and treated and paid them well'.[72]

Lawson started on 25 shillings for a six-day week and earned a pay rise to 30 shillings a few months later.

He placed an alarm clock either on a tray or a sheet of tin to loudly wake him because of his deafness. The 5 a.m. shock was the terror of his late teens. Hoping to improve upon his three years of rudimentary education, and trying for the matriculation exam, Lawson also enrolled at a night school held in St James' Hall, just down Phillip Street from his home. For six months he took classes in grammar, mathematics and history. On most mornings Lawson would have given his soul for another hour's sleep, especially after a long night's studying.

Each morning before leaving home he would make a breakfast of bread and milk over a spirit lamp, prepare a lunch

Train carriages at the Hudson Brothers factory at Clyde at the time Lawson worked there as a painter. State Library of NSW, PXE 1712, FL8488175

of bread and butter or bread and meat, and then start on the three-kilometre walk from Phillip Street to the old Redfern Station, situated in what is now Sydney's Prince Alfred Park. He would make his way through Hyde Park, down Elizabeth Street and through Belmore Park to the railway station, all the while haunted by the 'wan and weary'[73] faces in the street, and the 'wretched rag covered forms on the benches and under them, and on the grass' that was the city's homeless. Deafness had made his eyes keener, and he stored stark, confronting mental images of the drunks and downtrodden sleeping under the verandas around the old Central Markets. He remembered, one morning, seeing 'a horrible old bundle of rags and bones, that had been a woman, struggle up from the wet grass and staggering by try to drink from an empty bottle'.[74]

On the special 'Worker's Train' to Granville, Lawson would study his English history lessons when he could keep his eyes open. A 'nasty guard' frequently woke him around Homebush to check his ticket.

Coach-painting was an involved trade and it paid at the same rate as the blacksmiths, body makers and upholstery trimmers, although apprentices were paid only a fraction of the tradesman's rate.[75] It often took more than a week to properly paint a carriage.[76]

The hardest part of Lawson's work was the 'rubbing-down' of the carriages to a polished surface, especially when the old varnish was as hard as flint. On cold winter mornings blood would ooze from Lawson's fingertips. Shy, deaf, with a resulting speech impediment and different from other boys, Lawson was suspected of 'being of the Sunday school sort',[77] and therefore tormented by the workplace larrikins, who bullied him, threw his lunch on the ground and believed he was 'half ratty', especially after he majestically declared that he 'would rise above them all yet'.

Lawson usually returned from work at 6.30 p.m. and hurried down to the night school for a 7 p.m. start three times a week. On other nights he went to the School of Arts with an idea of learning drawing and Latin, after someone said that the ancient language would improve his English.

He took the university 'metriculation [sic] examination twice and failed'. On the second try, he couldn't hear the dictation, so 'I was taken into another room by an old man without teeth who dictated in Irish. I failed in everything save English history and English composition.' Lawson wished that he had his father's head for mathematics.[78]

He applied for a job as a letter carrier but was deemed too frail for the work. He twice tried to pass the Civil Service examination without success.

Most of Lawson's 30 shillings a week went into Louisa's purse, but Lawson used some of it to pay his night school fees and to buy his own clothes, which he washed and mended. Sometimes, he looked at the ships docked in Sydney Harbour and wished he could sail away to start a new life in America. He lived a lonely, solitary existence; his time was occupied almost totally with work or study. He did not follow or play sport and when he went for long walks it was by himself.

By the age of eighteen, Lawson was 'painfully shy and extremely sensitive ... sensitive about my deafness, my lack of education, my surroundings, my clothes, slimness and paleness, my "h's", handwriting, grammar, pronunciation (made worse by deafness) – everything almost'.

He was terribly shy of strange girls, too, 'and, if a girl I knew took any notice of me I would reckon that she was only either pitying me or laughing at me'.[79]

Chapter 4

Then came the unexpected and inexplicable outburst of popular feeling
(or madness) – called then the Republican riots – in '87 ...
And I had to write then or burst.
HENRY LAWSON ON THE IRRESISTIBLE MOTIVATION TO BEGIN WRITING[1]

LOUISA LAWSON had left the farm animals for good but
her home in Phillip Street was a pigsty. She had her sleeves
perpetually rolled up but it was rarely to do the dishes, more
to change the world. The abhorrence for housework she had
displayed at Eurunderee had followed her for the 280 kilometres
south-east to Sydney. The writer Mary Gilmore, who once lodged
with Louisa, would later complain that Lawson's mother was
the 'dirtiest housekeeper she ever knew'.[2] The unkempt abode,
though, quickly became a welcoming hotbed of radical thinking;
a cauldron for those of both sexes with an interest in feminism,
republicanism, journalism and spiritualism.

Louisa began attending spiritualist meetings at the dance hall
Leigh House in Castlereagh Street, and Lawson and Gertrude
attended the Sunday school there. Gertrude remembered that at
fourteen Lawson was a religious fanatic, at sixteen a Christian
spiritualist and at seventeen a republican rebel, who became a
disciple of the nationalist politicians of his time.

In her new surrounds Louisa quickly proved herself as a natural
leader with a commanding presence. She drew influential people
into her inner circle, including the thirty-year-old Edinburgh-

born journalist George Black,[3] who wrote for the *Australian Star* newspaper. Black was making headway in political circles despite a scandalous and stormy private life. On his voyage to Australia in 1877, he had an affair with Mrs Georgina Duggan.[4] A punch-up with her aggrieved husband saw the Scot placed in irons. When he arrived in Victoria the scandal led to his dismissal as a sheep-station book-keeper. He and Mrs Duggan moved to Sydney where Black scratched out a living as a struggling journalist. The couple never married but they had twelve children together.

Louisa's literary hero Henry Kendall had died a few months before she arrived in Sydney and late in 1884 Louisa visited Kendall's grave by the sea at Waverley Cemetery. She was appalled to find a 'wretched mockery of a monument'[5] with just a little tin wreath of roses, a salt-encrusted blue scroll with his name painted on it and a rough wooden cross. Lawson had been inspired by Kendall's work too, remarking that Kendall, like him, had also been 'a pale delicate shy and sensitive boy' who was called 'barmy'; in his case because he mumbled verses to himself.[6] Louisa launched a campaign to give Kendall what she believed would be a more fitting monument. She sold a sketch of the grave by an artist friend to the *Sydney Mail* magazine and while there started a fundraising drive by soliciting £2 from the editor and £5 from Mrs Eliza Bennett, the wife of newspaper magnate Samuel Bennett. Mrs Bennett told Louisa to see her sons at the *Evening News* office. They declined to contribute unless the New South Wales premier endorsed the plan, so Louisa harangued the imperious Sir Henry Parkes until he produced another £2, which the Bennett brothers matched.[7] To ensure there was enough space for a memorial over the grave, Louisa bought the plot next to Kendall's. Before long she had £80 in donations, but with other committees becoming involved she was pushed aside from official duties. Waverley Municipal Council decided the monument should be in a more prominent position and donated a larger area on higher ground. Kendall's body was exhumed and moved to the new plot and in 1886 the governor, Lord Carrington, unveiled an eight-metre-

Lawson at eighteen. University of Sydney, Lawson Collection.

Henry Kendall. National Library of Australia, 3084988

high memorial in Italian marble over the grave.[8] Louisa was left with the vacant burial plot she had purchased.

Still, her literary ambitions had come alive. In a time when republican sentiments were growing strong amid Sydney's working classes agitating for social reform, she began writing poems of fervent patriotism such as 'Australia' and 'An Australian Song'.

Lawson followed his mother's lead and with some juvenile doggerel penned his first recorded poem, 'Shadows Before', which he signed 'Hal, May 1885'.[9]

LAWSON CONTINUED HIS work at Clyde for a few months in 1884 before transferring to the company's railway branch workshops at Wickham, near Newcastle, where he also studied at the School of Arts. He was an emotional wreck, though. Tall, stick-thin and pale, he complained that 'all esprit and moral courage' – if any had survived his childhood – had 'been bullied and ground out' of him. It made him 'pander to the vanity of ignorant bosses', including a little foreman 'with a tremendous opinion of his "position"'.[10]

Lawson sent home every penny he had, and with Niels also sending all of his weekly earnings to support his estranged wife and children – less 5 shillings that he kept for his own basic needs – Louisa kept her brood in Phillip Street well fed and clothed. But after a short time in Wickham, Lawson recalled, 'I was soon wanted at home, or my board money perhaps, for I came back to Sydney and worked at [Hudson's] Redfern branch shops.' One morning he helped paint some beams which had been used on the gallows to hang Sydney's Mount Rennie rapists. He was given a stint as a clerk in the Redfern office. 'My tribe wanted a gentleman, or the appearance of a gentleman in the family, but they wanted every penny I could earn also,' he wrote. 'I couldn't write a simple business letter, I wasn't worth five shillings a week in the office.'

He was sent into the timber yard to learn 'measuring up' but was hopeless.

He appealed for another trial in the office, but it was no use and he resigned.

He moved on to Castlereagh Street and a cantankerous coach-painter with a 'horse face and a skin disease … He seemed to hate me especially – because of my clean skin and effeminate appearance probably. He used to call me a "B—y woman!" "Come out from under that carriage and let me see what yer doin', yer b—y old woman!" etc. He used to sack me every other day, but the first evening or two he sent his little girl after me to tell me I could come in the morning; so I got used to it …' [11]

It was 'a blessed relief' when Lawson found another job in Castlereagh Street, at No. 267, this time with carriage-builder William Kerridge, 'a little old gentleman with snow white hair and a white frill beard [who] was always in a hurry – an old fashioned bird like, pecking and jerky hurry'.[12] 'Kerridge's Carriages' regularly won prizes at the Sydney Show. Lawson spent two happy years in his employ until the work dried up.

Many times in the months after that, Lawson went without work and he formed a kindred spirit with the destitute. He knew what it was like to wait in front of the *Sydney Morning Herald* office at 4 a.m. during bitterly cold winters; to be 'one of the haggard group striking matches' as the unemployed ran their eyes down the 'Wanted' columns on the damp sheets posted outside the building. He knew what it was like to tramp long distances and be one of a hopeless crowd of job applicants turned away; what it was like to drift about the streets in shabby and patched clothes, and feel 'furtive and criminal-like'.

Louisa gave him no comfort. 'I [also] knew,' Lawson wrote, 'what it was to go home to a cold, resentful, gloomy and unbelieving welcome, and blind unreasoning reproaches at the very least.'[13]

THE CRAMPED CONFINES OF A SMALL, untidy, crowded house in a bustling city made Lawson restless and he would walk for hours alone with his thoughts, memorising the faces of the down-and-outs for future use. Throughout his life, in times of turmoil Lawson would find an outlet in the basic carpentry skills his father had taught him. While Niels had taken an axe into the bush to work out his grief or stress, Lawson often took to the hammer and nails and, at Phillip Street, built an outside room for himself out of packing cases given to him by a carrying company nearby. He roofed it with zinc lining and fitted a sliding window. Along one side he made a bunk out of bags under the window and he made a bench and a fixed stool. He covered the walls with illustrated newspapers.

For a short time in 1885 the family left Phillip Street for a smaller cottage in Clarence Lane at The Rocks. It was a slum area populated by wharf labourers and street gangs, and while Lawson had been unhappy in the poky Phillip Street home, he was glad to move back there before long.

Lawson's brother Charlie was becoming used to even more cramped conditions in prison. Two months shy of his sixteenth birthday, he appeared at the Condobolin Police Court on 27 April 1885 and received three cumulative sentences of four months' hard labour for stealing a saddle and bridle, blankets and a coat. He was brought from prison again to face the Forbes Quarter Sessions on 3 July 1885 and was sentenced to four years for horse stealing.

THERE WAS A LOT OF ANGST in Sydney during 1887 as the fiftieth anniversary of Queen Victoria's reign approached on 20 June. Australian republicans whipped up an electric atmosphere of fervent nationalism opposed to the colonial monarchists.

The Queen's jubilee coincided with the upcoming centenary of the First Fleet bringing European settlers to Australia on 26 January 1788, and the popular 'Bushman's Bible', the weekly *Bulletin* magazine, continued to fan the flames of nationalism as Australian-born Europeans outnumbered the immigrant population for the first time.

The Bulletin had first appeared on newsstands in 1880. Eventually it was selling 80,000 copies a week and it unified a large part of the populace when the continent was still composed of disparate colonies, often suspicious of each other.

Its founder and editor was Jules François Archibald, who had been born John Feltham Archibald[14] in Geelong twenty-four years earlier, the son of an Irish–Catholic police sergeant, but fancied a more exotic handle.

The Bulletin described itself as a 'journalistic javelin'[15] and shouted with an Australian nationalist voice; a voice that in hindsight could have come from the Ku Klux Klan and which grew louder and louder among white workers across the Australian landscape with a policy to 'howl for the undermost dog'.[16]

One of the young 'versifiers'[17] who first came to prominence writing for Archibald was a Sydney solicitor named Andrew Paterson.[18] He contributed his early work under the alias of 'The Banjo', the name of a country racehorse his father had once owned.

Banjo called *The Bulletin* the 'most unsatisfied paper in Australia',[19] as it represented the great bulk of Australians who, he believed, were demanding a better deal. To them 'it represented a new gospel'.[20]

Lawson dived headfirst into the wave of republicanism, and began to emerge from his mother's house on weekends to hear lectures by George Black, soon to be elected to the New South Wales Legislative Council, and other political agitators, the socialist William Henry McNamara,[21] a New Zealand freethinker and politician named William Whitehouse Collins[22] and the Lancashire-born Thomas Walker.[23]

There were also, Lawson said, 'a host of Yankee free-thought and socialist lectures. I gathered at the rising of the moon ... and dreamed of dying on the barricades to the roar of the "Marseillaise" – for the young Australian Republic.'[24]

Thomas Walker was one of the more strident speakers against the monarchy. His extraordinary journey eventually saw him become the Minister for Education in Western Australia despite one scandal after another. He had started his working life as a Wesleyan child preacher in England and then became a spirit medium in Toronto. During a seance there, Walker burned himself with phosphorus that he was using to make 'illuminated writing' and 'spiritual lights'. Another participant, John Saunders, helped extinguish the flames but died from tetanus three weeks later due to the burns he received on his hands and left foot. A coroner's jury found that Walker had 'feloniously' caused Saunders's death, but Walker had left Canada the morning after the accident. He was invited to speak on spiritualism in Great Britain, South Africa and Australia, and his first lecture in Melbourne, chaired by future prime minister Alfred Deakin, was said to have been delivered in a trance.[25]

Walker became a populist campaigner as a democratic republican and protectionist. His secretary was William Keep, a weedy twenty-five year old who had been a draper's assistant in London and now listed his occupation as 'van proprietor' of St Peters. George Black brought Keep to Louisa's house in Phillip Street and introduced him as a young man who had some experience as a printer's assistant. Together Louisa and Keep hatched a plan to publish *The Republican* as the mouthpiece of a new political movement.

Sydney was ripe for it.

On 3 June 1887, a boisterous public meeting was held at Sydney Town Hall. Mayor A.J. Riley[26] had organised the gathering to discuss ways of celebrating the Queen's jubilee. But agitators in the crowd strongly opposed any celebration. A 'large majority' supported an amendment that declared: 'That, in the opinion of this meeting, the proposal to impress upon the children of the colony the value of the Jubilee year of a Sovereign is unwise and calculated to injure the democratic spirit of the country.' Riley called for three cheers for the Queen, but received hissing and hooting instead.[27]

When the crowd 'cheered for an Australian Republic', Lawson knew he 'had to write then or burst'.[28]

Work had dried up for the gangly twenty year old. He was mostly working at house painting now, and odd jobs,[29] trying to make a living while attempting to have his voice heard over men and women of much greater learning.

He submitted a poem, under the byline 'Youth', to *The Bulletin* in the hope that he could lend his voice to the republican cause. J.F. Archibald had seized on the discord in Sydney over the jubilee. In his magazine on 2 July 1887, Archibald said the issue was about 'Royalty versus Republicanism': 'Let there be no mistaking the issue! The recent Sydney troubles have been between the people of Australia and Imperial Officialdom ... and the traitors to the cause of the colonies have been paid, if not with Imperial gold, with at least Imperial titles.'[30]

Mayor Riley called another public meeting on 10 June 1887, but made it by invitation only, hoping to keep out the dissenters. The republicans invited themselves anyway, and Premier Henry Parkes watched helplessly from the stage of Sydney Town Hall as gatecrashers created mayhem and police had to be called in to disperse the crowd.[31]

Five days later, a third meeting about the jubilee was held, this time at the Exhibition Building in Prince Alfred Park, and with a much bigger police presence boosted by volunteers from the military and local football clubs, as well as a smattering of prizefighters loyal to the Queen. Some of the reinforcements came with sticks in their hands and slouch hats on their heads. It was said to be the largest public meeting ever held in Sydney. While a resolution was put to the crowd of 12,000 by semaphore and carried by an overwhelming vote, the presence of many agitators sparked 'a number of exciting hand-to-hand combats ... between the occupants of the platform and those who were endeavouring to get a place on it'.[32]

Just three days later, on 18 June 1887, Lawson's dark eyes lit up like never before. In the 'Correspondence' section of *The Bulletin*, Archibald replied to his hopeful recruit:

'Youth,' Archibald wrote: 'The opening lines are the best –

> Rejoice! Rejoice! rise high the ringing cheers!
> Rejoice! because another fifty years
> Our weary backs have born with scarce a groan
> The cumb'rous, useless burden of a throne.'[33]

Nothing – not immersing himself in the word images of Poe or Dickens or Twain or Marcus Clarke or Henry Kendall – had stirred Lawson's desire to be a writer like this brief throwaway mention of his anonymous work.[34]

Lawson was emboldened to try again as *The Bulletin* continued fanning the flames of nationalistic fever and xenophobia.

The magazine promised to fight for Australians but only those it deemed to be truly Australian – as defined by Archibald. Archibald defended the change of *The Bulletin*'s banner from 'Australia for Australians' to 'Australia for the White Man'.

> By the term Australian we mean not those who have been merely born in Australia. All white men who come to these shores – with a clean record – and who can leave behind them the memory of the class-distinction and the religious differences of the old world; all men who place the happiness, the prosperity, the advancement of their adopted country before the interests of Imperialism, are Australian.[35]

The editorial went on to explain that 'No nigger, no Chinaman, no lascar,[36] no kanaka, no purveyor of cheap coloured labour is an Australian'.

LAWSON REMEMBERED TRUDGING home through a storm at Hyde Park one night after working late on a painting job at Paddington. There was rain and wind, and fallen branches and the sickly glow of gaslights on the wet asphalt. There were poles and scaffolding about in preparation for the jubilee celebrations.[37] Lawson thought about the Australian colonies being beholden to a foreign monarch and started rolling words around in his head for a poem he would call 'Sons of the South', about a brotherhood among Australians and a rejection of British rule. By lamplight after work, Lawson wrote down the verses of his call to arms. He wrote the byline using just his initials, 'H.A.L.', and 'screwed up courage' to go down to *The Bulletin* office at 24 Pitt Street after hours, intending to drop his work into the letterbox. He arrived at a small, shabby brick building hidden away among ship chandleries, wool stores and fish shops, with the smell of a recent catch wafting down from the cramped alleyway just off Pitt Street. He climbed a narrow, dusty flight of stairs into a narrow and dusty passage, with 'hardly room for two men to walk abreast'.[38] But, just as Lawson was contemplating whether to deliver the envelope or take his poem home and have another look at the spelling, the door opened suddenly and 'a haggard woman stood there'.[39] Lawson shoved the poem into the cleaner's hand and fled with embarrassment, like someone who was in a place where he didn't belong. Yet, he wrote later, 'it was my first song and sincere – written by a bush boy who was a skinny city work boy in patched pants and blucher boots'.[40]

Lawson lacked the courage to go near *The Bulletin* office again for a long time but he would lie awake at night and rise very early to slip down to the nearest newsagent on Thursday mornings, peeping into each new edition of the magazine. Each time he was disappointed.

LOUISA LAWSON AND WILLIAM KEEP got hold of an old printing press that had been used in the country west of the Blue Mountains and Lawson helped them establish a new and rudimentary publishing venture, *The Republican* newspaper.

The life of the '*Republican* was a tragecal [sic] farce', Lawson wrote, even though the slightly built Keep had 'the vitality, energy and blind self-confidence of a dozen fat men'.[41] While Louisa did much of the writing and editing, Lawson and Keep had to turn the press by hand and 'it ran like a dray most of the time'. The bed of the press was uneven and worm eaten, and Lawson could never tell when the machine was likely to go wrong, or why it went right at times. Keep invented some new roller composition, 'out of treacle and stuff', and in hot weather those rollers would bring the flies and pick up loose type. The paper was illustrated with portraits that came out black or blank or half and half, or smudged according to Keep's cheerful digging or pasting on the cylinder. 'But he'd get 'em right in time,' Lawson said, 'or at least recognisable as being intended to represent portraits.' Whenever there was 'a breakdown, or smash up somewhere', Keep would go round briskly and cheerfully in front of the machine, behind it and under it, and squeeze between it and the wall, with a couple of spanners and a screw wrench for odd nuts; and screw up a nut here, and loosen one there, and try her again, until at last, by some accident, or wonderful combination of accidents incomprehensible to Lawson, he'd get her going all right.[42]

Keep used to buy damaged lots of paper, of different colours and sizes, from fires and old stock, and he'd cut the longer sheets to size with a carving knife. He and Lawson would soak the paper in a tub of water the night before going to press. When there was the inevitable breakdown of the press on hot nights Keep would peel to his pants and shirt and rustle up every damaged or soiled sheet of paper from the floor and put it through the press again.

The night after printing, Lawson and Keep would fold the paper and carry it in a clothes basket to the post in the early hours; and before daylight have breakfast at the old coffee stall outside the *Herald* office where Keep would 'argue politics and free thought and other things with cabmen and others'.[43]

The first issue of *The Republican*, dated 4 July 1887, emerged hot and sticky from the press and sold at threepence a copy from what

Keep called the Progressive Publishing Company. In the male-dominated Victorian era, he, rather than Louisa, took responsibility for the journal and gave the office address of the newspaper as 45 Stanley Street, Hyde Park, which in fact was a room for his mail-order bookselling depot.

Through the pages of *The Republican*'s debut edition, Keep and the Lawsons promised to bolster the fight for a 'Flag of a Federated Australia, the Great Republic of the Southern Seas'. An article headlined 'Parkes's Despotism' called for funds to 'assist Mr Thomas Walker in his fight against the despotism of Czar [Henry] Parkes and the religious bigots of Sydney'.[44]

The Republican was off and racing with its nationalistic war cry, but despite the passion of mother and son for the cause, Lawson knew it was still a fledgling publication with a voice that only a few subscribers were hearing. *The Bulletin* had a circulation exponentially greater than this callow journal.

Lawson still waited on word about the poem he'd delivered to Archibald's office but in the meantime, he applied for work as a carriage-painter in the Railway Department and submitted two references, one from Hudson Brothers, the other from William Kerridge, dated 10 July 1887, which declared that Lawson was 'very steady, very attentive to his work, [a] hard working man and worthy of any employment'.[45]

Lawson failed to get the job, but finally in *The Bulletin*'s 'Correspondence' column on 23 July 1887, Archibald boosted the flagging spirits of the budding writer.

'H.A.L.: Will publish your "Sons of the South",' Archibald wrote. 'You have good grit.'[46]

In the same issue on the facing page, Archibald ran a cartoon of a well-to-do black man elegantly dressed in a top hat, tails and cane. The caption read, 'From the Zoo – Things we see when we come out without our gun'.[47]

It was that kind of magazine. *Bulletin* writers and cartoonists regularly mocked Aboriginal people, British, Chinese, Japanese, Indians and 'Hebrews', even though Archibald married the daughter[48] of a Jewish merchant. The public couldn't get enough of the weekly journal, though, and Lawson was over the moon with the promise of publication. A week later Archibald responded to a third Lawson poem, 'The Distant Drum',[49] by writing in the 'Correspondence' column: "'H.A.L": "The Distant Drum" is vigorous, but some of the lines are faulty; it is worth re-writing.'[50]

Faint praise was better than none, and Lawson waited in eager expectation for 'Sons of the South' to appear in print. And waited. And waited …

Each new issue made his heart skip a beat as he looked in vain for his verses. How he longed to see his words on the page.

MONEY WAS TIGHT IN THE LAWSON household and at *The Republican*, which frequently changed address.

Lawson and Keep had to shift the old press about 'a good deal, on account of the rent'.[51] Keep would sometimes get work as a clerk and donate his wages towards printing the next issue. He would tackle anything, Lawson said, and 'went on the platform once, for the first time in his life, and at five minutes notice, and gave a lecture, when he was managing for Tommy Walker and Walker fell ill'.[52]

Once they moved the press to a long narrow room on the top of a building in George Street, with a large window front and back. Keep slung a hammock and slept beside the machine. One Sunday morning, Keep had cleaned up and set fire to a lot of wastepaper in the fireplace, and 'was pottering round happily, and lovingly round the old press, with a screw wrench, getting ready for the monthly fray' when there was 'a crash below and a tremendous clattering and bumping on the stairs', and Keep, thinking that part of the building was collapsing, prepared to leap out of the front window when the door burst open and several big, helmeted firemen charged in.

There were already two horse-drawn fire engines in George Street, and more coming, and the opposite side was lined with upturned faces and gaping mouths. Keep had left both windows open and the wind from the back window had blown the smoke from the wastepaper through the front one.[53]

Chaos aside, the second edition of *The Republican* appeared on 6 August 1887 and declared that the position of New South Wales governor should be given to an elected official and that the office-holder should not be responsible to Queen Victoria but to 'the people of this country'. The journal also announced the establishment of the Australian Republican Union.

By the time issue four of *The Republican* appeared,[54] Keep and Louisa were taking no chances with the laws regarding sedition and libel, so the journal's editor was listed as Archie Lawson of 138 Phillip Street. The edition contained the first piece of published prose attributed to Lawson, an opinion piece written on 20 September 1887 entitled 'Australian Loyalty: Sentimental and Political'. Lawson vented his spleen, calling for Australia to reject 'landlordism, the title worship, the class distinctions and privileges, the oppression of the poor, the monarchy, and all the dust covered customs that England has humped out of the middle ages where she properly belongs'.[55] Some of Lawson's words were soon reprinted in a Newcastle newspaper[56] but the byline he craved was still to be set in type.

EACH WEEK LAWSON CONTINUED his fruitless missions to the newsagents, flicking through the latest edition of *The Bulletin*, hoping to see his work. At last, sick with disappointment, this shy, nervous young man, who asserted himself only through paper and ink, plucked up the courage to visit Archibald himself.

He arrived at Pitt Street, and with his skinny legs shaking and bony knees knocking together, he climbed the narrow, dusty stairs again.

Lawson passed small cubicles of rooms, piles of newspapers all about the floor, and walls that were decorated with ink stains and newspaper illustrations, caricatures of Henry Parkes and Queen Victoria, and cruel drawings of Chinese coolies with exaggerated eyes and teeth.

The nervous youngster was invited into Archibald's office to see a small, intense, bespectacled man, copy in one hand, pen in the other, sitting at his roll-top desk and shaping the way thousands of Australians thought.

Archibald looked much older than his thirty-one years. He had a moustache and spade beard, a hawk nose and quick movements. He was long in the arms and shabby in his dress;[57] an editor who described himself as a 'soler and heeler of paragraphs',[58] a man who discovered and promoted poets, who would pounce on a piece of verse with potential and polish it for weeks. A self-starter, his journalistic career had been meteoric. At fourteen he was apprenticed in the print works of the *Warrnambool Examiner;* delivering morning papers before work and practising his shorthand in the evenings. At eighteen he left for Melbourne, with a plan to become editor of *The Argus,* but he ended up as a compositor on the *Herald* and then a reporter on the Melbourne *Daily Telegraph.* He took a job as a clerk in a Queensland engineering firm and toured remote goldmines of north Queensland before John Haynes,[59] a journalist with Sydney's *Evening News,* found him a clerk's job on that paper. Archibald soon became a reporter there, and in 1879 he and Haynes, with about £140 in savings between them, bought a small case of battered display type, put a deposit on a second-hand press and rented the ramshackle Scandinavian Hall at 107 Castlereagh Street, where they used packing cases for a desk and counter. The pair worked around the clock selling advertising for their new magazine.[60] By the time Lawson ambled into his office in 1887, Archibald had bought out his other partners, Haynes and William Henry Traill,[61] and was one of the most powerful and influential figures in the Australian media.

Archibald seemed surprised to finally meet 'H.A.L.', a deaf lad wearing a painter's apron, carrying a paint pot and a roll of foolscap with a paintbrush secured inside it and his lunch in his pocket. He told him that 'Sons of the South' was on hold for a special edition and he gave Lawson some writing tips; told him 'not to strain after effect', to 'avoid anti-climax' and to 'blot out every word you can do without'.[62]

After tinkering with Lawson's copy and changing the title to a more dramatic, more topical 'A Song of the Republic', Archibald finally ran it in a prominent spot on page five of the 1 October 1887 issue.

Forget about H.A.L. – the byline was 'Henry Lawson', and though the author was self-conscious and plagued by self-doubt, his words roared from the pages of the magazine.

'Sons of the South, awake! arise!'[63]

Chapter 5

*In publishing the subjoined verses we take pleasure in stating that the
writer thereof is a boy of 17 years, a young Australian, who has as
yet had an imperfect education and is earning his living under some
difficulties as a housepainter, a youth whose poetic genius
here speaks eloquently for itself.*

J.F. ARCHIBALD DECLARING LAWSON A RISING
STAR OF THE LITERARY WORLD[1]

THERE WAS CONSTANT CONFLICT between mother
and son at Phillip Street but Lawson was grateful that Louisa
was trying to advance his writing career. She encouraged him
to try his hand at ballads and recollections of the bush, and so
he summoned the spirit of Edgar Allan Poe in writing 'The
Legend of Coo-ee Gully'.[2] He continued his nationalistic theme
with 'The Hymn of the Socialists'.[3] Working on *The Republican*
eventually gave him the poem 'The Cambaroora Star'[4] about a
bush battler with a little printing press.

The fourth issue of *The Republican* reprinted Lawson's 'A
Song of the Republic', and reported the establishment of both
the Australian Socialist League and the Anti-Chinese League.
Lawson also gave *The Bulletin* 'The Wreck of the "Derry Castle"',[5]
about the sinking of an Irish-registered ship off the sub-Antarctic
Auckland Islands.

Fred Broomfield,[6] an English-born accountant who was
working as a sub-editor on *The Bulletin*, remembered Lawson
arriving at the office, 'a tall, nervous, shabbily-dressed youth with
what seemed to be an impediment in his speech'.[7] Broomfield

One of Lawson's early mentors, Fred Broomfield of
The Bulletin. State Library of NSW, FL465861

was the only person in the office after hours. Despite repeated
encouragement from Archibald that Lawson had potential as a
writer, Lawson presented the envelope containing 'Derry Castle'
to Broomfield with trepidation and 'hurriedly bolted without any
explanation whatsoever'. Broomfield said when Archibald scanned
'the ill-written manuscript' later he crushed it in his hand and
threw it into the bin 'with a chuckle about "bards who had not
learned to spell"'.[8] Broomfield was curious, though. He fished
Lawson's work from the bin. 'It was crudely written,' Broomfield
recalled, 'the spelling was original, and it required concentration to
decipher. But I persevered and wrote out a good copy of two sets
of verses.' Lawson confirmed the account years later in the poem
'Dind's Hotel',[9] when he wrote that Broomfield had become his
'literary dad'.[10]

THE EXCITEMENT OF PERHAPS seeing another poem in print was tempered by Lawson's increasing discomfort over his deafness and speech. So with the money he saved from painting, he travelled to Melbourne to receive treatment at a clinic established by Dr Andrew Sexton Gray,[11] a 61-year-old Irishman from Limerick who had once been an assistant to Sir William Wilde, father of the writer Oscar Wilde, at Dublin's St Mark's Ophthalmic Hospital.[12]

Lawson made the journey south on the steamer *Wendouree*, in the luxury of saloon class, to cheer himself.

'It was glorious,' he said. 'We were a happy little party from the skipper down, and there was a nice natural girl who drew me out of myself a bit, and banished my shyness.'[13]

For an awkward young man embarrassed by his deafness and speech, the steward's surprising 'Tea or coffee, sir?' made Lawson feel special.

'I must have looked Bushy enough with my carpet bag, and a few washed and mended clothes,' he wrote later. 'I had a shop suit bought at a store on the mountains, and the cloth was like coarse corduroy dyed blue and the pants too bulky and short.'[14]

Lawson arrived in Melbourne with a letter of recommendation from a young woman who boarded at Louisa's place in Sydney, and he stayed with a Mrs Kelly in West Melbourne. After taking a horse-drawn cab to his lodgings – his first dealings with a cabman – Lawson had about a week's board money left. The excitement of the steamer ride south had gone and Lawson felt 'utterly demoralised, alone in a strange city at the door of my first boarding house'; a dingy little one at that, in a shabby, dusty street of two-storeyed terraces. The house was one room and a passage wide and two rooms deep, with a kitchen behind where Mrs Kelly 'was supposed to sleep – if she slept at all – and a room over it sacred to the lady lodgers'.[15] Mrs Kelly was a little elderly Irish woman, 'with one rusty, black best dress and shawl, a bonnet like an old spider's cob-web in a corner', and a face like a small apple that had been left for a long time in a sunny window.

The 'head boarder' was a stout gentleman in a rusty walking coat. He was the manager in the storeroom of a modest ironmongery, with a staff of himself, a storeman and the van-man. But he had the combined presence 'of country newspaper proprietor, schoolmaster, and storekeeper, with the hoggish throat of a Yankee lecturer or quack medicine seller and showman, and he had the balcony room to himself'.[16] There was also a stout lady, 'fair fat and forty and decidedly haughty, a schoolmaster's wife or something ... whom they called "the Queen"'. She used to sit on the paper at breakfast, and monopolised the bathroom for an hour or so every Sunday morning when the 'gentlemen' wanted to use it.[17]

Lawson shared a room with two other men; one he remembered as 'Tom Punt', an easy-going youngster who worked on the railways, and 'Bob Heckler', a commercial traveller, who was always behind with his board but who had 'a cheerful sanguine' disposition. Heckler had pawned his spare boots and pants to buy tobacco but read all the advertisements that offered easy money. He took Punt into his confidence, talked him into buying a range of hops and other herbs, and together they started making a secret potion that would resemble Warner's Safe Cure, a popular range of medicines. They brewed their concoction in a saucepan, kept it in bulk in a water jug, readied it in the washbasin and stored it in bottles until they broke the jug – and something else – and the bottles began to explode in the small hours. Mrs Kelly brought an end to their enterprise and 'Punt and Heckler's Only Cure' went down the sink by night.

Another boarder, 'Miss Smith', was a young dressmaker who was touched by Lawson's shyness and tried to teach him how to walk with women without getting in their way.[18]

On Saturday nights Lawson would often accompany Miss Smith and Mrs Kelly to the markets. Mrs Kelly would carry her shopping in an old pram that listed to port and went in circles if let go. She said she used to wheel her little grandson in it but he 'died of diptheery'.[19]

DR ANDREW SEXTON GRAY had arrived in Victoria with his wife Elizabeth in 1859 and worked as the railway surgeon during the construction of the Geelong–Ballarat line. He saw a prevalence of eye and ear diseases in Victoria, particularly among miners working in the goldfields where living conditions and sanitation standards were usually poor.

By the time Lawson arrived in Melbourne, Gray ran the Victorian Eye and Ear Hospital on Victoria Parade. He was a sharp-eyed little terrier with a neat beard and a fiery reputation. He believed strongly in bloodletting. When operating he was literally armed to the teeth for he carried his Graefe knife in his mouth while his hands were filled with other instruments.[20]

Lawson had high hopes for the Melbourne medical men but 'they did little or no good'.

They said it was chronic catarr [sic] or something and used to put an instrument shaped like a gas blower pipe up my nose, and turn it round inside my head with the point towards my ear and blow into it with an India rubber bulb.[21]

But whether it was the pipe up his nose or the change of surrounds, Lawson's mood improved dramatically in Melbourne. He went to the theatre to see *The Silver King* starring English-born George Titheradge. Lawson heard the performance better than he'd ever heard a play before.[22] Deafness thwarted Lawson's own ambitions to try acting but he kept receiving treatment at Dr Gray's clinic for several months.

LAWSON FOUND JOBS at the Yarra Bank Works for railway car construction at West Melbourne and then at the Melbourne Tramway and Omnibus Company in North Fitzroy. He remembered 'a would be bully' at that place who he 'put down' and, using the crude language of *The Bulletin*, what he called 'a mighty buck nigger night watchman with awful rolling eyes ... and a sudden guffaw like a grave yard eruption'.[23]

By the end of 1887 Lawson was earning 6 shillings a day as a coach-painter in the Melbourne suburb of Windsor. He was varnishing an old hearse one day when an envelope arrived for him containing the Christmas edition of *The Bulletin*. Trembling with anticipation, he tore it open and glanced through it, his heart beating overtime and his mouth dry. Then he saw not just 'Derry Castle', but another poem he had submitted, the first published about his old home: 'Golden Gully',[24] the first dealing with his evocation of the Australian landscape and the emotions it created in him.

Lawson was overcome with shock and then waves of relief and joy. He hid the magazine in the hearse he was 'rubbing-down', fearful that the journal might be confiscated by his boss, 'a fierce Wesleyan' who did not approve of such a revolutionary rag. Lawson rubbed the finish on the hearse as hard as he could with the pumice stone until his heart didn't thump so much and he felt calmer. Every now and then, when his workmates weren't looking, he stole glances at his two poems and what Lawson called Archibald's 'kindly editorial note' accompanying 'Derry Castle' 'to the effect that I was a mere lad ... earning a living, under difficulties, at house-painting, and that my education was, as yet unfinished (N.B. – I couldn't spell), and that my talent spoke for itself in the following poem'.[25]

Archibald had anointed the nervous lad as a rising star on the Australian literary scene and in telling Australia that the boy was only seventeen, he had shaved three years off Lawson's age as well.

'I felt strong and proud enough to clean pig-sties if need be, for a living for the rest of my natural life – providing *The Bulletin* went on publishing the poetry,' Lawson wrote. 'I was in print and in the Xmas number of a journal I had worshipped and devoured every inch of for years.'[26]

LAWSON LOOKED UP PETER MCINTOSH, an old miner who had been at the Ballarat gold rush before joining Niels on the diggings in Log Paddock. He had since retired to the seaside village of St Kilda and eventually became Peter Maginnis in a piece of Lawson prose.[27]

Lawson then caught the train to Ballarat and wrote an ode to the statue of Robert Burns there.[28] He walked on further to see the monument to the fallen on the site of the Eureka Stockade where three decades earlier miners, protesting unfair taxes, had fought soldiers and police under their Southern Cross flag of rebellion. Then he saw their graves in Ballarat Cemetery and mulled over the idea that 'twenty minutes freed Australia at Eureka Long Ago'.[29] 'Eureka',[30] 'Flag of the Southern Cross'[31] and a much later work, 'Australia's Forgotten Flag',[32] among others came from that visit.

Lawson had long had an idea of studying art, and he practised sketching at Mrs Kelly's. Bob Heckler had a plan that they could both get rich, with Lawson touching up photographic enlargements for a young, well-to-do amateur photographer and his artist friend at Windsor. Lawson's work wasn't neat enough, though, as he tried to colour the monochrome faces of studio portraits. Instead, the photographer hired him to do carpentry work and painting on an old produce store at Windsor that he hoped to use as a photographic studio and framing shop. Lawson signed on for 30 shillings a week and 'batched' on the premises but his pay soon dwindled to 25 shillings and then 20.

He returned to Sydney in the cheaper steerage class. There was no improvement to his hearing and his pockets were empty. In early 1888, he started painting some cottages his father had built at Mount Victoria in the Blue Mountains. He was earning 8 shillings a day when he received his first cheque as a writer – £1 7s – from *The Bulletin*.[33] Other publications became interested in his writing too, and he started contributing satirical verses to the *Lithgow Enterprise*, a struggling country newspaper run by John Farrell,[34] a 37-year-old poet and journalist. Farrell had previously been a gold-miner and farmer in Victoria, and a brewery owner in Goulburn. Lawson wrote that as a lad he worshipped Farrell's verses even more than he did those of Adam Lindsay Gordon, 'perhaps because he was so new and real'.[35] 'Keep on at writing,' Farrell told Lawson after his first submissions. 'I am sure you will achieve very fine success yet.'[36]

Lawson welcomed every chance to escape his mother's tight rein in Sydney and join his father in the mountains for construction and painting work. He also worked alongside his grandfather in various bush chores. In the bush working camps he found alcohol helped him overcome his shyness.

Lawson reckoned that by 1888, Niels had built most of Mount Victoria's township, 'save the few houses that were there in the old coaching days'.[37] Living alone, though, had made Niels careless of his health and personal appearance and more 'cantankerous', though seldom so with Lawson.[38] Niels was now in his mid-fifties and ageing fast, but for a small man he was still strong and could 'climb anywhere' and could keep his footing on the steepest parts of a roof or highest ridge pole, perhaps because of his training at sea.[39]

He had an idea of going back to Norway before he died and taking at least his youngest son, Peter, now fifteen, with him, leaving the rest of the children provided for as well as he could.[40] At the time, Peter was attending a small private school at Mount Victoria run by Henry Rienits, a friend of their father. Although Louisa sometimes caught the train up to visit her youngest son,[41] a gulf between Niels and his children had developed in the five years since Louisa had left him. Lawson's sister Gertrude was to write that 'not one of us really understood Father. If we had of known the real man we would have been kinder.'[42] Elizabeth Tierney felt that the long absences from his children had made Niels 'crotchety'.[43]

On his visits to the mountains, Lawson took long walks along the road to Cox's Pass and drank in the solitude, far away from Sydney's revolutionary republicanism. 'A May Night on the Mountains'[44] showed the influence of his mother's hero Kendall, and that Lawson thought deeply about mankind needing a moral overhaul as much as a political one. Often Lawson and his grandfather went about 'humping palings and rails out of gullies'.[45] Henry Albury, now in his early sixties, remained as imposing as ever. He relayed countless yarns about bush life. And death.

Amongst other things he was an undertake[r]. He buried many and under all sorts of conditions – some in sheets of bark; and he was in great demand at burials. He usually had a coffin cut out roughly and stuck up over the tie-beams of the kitchen to season, and wait.[46]

Lawson later penned the short story 'The Bush Undertaker'[47] about an eccentric old shepherd and his beloved dog, Five-Bob, and their odyssey to bury one of the undertaker's old alcoholic friends. The undertaker, disorientated by the heat and isolation, amuses himself during a hot Australian Christmas by excavating a 'blackfellow's' skeleton from its bush grave. Then he stumbles on the corpse of his friend Brummy, 'dried to a mummy by the intense heat of the western summer'.[48] A black goanna watches all. The Aboriginal bones, which are white, are dug up as collectables; while the white man's corpse, now 'black' from decomposition, is returned for what passes as a Christian burial.

On one level it is a tale of the maddening effects of loneliness on the isolated shepherd in 'the grand Australian bush – the nurse and tutor of eccentric minds, the home of the weird'.[49] But it also shows Lawson's awareness of the arbitrary nature of compassion, the failure of the white population to deal justly with the original inhabitants and, with the symbol of the goanna, its uneasy relationship with a land they often imagined to be haunted.[50]

Albury was now an endless source of material for Lawson's writing. Often, he worked alongside his teenage son Ernie, who was four and a half years younger than Lawson. Sometimes Albury's younger brother Abel joined them.

Abel would listen to commercial travellers, canvassers, and confidence men and spielers of all descriptions, until they seemed to have amused themselves sufficiently, and then he'd say, laconically, "Leggo me ear".[51] The expression played out in a memorable Lawson sketch.

When Henry Albury visited Sydney, he would ride his skinny old horse bareback across the Blue Mountains until he arrived at Parramatta. One of Lawson's oldest friends remembered Albury at the time as 'a very handsome man, with a big, deep, soft voice, though what he said could be very disconcerting'.[52]

Albury was eccentric and prickly, but endlessly fascinating, whether it was hiding presents in the bush for his offspring or marching down the middle of Sydney's crowded George Street towards Redfern Station with a razor-sharp adze and saw in his carpenter's bag slung across his wide shoulders, seemingly oblivious to the fear and discomfort of startled pedestrians ducking just in time to preserve eyes and ears.

Lawson said that his grandfather might have been illiterate but he was 'a dumb poet, a poet of the trees'.[53] He was anything but empathetic. He sold mountain ash timber instead of the superior stringybark to unsuspecting customers whenever he could, but he always had a soft spot for his family. In his old age when the children were scattered, he was known to journey down the mountains alone to Mulgoa just to have a look at the old church where he was married.[54]

He also had 'sight like a blackfellow', Lawson said, 'and was a first class Bushman of the old school. He was a humourist of the loud voiced order ... He nearly always shouted at the top of his voice, and it was a big voice. I got on well with him and was, I think, the only one in the family who could get him to sing ... Like most illiterate men he remembered nearly all he had ever seen or heard.'[55] Drink cost him most of the land he bought.

THE NEW SOUTH WALES PREMIER Henry Parkes spent much of the early part of 1888 trying to have his colony renamed 'Australia' in time for Queen Victoria's birthday on 24 May 1888. He had moved 'The Colony of Australia Bill', though 'newspapers, with few exceptions, condemned it as an attempt to appropriate to [NSW] a name which belonged to all the Australian colonies in common'.[56]

Lawson was back in Sydney, working alongside his mother and William Keep, cranking out *The Republican*, and writing political essays for it. He argued against closer ties between England and the colonies and any other moves to appease Australia's 'contemptible toadies'. 'Why on earth do we want closer connection with England?' Lawson asked in a *Republican* editorial on 7 January 1888. 'We have little in common with English people except our language. We are fast becoming an entirely different people. ... for the present let our colonies try to cultivate a still more brotherly feeling for each other, and the day will come when the sons of all the colonies can clasp hands and say truly: "We are Australians – we know no other land!".'[57] Lawson began using the pen-name 'Caliban' for political commentary.

For *The Bulletin*, he submitted 'Song of the Outcasts'[58] about those like him who saw nothing to celebrate during the Queen's jubilee. Lawson's deafness and his old schoolteacher John Tierney's Irish accent combined to make him believe that these lines in his poem rhymed:

I heard beyond the cheering, and beyond the trumpets' blare,
The steady tramp of thousands that were marching in the rear.

He was acutely embarrassed by the realisation that 'rear' was not pronounced 'rare' and in later years changed the poem to 'The Army of the Rear'[59] with altered verses.

By early 1888, George Black was winning acclaim among the Sunday crowds at Sydney's Domain, where he railed against the monarchy and Britain's class system. The Australian Republican Union was faltering though, with declining membership and poor attendances at their meetings. So it was that on 29 January 1888, three days after the centenary of the First Fleet's arrival in Australia, Black stood on a stump beneath the giant fig trees at the Domain and before a crowd numbered between 1000 and 2000 to announce the formation of the Australian Republican League. Supporters walked about the crowd handing out a scathing letter from Black to Queen Victoria, which then appeared in the Lawsons' newspaper.

Black remembered Lawson then as a 'gawky and morose youth, greatly handicapped by deafness' who always seemed to be going somewhere 'to a job or in search of one – and was perpetually coming back more disheartened with each return'.[60]

In an essay for *The Republican* on 4 April 1888, Lawson called for school students to be taught more about Australian history than British, to be taught about the diggers who died at Eureka and to 'acquire a preference' for their own national song rather than 'God Save our Gracious Queen'. This was Australia, he said, 'and not a mere outlying suburb of England'.[61]

Louisa contributed a 'Women's Column' to *The Republican*, campaigning for women's voting rights, among other claims for equality, and it gave her the idea for a publication specifically for a female audience. She had found many friends and admirers in the Progressive Spiritualist Lyceum at Leigh House, including the feminists Rose Scott and Susannah Gale, and predicted the dawn of a new age for women.

There wasn't a great deal of money in publishing though. Lawson ran a work wanted ad for himself: '"Caliban", Author of "Under the Emu Flag", wishes position on a bush-town paper. Anti-royalist. Address, 138 Phillip Street, Sydney, N. S. W.'[62]

ON 15 MAY 1888, Louisa launched her new feminist newspaper, *The Dawn*, publishing it under the pseudonym Dora Falconer from 138 Phillip Street. On its first front page, she declared her manifesto: 'There has hitherto been no trumpet through which the concentrated voice of womankind could publish their grievances and their opinions. ... Here then is DAWN, the Australian women's journal and mouthpiece.'[63]

Louisa later told *The Bulletin* that because she was female, her mother burnt her books when she was young and her husband, 'a clever, capable man', frowned upon her 'impulse to imaginative work'. Friends and relatives, she said, looked askance at her 'queer ways' and she had been repressed all her life.[64] She had no time for the weak or the foolish, and like her father she didn't care who she offended.

Louisa claimed that even the Post Office had been against her, initially refusing to register *The Dawn* to send through the post as

THE DAWN.

A Journal for Australian Women.

EDITED BY DORA FALCONER

Vol. I. No. 1.   SYDNEY, MAY 15, 1888.   PRICE, 3D.

About Ourselves.

"WOMAN is not uncompleted man, but diverse." says Tennyson, and being diverse why should she not have her journal in which her divergent hopes, aims, and opinions may have representation. Every eccentricity of belief, and every variety of bias in mankind allies itself with a printing-machine, and gets its singularities uttered about in type, but where is the printing ink champion of mankind's better half? There has hitherto been no trumpet through which the concentrated voices of womankind could publish their grievances and their opinions. Men legislate on divorce, on hours of labor, and many another question intimately affecting women, but neither ask nor know the wishes of those whose lives and happiness are most concerned. Many a tale might be told by women, and many a useful hint given, even to the omniscient male, which would materially strengthen and guide the hands of law-makers and benefactors aspiring to be just and generous to weak and unrepresented womankind.

Here then is Dawn, the Australian Woman's Journal and mouthpiece—

The debut issue of Louisa Lawson's feminist newspaper *The Dawn*. National Library of Australia.

a newspaper. She claimed that one day a man from the *Christian World* magazine, smartly dressed in a white flannel suit and straw hat, came round to borrow a picture for his publication. Louisa wouldn't lend it to him because she'd paid a pound for it. The *Christian World* man sneered at the girls around him so Louisa took up a watering pot full of water that she had for sweeping the floor, and threw it all over him.[65]

She told *The Bulletin* that Lawson was an enormous help in getting the magazine rolling, though, and that Niels always thought Henry was 'a tiger for work. Poor boy!'[66]

When we were starting *Dawn* he used to turn the machine for us; he would just get some verse in his head and go on turning mechanically, forgetting all about us. He didn't like to be interrupted when he was thinking, so often when the issue was all printed off we would go upstairs to supper and leave him there turning away at the empty machine, with his eyes shining.[67]

TWO MONTHS AFTER *THE DAWN*'S LAUNCH, and while returning from another fruitless search for permanent work, Lawson found himself on a rainy winter's night at Sydney's Petersham train station. He was 'alone and tired with a shoddy overcoat coarse as sacking and warm as [a] refrigerator'.[68] By the weak light of the sickly gas lamps, he looked at the wet shining asphalt, the posters on the mean brick walls, and the light glistening on the enamelled iron notice saying 'Second Class wait Here'.[69] Lawson was about to become 'the poet of the great tribe of the Down-and-out'.[70]

Having just celebrated his twenty-first birthday, he sent his newest, and as yet most poignant, work to Archibald, who reshaped it a little and published it in *The Bulletin* on 28 July 1888 as 'Faces in the Street':

> Drifting past, drifting past,
> To the beat of weary feet —
> While I sorrow for the owners of those faces in the street.[71]

Archibald paid Lawson a guinea for it and Lawson had struck a nerve with the poor, the downtrodden and those crying out for social reform. Only a few weeks before 'Faces in the Street' was published, Thomas McIlwraith's National Party scored a remarkable victory in the Queensland elections after running on a platform that included the formation of a federated independent government for the Australian colonies. The word 'national' was much more user-friendly for the republican cause.

So it was that some of the leaders of the republican movement met at Sydney's Royal Hyde Park Hotel on 12 July and formed the

Australian National Association.[72] 'Archie Lawson', now operating the old press out of Ramsay Street, Summer Hill, in Sydney's inner west, 'printed and published' the first issue of the *Australian Nationalist* on 8 August 1888, explaining that it was the new title of *The Republican* and its aim was to help pave the way for a 'United and Independent Australia in the near future'. Lawson saw a future when 'Australia shall become a great and progressive Commonwealth, free from the incubi of Kings, despotic rulers, land monopolists, and hereditary Have-alls',[73] but the paper lasted only one issue. *The Dawn* was proving far more popular than Lawson's red rag.

Lawson put political propaganda aside to return to his bush roots with 'Lachlan Side'[74] and what was to become one of his most popular poems, 'Andy's Gone with Cattle',[75] about the loneliness a family feels when their man is away droving.

He wrote a sequel six weeks later.[76] Lawson paid a visit to Eurunderee but it only summoned mostly bad memories in 'Beaten Back',[77] the tale of a lost property. The trip expanded Lawson's social circle on job sites at Mount Victoria, though, after he met a young plasterer named Arthur Parker in late 1888. Parker was selling a shotgun and one of his relatives told him of a young man who wanted to buy one and who was painting a row of four cottages called 'Buena Vista' that Niels had built on the Bathurst Road. Lawson was living with Niels in a one-room cottage behind Mount Victoria's wooden church. Niels had several men working for him at the time 'but still worked and lived as hard as ever'.[78] Parker always called Lawson 'Harry' and remembered him as 'a tall, thin boy, pale and very delicate looking, with deep dark eyes … quiet, earnest and dreamy; intensely shy and very reserved until you got to know him'.[79] Lawson didn't buy the gun but soon he and Parker were working together on houses with Parker's brother Charlie and his brothers-in-law, Jack and David Jones, and a few others. Lawson called them the 'Mountain Push'[80] and in their free time they would explore the spectacular countryside down into the Kanimbla Valley. The mountain sojourns gave Lawson the inspiration for works such as 'Cherry-Tree Inn'[81] and

'The Third Murder',[82] based on a visit to a supposedly haunted mansion called Lowther House by Lawson and his brother Peter. 'The Hairy Man'[83] was a bunyip story written after Lawson saw Jack Jones, a plumber, wearing a possum skin suit for a lark.[84]

Among those friends, Lawson wrote, 'there was between us that sympathy which in our times and conditions is the strongest and perhaps truest of all human qualities, the sympathy of drink. We were drinking mates together ...'[85]

Alcohol became Lawson's tonic for his shyness, melancholy and whatever else troubled him.

The team camped together in a tent on job sites. Parker always remembered Lawson as a hard worker putting the first coat of paint on cottages – and all over himself – in a day. Often swagmen tramping by would stop at the tent for a smoke and a feed, and Lawson would fry sausages for them, getting paint on the sausages as well.

Lawson was fascinated by the spectacular mountain scenery, the gorges and ravines, the majestic formations inside the Jenolan Caves. Local legends about ghosts intrigued him, too, and he would often go tramping at night. Once he roused Parker out of bed at 9 p.m. to walk through Blackheath to look at the cavernous Govetts Leap by moonlight. He was always embarrassed by his deafness and if people shouted at him, he would roar back 'Don't shout; I'm not as deaf as that'. He seemed to hear well enough if people spoke slowly and clearly. Sometimes he visited concerts with his mates and tried not to fall on his face on the new roller-skating rink at Blackheath.[86]

Arthur Parker began cutting Lawson's work out of *The Bulletin* and other publications to keep in a scrapbook for him and Lawson told Parker that he'd like to write less poetry and more prose. 'His whole soul was in his writing,' Parker wrote, 'and in his hopes for Socialism.'[87]

It was now that Lawson decided to convert one of his grandfather's campfire yarns into a piece of prose that would cement his reputation as a writer around Australia. Lawson wrote seven short chapters in the style of Bret Harte, telling the tale of the death of nine-year-old Thomas Aspinall down a fifteen-metre mineshaft that the boy's father was working at the New Pipeclay Diggings on 1 February 1865.[88] 'His Father's Mate' became a harrowing and haunting tale, full of Victorian-era melodrama and tear-jerking sentimentality. George Black, now working as a *Bulletin* sub-editor, said the story arrived at the magazine as a 'very crude composition', unpunctuated, with bad spelling and a sloppy arrangement of paragraphs.

Black said he and 'the chief' (Archibald) condensed it in places and remodelled it. After three re-typings it was sent by vacuum chute to the composing room.[89] 'His Father's Mate' appeared in *The Bulletin* on 22 December 1888 and was an instant hit. At Mount Victoria, Niels was completing a row of cottages called the Sanitorium and also working on Rienits's school. He was asking every person he met 'Have you seen my son Henry's story in the Sydney *Bulletin*?' And though he was a quiet man, he asked the question in a voice for all the world to hear.[90] Niels was aghast at Henry's drinking, though, and sent a telegram to Louisa asking her to find work for him away from the Mountain Push.

Louisa was now in full stride publishing *The Dawn* from an office at 26 Jamieson Street, Sydney. Her list of contacts expanded and her influence grew. On Lawson's behalf she renewed his application for a job on the railways, suggesting that perhaps his submission from the previous year had been lost or forgotten. She even sent off a request to Premier Henry Parkes asking for his help in finding her boy work as a carriage-painter. She sent Parkes Lawson's poem 'Andy's Gone with Cattle' and its sequel, and Lawson was given an audience with him. Parkes, though, told Lawson that poetry was not a prerequisite for such a position, and that his experience was not sufficient for the job. Louisa was not pleased and while she thanked the premier for his 'kind attention' over the matter, she pointed out that she did not believe Lawson's 'as yet unperfected poetic faculties make him any less a good workman'. Her son's 'over-modesty' did him no favours, she said, and while Lawson told Parkes he had been painting for only three years, Louisa said he had actually been doing it for seven 'and is able to do any work which can be given him in his trade'.[91]

ON NEW YEAR'S EVE 1888, Lawson was on a scaffold whitewashing a ceiling at the Deaf Dumb and Blind Institution in Sydney's Darlington when his brother Peter brought a telegram from Mount Victoria. With a trembling hand, Lawson read that Niels had died suddenly that morning.

Lawson was stunned.

He recalled that Niels 'was camping in a room of one of the new cottages, and, the night before his death he had two or three young fellows up to see him who used to discuss Henry George's *Progress and Poverty* and other democratic subjects with him, and always got onto mathematics ... Next, morning they told me, he went down to work at the school building as usual, and though he complained of "feeling queer" ... he returned to the cottages for a keg or small drum of white lead, instead of letting one of the men go for it.'

About halfway back from the cottages, Niels began to feel worse and broke into a trot, the quicker to reach his bunk. A friend ran for a doctor and then Niels asked him to run for his friend, Constable Brassington, as he had something to tell him. The constable came at once, but by then Niels was sitting dead on his bunk, leaning back against the wall.[92] He was just fifty-six.

The young doctor Edward Hume Morgan[93] told Lawson it was heart disease and 'an old thing'. Lawson wrote later that he reached Mount Victoria by the midnight train when the New Year's bonfires were blazing and rockets were going up. Some of his father's friends told Lawson that it was the only time they had ever seen Niels rest. The similarities between his father's death and the sudden demise of the worn-out dad in 'His Father's Mate' only added to Lawson's shock and grief.

Dr Morgan recorded that Niels died on 31 December 1888 from 'fatty degeneration of the heart'. He was buried by local undertaker Fred Wilson the next day in the Hartley Vale Cemetery in the shadow of Mount York. Even though they had been apart for five years there was still affection between Niels and Louisa, and she paid for a decent burial. Lawson claimed that he and Peter had both arrived for the funeral, but the burial register recorded that Louisa's foreman William Keep was the only witness.

Lawson's sister Gertrude would later write that 'Henry's grief was terrible to witness. Dry eyed he moaned, If I could only cry, Mother. If I could only cry.'[94]

In 'A Foreign Father', Lawson wrote that his father 'died before I began to understand and appreciate him. He was a stranger and a foreigner to his own family – as are many of our foreign fathers in Australia. He had different notions, to us Australians, about family life. He had a different past to look back to, in a foreign country amongst strange people, that we could never realize. We spoke English, or, rather, Australian; he spoke broken English which was worse as he grew older.'[95]

And in the same account: 'I went away and leaned on the cemetery fence, and watched the sun going down on the bush; and hated the bush, and the country, "my country"! and the English that owned it – the squatters and the bank shareholders who lived in luxury in the city – the hundreds who lived in idleness because of the wasted lives of toil of thousands of men like the man that lay yonder under the new mound of hard, lumpy clay that was already drying in the drought. And I wished that I could write.'[96]

Years later Lawson said Niels had 'left a tidy sum' to him, 'But I'd give all the money to hear him say, "Will you get up and bile the billy, Sonny?"'[97]

Lawson poured his soul out in his writing in the years to come, expressing his love and admiration for the poor people of the bush and the inner-city slums. For the little battlers like his father. He yearned to be their voice.

Chapter 6

*About this time Henry became acquainted with Miss Mary
J. Cameron. She was a school-teacher; her mother was a journalist and
an advocate of women's rights. Through her mother's acquaintance with
Mrs Lawson, Miss Cameron came to know Henry
and the poet fell in love with her.*

LAWSON'S FRIEND AND FELLOW WRITER BERTRAM STEVENS[1]

LAWSON CONTINUED TO WORK in the mountains off
and on for a few months after his father's death and finished
painting the last cottages that Niels had built. Niels had been
a thrifty man, so on 18 February 1889 his estate was valued at
£1103 for probate,[2] his land at Sapling Gully valued at £400. The
amount represented a small fortune – enough to sustain Louisa's
new baby, *The Dawn*, for years.

The mountains also continued to be a goldmine for Lawson's
writing. Not long after his father's funeral, Lawson was driving
a cart from Mount Victoria down the range to the cemetery. He
was carrying a load of sturdy wooden pickets to protect Niels's
grave from wind and rain. Arthur Parker and Jack Jones overtook
Lawson on the road as they made their way to help an old settler
move his possessions to another part of the valley.

That night, at the foot of the mountain pass, the trio
met again, and in the ghostly moonlight, Lawson's young
companions told him an eerie story about the ghost of the
murdered teenager Caroline Collits, dressed in black, which

would appear to travellers late at night, her long, dark hair streaming out in the wind and her arms raised to the heavens. Some said that her eyes shone in the dark like a tiger's, others that she was headless.[3] Lawson later wrote 'The Ghost at the Second Bridge'[4] for *Freeman's Journal*.[5] At just twenty-one, Lawson was finding a steady market for his work, though each piece only earned him a few shillings. He wrote under his own byline and the pen-names 'Rumfellow', 'The Ghost' and 'Joe Swallow'. His poems had a freshness that few Australian writers of the time could match and he spoke to the working-class Australians in the city and country in language they could understand, even if he often wallowed in sentimentality.[6] Archibald was nurturing a large stable of writers that included Banjo Paterson, Victor Daley,[7] Phil Mowbray[8] and Ted Dyson,[9] and Lawson found that any of his poems or stories that *The Bulletin* couldn't or wouldn't use would readily find a home elsewhere. There was always *Freeman's*, which ran his poem 'To the Irish Delegates'[10] in support of Irish home rule during a visit to Australia by three Irish members of the House of Commons. But the editor Tom Butler was always telling Lawson that the publication rarely paid for contributions.

There was also *Australian Town and Country Journal* which usually paid 10 shillings and sixpence for his work. It published 'Andy's Gone with Cattle' in 1888 and then ran eleven of Lawson's poems in 1889, everything from odes to the bushman in 'The Ballad of The Drover',[11] to 'Cinderella'[12] and his first romantic work 'Oh Cupid, Cupid; Get Your Bow!'[13] The *Illustrated Sydney News* ran another of his shipwreck poems, 'The "Seabolt's" Volunteers'.[14]

Lawson used Henry Albury as the model for poems such as 'The Mountain Splitter'[15] and much later, the short story 'Grandfather's Courtship',[16] in which the hard old man tells his delicate grandson:

I was a young man then Henery, about your age – but they did say I was something to look at ... and I didn't wear la-di-dah clothes, an' write poetry for papers ...[17]

Albury told Lawson about the death of the Mudgee policeman Senior Constable Hugh Campbell, who was thrown from his horse and killed while chasing two bushrangers on the road to Guntawang in 1868.[18] The poem 'Ben Duggan', later known as 'Talbragar', was the result.[19]

Working as a coach-painter had already given Lawson the ideas for short stories about the hard slog of manual work for the urban poor in 'Arvie Aspinall's Alarm Clock'[20] and 'A Visit of Condolence'.[21] 'Jones's Alley'[22] was based on his time living in the slums around Clarence Lane and the cruelty of old workmates resurfaced in 'Two Boys at Grinder Bros'.[23]

More and more Lawson was focusing on exploring the human condition in his writing, rather than the red flag of republicanism. Still, the death in 1889 of Peter Lalor,[24] the Irish-born leader of the rebels at Ballarat thirty-five years earlier, prompted Lawson to write 'Eureka'[25] as a tribute to the ordinary man's struggle against tyranny.

In early 1889, the Mountain Push began working on the new sixty-room Centennial Hotel in Blackheath.[26] Arthur Parker recalled:

The tradespeople sought our custom, but did not want us at the local dances and other social events. Henry came to see us and we told him our sad tale. He wrote for the [Lithgow] *Mercury* an article called 'The Scrub Aristocracy'. [With] Lawson's assistance, we were received into the social fold, and all went well.[27]

Lawson's mentor John Farrell wrote extensively for Sydney's *Daily Telegraph* in support of the tax reform ideas put forward in Henry George's book *Progress and Poverty* and Farrell escorted the American on a tour of Australia in 1889. Farrell was appointed editor of the *Daily Telegraph*, then a broadsheet newspaper, but soon decided he could not cope with the pressure and resigned three months later, though he continued to write articles for it.

Banjo Paterson, meanwhile, had joined the well-connected lawyer John Street in a Sydney law firm, Street & Paterson, at 105 Pitt Street, but he said he gained much more enjoyment in writing his rollicking, often humorous sketches and poems than he did writing legal letters of demand on behalf of banks, trying to extract money out of farmers who had nothing.

While both young men were bush bred and living in the city, Paterson, two years older than Lawson and far more learned in the ways of the world, had enjoyed many more material advantages. The republican mantra of *The Bulletin* was socially dangerous for Paterson, though, given his rich friends and business associates, so his work continued to appear under the 'Banjo' byline.

To Archibald, Paterson and Lawson were the emerging 'twin deities of Australian literature'.[28]

The artist Norman Lindsay,[29] who knew them both, said Banjo 'compacted in himself the best of the Australian ego', the rugged outdoorsman who regarded 'life as a high adventure in action, even to the risk of a broken neck'.[30] Much of Banjo's writing was outrageous fun as he had a lot to love about life. Not only did he have a successful legal practice, he mixed in the upper echelons of society and, with a beautiful fiancée,[31] had none of Lawson's reserve around women. He was a strapping athlete; a champion rower, tennis player and amateur jockey who played polo, and was once described as 'one of the keenest of sportsmen, a dashing cross-country rider, thin, wiry and hard as nails'.[32] Lawson, by contrast, was pale and sickly, and handicapped by his deafness and his domineering mother. He saw pain and suffering in the bush battler's eternal struggle against the unyielding elements. Norman Lindsay said that Lawson's Australia reflected his own demons, his own sadness 'sodden with self-pity ... that of the underdog'.[33]

Over the years, Lawson and Paterson often sat and yarned over their pipes about the inspiration for their works. Lawson told Banjo once that 'I can catch ideas anywhere, but I can't always make 'em go in harness. Simple stuff is the best. One day I picked up a pair of pants and found they had a hole in the stern and I wrote, "You've got to face your troubles when your pants begin to go". That hit them where they lived, for most of them had to face their troubles in life.'[34]

Archibald published Lawson's prose tearjerker 'The Story of Malachi'[35] in June 1889. It told the tale of a Lawson-like boy; tall, thin, round-shouldered, shabbily dressed that everyone took for a fool, but who eventually left them heartbroken by his gallantry.

There was 'The Song of the Waste-Paper Basket'[36] about a receptacle which devoured the rejected thoughts of both genius and fool, and then 'The Ghost',[37] in which Lawson rejects an evil apparition's claim that 'Self and Pity ... is the motto of the world' with the assertion that it is instead 'Brotherhood and Love and Honour!'[38]

Louisa was often at loggerheads with her son, who accused her of neglecting Niels in the last years of his life and they are said to have fought over the publication of 'The Ghost' which Louisa reckoned was in part a criticism of her striving for material riches from *The Dawn*.[39] As Christmas 1889 approached, the *Australian Town and Country Journal* ran three of Lawson's poems. 'The Teams'[40] displayed Lawson's keen eye in observing the bullockies in Golden Gully during his childhood. 'Brighten's Sister-in-Law',[41] which ran alongside a drawing of an angelic child, highlighted a man's love for his offspring, and the women who were saviours among the hard, rough men of the bush. 'Mount Bukaroo'[42] lamented the toil in vain of so many pioneers in a land that was so unforgiving.

On the same day, in the Christmas 1889 bumper edition of *The Bulletin*, Archibald showed off the best Lawson and Paterson had to offer. He ran two of Lawson's poems.

'The Roaring Days'[43] was an ode to men like his father who had gone prospecting everywhere from Ballarat to Log Paddock only to realise that those glorious, exciting days had passed and that with gold mining now the preserve of big companies:

> The mighty bush with iron rails
> Is tethered to the world.[44]

On the same *Bulletin* page, 'The Legend of Mammon Castle'[45] was a piece of doggerel with a socialist flavour.

Archibald featured four pieces by Banjo, with the most enduring tucked away in the bottom right corner of page seventeen. Its arresting tempo bound along like one of Banjo's horses taking off at Randwick racecourse. It was another of his homages to the great Australian outdoors and those he said were fortunate to ride the wide open spaces; who were done with the boss and the balance sheet and lived for the free life, bolstered by the bush air and the sunshine.[46]

The poem had its genesis in a letter of demand from Street & Paterson to a drover Banjo had met down near the Lachlan River some years earlier. One of the drover's mates sent a letter back with handwriting so appalling it looked as if it had been composed with a thumbnail dipped in tar.[47]

The poem was called 'Clancy of the Overflow'.[48]

It appeared almost as an Archibald afterthought, buried under an illustrated short story called 'Flowers for the Dead', by Francis Adams,[49] a champion of socialist and feminist causes who was also then writing leaders for the *Brisbane Courier*.

AN OVEREXTENSION OF THE 1880s property boom and the bursting of its bubble in 1889[50] led to a sudden collapse of investment in both Australia's pastoral industry and urban development. Soon there would be a fall-off in capital inflow from Britain, and a drought that brought man and beast to their knees. *The Bulletin*'s republican rhetoric was being read against a background of unprecedented industrial agitation.

Wool and wheat prices were falling. Unemployment skyrocketed. Employers in the city and the bush complained that they could no longer be generous with concessions such as the eight-hour day and other union demands. Many proposed 'freedom of contract' using cheaper non-union labour – or 'scabs', as their enemies called them.

The Australian colonies entered their worst ever financial crisis[51] and *The Bulletin* exposed the plight of the homeless in

Sydney in 'A Search for the Shelterless'[52] which influenced Lawson's later essay '"Dossing Out" and "Camping"'[53] for *The Worker* newspaper. Lawson found 'at least two hundred poor beggars' sleeping on the pavements, 'grotesque bundles of rags lying under the verandas of the old Fruit Markets and York-street shops, with their heads to the wall and their feet to the gutter ... driven in from Hyde Park and the bleak Domain by the rain and cold and the wind'.[54]

Lawson and his family had Niels's estate as a buffer against the financial headwinds, but that did not lessen any of their personal turmoil on 4 March 1890 when Charlie Lawson, now a habitual criminal using the alias Mark Allen, appeared before Judge Ernest Brougham Docker at the Forbes Quarter Sessions on charges of larceny and receiving. Charlie was sentenced to three years' hard labour in Darlinghurst Gaol.[55] A newspaper reporter in court noted that the prisoner was 'about 22 years of age' and had for the last seven years 'spent the whole of his life in gaol on various charges of stealing, many of his sentences being concurrent'.[56]

LAWSON WAS NOW nearing his twenty-third birthday and despite his reticence around women, he fell for an adventurous young schoolteacher, Mary Cameron, better known in Australian history by her later title Dame Mary Gilmore.[57] Mary was a young woman of extraordinary gumption who had just started teaching at Neutral Bay Public School. She was born near Crookwell, about 250 kilometres south-west of Sydney. She became a pupil-teacher at the age of thirteen at a small Cootamundra school run by her mother's brother, and for the next decade worked at Riverina schools of varying sizes. In October 1887 she was made a temporary assistant at Silverton Public School near Broken Hill on a salary of £114 a year with £24 in allowances to compensate for hardships at the remote posting. She complained that in her first eighteen months there, she saw rain only twice – and it was destructive – and that each summer heralded an outbreak of 'Barrier Fever' as a result of contaminated water, extreme heat and poor sanitation.

Lawson's early love interest, young schoolteacher Mary
Cameron, later became the socialist writer Dame
Mary Gilmore. Her relative Scott Morrison became
Australia's Prime Minister in 2018. State Library of NSW,
PXD 905/1-130

When Mary met Lawson early in 1890, she and her mother,
Mary Ann, were lodging together at Kate Dunn's boarding house,
'Kieta', at 5 Bligh Street, Sydney. Mrs Cameron had separated
from her husband and was writing a social column for the *Town
and Country Journal.* She had become friends with Louisa Lawson,
a kindred spirit, and claimed that in Louisa she had found 'the one
perfect woman in the world'.[58]

Louisa was overcoming the prejudices of the day to make *The
Dawn* a tool of empowerment for Australian women. The New
South Wales Typographical Association, which did not allow
women members, protested Louisa's use of female printers, claiming
that typesetting was such arduous and unhealthy work that in
employing girls, Louisa was 'dooming them to an early death'.[59]

Some of *The Dawn*'s employees needed police protection against union threats of violence and many of the unions withdrew their custom to shops which advertised with it. Many husbands forbade their wives and daughters to read Louisa's publication.[60]

Yet Louisa went on increasing her business so that she eventually had a staff of ten women, with her newspaper campaigning for a married women's union and the establishment of creches for the benefit of the overworked mothers of large families and those forced into paid work.

She also campaigned vigorously for New South Wales to adopt the divorce laws of Victoria. In what could have been a foregleam of what she would one day see in her own family, Louisa told *Dawn* readers in an article headlined: 'The Divorce Extension Bill, Or The Drunkard's Wife' that 'The fate of the Victorian divorce extension bill is a source of keen anxiety to many a miserable wife who has the mis-fortune to be linked for life to a drunkard ... With all due reverence for the sanctity of marriage, can there be anything sacred in the bond which binds a good woman to a sot, felon, or brute?'[61]

Mary Cameron, two years older than Lawson, was a strong, confident young woman who combined an 'alert manner and abrupt speech' with 'an active and original mind'.[62]

Lawson called Mary 'the best friend a man ever had'[63] and he became a frequent visitor to 5 Bligh Street. Mary later claimed much of the credit for Lawson's early development as a writer, and said he fell in love with her 'at first sight'.

They shared a disdain for bush snobbery and Mary would one day write of the bush aristocracy she had seen at the Wagga Wagga Race Ball and how a chalk line was drawn across the floor which the 'lower classes' were not to cross.[64] While Mary admired Lawson's writing, he was not really the type of rugged outdoorsman that the young schoolmistress found attractive.

'There was a curious immaturity about Lawson at that time,' she wrote. 'He was in the sappy twig stage of development. The handsome face and masculinity of later years had not then come into being. The face was weak, the chin underdeveloped. The look is effeminate ...'[65]

Lawson wasn't too savvy about how to show a girl a good time either, taking Mary not to the bright lights or the theatre but rather to the slums of Lower George Street and The Rocks for an education on Sydney's poverty. Mary had seen the destitute around Silverton but the privations of frontier life were eased by the constant hope that one lucky strike could change a family's fortunes. Sydney's underbelly was an eye-opener:

> He used to take me out to see the wrong things, the things
> repressive of the rights of Australia; the things like a blot
> upon her and which prevented her being herself – the low
> wage workers, the Chinamen working at treadle-saws
> in underground cellars lit only by a grating in the street,
> the huddled houses by the old Argyle Cut, and the Rocks
> where women hung their washing out on the roof and from
> windows, and where pale seamstresses sewed at a foot or a
> hand machine from daylight till dark for a few pence …[66]

In March 1890, Mary's mother left the *Town and Country Journal* and before taking a new job at Sydney's *Daily Telegraph* she went back to the Riverina for a six-week holiday in Junee. Mary boarded with the Lawsons, and while she was appalled at the untidiness of Louisa's home, Louisa was appalled at the thought of losing her son.

She quickly arranged for Lawson and his brother Peter to sail for Western Australia to chase job opportunities, since like Melbourne thirty-five years before, the west was undergoing a population boom fuelled by gold rushes. Louisa explained to Mary that if Lawson was to marry, he needed to make some real money, but perhaps Louisa was really hoping the tyranny of distance would end the relationship.

Lawson's eccentricities – 'his mannerisms and queer ways' – were often the subject of comment at home, and faced with losing Mary he decided to put his 'odd self to the test of feminine appreciation or disapproval' the night before he was to set sail. He approached Mary and calmly, as though asking her if she would like a cup of tea, asked the prim schoolmistress to marry him.[67] Mary later claimed that Lawson suggested a quick elopement – a visit to a registry office and a honeymoon trip to Western Australia, saying that he would arrange her ticket for the voyage the next morning. But Mary demurred, later explaining it was through 'some sense of unfitness, some realization that I was not ready for marriage'.[68]

LAWSON AND PETER SET SAIL for the west on 26 April 1890 aboard the new[69] French mail steamship *Australien*; at 153 metres, the longest vessel ever seen in Australian waters. It was bound for Marseilles via Albany and was described as 'a floating palace',[70] though the Lawsons roughed it in steerage. As they left Sydney Lawson counted '135 animated bundles of rags and bones sleeping around the goods sheds' at the wharf.[71]

Following the success of 'Clancy of the Overflow', Banjo Paterson had scored another hit with his epic 'The Man from Snowy River', which *The Bulletin* featured on 26 April 1890. Lawson had written his own less memorable tribute to the Australian horsemen, his 'A Word to Texas Jack',[72] pointing out that no fancy American showman of the type visiting Sydney at the time could ride the gullies and 'roarin' Darlin' in flood like a local.

Lawson had enjoyed a productive few weeks before the voyage, producing 'The Song of Old Joe Swallow',[73] 'The Black Tracker'[74] and 'To "Doc" Wylie',[75] a tribute to bush doctors like the one who had ministered to Niels. 'Middleton's Rouseabout'[76] told the story of Tom Middleton, a selector at Eurunderee Lawson had known, and his adopted son Andy. Andy was blown about by the wind with no plan for the future and no roots, and he might have mirrored Lawson when 'liquor and drought prevailed'.[77]

In an entirely different tone in 'Stand by the Engines',[78] Lawson lauded the heroism of the engineers who went down with the British-India ship *Quetta* on the night of 28 February 1890 after it struck a rock north of Cape York while carrying passengers and a load of mail and refrigerated meat from Brisbane to London.

There were 134 deaths, and there would have been more had the engineers not maintained their posts below deck to open valves and prevent an explosion.

Lawson's 'Over The Ranges And Into The West'[79] and 'To a Pair of Blucher Boots',[80] which appeared on the same day in *Freeman's Journal*, reflected his restlessness while 'The Glass On The Bar',[81] a tribute to mateship, was so prized by Archibald that he had Lawson write it out by hand for framing.

Two of Lawson's pieces, 'Faces in the Street' and 'His Father's Mate', were also being prepared for the July release of a *Bulletin* compendium, *A Golden Shanty*,[82] featuring the works of Banjo, Edward Dyson, Victor Daley, John Farrell, the late Henry Kendall and others.

THE LAWSON BROTHERS arrived in Albany on 5 May 1890, two days after his call to arms in 'Ireland Shall Rebel'[83] appeared in *Freeman's Journal*, prefacing the equally caustic 'The Statue of our Queen',[84] a condemnation of the new statue of Queen Victoria unveiled in Queen's Square on Sydney's Macquarie Street.

Lawson found Albany undergoing a construction boom, with bricklayers and carpenters in great demand and with housepainters so scarce that he had in the first hour after disembarking the choice of three bosses at 'top all-round wages'.[85]

He could make money quickly and wrote to Mary, who was still lodging with Louisa. Lawson's sister Gertrude revealed that Louisa 'who had never known the tender passion' crushed the budding relationship by concealing the correspondence,[86] unaware that Mary was not really that interested in a romance with her son. Mary said that Lawson later told her he had answered all of her letters, though none found their way into Mary's hand.[87] In any case Mary's mother returned from Junee after six weeks and Mary moved out of the Lawson home 'and broke off everything', though there remained strong bonds of affection with Lawson.

He took up lodgings at Victoria House in Albany and not long after saw a calico sign ten metres wide in front of a small brick cottage announcing 'Albany Observer. Biggest Circulation in West Australia. Best and Brightest Pennyworth In the Colonies'.[88] A day after Lawson had arrived in town, a 28-year-old Virginian named Lancelot Lindley-Cowen[89] had published the first issue of the four-page *Albany Observer* from the house for the West Australian Land Company. Lindley-Cowen had been an American naval lieutenant on the USS *Enterprise* and after arriving in Victoria had run the Mooroopna *Yeoman* and written on agricultural matters for the Melbourne *Leader*.[90] Now tapping into the economic boom of the west, he was offering a penny a line for contributors.

Lawson wrote to Lindley-Cowen asking for a chance to make a few pennies.

'You will no doubt perceive that I have not had the advantages of a good education,' he told the young editor, 'but if I could only raise myself from the cursed drudgery of day labour, I would soon make up for that.'[91]

Back in Sydney, *The Bulletin* had announced that 'The talented Henry Lawson has left for Western Australia', prompting an item in the *Western Australian Bulletin* asking 'Who's Henry Lawson?'.

Lawson wrote a response for Lindley-Cowen to run, with a mock German title 'Who's Dot Pulleteen?',[92] signing his work Henrich Hertzberg Lawson.

Just two days later, using the pen-name 'Joe Swallow' for the *Albany Observer*, Lawson wrote in support of development of the west, of cities growing as fair as Adelaide, as green as Ballarat, as busy as Sydney and Melbourne.[93] Two weeks later he made the case for decentralisation in the west, saying that it needed thriving inland cities to prosper. Bathurst, he complained, was 'the dullest, dreariest, sleepiest, deadest hole I ever set foot in'.[94]

In 'Nationality in Colonisation', Lawson told readers that 'Australia is not for the British ... but for the Australians', a people he said, 'evolved from the best nations on earth'.[95]

Lawson encouraged trade unionism in the west, the 'new religion'[96] which promised an international brotherhood of workers, though, in a carryover from the racism of the Australian goldfields, he admitted 'there is one great flaw in the theory of universal brotherhood: It is where the Chinaman comes in'.[97] The rapid population growth in China, he argued, was alarming.

There was no difficulty, he wrote, in including 'the progressive "Jap" in the scheme, and the American negro is already a man and brother. The American Indian, the African and South Sea savage, and the aboriginals of Australia will soon in the course of civilization become extinct, and so relieve the preachers of universal brotherhood of all anxiety on their account. The Chinaman remains to be dealt with ... the Chinese question is, I fear, one of the problems which we must leave to our children to solve.'[98]

While of little literary value, the articles for *The Observer* gave an insight into Lawson's juvenile thinking at the time.

WHILE LAWSON WAS IN THE WEST, grievances of Australia's coal miners and shearers were escalating to a nationwide maritime strike as trade unionists began a fierce and ugly campaign for better conditions.

By May 1890 shearers had started walking off the job at Jondaryan near Oakey on Queensland's Darling Downs and wharf labourers in Rockhampton were refusing to load bales of wool that had been shorn by non-union labour.

Industrial action quickly spread to seamen, wharf labourers, then gas stokers. Coal miners from Newcastle, Broken Hill and even New Zealand were locked out after refusing to dig coal for non-union-operated vessels.

Then authorities in Melbourne poured fuel on the simmering tension. On 30 August 1890, the night before a public meeting in Melbourne's Flinders Park that drew as many as 50,000[99] supporters for the strike, Lieutenant-Colonel Tom Price instructed his men of the Victorian Mounted Rifles how to deal with crowd unrest.

As a force of 1000 militia and mounted police and another 1000 special constables prepared to battle the unionists, Price said: 'You will each be supplied with 40 rounds of ammunition, leaden bullets, and if the order is given to fire, don't let me see any rifle pointed in the air; fire low and lay them out so that the duty will not have to be performed again.'[100]

Even though Price later explained that he only meant for his troops 'to hit the strikers in the legs ... not to kill them outright',[101] Mary Cameron said the words 'fire low and lay them out' had a profound effect on the rest of Lawson's life; on his attitude to the working man and the oppression he saw.[102]

Mercifully, the ammunition was not used. The platform for the great public meeting was decorated with a copy of the Eureka flag.

Within days, 28,500 workers were on strike and on 19 September squatters carrying their wool from Redfern station on drays to the wharves at Circular Quay under mounted police escort had blue metal and rocks hurled at them by a posse of unionists who had been joined by a gang of thugs from The Rocks. A magistrate read the Riot Act and the mounted police drew their swords and charged to disperse the mob.[103]

The west had not been the El Dorado Lawson had expected. Although he had written some pieces for *The Observer*, painting and carpentry work had petered out and he became lonely and disconnected from his mates at home. His deafness constantly embarrassed him.

On 30 September, now used to drowning his sorrows with drink, Lawson left Albany alone on another French ship, the *Salazie*. He was back in Sydney on 9 October 1890, broke and shabby.[104] With Mary gone from Louisa's home, he chose to stay instead on the veranda of Louisa's older sister Emma, now remarried and living in Dawes Point, near the harbour. Lawson had written some verses on the journey home. He sent two works to *Freeman's Journal*: the anti-British 'John Cornstalk'[105] and the morbid 'Lily'[106] based on a story his mother had told him from her girlhood when she and some friends found the body of a beautiful girl in a creek.

He walked to *The Bulletin* office the day after his arrival to sell a poem called 'The Fire at Ross's Farm'.[107] It told the story of a Romeo and Juliet-style romance against the backdrop of a land feud. Archibald paid Lawson a few shillings and Lawson spent it on booze. He returned to Aunt Emma drunk.[108]

Chapter 7

It was the first, the last, and only chance I got in journalism.

LAWSON ON AN OFFER TO WRITE FOR *THE BOOMERANG*
NEWSPAPER IN BRISBANE[1]

LAWSON WAS AT A LOOSE END when he came back from Albany; jobless, broke and drinking. He occasionally stayed with Louisa but was more often at Aunt Emma's, and spent weeks in what he called 'a third-rate hash-house' which may have been uncomfortable and confronting, but which provided him with some good copy[2] as he explored socialist politics.

The maritime strike had begun to unravel in November 1890 and a ready supply of non-union labour meant that by January 1891, Illawarra coal miners, the last workers to hold out, had given up the fight.

Wage cuts, some up to 30 per cent, then ravaged the maritime industry, but soon an army of shearers, working in a great arc through western Queensland and down into New South Wales, took Australia's war between labour and capital to new battlefields.

Lawson was right behind the unions. He worked for a while on a house at Waverley, which Arthur Parker was plastering, and he took his friend to join the Australian Socialist League, which was endeavouring to form a Labor party in New South Wales. Lawson introduced Parker to Labor advocates such as William McNamara, George Black, William Holman, Arthur Rae and Sam Rosa.

Lawson also found an important supporter in John Norton,[3] who had just been sacked as editor of the *Newcastle Morning Herald* for repeated drunkenness, but was now editor and part-owner of the *Truth*, a racy new weekly that focused on sport, crime and scandal.

Norton had known Lawson since Louisa was publishing *The Republican* as the Trades and Labor Council of New South Wales had accredited Norton as their official delegate to union congresses in London and Paris. Lawson wrote 'The Pavement Stones: A Song of the Unemployed'[4] and 'The Australian Marseillaise'[5] for Norton's *Truth*, suggesting that given the capitulation of the maritime strikers it might take strong, forceful women like Louisa – 'our starved and madden'd women' – to 'lead our armies on to strife'.[6]

Louisa was having less and less influence on Lawson, though, as he set out to master his own destiny, but she had readily printed in *The Dawn* his tragic poem 'The Water-Lilie', about another drowned child.[7] The poem prompted Jack Brereton,[8] a poet and later professor of English who became one of Lawson's closest friends, to detect 'signs of a greater delicacy of ear' in Lawson's writing.

The refrain was the call of the phantom child –

Come, mamma! come!
Quick! follow me!
Step out on the leaves of the water-lily!

'The use of the unaccented syllable for the rhyme,' Brereton wrote, 'has the kind of beauty that [Dante Gabriel] Rossetti often obtained by similar means. I asked Lawson how he came to use such a rhyme. He was apologetic. He should have made it clear, he explained, that he was imitating a child's way of stressing the word – "putting all the weight on the last syllable".'[9]

Brereton revealed that Lawson would compose his poems gradually, without setting them down on paper. 'Shut in from outward disturbance by his deafness, he would walk along, with that intense look of his, fitting his words to the chosen metre.'[10]

COMPARISONS TO ROSETTI didn't pay Lawson's bills, though, or for his ever-growing fondness for liquid entertainment. He wrote 'The Good Old Concertina'[11] for the *Town and Country Journal*. Just after New Year's Day 1891 he regaled the small staff at *The Bulletin* with a tale of Chinese cooks he had seen taking icing sugar into their mouths and blowing it over the cakes.[12] The Chinese were frequent targets for the magazine, especially given the fears among its blue-collar readership over foreign workers taking local jobs.

Lawson was not discouraged that things had not progressed with Mary Cameron as he found love again amid the ruins of his childhood at Eurunderee. Lawson went back to the Blue Mountains to work alongside his grandfather for a while, and stayed for a few weeks with Harry O'Brien, who was leasing the Lawsons' old home from Louisa. Also staying with O'Brien was his nineteen-year-old niece Bridget Lambert, Lawson's former schoolmate. She was the daughter of an Irish-born shanty keeper, and about to start work at £5 a month as a substitute schoolteacher at the Collingwood Provisional School just west of Mudgee.[13]

Lawson wrote 'The Free-Selector's Daughter'[14] for Bridget, the first of several odes.

Many years later he wrote of her again, changing her name to Bertha Lambert for 'The Bush Beyond the Range'[15] and it is said she inspired 'The Drover's Sweetheart'[16] and 'The Sliprails and the Spur'.[17]

It was rumoured they became engaged[18] but Bridget eventually broke it off just before Lawson made the biggest move of his life to date. An exciting opportunity to be a full-time writer soothed any wounds he felt over the end of the romance and Bridget retained affection for him all her life. Lawson was at Mount Victoria house-painting for 8 or 9 shillings a day at the time, with every prospect of a good run of work when ...

> one day as I was painting a ceiling, I got a telegram to say that the Brisbane *Boomerang* offered £2 per week and a position on the staff. I was doubtful of my abilities, and

wired to an old friend in Sydney for advice. He advised accept; so I accepted.[19]

The offer had come from 51-year-old entrepreneur Gresley Lukin,[20] who was buying the fledgling Brisbane newspaper.

Lukin was a Tasmanian, who as a young man had travelled to western Queensland and become a senior public servant in the fledgling colony before becoming editor of the *Brisbane Courier* and *The Queenslander*. After land and mining speculation bankrupted him, he became managing director of the Sydney newspapers *The Globe* and the *Sunday Times*.[21]

His Sydney office was just four doors down from Louisa's headquarters for *The Dawn* in Jamieson Street and it appears she put a word in for her son. In November 1890, Lukin began negotiating with the radical young journalist William 'Billy' Lane[22] to buy the Brisbane *Boomerang*. Lane had been one of the founders of the newspaper in 1887, at just twenty-six, writing most of the strident articles which propagated his socialist views.

Bristol-born Lane was a small, thin firebrand with a droopy moustache and blue eyes that burned behind gold-rimmed spectacles. He had a limp, a legacy of the club foot that had blighted his childhood in England, and a slight 'Yankee twang' that was a carryover from his time working in Canada, where he married, and the United States, where he was a young reporter on the *Detroit Free Press*.

Lane was the driving force behind the formation in 1889 of the Australian Labour Federation, an organisation of Queensland unions which replaced the Trades and Labour Council in Brisbane, and which, along with other labour organisations, was backing his new newspaper *The Worker*.

Lane idealised the bush worker and his words became like flames that ignited revolt among them as he urged the unions to fight for their rights and to prepare to defend themselves against capitalist standover men like Colonel Tom Price.

On 29 November 1890, Lane used *The Worker* to advise every working man in Australia 'to save every penny previously spent in drink until they have sufficient to purchase a reliable weapon – say a good Winchester'.[23]

A week later Gresley Lukin announced that from 1 January 1891, *The Boomerang* would be published under a new direction, and would support federation and a conciliation of capital and labour. The paper would retain a radical flavour, albeit somewhat toned down.

Even before Lukin offered Lawson a job, in *The Boomerang's* Christmas 1890 edition he published Lawson's tale 'The Third Murder',[24] based on his visit to the haunted house in the Blue Mountains during his youth.

Lukin also ran a contribution by Archibald Meston, a noted journalist and explorer, who once recalled with shame that not many years earlier settlers would shoot Indigenous people from the veranda of Fassifern Station near Boonah, either for fun or to test the range of their weapons.

Lawson was heading north at a time of unprecedented labour disputes in Queensland that threatened to become what the Brisbane *Courier* called an 'industrial Armageddon'.[25] The tension that had bubbled in the shearing sheds for years was about to explode with violent strikes and walkouts, as men downed tools and refused to work alongside low-paid Chinese labour.

The shearers struck the first blow of 1891 at the Logan Downs station near the town of Clermont in Central Queensland. Logan Downs was part of the great expanse of Australia controlled by George Fairbairn, a Scottish shepherd who had ridden on the sheep's back to a vast pastoral fortune. He and his sons, George Jr and Charles, had three million sheep and millions of hectares among their twenty-eight properties.[26] On 5 January 1891, George Taylor, an organiser for the Queensland shearers' Central District Union, led a walkout by 200 shearers and labourers who refused to sign a new work agreement. They formed a camp on the banks of Wolfgang Creek.

A 'strike committee' in Barcaldine, having met under the branches of the town's mighty ghost gum, announced on 1 February 1891 that 'the Queensland bush is to be a battleground

William 'Billy' Lane, editor of the union journal *The Worker*, encouraged Lawson's socialist passion. University of Sydney, Cosme Colony Collection

whereon is to be decided whether capitalism can crush Australian unionism altogether into the dust'.[27]

To start breaking the strikes, Victorian pastoralists organised 200 non-union workers to leave Melbourne on 3 February bound for Rockhampton. George Fairbairn Jr was at the High Level Wharf in Rockhampton along with twenty-eight policemen a week later to welcome the steamer *Derwent* and the 120 replacement shearers and eighty rouseabouts.[28]

As hundreds of unionists, their wives and children heckled the 'scabs', the police moved in to escort the strike-breakers onto trains bound for Clermont, Emerald, Barcaldine, Springsure and Capella,[29] but drays waiting to escort the shearers from Clermont to Logan Downs had their wheel lynch pins removed.

At Clermont, 200 armed men rallied behind union organiser Julian Stuart,[30] a twenty-four-year-old-year-old former schoolteacher who would one day write for *The Worker* and *The Bulletin*.

Guns, including Winchester repeating rifles, and bullets were stockpiled in large quantities[31] at Clermont, while at Emerald, shearers seized significant quantities of gunpowder. The *Brisbane Courier* warned Queensland that the men intended 'extreme violence'.[32] Ten thousand shearers had soon joined the protests and the Queensland Government feared civil war.

On the balmy evening of 20 February 1891, as the sun set over the Brisbane River, sixty soldiers from Queensland's permanent artillery marched up the gangway onto the steamer *Burwah* bound for Rockhampton and then onto a train to confront the shearers at the union strongholds. Each soldier carried a Martini-Henry rifle and together they had not only a state-of-the-art cannon that fired 4.5-kilogram shells but an American-made Gatling machine gun with six barrels that could spit out 900 bullets a minute.[33] Before long there were 1400 soldiers and fifty-eight heavily armed constables in Central Queensland. The reinforcements brought with them the Nordenfeldt machine gun.[34]

The shearers began burning effigies of the Queensland Premier Sir Samuel Griffith, then started lighting fires in the tinder-dry grasses across Central Queensland, torching millions of hectares.[35]

Hugh Blackwell, secretary of the Queensland Labourers Union, sent a telegram to colleague Alex Forrester declaring that 'The first shot fired will maybe cause the Australian Revolution'.[36]

LAWSON'S TRAIN LEFT FOR BRISBANE a few days later during the third week of the intercolonial federal convention in Sydney, where the crusty Sir George Grey,[37] a former colonial ruler in South Australia, New Zealand and the Cape Colony, was advising delegates from the Trades and Labour Council to press for one man, one vote when a constitution for a federated Australia was formed, rather than a 'plural vote' system based on property ownership.[38] One man, one vote was a principle Billy Lane was demanding for 'every liberty loving man'.[39] Even though Lawson was being paid £2 a week by *The Boomerang*, he still contributed to other publications and he wrote a poem supporting Lane's voting principle for *The Worker*.

The poem 'Original Labour Songs'[40] appeared in July 1891 just two weeks after the first general election contested by Labor candidates saw the Labor Electoral League of New South Wales win thirty-five of 141 seats, with George Black and Arthur Rae among those elected.

Lawson had arrived in Brisbane at a time when the Queensland capital had a population of 84,000,[41] and was still recovering from a flood that had submerged wharves along the Brisbane River, turned much of South Brisbane into mudflats and made hundreds of families homeless.[42]

The heat from all the arson in Central Queensland was firing up *The Worker* office in Brisbane as well, and Lane wrote that the blue Southern Cross flag of Eureka was flying over a canvas town of 1000 or so unionists at Barcaldine. 'There are meetings, games, and drills regularly,' Lane wrote. 'The boys are picking up military evolutions rapidly, and march now like soldiers. Camps are being formed at Hughenden, Barcaldine, Charleville, Muttaburra, Winton, Augathella, and St George. From these and the older camps, letters come to the *Worker*, all breathing the sternest determination to fight the Chinese and the squatter to the bitter end.'[43]

Lawson was only at *The Boomerang* a few days when he met twenty-five-year-old sub-editor Alfred Stephens,[44] who had been editor of *The Miner* in Gympie and who was now earning a whopping £5 a week from Lukin.

Stephens was a handsome man with a solid build, blond beard and wide, expressive blue eyes. It was said that his over-confident manner, 'head thrown back, the jutting beard, the resolute walk and the expanded chest', concealed a nervous, sensitive and vulnerable nature and he was deeply affected by touching lines of poetry.[45]

Stephens recalled that Lukin introduced him to Lawson, then 'a tall, dark, wiry young man with large luminous brown eyes ... From nine to five daily Lawson was at the office, usually walking up and down the room allotted to him, making verse painfully and persistently. For months I listened to him pounding out his rhymes, often aloud, as he paced to and fro.[46]

Stephens became one of Australia's most important literary critics, and recognised the mark of genius in Lawson's youthful writing. He encouraged him to expand the scope of his work.

'Lawson had the gift of putting himself in another man's place,' Stephens wrote, '... [He] had no exceptional intelligence; much of his mental field was uncultivated; his brain worked in a narrow channel; but within that channel its speed and power were extraordinary. His outlook upon life was the average man's outlook, coloured by his personal experience, deeply coloured by inherited idiosyncrasy. His talents were the ordinary man's talents raised to a higher power by the strength of the burning life behind them.'[47]

Lawson recalled that he 'wrote [paragraphs], sketches, and verse' for the £2 a week 'and barracked, spare times, for Democracy, in the Brisbane *Worker,* for nothing. I got very fond of the work, and was with difficulty kept out of the office on Sundays, publishing days, Saturday afternoons, and other holidays.'[48]

He began writing a *Boomerang* column called 'Country Crumbs' on 4 April 1891. He 'hashed up a couple of columns of pars, from the country papers every week, with the names of the papers attached – to curry favour with the country press'.[49]

In his first column, he related the recent drowning of sisters Bridget Kate Broderick, nine, and Mary Jane Broderick, six, in a waterhole at Walloon near Ipswich.[50] Lukin reprinted Lawson's 'Water-Lilie' and Lawson later composed 'The Babies of Walloon'[51] which his mother ran the following month in *The Dawn.* In Lawson's first *Boomerang* column he also wrote '... it is against our principles to shake hands with a Chinaman, because we are anti-Chinese to the backbone ...'

The Chinese remained at the heart of Queensland's labour struggles over non-union workers, but arrests among the shearers were now being made swiftly. Three days after Lawson's first 'Country Crumbs' column, Julian Stuart and five other prisoners were taken in chains and under heavy guard by special train from Clermont to the Barcaldine police station. There they were surrounded by a military outfit comprising 500 men: mounted troops and field artillery, infantrymen with fixed bayonets, Scottish pipers and drummers, and a brass band. A few shearers bellowed out 'scab protectors' but just in case the unionists were thinking of causing a ruckus, the military stationed the ambulance corps at the rear. It was a clear message that resistance was futile and would only end in a bloodbath.[52]

LAWSON REGULARLY PRODUCED poems for *The Boomerang* too, including 'Bogg of Geebung',[53] in which he satirised the romantic portrait of the town drunk in the bush, well aware of his own increasingly intemperate ways. Far more forceful were Lawson's political commentaries for Billy Lane as Queensland's strike leaders stared at long prison sentences.

Lane began visiting the strike camps, lecturing on socialist values and revealing a plan by which as many as 7000 striking unionists would be given land grants – as well as 'implements, rations and transport' in Argentina to raise sheep and cattle in what Lane envisaged as a socialist workers' paradise.[54] Lane and his friends had chosen remote South America in order to discourage the weak from signing on and his charismatic orations attracted more than 600 subscribing members to his New Australia Co-operative Settlement Association.

FOURTEEN OF THE UNION LEADERS[55] faced charges of conspiracy against the Crown in trials at the Rockhampton Supreme Court starting on 1 May 1891. Billy Lane watched through his round spectacles from the press table, though many believed he should have been in the dock over his rallying calls in *The Worker*. In Queensland's Legislative Assembly, Lane's writings were described as 'incendiary' and he was called 'an arch fiend … who stands behind the men, driving them on'.[56]

On the same day that the trials began, Barcaldine hosted a May Day labour parade to celebrate the eight-hour day won by

Australian unionists in the aftermath of the Eureka Stockade rebellion. There were 1340 striking shearers and their families taking part – a total estimated of at least 3000 people protesting against poor working conditions and low wages beneath the boughs of what became known as the Labor Party's Tree of Knowledge.[57]

While the trials were underway, Lane ran Lawson's 'Freedom on the Wallaby'[58] – 'Wallaby' being a term meaning 'to carry a swag'. Lawson drew on the memory of Eureka:

So we must fly a rebel flag,
As others did before us,
And we must sing a rebel song
And join in rebel chorus.
We'll make the tyrants feel the sting
O' those that they would throttle;
They needn't say the fault is ours
If blood should stain the wattle![59]

On 20 May 1891, the jury in the conspiracy trials returned its verdict of guilty. The fourteen accused were sentenced to three years' imprisonment, and eventually more than twenty strike leaders were sent to prison on St Helena Island in Moreton Bay for conspiracy, rioting or sedition.

On 23 May, Lane spoke slowly and deliberately to striking shearers at Barcaldine and between long puffs on his ever-present pipe told them about the promise of a society with no more bullying pastoralists, but rather a haven where workers 'could enter into co-operation untrammelled by the exactions of the present system, where all could work in their several occupations each for all and all for each'.[60]

Lane had dispatched an agent, Alf Walker, 'late business manager of the *Boomerang* newspaper ... to the Argentine to see if the project could be carried out'.[61]

Lawson never wrote in support of Lane's utopia but the idea of a working man's paradise built on mateship was the foundation of his own Australian socialist ideal of a universal brotherhood, so long as the brothers were from a European background.

The shearers officially called off the strike in Blackall on 15 June 1891 and at Hughenden three days later. The unions now encouraged members to enrol on the electoral roll and fight injustice with their votes, though Lane and Lawson still fired ink bullets.

In 'As Ireland Wore The Green', Lawson wondered if Australian workers would hide the colour and spirit of Eureka.[62] Readers of *The Worker* might have been inspired by it but Lawson was making powerful enemies.

In the Queensland Legislative Council on 15 July 1891, during a 'Vote of Thanks' to the lawmen who had broken up the Barcaldine strike camp, Frederick Brentnall,[63] a Wesleyan minister and chairman of directors of the Brisbane *Telegraph* newspaper, read out parts of 'Freedom on the Wallaby'. Brentnall was a sworn enemy of the Labor movement and pointed out the way Lane's paper had inflamed an already volatile situation among the shearers. There were calls in the chamber for Lawson's arrest for sedition, but he was ready to take on all comers and gave Brentnall a lashing with a follow-up poem, 'The Vote of Thanks Debate'.

> You hate the Cause by instinct, the instinct of your class.
> And fear the reformation that shall surely come to pass;
> Your nest is feathered by the 'laws' which you of course defend,
> Your daily bread is buttered on the upper crust, my friend.[64]

FROM 4 JULY, LAWSON BEGAN putting his 'Country Crumbs' column to verse but the idea lasted only three weeks and he went back to prose.

Instead, he wrote rousing poems for *The Worker*, deciding to use the rebellious pseudonym 'Jack Cornstalk' for 'Patriotic League'[65] and 'Spread the Truth',[66] which Archibald reprinted in *The Bulletin* three weeks later. He wrote, among others, 'The Way I Treated Father'[67] and 'On the Wallaby'[68] for *The Boomerang*.

But times were tough and as savvy as Lukin may have been, *The Boomerang* was failing to fly.

The financial depression around Australia showed no mercy. Talk of the journal falling was everywhere in the Brisbane office. Lawson remembered how deputations of compositors 'went up oftener to the sanctum to discuss the inadvisability of their taking shares in the paper in part-payment of wages'.[69]

Lawson penned his last 'Country Crumbs' on 12 September 1891, the same day that his poem 'Lay Your Ears Back and Fight'[70] appeared.

Despite Lukin stating publicly that *The Boomerang* was a raging success,[71] he had to let Lawson go. Lukin wrote to Louisa a week later to say her son had 'unquestioned ability and earnest democratic character' and that when *The Boomerang* was enlarged during better business conditions, he promised to make Lawson an offer to return.

Lukin embarked on a campaign to remodel and reinvigorate *The Boomerang*[72] and it struggled on as he raised the cover price a penny to fourpence because of new charges incurred by the Postal Act. But *The Boomerang* closed abruptly on 9 April 1892.

Although he was no longer on the staff, Lawson still contributed pieces for the paper's 1891 Christmas edition.

He sent Lukin the poem 'Watching the Crows',[73] which he had already sold to *Freeman's Journal* about crows circling a body in the bush. Lawson also sent Lukin the sketch 'Big Jack Dale'[74] and 'The Cambaroora Star',[75] about a struggling bush paper. Lawson called the poem '*The Boomerang*'s own epitaph'.[76]

Chapter 8

I came south, steerage, with £2. It wasn't the first time
I went saloon and came back steerage.
LAWSON AFTER LOSING HIS DREAM JOB AS A YOUNG JOURNALIST[1]

THE JAILING OF THE UNION MEN and the loss of a newspaper position that he loved cut Lawson to the core and he returned to Sydney using the cheapest steamer ticket he could buy. Hard times were all around him. Banks and businesses seemed to be closing every day. Relief societies were being formed to help poverty-stricken families, doling out meat, bread and tea. As many as a third of Australians were out of work and many men packed their swags with a few staples and left their families for the dusty roads seeking some sort of employment. Lawson had continuing problems with the 'Chieftainess', too. He could no longer spend a night under her roof without fighting. So, with his professional aspirations shattered, he was basically broke, humiliated and homeless. He poured out his pain for *The Bulletin* in 'The Shame of Going Back'.

When you've come to make a fortune and you haven't made your salt,
And the reason of your failure isn't anybody's fault —
When you haven't got a billet, and the times are very slack,
There is nothing that can spur you like the shame of going back;
Crawling home with empty pockets,
Going back hard-up;
Oh! it's then you learn the meaning of humiliation's cup.[2]

Lawson earned a few shillings here and there writing for Archibald, the *Truth* and *Freeman's Journal*, which tended to run anything of his with an Irish bent for its Catholic readership. Editor Tom Butler lapped up 'When The Irish Flag Went By',[3] written after Lawson and Louisa had buried their differences for an hour or two and watched the eight-hour-day demonstration through the centre of Sydney on 5 October 1891.[4]

Lawson quickly dashed off 'The Old Man's Welcome'[5] subtitled 'A Sequel to "The Shame of Going Back" in a recent "Bulletin"'. Archibald ran it, perhaps deliberately, next to an advertisement for Cuticura skin remedies that featured a drawing of a big baby crying.

Lawson was drinking more to boost his low moods, but by contrast Lawson's literary rival Banjo Paterson was riding high. There might have been a financial depression all around him but it seemed the well-off young lawyer was always in great spirits.

Though Paterson was adamant he was no poet, just a 'versifier',[6] 'Clancy of the Overflow' and 'The Man from Snowy River' had made him the most popular writer in Australia and he would soon be earning more from his writing than from his legal work.

Just a few weeks after Archibald ran Lawson's 'The Shame of Going Back', Paterson was one of the stars on show when the Sydney Polo Club threw open the invitation to 'a large gathering of ladies' to watch practice and enjoy afternoon tea in one of the Moore Park rooms on the Agricultural Society's grounds. The spectators included the club patron – the New South Wales Governor, Victor Child Villiers, 7th Earl of Jersey – and some of Sydney's most influential families.[7]

Lawson did not play polo and could not afford a pony. He stayed off and on with Aunt Emma, sometimes leaving her home for the flophouses of Castlereagh Street for a month or two before returning to her safe and comforting surrounds for a short spurt of spirited writing fuelled by midnight rambles through the seedier side of Sydney.

He would often roam the slums of The Rocks and Surry Hills, and he became an expert on the street gangs – or 'pushes' as they were known — that dominated the city's underbelly. He blamed poverty and bad government for the rising numbers of young hoodlums.

Lawson's 'The Captain of the Push'[8] is an enduring portrait of gang life in Sydney in the late nineteenth century:

> There was nought to rouse their anger; yet the oath that each one
> swore,
> Seemed less fit for publication than the one that went before.
> For they spoke the gutter language with the easy flow that comes
> Only to the man whose childhood knew the brothels and the slums.[9]

Lawson never coloured his work with expletives even though he swore often and mixed with rough crowds. Often, late at night Lawson would leave Aunt Emma's for a midnight stroll down to the Dawes Point Battery, reciting his verses to himself as he struggled for rhyme and metre. A night policeman on patrol deemed him a suspicious person and started following him. *The Bulletin* poem 'Constable McCarty's Investigations'[10] was the result.

Banjo Paterson rarely entered Lawson's dark world of poverty and despair. Street & Paterson 'solicitors and proctors' had moved office from 105 Pitt Street to more salubrious chambers in the Waltham Building at 24 Bond Street. For inspiration, one of Paterson's office walls was decorated with a magnificent watercolour painted by Frank Mahony,[11] depicting a mob of wild horses. Paterson told a reporter that he had already spent 'a good deal of money on paintings by local artists' and that he intended to 'add very considerably to his present art gallery'.[12]

Paterson's library contained books that had been written in the mid-1700s, and he had eclectic tastes. Some of Darwin's *On the Origin of Species* was cheek by jowl with Sterne's *Sentimental Journey*, first published in 1768. By contrast, Lawson was never a great reader, and 'at the height of his powers, devoted more of his time to the perusal of Deadwood Dick's dime novel adventures than to anything that could be called literature'.[13]

While Lawson had just written of crawling home with empty pockets and of not having a billet, Paterson was living in a swanky bachelor flat at 13 Bond Street, almost opposite his new office. It was decorated with souvenirs from his boyhood growing up in the bush, with a variety of stuffed birds and some of the possum-skin rugs his mother had made.[14] Soon he would move into an even grander city flat, complete with a Japanese valet.

ALTHOUGH LAWSON WAS OFTEN at loggerheads with Louisa, she helped him by running his work in *The Dawn* including 'The Helpless Mothers'[15] in support of the sisterhood. For now Lawson was both a Republican and a feminist, the fight for women's suffrage which Louisa championed being one step towards full democracy in Australia. Lawson made ends meet, selling poems and short stories while painting houses or carriages for 5 shillings a day for bosses who drove him hard. He recalled:

Hard times had come to Sydney, and it took a good, all-round tradesman to be sure of seven or even six 'bob' and fairly constant graft. When the trade failed me I used to write a column of red-hot socialistic and libellous political rhymes for *Truth*. I still believed in revolutions, and the spirit of righteousness upheld me. *Truth's* [editor] was eccentric, and the usual rates for outside contributions were from [5 shillings] upwards; but John Norton gave me 15s. to £1, for special stuff. He cursed considerably; and there were times when it wasn't advisable to curse back; but he saw that I, and one or two other poor devils of scribblers on their uppers, were paid ...[16]

Norton was one of the great iconoclasts in Australian publishing, once shocking the conservative majority of Australia by referring to Her Majesty Queen Victoria as 'flabby, fat, and flatulent'.[17] Writing under the name Joe Swallow, Lawson sent Norton 'The Rebel', a poem in which the bipolarity that often left him

Lawyer and writer Andrew Barton 'Banjo' Paterson was Lawson's great rival in Australian literature. State Library of NSW, PXA1559 174c

depressed and lonely was on full display. Lawson now claimed that with the 'strength of Truth and Right', he was 'immortal in the battles of the night'.[18]

Lawson wrote 'The Literary Friend'[19] both for *The Bulletin*, and for one of his mentors, Fred Broomfield, who was providing Lawson with constructive criticism over his metre and his rhymes. Lawson used the pen-name 'Cervus Wright' when he became Norton's attack dog, writing the poem 'The House of Fossils' about members of the Legislative Council who had just argued against full adult suffrage. He called the prominent politician and barrister Charles Edward Pilcher[20] 'P(h)ilcher'.[21] Lawson said the politician and civil engineer Edward Combes 'should go and dig another hole, and undertake himself'.

In 'Wales the First', he wrote of the Queen's playboy son Prince Edward, the heir to the throne: 'A bloated prince of parasites'.[22]

Lawson wrote eight such pieces for the *Truth* until Norton was sacked as editor for drunkenness. Lawson's last offering was 'The English Queen' about what he called 'a dull old woman', who had lived a 'useless' life with a 'loafer son', taking a fortune from her Empire while the poor starved.[23]

Archibald ran 'The Shanty on the Rise'[24] in which Lawson wrote of young Mary Buchholtz and a shanty kept by Robert Newton at Eurunderee. But the pay remained meagre. Not only did Lawson remain a struggling writer, but he also had to put up with other people stealing his work.

One of the pilferers was a young go-getter named E.J. (Ted) Brady,[25] from Carcoar. Brady was two years younger than Lawson but already making his mark on the Australian literary landscape, his imagination sparked by the colourful life of his father, an Irish-born policeman who had fought in the American Civil War.

Brady had worked as a tallyclerk on the wharves at Woolloomooloo, and he wrote vividly of ships and sailors, but he had lost his job during the maritime strike when he refused to be sworn in as a special constable. Instead, he wrote the poem 'Vive Anarchy'[26] for the *Australian Workman*, the official organ of the Sydney Trades and Labour Council.

Brady then joined a clerk's union, became secretary of the Australian Socialist League and a member of the Labour Electoral League. By the time Lawson was licking his wounds after returning from Brisbane, Brady was the *Workman*'s editor,[27] aged twenty-one, and though inexperienced as a newspaperman, earning £3 a week busily cutting articles out of other publications and using them in his own. He had heard all about Lawson from Billy Lane, Brady's colleague in the socialist press. He admired Lawson's work so much he decided to take some as his own.

An angry Lawson went to the *Workman*'s office to confront the thief.

At the time, Brady occupied a small, untidy cubicle adjacent to an untidier composing den in the nether part of an arcade which opened onto George Street, in the area known as Brickfield Hill, between Sydney Town Hall and what is now Central Station.

Brady had minimal staff and instructions to find articles where he could without paying. Brady later recalled:

> The sub-editor was an old hand named Scissors, well known in newspaper circles; and the chief-of-staff a person named Paste, who has stuck to the business since time immemorial. With the help of these two I lifted a recent thing of Henry's called 'The Cambaroora Star' without author's or publisher's permission, and reprinted it bodily in the *Workman*. I was sitting in shirt sleeves one sunny morning meditating over a new Fabian essay of Bernard Shaw's, which I intended to steal, when a lean, tall young

Lawson first met his great pal Edwin 'Ted' Brady after his rival lifted one of Lawson's poems and passed it off as his own. National Library of Australia, 43935365

man entered the cubicle, a lonesome looking person about two years older than myself. He examined me with reflective brown eyes, and inquired with a curious lisp if I was the editor. After I had proudly acknowledged the fact he informed me that he had come to thank me for the honor I had paid him in stealing 'The Cambaroora Star' for the official organ of Labor.[28]

After the initial shock of being caught red-handed, Brady removed his feet from the table, put down the article he was about to plagiarise and locked the drawer in which he kept girls' photographs, anarchistic literature and a 'loaded bulldog revolver of English pattern', and put on his coat.

The pair of young writers then went next door to a pub where they could drink large glasses of beer for threepence, and patrons could snack for free on broken ship's biscuits and small squares of cheese. They talked poetry and politics and the destiny of their un-federated continent. Despite a hostile beginning they parted reluctantly after many hours, and 'a friendship of a lifetime had been appropriately cemented'.[29] At the time Lawson was so broke that he often had to cadge tobacco off Brady, which he wrote about in 'Ned's Delicate Ways'.[30]

Lawson was inspired by Brady's own forceful writing and composed 'A Song of Southern Writers',[31] a lament about the priorities of his countrymen and what he saw as the narrow outlook of publishers pandering to the masses.

In the land where sport is sacred, where the lab'rer is a god,
You must pander to the people, make a hero of a clod!
...
To be buried as a pauper; to be shoved beneath the sod –
While the brainless man of muscle has the burial of a god.[32]

He used the pen-name 'Joe Swallow' just in case any publishers – or 'brainless men of muscle' – took offence. Lawson had also been deeply affected by the recent death of Barcroft Boake,[33] whose stirring verses about brave horsemen earned him comparisons with 'The Banjo'.

Lawson knew just how harsh life could be for an aspiring writer and Lawson saw a lot of himself in Boake's story; a young surveyor and a boundary rider who was trying desperately to make a living from his poetry. In 1892 Boake returned to Sydney from a stint as a surveyor around Wagga in a state of depression. On 2 May he left his father's house at Croydon and eight days later was found hanging by a stockwhip from the bough of a tree at Long Bay, Middle Harbour.[34]

Lawson saw in Boake's death comparisons with Adam Lindsay Gordon's struggle for acceptance and ultimate demise.

> Banish envy, Southern writer! Strike with no uncertain hand,
> For the sound of Gordon's rifle still is ringing through the land!
> Ah! the niggard recognition! Ah! the 'fame' that came in vain
> To the poor dead poet lying with a bullet through his brain![35]

In 'Charlie Lilley',[36] Lawson made a vain request to the Chief Justice of Queensland to move to New South Wales and fire up the new Labor members in the New South Wales Parliament, arguing that they were moving far too slowly to make any real change. He maintained the rage in his satirical 'Rise Ye! Rise Ye!'.[37]

Lawson's deafness, and especially his drinking, made it increasingly difficult for him to find work that he enjoyed. He lacked the application to write a novel about the urban poor for which 'Jones's Alley' and other works showed such promise, and instead he continued to work piecemeal for a guinea here and there.

Mary Cameron, now teaching at the Stanmore Superior Public School, implored him to 'write Australia, and again Australia',[38] and he returned to his rural roots with *The Bulletin* poem 'Corny Bill'[39] about a big-drinking garrulous storyteller in the mould of his grandfather. His sketch 'A Day on a Selection'[40] was a slice of life from his days at Eurunderee.

Two months later, Archibald published another of Lawson's sketches. It was a little more than 3000 words about hard times and heroics, love and loyalty, poverty and despair and a young man yearning for the love of his family.

It had started with the seed of an idea after Louisa told Lawson about the time a mad bullock had terrorised her, keeping her a virtual prisoner in her hut, and he later said the model was Louisa's sister Gertrude Falconer, the wife of Job Falconer, a squatter at Lahey's Creek, near Dubbo.[41]

Lawson called his sketch 'The Drover's Wife'[42] and even couched in the casual racism of the 1890s *Bulletin* it still resonates as a story of a woman's love for her children 130 years later. This is how it went:

The 'house' contains two rooms; is built of round timber, slabs, and stringy-bark, and floored with split slabs. A big bark kitchen stands at the end, and is larger than the house, itself, verandah included. Bush all round – bush with no horizon, for the country is flat. No ranges in the distance. The bush consists of stunted, rotten 'native apple trees'. No undergrowth. Nothing to relieve the eye, save the darker green of a few she oaks which are sighing above the narrow, almost waterless creek. Nineteen miles to the nearest civilisation – a shanty on the main road.

The drover – an ex-squatter – is away with sheep. His wife and children are left here alone.

Four ragged, dried up-looking children are playing about the house. Suddenly one of them yells:

'Snake! Mother, here's a snake!'

The gaunt, sun-browned bushwoman darts from the kitchen, snatches 'the baby' from the ground, holds it on her left hip, and reaches for a stick.

'Where is it?'

'Here! gone into the wood-heap!' yells the eldest boy – a sharp-faced, excited urchin of eleven.

'Stop there, mother!' I'll have the ... !' (he swears like a trooper). I'll have the ... !'

'Tommy, come here, or you'll be bit. Come here at once when I tell you, you little wretch!

'Damn you (that I should say such a thing!) come here!' she shrieks. Her voice is not very musical.

The youngster swears beneath his breath, and comes reluctantly, carrying a stick nearly as big as himself. Suddenly he yells, triumphantly:

'There it goes, under the house!' and darts away, with club uplifted. At the same time, the big, black, yellow-eyed dog-of-all-breeds, who has the greatest interest in the proceedings, breaks his chain and darts after the snake. He is a moment late, however, and his nose reaches the crack in the slabs just as the end of the snake's tail disappears. Almost at the same moment the boy's club comes down and skins the aforesaid nose. The dog takes small notice of this and proceeds to undermine the building; but he is subdued after a struggle and chained up. They can't afford to lose him.

The drover's wife makes the children stand together near the dog-house while she watches for the snake. She gets two small dishes of milk and sets them down near the wall to tempt the snake out; but an hour goes by and it does not show itself.

It is near sunset, and a thunderstorm is coming.

The children must be brought inside. She will not take them into the house, for she knows the snake is there and may at any moment come up through the cracks in the rough slab floor. So she carries several armfuls of firewood into the kitchen, and then takes the children there. The kitchen has 'no floor,' or rather an earthen one called a 'ground floor' in this part of the bush. There is a large, roughly-made table in the centre of the place. She brings the children in and makes them get on this table. They are two boys and two girls – mere babies. She gives them some supper, and then, before it gets dark, she goes into the house, and snatches up some pillows and bed-clothes – expecting to see or lay her hand on the snake any minute. She makes a bed on the kitchen-table for the children and sits down beside it to watch all night.

She has an eye on the corner, and a green sapling club laid in readiness on the dresser by her side; also her sewing basket, and a copy of the *Young Ladies' Journal*. She has brought the dog into the room.

Tommy turns in under protest, and says he'll lay awake all night and smash that nameless snake.

His mother asks him how many times she has told him not to swear.

He has his club with him under the bed-clothes, and the child next to him protests:

'Mummy! Tommy's skinnin' me alive wif his club. Make him take it out.'

Tommy: 'Shet up, you little …. ! D'yer want to be bit with the snake?'

Jacky shuts up.

'If yer bit,' says Tommy, after a pause, 'you'll swell up, an' smell, an' turn red an' green an' blue all over till you bust. Won't he, mother?'

'Now then, don't frighten the child. Go to sleep,' she says.

The two younger children go to sleep, and now and then Jacky complains of being 'skeezed.'

More room is made for him. Presently Tommy says: 'Mother! listen to them (adjective) little possums. I'd like to screw their blanky necks.'

And Jacky protests drowsily.

'But they don't hurt us, the little blanks!'

Mother: 'There, I told you you'd teach Jacky to swear.' But Jacky's remark makes her smile. Jacky goes to sleep.

Presently, Tommy asks:

'Mother! Do you think they'll ever extricate the (adjective) kangaroo?'

'Lord! How am I to know, child? Go to sleep.'
'Will you wake me if the snake comes out?'
'Yes. Go to sleep.'

***

Near midnight. The children are all asleep and she still sits there, sewing and reading by turns. From time to time she glances round the floor and wall-plate, and, whenever she hears a noise, she reaches for the stick. The thunder-storm comes on, and the wind rushing thro' the cracks in the slab wall threatens to blow out her candle. She places it on a sheltered part of the dresser, and fixes up a newspaper to protect it. At every flash of lightning, the cracks between the slabs gleam like polished silver. The thunder rolls, and the rain comes down in torrents.

'Alligator' (the dog) lies at full length on the floor, with his eyes turned towards the partition. She knows by this that the snake is still there. There are large cracks in that wall opening under the floor of the dwelling-house.

She is not a coward, but recent events have shaken her nerves. A little son of her brother in-law was lately bitten by a snake, and died. Besides, she has not heard from her husband for six months, and is anxious about him.

He was a drover and started squatting here when they were married. The drought of 18– ruined him. He had to sacrifice the remnant of his flock and go droving again. He intends to move his family into the nearest town when he comes back, and in the meantime his brother, who lives on the main road, comes over about once a month with provisions. The wife has still a couple of cows, one horse, and a few sheep. The brother-in-law kills one of the latter occasionally, gives her what she needs of it, and takes the rest in return for other provisions.

She is used to being left alone. She once lived like this for 18 months. As a girl she built, we suppose, the usual air-castles, but all her girlish hopes and aspirations are dead. She finds all the excitement and recreation she needs in the *Young Ladies' Journal,* and Heaven help her, takes a pleasure in the fashion-plates.

Her husband is a native, and so is she. He is careless, but a good husband enough. If he had the means he would take her to the city and keep her there like a princess. They are used to being apart, or at least she is. 'No use frettin,' she says. He may forget sometimes that he is married, but if he has a good cheque when he comes back he will give most of it to her. When he had money he took her to the city several times – hired a railway sleeping compartment, and put up at the best hotels. He also bought her a buggy, but they had to sacrifice it.

The last two children were born in the bush – one while her husband was bringing a drunken doctor, by force, to attend on her. She was alone on this occasion, and very weak. She had been ill with a fever. She prayed to God to send her assistance. God sent 'Black Mary,' the 'whitest' gin in all the land.

One of her children died while she was here alone. She rode nineteen miles for assistance, carrying the dead child.

***

It must be near one or two o'clock. The fire is burning low. Alligator lies with his head resting on his paws, and watches the wall. He is not a very beautiful dog to look at, and the light shows numerous old wounds where the hair will not grow. He is afraid of nothing on the face of the earth or under it. He will tackle a bullock as readily as he will tackle a flea. He hates all other dogs – except kangaroo-dogs – and has a marked dislike to friends or relations of the family. They seldom call, however. He sometimes makes friends with strangers. He hates snakes, and has killed many, but he will be bitten some day and die; most snake-dogs end that way.

Now and then the bushwoman lays down her work and watches, and listens, and thinks. She thinks of things in her own life, for there is little else to think about.

The rain will make the grass grow, and this reminds her how she fought a bush-fire once while her husband was away. The grass was long, and very dry, and the fire threatened to burn her out. She put on an old pair of her husband's trousers, and beat out the flames with a green bough till great drops of sooty perspiration stood out on her forehead and ran in streaks down her blackened arms. The sight of his mother in trousers greatly amused Tommy, who worked like a little hero by her side; but the baby howled lustily until his mother appeared in skirts again. The fire almost mastered her, but four excited bushmen arrived just in time.

She thinks how she fought a flood during her husband's absence. She stood for hours in the drenching downpour, and dug a drain to save the dam across the creek. But she could not save it. There are things that a bushwoman cannot do. Next morning the dam was broken, and her heart was nearly broken too, for she thought how her husband would feel when he came home and saw the result of months of labour swept away. She 'cried' then.

She also fought the pleuro-pneumonia, dosed and bled the few remaining cattle, and wept again when her two best cows died.

Again, she fought a mad bullock that besieged the house for a day. She made bullets and fired at him thro' cracks in the slabs, with an old shotgun. He was dead in the morning. She skinned him, and afterwards got 7s. 6d. for the hide.

She also fights the crows and eagles that have designs on her chickens. Her plan of campaign is very original. The children cry 'Crows, mother!' and she rushes out and aims a broomstick at the birds as though it were a gun, and says 'Bung!' The crows leave in a hurry; they are cunning, but a woman's cunning is greater.

Occasionally a bushman in the 'horrors,' or a villainous-looking 'sundowner,' comes and scares the life out of her. She generally tells the suspicious-looking stranger that her 'husband and two sons are at work below the dam,' for he always cunningly enquires for 'the boss.'

Only last week a gallows-faced swagman – having satisfied himself or been informed that there were no men on the place – threw his swag down on the verandah, and demanded tucker. She gave him something to eat, and then he expressed his intention of staying for the night. It was sundown then. She got a batten from the sofa, loosened the dog, and confronted the stranger – holding the batten in one hand and the dog's collar with the other. 'Now you go!' she said. He looked at her and at the dog, said 'Allright, mum,' in a cringing tone, and left. She was a determined-looking woman, and Alligator's yellow eyes glared unpleasantly. Besides, the dog's chawing-up apparatus greatly resembled that of his namesake.

***

She has few pleasures to think of as she sits here alone by the fire and watches for a snake. All days are much the same to her; but on Sunday afternoon she dresses herself, tidies the children, smartens-up baby, and goes for a lonely walk along the bush-track, pushing an old perambulator in front of her. She does this every Sunday. She takes as much care to make herself and the children 'look smart' as she would if she were going to 'do the block' in Sydney. There is nothing to see, however, and not a soul to meet. You might walk for 20 miles along this track without being able to fix a point in your mind unless you are a bushman. It is because of the madding, everlasting sameness of the stunted trees, the quality that makes a new-chum long to break away and travel as far as trains can go, and sail as far as ships can sail – and further.

But this bushwoman is used to the loneliness of it. As a girl-wife she hated it, but now she would feel strange away from it.

She is glad when her husband returns, but she does not gush or make a fuss about it. She gets him something good to eat and tidies up the children.

She seems contented with her lot. She loves her children, but has no time to show it. She seems harsh to them. Her surroundings are not favourable to the development of the womanly or sentimental side of nature.

***

It must be near morning now, but the clock is in the other room. Her candle is nearly done; she forgot that she is out of candles. Some more wood must be got to keep the fire up, and so she shuts the dog inside and hurries round to the woodheap. The rain has cleared off. She seizes a stick, pulls it out, and – crash! the whole pile collapses, and nearly frightens her to death.

Yesterday she bargained with a stray blackfellow to bring her some wood, and while he was at work she went in search of a missing cow. She was absent an hour or so, and the black made good use of his time. On her return she was astonished by seeing a great heap of wood by the chimney. She gave the black an extra fig of tobacco, and praised him for not being lazy. He thanked her, and left with head erect. *But he built the wood-heap hollow.*

She is hurt now, and tears spring to her eyes as she sits down again by the table. She snatches up a handkerchief to wipe the tears away, but pokes her eyes with her bare fingers instead. The handkerchief is full of holes, and she finds that she has put her thumb through one, and her forefinger through another.

This makes her laugh suddenly, to the surprise of the dog. She has a keen, very keen sense of the ridiculous; and sometime or another she will amuse bushmen by relating this incident.

She was amused once before in a manner similar in some respects. One day she sat down 'to have a good cry,' as she said – and the old cat rubbed against her dress and 'cried, too.' Then she 'had to laugh.'

***

It must be near daylight now. The room is very close and hot because of the fire. Alligator still watches the wall from time to time. Suddenly he becomes greatly interested; he draws himself a few inches nearer the partition, and a thrill runs through his body. The hair on the back of his neck begins to bristle, and the battle light is in his yellow eyes. She knows what this means, and lays her hand on the stick. The lower end of one of the partition slabs has a large crack on each side of it. An evil pair of small, bright, bead-like eyes glisten at one of these holes. The snake – a black one – comes slowly out, about a foot, and moves its head up and down. The dog lies still, and the woman sits as one fascinated. The snake comes out a foot further. She lifts her stick, and the reptile, as though suddenly aware of danger, sticks his head in through the crack on the other side of the slab, and hurries to get his tail round after him. Alligator springs, and his jaws come together with a snap. He misses this time, for his nose is large, and the snake's body close down in the angle formed by the slabs and the floor. He snaps again as the tail comes round. He has the snake now, and tugs it out eighteen inches. Thud, thud, comes the woman's club on the ground. Alligator pulls again. Thud, thud. Alligator pulls some more. He has the snake out now – a black brute, five feet long. The head rises to dart about, but the dog has the enemy close to the neck. He is a big, heavy dog, but as quick as a terrier. He shakes the snake as tho' he felt the curse of Toil in common with mankind.

The eldest boy wakes up, seizes his stick, and makes to get out of bed, but his mother forces him back with a grip of iron. Thud, thud; the snake's back is broken in several places. Thud, thud; the head is crushed, and Alligator's nose skinned again.

She lifts the mangled reptile on the point of her stick, carries it to the fire, and throws it in. Then she piles on the wood and watches the snake burn.

The boy and dog watch, too. She lays her hand, on the dog's head, and all the fierce, angry light dies out of his yellow eyes. The younger children are quieted, and presently go to sleep. The dirty-legged boy stands for a moment in his shirt, watching the fire. Presently he looks at her. He sees the tears in her eyes, and, suddenly throwing his arms round her neck, exclaims:

'Mother, I won't never go drovin'; blast me, if I do!'

And she hugs him to her worn-out breast and kisses him, and they sit thus together while the sickly daylight breaks over the bush.

Chapter 9

So, no doubt, the bush is wretched if you judge it by the groan
Of the sad and soulful poet with a graveyard of his own.
BANJO PATERSON ON LAWSON'S GRIM VIEW OF THE AUSTRALIAN BUSH[1]

'THE DROVER'S WIFE' was the way that Henry Lawson saw the real Australia of the depression-hit 1890s – a ceaseless struggle for the battler against overwhelming odds. Whether it was the gaunt bush-woman fighting with every bit of strength she had to save the lives of her terrified children, or the pale, frail, factory boy being crushed by capitalism as he tried to help his destitute family, Lawson witnessed struggle at every turn. The fight by a little collection of colonies for republicanism against an ancient Empire; the mateship and larrikinism of the Australian worker – they all became fuel for the fire that blazed inside Lawson as he tried to truly portray the experiences of Australia's poor and downtrodden.

Lawson did not see Australia through the same rose-tinted glasses worn by 'The Banjo'. He claimed Paterson was selling an illusion that elevated the drover, the stockman and the rouseabout to demi-gods, and that he had turned the harsh, unyielding bush into an Australian fantasyland of

... the vision splendid of the sunlit plains extended,
And at night the wond'rous glory of the everlasting stars.[2]

As well as Lawson and Paterson, Archibald was nurturing many other emerging writers through *The Bulletin*.

John Farrell and Ted Brady had already made their mark and Bristol-born university lecturer Arthur Jose[3] was starting to have his poetry published. Ballarat-born Ted Dyson[4] wrote many of his ballads about the mines but was looking further to the far horizons of the bush and the outback plains. Will Ogilvie,[5] a young Scot, was working as a drover, horse-breaker and rouseabout and had begun to supply newspapers with bush verse.

Lawson and Paterson were unquestionably the two big guns of *The Bulletin*, though, and readers were lapping up Paterson's ballads of escapism, of yearning for and celebrating a bush idyll that Lawson said did not exist.

By the time 'The Drover's Wife' appeared in the middle of 1892, Lawson was twenty-five and had established his reputation for pulling no punches in writing about Australian life as he saw it. The bush had been nothing but hard toil for Lawson since he could remember and he had heard more than enough about Banjo's cracking whips, flying horses and loveable country rogues.

Rather than tramping anywhere with his swag though, Paterson was a mainstay of the city establishment, having followed the example of his grandfather Robert Barton by becoming a member of Sydney's exclusive Australian Club in February 1892. Banjo soon regarded the club and its plush surrounds as his second home.

In 'The Drover's Wife', Lawson could have been telling the story of Paterson's mother Rose,[6] who struggled through most of her short life on remote bush properties in danger and despair, bringing up her children while her husband was away riding fences or droving.

Paterson carefully concealed his own family trauma, though, including the death of his broken-down, worn-out father[7] from an overdose of the opium-based medication laudanum that he was using to dilute the pain of his constant lumbago. Lawson was far more forthcoming about the trauma he experienced in a bush family, using its quirks and misfortunes for material.

He challenged Banjo to a duel. In print.

Archibald welcomed the idea for what became known as 'The Bulletin Debate' as a way to stir controversy and boost readership for his magazine.

On the surface, Lawson was fighting out of his division, a shy, awkward and frail-looking deaf man with a speech impediment going up against Australia's favourite real-life action hero. But Lawson believed he had a strong case and while Arthur Jose said that the 'Bulletin's two chief bards were usually on the edge of animosity',[8] the pair initially treated their rivalry as a good-natured contest that could make them both a few quid.

The 'write-off' had started with a handshake late in June 1892, a few weeks before 'The Drover's Wife' appeared. Paterson recalled ...

one day [Lawson] suggested that we should write against each other, he putting the bush from his point of view, and I putting it from mine. 'We ought to do pretty well out of it,' he said. 'We ought to be able to get in three or four sets of verses each before they stop us.' This suited me all right, for we were working on space, and the pay was very small – in fact, I remember getting exactly thirteen and sixpence for writing 'Clancy of the Overflow' – so we slam-banged away at each other for weeks and weeks; not until they stopped us, but until we ran out of material.[9]

Lawson was up for the challenge, writing to his 'Dear Gran' Harriet Albury that he was now doing well, 'better than I ever did before', and was confident his writing would only become more popular.[10]

The contest started with Lawson's 'Borderland'[11] on 9 July 1892.

Sunny plains! Great Scot! – those burning wastes of barren soil
  and sand
With their everlasting fences stretching out across the land!

Desolation where the crow is! Desert! where the eagle flies,
Paddocks where the luny bullock starts and stares with reddened eyes;

The bush, Lawson argued, was full of treacherous tracks; dark and evil-looking gullies; dull, dumb flats and stony rises; lizards and snakes. It was either heat and dust or destructive floods. The paradise painted by men like Paterson was just a mirage.

Lawson did not name Paterson in 'Borderland', referring only to 'Southern poets', his derisive term for the well-paid authors pandering to the masses:

I believe the Southern poets' dream will not be realised
Till the plains are irrigated and the land is humanised.
I intend to stay at present – as I said before – in town
Drinking beer and lemon-squashes – taking baths and cooling
    down.[12]

Banjo hit back in *The Bulletin* two weeks later with 'In Defence of the Bush (On Reading Henry Lawson's "Borderland")'.[13]

So you're back from up the country, Mister Lawson, where you went,
And you're cursing all the business in a bitter discontent;
Well, we grieve to disappoint you, and it makes us sad to hear
That it wasn't cool and shady, and there wasn't whips of beer,
And the looney bullock snorted when you first came into view,
Well, you know it's not so often that he sees a swell like you;

The bush had moods and changes, Paterson explained, and Lawson would tell a happier tale if he saw the rains return and the dust bowls turn into fields of waving grass and the rivers transform into refreshing torrents. True bushmen, Paterson said, would 'be loyal thro' it all'. Paterson's rebuttal appeared in the same *Bulletin* issue as 'The Drover's Wife' and Paterson referenced Lawson's work asking of his young rival's visit to the bush:

And the women of the homesteads and the men you chanced to meet,
Were their faces sour and saddened like the 'faces in the street'?
And the 'shy selector children', were they better now or worse
Than the little city urchins who would greet you with a curse?

Paterson landed his final blows by further interrogating Lawson about the merits of city life:

Did you hear no sweeter voices in the music of the bush
Than the roar of trams and buses, and the war-whoop of 'the push'?
... You had better stick to Sydney and make merry with the 'push',
For the bush will never suit you, and you'll never suit the bush.[14]

Ted Dyson sided with Lawson, refuting that Clancy of the Overflow really had it so good under the bush stars, and a week later Archibald ran Dyson's 'The Fact of the Matter'.[15]

The battle of the bards became a literary sensation and two weeks later, on 6 August 1892, Archibald ran Lawson's 'In Answer to "Banjo" and Otherwise',[16] as Lawson rained rhyming blows all over Banjo's reputation. The tirade was later sarcastically renamed 'The City Bushman':

Would you like to change with Clancy, go a-droving? tell us true,
For we rather think that Clancy would be glad to change with you, ...
Did you ever guard the cattle when the night was inky black
And it rained, and icy water trickled gently down your back.
Till your saddle-weary backbone started aching at the roots
And you almost heard the croaking of the bullfrog in your boots? ...
... you'll find it very jolly with the cuff-and-collar push,
And the city seems to suit you, while you rave about the bush.[17]

Lawson added a socialist bite, telling Paterson:

Droving songs are very pretty, but they merit little thanks
From the people of country which is ridden by the Banks.

Archibald ran two more contributions siding with Lawson over successive weeks. 'The Overflow of Clancy',[18] which was signed 'H.H.C.C.', may have been written by Lawson, though the poet Humphrey Cripps-Clark[19] was a contemporary. 'Banjo, of the Overflow', by Francis Kenna,[20] savaged Paterson's romantic vision.

In the 'Grog-An'-Grumble Steeplechase'[21] Lawson was back poking fun at the image and characters of Banjo's 'Open Steeplechase'.[22]

Banjo struck back again with 'In Answer to Various Bards',[23] scoffing at the melancholy of a poet 'with a graveyard of his own', a line he came to regret. He is said to have developed that putdown after seeing an early draft of Lawson's 'Poets of the Tomb',[24] and perhaps with the knowledge that Lawson was writing a short story based on his grandfather's coffin-making pastime, 'The Bush Undertaker',[25] for editor George Essex Evans's new magazine called *The Antipodean*. Lawson was delighted that 'The Bush Undertaker' was soon reprinted in *The Scotsman*.

Paterson had all the ammunition he needed and wrote:

Well, I've waited mighty patient while they all came rolling in,
    Mister Lawson, Mister Dyson, and the others of their kin,
With their dreadful, dismal stories of the Overlander's camp,
How his fire is always smoky, and his boots are always damp;
And they paint it so terrific it would fill one's soul with gloom,
But you know they're fond of writing about 'corpses' and 'the tomb'.[26]

Paterson ended his attack on an amicable note, though:

But that ends it, Mr. Lawson, and it's time to say good-bye,
    We must agree to differ in all friendship, you and I.[27]

A week later Lawson's 'The Poets of the Tomb'[28] appeared in *The Bulletin* as he tried to answer a growing brief of evidence that he specialised in gloom, writing that 'An honest man alive is worth a million under ground'.

A few weeks later, in the Christmas 1892 edition of *The Bulletin*, Archibald published Banjo's comic 'The Man from Ironbark'[29] about a befuddled bushman running amok in a Sydney barber shop. Archibald was so impressed with what many still regard as Banjo's most humorous work that *The Bulletin* took out its entire first editorial page with illustrations. When Lawson wrote a parody of the poem for *The Bulletin*, Archibald refused to run it, so instead Lawson sold 'The Man from Waterloo (With Kind Regards to Banjo)' to *Truth*.[30]

Two years later, Paterson had one last go at Lawson in 'A Voice from the Town',[31] but he always knew he had a head start over his rival in life and felt a degree of sympathy for him.

'Henry Lawson was a man of remarkable insight in some things and of extraordinary simplicity in others,' Paterson wrote. 'We were both looking for the same reef, if you get what I mean; but I had done my prospecting on horseback with my meals cooked for me, while Lawson had done his prospecting on foot. Nobody realised this better than Lawson.'[32]

Paterson said that Lawson had put his case about the bush 'better than I did, but I had the better case, so that honours (or dishonours) were fairly equal'.[33]

While the great debate raged, the glaring disparities between Paterson's affluent lifestyle and Lawson's dangerous slides into depression were never more obvious. Lawson began to haunt Archibald's office smelling of booze and telling him of all the characters he had met drinking at The Rocks. It seemed whatever money Lawson had was going on booze as he tried to dull his inner pain. Even Lawson's clothes were falling apart. His boots were down at heel and, to his embarrassment, the seat on his only pair of trousers was wearing thin. Lawson decided to use the humiliation as material for a new poem.

In December 1892 he walked down to Ted Brady's flat on the ground floor of an umbrella repair shop in Regent Street, Redfern, and the two headed for a seat in Belmore Park to assess Lawson's latest work which he had written the night before.

Lawson started reading about what it was like to wear a pair of trousers that badly needed 'a patch behind'.

> You will face the doubtful glances of the people that you know;
> But – of course, you're bound to face them when your pants begin
>   to go.[34]

Archibald had become increasingly worried by Lawson's drinking and by the company his young protege was keeping. Soon he would hatch a plan to get Lawson out of Sydney, believing it might also provide him with some vivid new sources for poems and short stories. While Lawson may have decried the terrors and torments of the bush, Archibald decided to send him packing to the wild west.

Chapter 10

A reckless spirit he was even in those days, quick to feel the smart of a slight, impatient at small obstacles, and when the mood was on him, morose almost to grumpiness … but withal, an affectionate and sincere friend.

LAWSON'S CLOSE COMPANION, JIM GORDON[1]

NOT ONLY HAD LAWSON'S pants begun to go, but his pockets were bare too, and his brother Charlie, just out of prison, was now facing another long lag after a violent burglary.[2] Charlie had been robbing a Mudgee doctor's house at 4.30 a.m. on 25 August 1892 when a police constable, walking the beat, surprised him. The young tearaway attacked the policeman with a sword, but missed and sliced through a door instead before being handcuffed.[3]

Soon after, Lawson arrived at Ted Brady's Redfern flat in one of his blackest moods. Brady was now writing mostly for *Truth* and *The Bulletin*, but earning little. He and Lawson walked to Archibald's office in Pitt Street to see what business they could drum up there.

Archibald, keeping his hand on the copy he was revising, screwed partly round in his chair and regarded the two young writers with what Brady thought 'was an uncivil eye'.[4] As Lawson went downstairs, Archibald, still holding his manuscript, suddenly wheeled right round and asked Brady, 'What's the matter with Lawson?'[5]

'He's all right …,' Brady started, but Archibald cut him off.

'No, he is not all right. He is coming here in the morning with tobacco-juice running down his jaw, smelling of stale beer.'

'Look,' Brady cried, seized by an inspiration. 'I think if Lawson got away to the bush he would be all right.'

Archibald turned back in his chair and regarded his manuscript thoughtfully. That wasn't such a bad idea. Though Lawson wrote movingly of bush characters and their surrounds, Archibald wondered just how much of Australia's interior he had seen beyond Grenfell and Mudgee.

'Why doesn't he go back to the bush?' Archibald demanded over his shoulder.

'No money,' Brady ventured.

Archibald could fix that. The prospect of Lawson writing about outback life and personalities excited him, though he was not about to make Lawson wealthy even if 'The Drover's Wife' was being lauded as a piece of literary brilliance. Fresh air and new horizons could perhaps quell the demons tormenting his sad star and produce more material to lift *Bulletin* sales.

Archibald gave Lawson £5 in spending money and a £4 one-way ticket to Bourke, 760 kilometres north-west at the end of the railway line from Sydney. Bourke was the largest inland port in Australia, where drays delivered huge loads of wool to be carried on barges down the Darling River. It was also the gateway to the arid outback.

Lawson sent a poem, 'A Stranger on the Darling',[6] to Bourke's *Western Herald* under the pseudonym Joe Swallow, and he hoped to gain some journalism work in the western town, just as he had done when he sailed to Albany. He packed his paintbrushes just in case.

He also submitted a poem to Archibald referencing Mary Cameron, 'Mary Called Him "Mister"',[7] and two of *The Bulletin* staff, including Alfred Stephens – his old sub-editor from the *Boomerang* who was now editing *The Bulletin*'s 'Red Page' of literary gossip and reviews – escorted him to Redfern Station to ensure the deaf, shy and brooding wastrel got on board the train.

They bade Lawson Godspeed to what they said was 'a land of health and a wealth of copy that should be [an] answer to any aspiring writer's dream'.[8]

Bourke was a staunch union town that had given support for the shearers during their strike, so Lawson knew he would meet men of a kindred spirit.

The town offered him a new start with a population of more than 3000 when all the shearers were in town, with their fat cheques, 'gloriously drunk and happy, in love with all the world'.[9] There were about 200 businesses,[10] wide streets and brick buildings with iron roofs that reflected a dazzling sun.

Lawson arrived at Bourke late on the afternoon of 21 September 1892,[11] after thirty-six hours of rocking and rattling along the line. 'At 5.30 we saw a long line of camels moving out across the, sunset,' he wrote. 'There's something snaky about camels. They remind me of turtles and goannas. Somebody said, "Here's Bourke."'[12]

He called the western town 'the metropolis of the Great Scrubs'[13] and years later remarked of the heat and the isolation, and the mateship of working men, that 'If you know Bourke you know Australia'.[14]

He promptly wrote to his Aunt Emma with a degree of justification over his point of view in The Bulletin Debate. 'The bush between here and Bathurst is horrible,' he told her. 'I was right, and Banjo wrong.' Most of the 'alleged' bushmen hated being out here, he continued. He had endured an argument with a shearer about how many sheep could be shorn in a day, and he had met one braggart so full of bluster that he was convinced bushmen 'were the biggest liars ever the Lord created'. He said Bourke was 'a much nicer town than I thought it would be' and that he would be 'able to hang out all right … Might take a job if I see a chance'.[15] Soon, though, he was saying that Bourke was a 'hostile wasteland',[16] so hot that when the dead from there went to hell they sent home for their blankets.[17] The town had an air of impermanency, as though all who lived there were travellers wanting to go somewhere else.

Lawson took a room at John Lennon's two-storey Great Western Hotel – but if Archibald and Brady had hoped the outback heat would dry up Lawson's drinking, they were wrong. He gave Bourke the nickname 'Comeanaveadrink', as among its wide and welcoming streets there were only three churches but nineteen pubs. He told his aunt that he had a problem and these establishments were not helping him overcome it. 'I'm an awful fool,' he wrote, explaining that he had hardly unpacked his swag when some Great Western barmaids, 'ex-actresses ... as cunning as the devil', sent him to bed 'boozed'. He promised that he had learnt his lesson and knew that to escape the demon drink 'I must take to the bush as soon as I can'.[18]

Lawson earned a guinea from the editor of the *Western Herald* for a poem[19] praising William Walter 'Baldy' Davis,[20] who had been recently deposed as the Member for Bourke. Lawson told Aunt Emma that Davis was the *Herald* editor's brother and 'a very rich and very good natured squatter'. Three days after Lawson's poem appeared, 23-year-old Charlie Lawson, in and out of jail since he was thirteen, appeared briefly at the Mudgee Circuit Court, pleaded guilty to burglary and was sentenced to seven years in jail.

BOURKE HAD AN ELEMENT of socialism that Lawson found appealing: 'There was no poverty in Bourke – as it is understood in the city,' he wrote, 'there was plenty of food; and camping out

A camel team at Bourke carrying supplies. State Library of NSW, FL1710928

and roughing it come natural to the bushmen. In cases of sickness, accident, widows or orphans, the chaps sent round the hat ... If a chap was hard up he borrowed a couple of quid from his mate. If a strange family arrived without a penny, someone had to fix 'em up, and the storekeepers helped them till the man got work.'[21]

The Salvation Army did good business. There was 'the thoughtless, careless generosity of the bushman, whose pockets don't go far enough down his trousers ... and who contributes to anything that comes along, without troubling to ask questions, like long Bob Brothers, 'The Giraffe' of Bourke, who, chancing to be "a Protestant by rights," unwittingly subscribed towards the erection of a new Catholic church, and, being chaffed for his mistake, said: "Ah, well, I don't suppose it'll matter a hang in the end, anyway it goes. I ain't got nothink agenst the Roming Carflicks."'[22]

Lawson took a job painting the Great Western and he became friends with many of the shearers who drank there, sharing beers, listening to their yarns, watching their bareknuckle fights. He saw their sense of mateship in a harsh environment as vital, just as it had been for the men during the strike in Queensland a year earlier.

Under the byline 'Tally', Lawson wrote some political poems for the *Western Herald*, one of two local papers in town. In the vein of the Bulletin Debate, it was also suspected that he wrote for its rival the *Central Australian and Bourke Telegraph* as 'Smoko', though the works appeared 'as one poet writing against another poet'.[23]

He had his photograph taken, and told his aunt that the *Western Herald*'s editor wanted to give him a 'notice', but that he 'preferred to keep dark for a while'. The notice and photograph were not published.

There was still little money in poetry, though, and not much more in painting. Archibald's £5 was soon gone. Lawson stayed in different pubs and the union men made him feel like a true comrade. He formed some strong friendships with unionists such as Thomas Hicks Hall, William Wood[24] – who Lawson mistakenly called 'Billy Woods' – and particularly with Donald Macdonell,[25] a shearer who would soon become secretary of the Bourke branch of the Amalgamated Shearers' Union of Australasia and later the Member for Cobar in the NSW Legislative Assembly, as well as the agriculture minister and colonial secretary.

Lawson also became friendly with another local member, Hugh Langwell,[26] and he wrote the political ballad 'Martin Farrell' which depicted the struggle of a dying swagman trying to reach the polling booth to vote for 'Hughie'.[27] His dealings with the union men were the catalyst for his short stories 'Send Round the Hat'[28] and 'That Pretty Girl in the Army'.[29]

For a time, Lawson slept in a skillion at the back of the union office, and at other times slept outside in 'the Park', or town square, like others in the 'free' or unwed portion of the male population ... 'the wives and daughters of the town slept, or tried to sleep, with bedroom windows and doors open, while husbands lay outside on the verandas'.[30]

Lawson found work painting for a Bourke builder named John Hawley, who recalled that the young poet 'was energetic, very punctual to his work, kept to himself, and did not yarn freely to others'. Lawson had to be coaxed into admitting that he was the well-known poet, and Hawley realised that after several weeks of getting to know Lawson, 'the poetry that read as though it flowed easily from his pen, was only achieved by much and persistent burning of the midnight oil'.[31]

Lawson often viewed Bourke life from the front veranda of Watty Braithwaite's[32] Carrier's Arms. The Salvation Army 'used to pray, and thump the drum, and sing, and take up collections every evening outside' the pub, '... perhaps because Watty was considered the most hopeless publican and his customers the hardest crowd of boozers in Bourke'.[33] As Lawson would write in 'That Pretty Girl in the Army':

The band generally began to play about dusk. Watty would lean back comfortably in a basket easy-chair on his wide veranda, and clasp his hands, in a calm, contented way, while the Army banged the drum and got steam up, and

Lawson photographed by Charles Wilson in Bourke, NSW, in 1892. State Library of Victoria, H30827

whilst, perhaps, there was a barney going on in the bar, or a bloodthirsty fight in the backyard. On such occasions there was something like an indulgent or fatherly expression on his fat and usually emotionless face. And by and by he'd move his head gently and doze. The banging and the singing seemed to soothe him ...[34]

Six weeks after Lawson arrived in Bourke, and while Banjo Paterson was thrilling big crowds with a series of polo performances at Rosehill,[35] Archibald published Lawson's short story 'In a Dry Season',[36] which ends with 'P.S. Never tackle the bush without a good mate. With one you can do anything and go anywhere.'[37]

The hard-drinking and destitute 25-year-old found a good mate that November in eighteen-year-old Victorian Jim Gordon,[38] another battler who, like many of the unemployed, had gone bush chasing work to supplement his station overseer father's miserable wage. A 'tenacious chest cold' had sent Gordon from the chill of country Victoria to the 'dry, clear' air of the outback.[39]

Lawson was living in a small house beside the local billabong with two Swedish men who were almost as broke as him and who existed in clouds of smoke from the cheapest, blackest pipe tobacco they could afford.[40] According to Gordon, who later found success as a writer under the pseudonym Jim Grahame, he and Lawson felt an immediate bond when they passed each other in Mitchell Street, the main thoroughfare of Bourke.

'I had noticed this long-necked, flat-chested stripling eyeing me off each time we passed,' Gordon wrote. 'And I noticed too that he had the most beautiful and remarkable eyes I have ever seen on a human being ... soft as velvet and of a depth of brownness that is indescribable ...[41] I was lonely, and somewhat frightened and home-sick, and he was alone, pacing the footpath up one side and down the other.'[42]

Lawson, tall at six feet (183 centimetres) and sickly thin with delicate mannerisms, seemed very different to the other rugged, rough men in town – his aunts after all said he should have been a girl – and he was growing an impressive, drooping moustache that hid his thin lips and feminine mouth.

After following Lawson for the full length of the square, Gordon met him as he turned to retrace his steps.

Gordon said: 'Good day mate' and Lawson lifted his head suddenly with 'the look of one who was embarrassed at being caught day dreaming'. After staring into the teenager's eyes, Lawson replied, 'Hello, have you been shanghaied too?' and chuckled softly.[43]

Lawson knew Gordon was another outsider by his untanned skin and by the dark-coloured, heavy clothing of Victoria that he was wearing.

Gordon had only been in town three days but told Lawson he was already 'as homesick as a motherless calf'.[44]

'Where are you staying?' Lawson asked. Gordon told him he was living at a hotel but that his 'sugar bag' – his money – was running low. Lawson became animated, gripped Gordon's hand and said, 'Come and camp with me.'[45] There has been speculation ever since that the intensity of the friendship was more than platonic.[46]

They stopped in front of a pub and Lawson asked Gordon if he drank. When he said 'no', Lawson lied and said he didn't either. Perhaps having a sober mate kept him that way for a while too. As they were passing a grocery store on the way to Lawson's tiny house, Gordon went in and hurriedly bought some tinned food and half a loaf of bread.

Lawson's house was the smallest to have three rooms that Gordon ever saw, but it was well built, with stone, and it had an open fireplace, though firewood seemed to be a problem and the fire was sometimes stoked with a cow's shinbone and dry cow dung. There were no bunks or furniture of any kind, and the only cooking utensils were billy tins and a frying pan. Lawson owned none of them, but his housemates were socialists in every sense, and what they had Lawson was welcome to share. Gordon soon fell into their ways and it was not more than an hour before they were eating his sardines, and he was chewing on their cold corned beef, which was as hard and shiny as a piece of mahogany, having been cooked, Gordon surmised, for a month.

The next morning over breakfast Gordon learnt that his new friend was 'Lawson! the man who had written all those splendid verses ... in *The Bulletin* and elsewhere'.

'I could hardly believe it,' Gordon recalled. 'I had always visualised him in the lap of luxury, enjoying the admiration and plaudits of half the people of Sydney.'[47]

But the life of a popular writer in Australia could be very different to that.

Only a couple of days after Gordon had moved into Lawson's share house, they were working together for a 'rich old American who had bought a whole square of the town and had completed building a big hotel on one corner and small cottages on the remaining portion'. Gordon had limited experience with a brush but began painting the picket fences while Lawson started on the cottages, working with a speed and diligence that his teenage workmate found amazing, even though they were toiling all day under a burning sun for a meagre £1 a week.[48]

Gordon was sacked within a few days, though, because of his lack of knowledge in blending paints and Lawson quit soon after, sustained for a while by a cheque from *The Bulletin*. The pair decided to look for jobs elsewhere but Gordon's chest cold flared up again and he needed medical attention.

'It was during that period that Lawson showed the true spirit of mateship,' Gordon wrote. 'We had pooled our money, and, owing to medical expenses, I was getting far more than my share, but he made light of it. "Money is nothing between mates," he'd say. It was just the same with the food – often he'd bring home some small delicacy to tempt my appetite.'[49]

Lawson and Gordon decided to leave Bourke and chase work on the vast sheep stations, the only settlements in much of that immense and largely uninhabited countryside, covered as it was by dust and mulga. Just before they left, though, a member of the Australian Workers' Union was drowned in the Darling, and Lawson and Gordon attended the funeral. It was a hot day, and all were bareheaded, but an over-officious publican opened an umbrella and held it above the priest's head. Lawson nudged Gordon. He had found material for his short story 'The Union Buries Its Dead'.[50]

Lawson joined the General Labourers' Union on 23 November 1892, paying 10 shillings to become ticketholder No. 2581. The following morning, he wrote to Arthur Parker, telling his old plastering mate that he was 'pretty drunk' but was about to start down the Darling to get work in a shearing shed. So it was that Lawson set off with Gordon in spring sunshine, crossing the river by punt and then starting a tramp of hard slog for sixty kilometres south-west. They were both wearing boots that were made for the pavements of the city rather than rough unmade bush tracks in country that was shimmering with mirage, only the occasional sandhill breaking the everlasting flatness stretching to the horizon.

Along the way they came upon a recently vacated surveyor's camp, and scavenged amongst the cast-off boots to replace their own inadequate footwear. Gordon wore size eight, while Lawson, who was an inch or so taller, took sevens, or at a pinch, sixes. This was about his only vanity, Gordon recalled, that for whatever reason he was proud of his small feet. Lawson came away with an odd blucher and an ordinary lace up, while Gordon found a dilapidated pair of Cossack boots.[51]

They slept at the abandoned camp. Gordon said Lawson 'never shore a sheep in his life',[52] but the next day they were enrolled at the Fort Bourke sheep station, as rouseabouts, picking up the wool and carrying it to the wool rollers at long tables. They spent three weeks at Fort Bourke, with Lawson's bipolarity evident. He was moody most of the evenings, 'as a rule lying on his bunk from tea time until the lights were out, talking very little and gazing at the cobwebby, corrugated iron roof'. As the other men joked and yarned about their work, Lawson was increasingly withdrawn, isolated by his deafness and agitated by the enforced sobriety among station workers. Though he wrote of great mateship in the bush, 'He was a man apart, having little in common with those whom he worked with,' Gordon said.

> There were nights tho' that he would suggest a walk, and we might stroll a mile or so by some dusty bush track, at times meeting the Royal Mail coach on its long night journey to Wanaaring … One day he was a bushman and the bush was paradise, and perhaps the day following he would be in the dumps and the bush was all gloom and heartbreak.[53]

The fierce sun and unforgiving country exacerbated the good and bad in men and women, and Lawson was able to capture the spirit of unique characters. Gordon believed that Lawson's deafness served him well at the shearing sheds, as he could lie in his bunk 'in a rouseabouts hut, amidst the clatter and rattle of the dishwashing, and the battle of the tongues of the yarn-spinners and card players after tea, and write until he was sleepy. What he saw today he seldom wrote of tonight, but in six months, or a year, or two years – that was his method.'[54]

Lawson was in high spirits on the morning the pair left Fort Bourke, taking the river road that in a few days led them on to Toorale (pronounced Toorally) Station and the confluence of the Warrego, which Lawson called 'an alleged river with a sickly stream that looked like bad milk'.[55] The station was owned by the Irish-born pastoralist Sam McCaughey,[56] later Sir Samuel, who by the early 1890s had acquired more than a million hectares of Australia, including a stretch of more than 150 kilometres along the Darling.

It was almost the end of the shearing season but the two young mates earned a small wage at Toorale, though 'a shearing shed', Lawson observed later, 'is perhaps the most degrading hell on the face of this earth.'[57]

His time on McCaughey's million hectares gave him the poem 'The Boss's Boots',[58] named for the pair worn by Jimmy James, the dapper little manager of Toorale's shed.

When the shearing finished in mid-December, Lawson and Gordon trudged back wearily to Bourke for Christmas.

William Wood recalled that on Christmas Day, he, Lawson, Donald Macdonell, Thomas Hicks Hall, and another friend, Teddy Thompson, all had lunch together. Then they all went back to Wood's house, and as Mrs Wood was away visiting relatives, the men stripped down to their underpants and sat under a water spray on the veranda drinking beer for the rest of a hot afternoon as the mercury hit 115 degrees Fahrenheit in the shade.[59]

Later that night they went boating on the Darling and camped on a bend, boiling their billy and yarning over a smoke into the late evening before drifting gently downstream.[60]

Two days later Lawson and Gordon set out again with their swags and water bottles and wide, battered hats heading north to the main Bourke–Wanaaring road. With them was another mate.

They followed a track that led to Goonery, an outstation of Toorale, and from there they camped for a couple of days at a small wayside pub called Gumbalie. It was there that Lawson saw for the first time Aboriginal people in their tribal state, 'a big camp of them together, depending mostly on game and fish for an existence'. A few of them came to the camp, expecting food and tobacco. They got a little of both but looking at their emaciated bodies, Lawson took pity and could only exclaim: 'They're a dying race, Jim, and they know it. I can read it in their eyes — I can read it in their eyes. I was suckled on a black breast, Jim.'[61]

Gordon and Lawson cast off their mate after he allowed them to drink water from a tank that was contaminated by a dead two-metre carpet snake, and then showed them the remains of the reptile.

On the banks of the Warrego, Lawson and Gordon spent most of New Year's Eve hunting round in the dark and feeling on the ground for camel and horse droppings with which to build fires and make smoke to ward off the mosquitoes which started at sunset and left off at daybreak, when the flies got to work again.[62]

The walk took them on more than 200 kilometres of a meandering odyssey across some of the driest and most unforgiving country on earth. They hoped to find work at stations along the way, but all they found was a ceaseless sun baking their heads and the hot earth burning the soles of their tattered boots.

On and on, Lawson and Gordon trudged like the explorers Burke and Wills stumbling to their doom. 'Time means tucker,' Lawson wrote in his poem 'Out Back', 'and tramp you must … To live you must walk. To cease walking is to die.'[63]

Occasionally Lawson and Gordon met other swagmen looking for food and shelter, or bullockies driving their teams across the rough, rutted tracks. Many of the station owners told them there was no work and to keep walking. 'You have no idea of the horrors of the country out here,' Lawson told his aunt. 'Men tramp and live like dogs.'[64] They survived on cornmeal flatbread called 'Johnnycakes' and 'cadged a bit of meat here and there at miserable stations'.[65]

At night, Lawson and Gordon took comfort in the cooler weather. They camped under the black canopy, gazing at Paterson's 'wond'rous glory of the everlasting stars' but wishing they were in a town with a roof over their heads. Lawson complained that it had been two months since he had slept in a proper bed. Gordon described how the two thin, bony men slept out in all weathers, and scraped hollows in the soil for their hip bones. They felt degraded like animals.[66]

Lawson could be 'fussy' and he complained about the way Gordon rolled his swag and the way Gordon's billy can bumped and stained the younger man's moleskin trousers. Lawson covered his billy with a calico sheath. They would also argue about the water bag, as even though it had been a wet season and they were at times walking through water, Lawson always insisted on keeping the water bag full 'in case of accidents'.

Other times he saw beauty everywhere and suggested in 'The Song of the Darling River'[67] that floodwaters should be preserved and rivers protected. Sometimes he would be too tired to lift his head at night so he would just lie back and marvel at 'The Western Stars'.[68]

It took Lawson and Gordon more than two weeks of tramping to reach Hungerford, which straddled the remote border of Queensland, though it was so hot Lawson called it 'the border of Sheol'.[69]

'I believe [Burke] and Wills found Hungerford,' Lawson wrote, 'and it's a pity they did.'[70]

Lawson didn't even see the town until they were 'quite close to it', the reflection of the sun bouncing off 'two or three white-washed galvanized-iron roofs' rising out of the mulga.[71]

He wrote that he was 'a beaten man',[72] having carried his swag 200 miles (320 kilometres) since he had last written to Aunt Emma. He was ready to leave the next day – 17 January 1893 – for Bourke, '140 miles by the direct road' but would go 'off the track to try to get a few weeks work on a Warrego station'.[73]

Hungerford consisted of two houses and a humpy in New South Wales, and five houses in Queensland. 'Characteristically enough, both the pubs are in Queensland. We got a glass of sour yeast at one and paid sixpence for it – we had asked for English ale. The post office is in New South Wales, and the police-barracks in Bananaland. The police cannot do anything if there's a row going on across the street in New South Wales, except to send to Brisbane and have an extradition warrant applied for; and they don't do much if there's a row in Queensland. Most of the rows are across the border, where the pubs are.'[74]

In Hungerford, Lawson and Gordon worked for a few days on a wool scour. Lawson gained weight and while he was cheerful and content for a while, he became increasingly sick of his surrounds and yearned for the busyness of Sydney.

On the return walk to Bourke, Lawson was restless and drove Gordon hard, wanting him to cover many more miles than they planned. They were given assistance by 'Baldy' Davis, the owner of the 100,000-hectare Kerribee Station and the subject of Lawson's poem for the *Western Herald*. Davis supplied them with as much food as they could carry and added a pound note for good luck. It contrasted sharply with the meanness at other stations. Lawson made the squatter, whose head had been scalded as a child and who always wore a curly auburn wig to cover the scars, the hero of his sketch 'Baldy Thompson'.[75]

Lawson and Gordon finally plodded into Bourke in February 1893; Lawson to resume his work as a painter – sometimes painting inside the Great Western bar – and Gordon to wander off for more station work. The relationship ended abruptly and they would not see each other for a quarter of a century.

Lawson told Aunt Emma on 6 February 1893 that while Archibald had written to him asking for copy, he would have to wait because he was writing for the *Western Herald* in order to buy some clothes. He promised to 'find the means of getting back to Sydney – never to face the bush again'. 'My boots were worn out and I was in rags when I arrived here,' he wrote, 'you should have seen the last hat I wore. I find that I've tramped more than 300 miles since I left here last. That's all I ever intend to do with a swag.'[76] Lawson had been offered a job editing a newspaper in New Zealand but he doubted his ability to edit, and said he hoped for a position on the staff instead.

He spent two anxious weeks making arrangements with a firm of stock agents, 'J Anderson & Co', for a drover's pass that would allow him to travel with a consignment of livestock. He turned the company into 'Peter Anderson and Co' for some of his verses.

IT WAS WHILE HE WAS AT BOURKE that Lawson received a Christmas card from another of *The Bulletin*'s bush poets, infamous as a rogue around north Queensland and western New South Wales. The card was sent from Walgett and written in doggerel. It congratulated Lawson for his victory over Banjo in The Bulletin Debate, and it reached Lawson via Archibald's office in Sydney after Lawson had returned from Hungerford. It was sent by a wild horseman, 'handsome adventurer'[77] and bush poet named Harry 'Breaker' Morant.[78]

Paterson's uncle Arthur Barton had warned 'The Banjo' that 'The Breaker' was a conman – but a charming one, nonetheless.

Morant drifted about Queensland doing odd jobs, working for a while on a newspaper in Hughenden and creating a legend around himself as a horse-breaker. He headed south-west to Winton, lying to everyone that he was the son of Britain's Admiral Sir George Digby Morant, and that he had studied at the Royal Naval College. He was notorious for borrowing horses and money and giving neither back.

In June 1893, Lawson finally boarded a train with a free pass to oversee 'five trucks of cattle'[79] to Nyngan, before taking a passenger train from there to Sydney. It rained all the way home, the sky 'like a wet grey blanket; plains like dead seas, save for the tufts of coarse grass sticking up out of the water'.[80]

Lawson said he had 'escaped'[81] the bush. He was rich in experience and material for his writing but still broke, depressed and drinking.

He had seen enough of the west never to venture near a shearing shed again. His *Bulletin* sketch 'Stragglers'[82] in which the shearers are described with the term used for lost sheep, depicted the harsh conditions of the sheds, men who resembled the living dead, tramping along dusty tracks for a little money and tucker.

'The Shearing of the Cook's Dog'[83] highlighted workplace bullying and double standards over democracy and socialism in the west, while 'A Typical Bush Yarn',[84] which later morphed into 'Two Sundowners',[85] mocked the ideas of a workingman's brotherhood which was being promoted during a visit to Bourke by Billy Lane.

Lawson later said that most of his 'hard-up experiences' were disguised but not exaggerated,[86] though his stories were often distortions including 'The Paroo "River"',[87] in which he wrote that his companion was a 'native of the land' when in fact it was the Russian-born writer Ernest de Guinney, who, among others, walked part of the outback journey with Lawson and Gordon. De Guinney had been in Bourke recruiting for Lane's New Australia movement and the utopian workers' colony in South America.

'I have been accused of painting the bush in the darkest colours from some equally dark personal motives,' Lawson wrote. 'I might be biased – having been there.'[88] Lawson was not writing of the bush as a journalist, though, but as an artist.

Back in the big smoke, he encouraged other Australian writers to 'leave off trying to make a paradise out of the Out Back Hell' and describe it as it really was. For Archibald – and by extension Banjo Paterson – he wrote 'Some Popular Australian Mistakes' about the bush. Among them was 'No. 17. It's not glorious and grand and free to be on the track. Try it.'[89]

Alfred Stephens likened Lawson's journey through the heat and dust to that of 'a damned soul swagging it through purgatory'.[90] 'Lawson hates the bush,'[91] Stephens wrote, saying that his time around Bourke coloured everything Lawson later wrote about Australia.

By contrast Jim Gordon argued: 'Lawson loved the bush, and mostly all contained therein – its rivers and old homesteads with their straggling bridle-paths and winding tracks. He saw beauty in the plain with its cruel mirages, and found charm in the great silences of the nights of the Never-Never. None of them were lost romances to him.'[92]

Three years after leaving Bourke, Lawson wrote his poem 'To An Old Mate', with references to Gordon:

I remember, Old Man, I remember –
The tracks that we followed are clear –
The jovial last nights of December,
The solemn first days of the year.[93]

Lawson's one and only time in what he called the 'Out Back' was crucial to his later prose and the foundation for his reputation as the man who portrayed Australia as it really was. The bush could be harsh, horrible and deadly, but so many of the people were pure gold.

Chapter 11

An' if you meet a friend of mine who wants to find my track,
Say you, 'He's gone to Maoriland, and isn't coming back'.
LAWSON ON JOINING THE EXODUS OF AUSTRALIA'S WORKERS OVERSEAS[1]

AUSTRALIA'S FINANCIAL COLLAPSE had worsened by the time Lawson returned to Sydney in June 1893. Eleven major Australian banks had recently been forced to close their doors, and in Melbourne one in ten homes was being repossessed. Unemployment skyrocketed and political activism intensified, with socialist speakers drawing big audiences in Sydney. Lawson, though, had never had it so good. One of the most feted writers in Australia was now almost making a decent living.

Everywhere he looked there was material for his writing and demand for his work was high. Archibald's investment in Lawson's western adventure resulted in characters that would firmly establish Lawson as the authentic voice of ordinary Australians, and *The Bulletin* editor continued to mentor the writing of his wayward protege. Lawson called Archibald 'the king of sub-editors' and claimed that 'Archie' didn't touch a line of prose without improving it, though he rarely changed verse because it wasn't his forte.[2]

'You couldn't quarrel with Archibald,' Lawson wrote years later. 'In the old days a writer would go up the *Bulletin* stairs furious and boiling over about broken promises with regard to publishing copy within a reasonable time, or rates of pay; and come down a few minutes later soothed, and even remorseful ... But with a more deeply rooted sense of injury against the Management, which, it would now appear (though Archie never actually hinted it) was all to blame, as usual.'[3]

As well as *The Bulletin* and other publications, Lawson agreed to supply the Sydney version of *The Worker* with regular articles for 12 shillings and sixpence each,[4] and he supplied thirteen of them in 1893, including 'An Old Mate of Your Father's' in which he wrote of the old diggers 'getting few and far between' who sometimes came to see Niels. Lawson wrote that he had a yarn with one, and afterwards got to thinking 'whether those ancient friends' were 'better and kinder to their mates than we of the rising generation are to our fathers'.[5]

Lawson had also become a regular at a bookshop that socialist William McNamara[6] and his diminutive but forceful new wife Bertha Bredt[7] had opened at 238 Castlereagh Street.

The daughter of a struggling Prussian civil servant, Mrs McNamara had been driven from her home in what is now Poland by poverty as a small fifteen year old with sparkling blue eyes. She arrived in Melbourne in 1869, staying with an uncle before moving to Bairnsdale to work as a governess for a wealthy aunt. It was there, at the age of eighteen, that she married Peter Hermann Bredt, a Prussian-born accountant almost twice her age. Peter Bredt became Bairnsdale's shire secretary and he and Bertha had nine children.

When Peter died in 1888, Bertha tried to keep her family together in Bairnsdale but was forced to move back to Melbourne as a penniless single parent. She worked as a travelling saleswoman, selling jewellery and sewing machines to support her six surviving children, three sons and three daughters. She joined the fight for a fairer deal for the working classes. Although her English was far from perfect, she published the pamphlet *Home Talk on Socialism* in 1891.

The next year she married 35-year-old McNamara at Melbourne's Collingwood Registry Office. Before long she was known as 'The Mother of the Labor Movement'.[8]

The McNamaras' bookshop became a meeting place for all those with a passion for the labour movement and it was at a dosshouse next door that Lawson met the ruggedly masculine political anarchist Arthur Desmond in June 1893.

Lawson was captivated by this charismatic speaker who was spouting the gospel of Friedrich Nietzsche, that the strong must rule the weak.

Desmond was a Social Darwinist who wrote under the pen-name 'Ragnar Redbeard'. He had stood unsuccessfully for parliament in New Zealand in 1884, telling the electors of Hawke's Bay that they were serfs who must rise up and overthrow the tyrants. He came last of the three candidates with just 190 votes, but somehow believing he was a reincarnation of the Norse god Wodin, he powered on, preaching revolution and racial superiority. Soon he would publish the tome 'Might Is Right'[9] in which 'Jews, Christians, [Freemasons] and politicians of every race, creed, and color [took] a hard drubbing under phrases that removed the hide without anaesthetic'.[10]

Desmond had arrived in Sydney in 1893 to shake up the political landscape. With trouble again flaring on the sheep stations of Queensland, his Active Service Brigade – a collection of political terrorists – distributed a leaflet telling shearers: 'The squatter kings, callous and brutal, intend to try and reduce your wages from the beginning of 1894. ... Remember that it is better to belt one squatter than half-a-dozen scabs. Go to the fountain head – the head of the police, the head of the military, the head of the specials, the leading men of the employers' union, the head of the Government. Strike to the earth all who illegally use their authority, position, or wealth to enslave you.'[11]

In the front room of a cottage in Rose Street in Sydney's Darlington, Desmond and a big teenage Labor idealist named Jack Lang,[12] a future New South Wales premier, printed the journal *Hard Cash*, 'a militant journal that attacked the banks, and exposed the doings of the wealthy corporations and companies'.[13] Lang was a product of the inner-city slums, and though he had sold newspapers as a child to help his family, they were still so poor that in the mid-1880s, he was sent to live with his mother's sister on a farm near Bairnsdale. He returned to Sydney aged fourteen, working on a poultry farm at Smithfield, and then driving a horse-drawn bus through Merrylands and Guildford. Lang became interested in politics during the banking crisis, frequenting radical bookshops such as McNamaras' and helping with newspapers and publications of the infant Labor Party. Australia's future Labor prime minister Billy Hughes,[14] a former umbrella repairman and ship's cook, helped Desmond produce the Labor journal *New Order*, which Hughes said was designed to 'overthrow the hordes of Capitalism, spread enlightenment throughout the Universe [and] awaken the slumbering masses'. Hughes called Desmond 'our regular poet' and described as 'appalling' his command of 'scarifying language'.[15]

Lawson was spurred into action to respond to Desmond's writings, turning his back on his long-held promotion of 'Brotherhood and Love And Honour' from his poem 'The Ghost'. *The Worker* ran Lawson's 'A Leader of the Future' in which he predicted that while Jesus had preached 'peace and goodwill and brotherhood' the sword spoke louder, and that the great world leader of the future would most likely 'rise on the top of a barricade' and 'come with a blood-stained bandage round his forehead. … His uniform will be the uniform of the unemployed.'[16] On the same page *The Worker* ran Lawson's 'The Waving of the Red',[17] the blue banner of Eureka's revolution having changed hue.

Lawson was in a more convivial mood for *Truth* though, which was now under the stewardship of William Henry Traill,[18] a member of the Legislative Assembly representing South Sydney and Archibald's former business partner at *The Bulletin*. Lawson supplied Traill with 'The English Ne'er-do-well',[19] about the loafers and cads turned into bush heroes by some of Lawson's poetic rivals, and he gave Traill 'The Other Gum' in reply to a reader who in rhyming couplets accused Lawson of throwing bricks at the humble bush workers.[20]

MCNAMARAS' BOOKSHOP WAS next door to the Labour Bureau of Larry Petrie,[21] a one-armed Scot, who was helping unemployed men find work when apparently not looking for explosives to blow up the capitalist system. Police activity around the Labour Bureau, and the anarchists it attracted, forced the McNamaras to move their Bookstore and Cosmopolitan Lending Library across the road to No. 221 Castlereagh Street, but in both locations, it was a hotbed of radical thought. Lawson spent much of his time drinking and thinking alongside activists such as Thomas Batho, Ted Brady's comrade from the Socialist League, who wrote for the *New Order* under the pen-name 'Vag', and Arthur Yewen, who attempted in vain to organise a successful workers' commune in Frenchs Forest. Lawson attended lectures at Leigh House, further along Castlereagh Street, listening to the militant views of the feminists Rose Summerfield and Rose Scott, the bombastic Petrie, and the tall and wiry William Arthur Holman,[22] another future premier of New South Wales.

Holman was the *New Order*'s reserve poet behind Arthur Desmond, and Billy Hughes wrote that to watch him hammering away 'on a hired typewriter (that might at any moment be seized by the myrmidons of Capital) was a sight for the gods!'[23]

While these men and women were attempting to change the social and economic structures in Australia from within, Billy Lane was putting together the final touches for his workers' utopia – 'a place where strikes shall not exist and capitalists will be unknown'.[24] With the economic situation in Australia dire, Lane had finally secured 187,000 hectares of unsettled land free of charge in Paraguay, a troubled country keen to attract white farmers after much of its European population had been wiped out by warfare. Lane's New Australia Co-operative Settlement Association then paid £1350 for a 598-ton barque, the *Royal Tar*.[25]

Billy Lane, together with his wife and children, was about to lead more than 200 settlers sailing out of Sydney Harbour on 16 July 1893 bound for Cape Horn and then Montevideo and Asuncion. They were £1000 short of cash to fund the new settlement but Rose Scott mortgaged her house for £300 and there was a sudden surge of donations from Queensland.[26]

Lawson had looked on with disappointment as Mary Cameron began a relationship with one of the men heading to Paraguay, the ruggedly handsome 31-year-old bushman David Russell Stevenson, who claimed to be a second cousin of the writer Robert Louis Stevenson. Physically, Stevenson was everything Lawson was not. Billy Lane's younger brother Ernie[27] called Stevenson 'a brainy, unscrupulous individual, with a couple of avowed adherents'.[28] He was a ladies' man with a roving eye who once tried it on with Jenny Lane, the wife of Billy Lane's brother John, so forcefully that she had to fight him off with a whip.[29] Mary fell for Stevenson, though. He was working in the office of the *New Australia* editor Walter Head in 1893 when she first met him. 'The attraction was mutual,' she recalled. Sometimes rather than catch the ferry from the city to his lodgings in Balmain, Stevenson would strip naked, tie his clothes in a bundle on his head and swim across Darling Harbour.

When he asked Mary to marry him, she said yes, but even though she was now almost twenty-eight, she claimed that her mother insisted before they wed that Stevenson would have to go to Paraguay first to make sure everything was above board before Mary joined him. He agreed.

The 'Paraguayan Paradise' was to be called 'New Australia' and was to be established 176 kilometres south-east of Asuncion, where John Lane, a schoolmaster from Queensland's Darling Downs, said the soil was rich and the weather mild all year.[30] The settlers were to be bound by strict rules around temperance and racial exclusivity. *The Bulletin* declared the plan 'madness', and called the voyage 'one of the most feather-headed expeditions ever conceived'.[31]

While Lawson suspected that the South American experiment was doomed, Mary was among Lane's greatest supporters. Lawson spent a great deal of time with Mary late in 1893 and his 'ferocious poetry' was likely the model for Lane's radical writer Arty in his book *The Workingman's Paradise*:

Whenever you get into your blue fits you always pour out blood and thunder verses. The bluer you are the more volcanic you get. When you have it really bad you simply breathe dynamite, barricades, brimstone, everything that is emphatic.[32]

Mary had started writing on the South American utopia for the journal of the New Australia Association and for *The Hummer*, the journal of the Australian Shearers Union. Arthur Rae,[33] who represented Murrumbidgee in the New South Wales Legislative Assembly, was one of *The Hummer*'s editors. *New Australia* had reprinted Lawson's 'Otherside'[34] from *The Bulletin* on the front page of its first edition on 19 November 1892, in which he wrote of a utopia where there was 'more Humanity than Pride'.

Five months after the *Royal Tar* left Sydney, Mary wrote of Billy Lane, her Messiah: 'The heaven is already working, for the spirit of the man whose teaching has made us what we are, is a living force.'[35] Lawson knew he couldn't compete with Lane, or big Dave Stevenson, for Mary's heart and mind. If he still had any thoughts of marrying Mary, he knew they had sailed to South America. On 21 October, *The Bulletin* ran his poem 'The Rejection'.[36]

Lawson and Mary remained close though, and on 26 August 1893, their prose pieces appeared side by side in *The Worker* – Lawson's 'Australian Rivers: On The Darling No. 1' and Mary's 'In The Night'.

LARRY PETRIE SOON PROVIDED Mary with an even more stirring piece. Ernie Lane, who did not have the money to sail on the first voyage to Paraguay, said Petrie was in the 'super-class' of rebels, raising his only arm to sing 'The Marseillaise' in a strong, baritone voice to gather a good crowd around him in the Domain or on street corners, 'calling on the workers of Sydney to take up arms and man the barricades'.[37] Just after the *Royal Tar* departed for South America, there was a strike on the coastal steamers. Ship owners manned some of the vessels with non-union labour.

'Larry considered that scabs were the lowest things in the world,' Ernie Lane recalled, 'and vowed he would travel on one of the scab boats and blow it and the scabs up.' Deaf to all reasoning, Larry duly boarded the *Aramac*, bound for Brisbane, and, sure enough, when the ship was off Cape Moreton, an explosion did considerable damage.[38] The bomb went off at midnight on 27 July, when the 2114-ton vessel, carrying 144 passengers and crew, was about seven kilometres off Point Lookout.

No one was killed but that was put down to sheer luck. Two men suffered cuts, and the damage to the ship was extensive. Portions of half-burnt mattresses and boards were strewn about in all directions.[39]

Mary feared that Petrie would hang for the crime. A year or so earlier, he had told Mary he had 'planted a bomb in the outfall vent on the right hand side of Circular Quay to blow up the shipping and that part of the Quay'.[40] She and some friends, including Arthur Rae and the future Labor prime minister Chris Watson, decided to remove it at their peril.

'When it came to dark,' Mary wrote, 'the men met at the sewer, and Arthur being the small one at just five feet tall [150 centimetres], had to crawl in and get the bomb.' When Rae came out with the bomb and stood up, white-faced and shaking, he said, 'I never knew before why God made me so small but I know now.'[41]

While Petrie was holed up in Boggo Road jail after the *Aramac* bombing, Mary remembered a tale he had told her of when he was lost in the bush and dying of thirst, and how a boundary rider looking at circling crows above wondered if the body in the distance was a sheep or a man. She wrote '"I Have to Thank the Crows for the Saving of My Life" – L De Petrie'[42] and *The Worker* ran it alongside Lawson's third instalment of his Darling River series.

Next day Lawson came flying out to the boarding house where Mary now lived near Sydney University.

'You have beaten me,' he told her, 'and you have beaten me on my own ground.' Lawson went over her poem line by line, and according to Mary, who was prone to exaggeration at times, he then became downcast, saying there was no longer room for the two of them in such a small market as Sydney. To appease her friend, Mary said she would stop writing poems about the bush, which for a long time she did.[43]

Petrie was released three months after the *Aramac* bombing due to a lack of evidence but Mary claimed that he had confessed to her.[44]

DESPITE ALL THE SOCIALIST AGIATION, Sydney's economic climate worsened. Many of Lawson's mates from the building trade – the Mountain Push men – and long Bob Brothers, the Bourke 'Giraffe', were leaving New South Wales, hoping to make a go of it in Western Australia or New Zealand, where there was work on new railway lines and other infrastructure projects.

Lawson wrote that 'there were ten of us there on the wharf when our first mate left for Maoriland, he having been forced to leave Sydney because he could not get anything like regular work, nor anything like wages for the work he could get. He was a carpenter and joiner, a good tradesman and a rough diamond. He left his wife with her people and four pounds ten, until such time as he could send for her.'[45]

Lawson's role at *The Worker* was souring, despite him writing some outstanding prose about Bourke and the Darling as well as 'Macquarie's Mate'[46] and 'The Mystery of Dave Regan'.[47] He sent 'The Man Who Forgot'[48] to the *Truth*. Lawson had hoped his work might see him appointed *The Worker*'s permanent editor but perhaps his drinking or his mercurial nature raised concerns and 'that mysterious inner circle, the trustees and their friends' thought otherwise.[49]

Lawson was losing his battles with the booze and in his poem 'Sweeney'[50] he wrote how he was haunted by the memory of a dishevelled, battered drunk he had encountered in Bourke:

... perhaps, his face forewarned me of a face that I might see
From a bitter cup reflected in the wretched days to be.[51]

On 11 November 1893, acting editor Arthur Rae published a paragraph in *The Worker* to say that J Medway Day[52] of the weekly Adelaide *Voice* would be taking the paper's reins. Disgruntled, Lawson left town a week later for New Zealand after deciding to pull himself together and 'battle round' to raise the price of a steerage ticket, and maybe a pound or two over. 'There may not be anybody to see me off,' he wrote, 'but some of the boys are sure to be on the wharf or platform "over there," when I arrive.'[53]

His *Bulletin* connections convinced the Union Steamship Company to offer Lawson a first-class ticket on the 2003-ton *Waihora*, which sailed on 18 November 1893, but he declined the luxury to travel among the battlers in steerage where there was better 'copy' for a writer. There were about fifty male passengers, including half a dozen New Zealand shearers, two of whom came on board drunk. The others were chiefly tradesmen, labourers and clerks, driven out of Australia by hard times.[54] There were five 'grass widows' on board, too, and every one of them had a baby. They were heading to join their husbands who'd gone ahead of them to 'Maoriland' looking for work.[55] There were hundreds of cases of oranges roped together on deck and the captain said he'd 'give any man three months that he caught at those oranges', but a steward was sweeping orange peel out of the steerage for the next three days.

Late every night, a steward turned off the electricity, but there were two lanterns dimly burning in Lawson's part of the steerage, where the passengers were 'stowed away like sheep'.[56]

Lawson penned 'Coming Across: A Study in the Steerage'[57] for which the *New Zealand Mail* paid him 5 shillings. He later wrote that 'towards the end of '93 I landed in Wellington with a pound in my pocket'[58] but he actually arrived in Auckland on 23 November and went to see Maori carvings in the local museum. He looked for newspaper work, but told Aunt Emma he couldn't 'get a show', so he spent his last pound on a ticket to Wellington, where he had friends. He arrived there on 27 November, the day before 90,000 New Zealand women went to the polls, making that country the first in which women had the right to vote in parliamentary elections.

Lawson acknowledged the milestone in his poem 'For'ard'.

> But the curse of class distinctions from our shoulders shall be
> hurled,
> An' the influence of woman revolutionize the world.[59]

He eventually sold the poem to *The Worker* but recalled how he also received a guinea for it from the *New Zealand Mail*, 'including five shillings from the editor's pocket'.[60]

He also sent a report about this victory for women's rights to Louisa for *The Dawn*, telling readers that the wild fears of the anti-suffragists had proved to be unfounded. There was 'no drunkenness or disorder of any kind'.

'The thing has quite immortalized New Zealand ... Men and women worked together like brothers and sisters. ... The people here seem far more intelligent and liberal than in N.S.W.'[61]

For a short time, Lawson was flat broke and could find none of his old pals. He wired Archibald for help, but in the meantime he was forced to sleep rough in the Wellington harbour reclamation known as 'The Rec', making his bed in one of the huge water pipes that were being stored there for the construction of the city's reticulation system. All he had with him were some shabby clothes, a couple of blankets, some exercise books, pen and ink, and a shilling Routledge dictionary. Lawson had gone some days without a proper meal when his plight was observed by Herbert Talbot, one of the compositors on the *New Zealand Times* newspaper, who reported it to staff writer Tom Mills,[62] an avowed admirer of Lawson's writing. Mills, who was also a contributor to *The Bulletin*, was aghast. He regularly lectured on Lawson's work at the literary and debating societies of Wellington.[63]

Mills asked Talbot to find Lawson straight away and bring him to the *Times* newsroom, and that night Mills met one of his heroes, a man he called 'a rather taciturn and gawky Australian genius' who was 'very shy of the limelight'.[64]

Mills immediately asked Lawson why one of the finest writers in Australia was sleeping in a New Zealand water pipe.

Lawson told him he'd met plenty of fellows who wanted to drink with him, but he was only ever offered beer, never bread or a bed. Mills's family was away, so he invited his literary hero to stay in his tiny cottage for two weeks. He found Lawson to be an ideal house guest – always having a hot and tasty meal ready for his host no matter what hour of the early morning Mills arrived home from work.

Lawson was always reciting the verses of Paterson, Kipling, Boake or Kendall, and with The Bulletin Debate still not fully settled, would become prickly over 'The Banjo's' work, saying his well-heeled rival was not a true bush poet but only a city man who visited the bush. When Mills suggested that critics were favourably comparing Lawson's work to Rudyard Kipling's, Lawson bristled more, declaring that he had been writing verses 'like Kipling' long before Kipling had.[65]

Mills noted that Lawson's hearing was poor indoors. 'Strange to say, his hearing was good – even sharp and sensitive – in the open and on the crowded thoroughfare.' Often Lawson pulled Mills up sharply as they walked down Cuba Street into town telling him firmly: 'You needn't shout, Tom – I'm not deaf, you know!'[66]

Mills also was astonished by the amount of work Lawson put into his writing. Sometimes Lawson sat at Mills's dining table for eight hours to compose a few verses or a few paragraphs of prose. He told Mills that he was his own worst critic, 'next to my mother', and Mills would sometimes watch him work all night on a piece and, despite needing the money from a sale, toss it into the fire the next morning as 'not good enough'. Mills called Lawson 'The People's Poet' and Lawson liked the sound of that.[67]

He convinced some of Wellington's more prominent citizens to give Lawson a hand, and some who contributed included Lawson's old boss Gresley Lukin, who was about to start a twenty-year stint as editor of Wellington's *Evening Post*. Charles Wilson, editor of the *Times*, also threw in some money as did the brothers Herbert and John Baillie, who ran a bookshop together in Cuba Street. John Baillie, a renowned artist, took a striking photograph of Lawson in the back room of their shop one afternoon as Lawson sat uncomfortably in the clothes in which he had slept for days.

Lawson wrote to Aunt Emma asking for a more flattering photograph, which appeared in Wellington's *Fair Play* magazine on 16 December, two weeks after the journal had described him as 'slight, with a light brown moustache, a quiet manner and deaf'. He wrote 'That There Dog o' Mine' for the *New Zealand Mail* and sent Archibald 'In the Days When the World was Wide',[68] in which he announced an end to idealistic reminiscence and an acceptance of the world as it was. But whatever money Lawson was earning from New Zealand publications he was drinking in Wellington bars. His frustration at not finding full-time work and his desire to go home were reflected in 'I've Drawn New Zealand Blank' under the byline 'The Exile'[69] and 'A Respectable Young Man with a Portmanteau'[70] about a stranded Australian journalist.

Then Edward Tregear, the first Secretary of New Zealand's Labour Department, found work for Lawson as a painter, and Lawson urged Mills to come and watch him applying his brush to a small door at the Government House grounds on Molesworth Street.

It was the only painting work Lawson obtained, though, and he was destitute again before long. He left Wellington with a mate at the end of January 1894 to work at a sawmill in the Hutt Valley, for a boss who had contracted to supply the mill with logs.

We two bullocked in a rough, wet gully for a fortnight – felling trees, making a track for the bullocks, and "jacking" logs to it over stumps and boulders. But we were soft and inexperienced, and at the end of the fortnight the boss said we weren't bushmen – which, strange to say, hurt me more than any adverse criticism on my literary work could have done at the time.[71]

Lawson's mate became the basis for his 'Steelman' sketches, though Steelman's character could change from a devoted family man to a cynic, spieler,[72] and sometimes conman, who knew every lurk, once coaching Lawson how to fake consumption and Scottish ancestry when they were to put the bite on a family of Scottish settlers.[73]

Not far from Palmerston North, Lawson found work at the *Pahiatua Herald*, in the middle of a prosperous farming district of 8500 people. Another reporter there, Anthony Cashion, wrote that the locals welcomed the famous Australian writer to their dinner tables and Lawson visited many of the nearby areas including the Makuri Gorge, the Manawatu Gorge, Woodville and Kaitawa. In his short story 'Stiffner and Jim',[74] Lawson wrote of going down to Canterbury in the direction of Christchurch looking for work on the new railway line, and the area also seems to be the setting for another Steelman adventure in 'The Geological Spieler'.[75]

Lawson had more of a talent for verse than hard news, though, according to Cashion. He said that when Lawson was sent to cover the opening of the Mangatainoka Brewery, Lawson's report was a model of brevity and wit: 'The Mangatainoka Brewery was opened one day this year. It was a gigantic success and ended in oblivion.'[76] It was an amusing tale but the brewery had actually opened in 1889, five years before Lawson arrived.[77]

Lawson did stay in Pahiatua, though, for six weeks and contributed four pieces for the paper, starting with 'First Impressions of Pahiatua'.[78]

His farewell piece for the *Herald* was his humorous poem 'The Home of the Gods',[79] a tribute to some of the people he had met in that rural heartland, including a bookseller named George Moore. One of Moore's daughters, Gertie, was besotted by Lawson and his writing, and a walk she took with him on Easter Monday 1894 inspired her own poem 'Waiting: A Bush Idyll', for the *New Zealand Mail* three years later.[80] Lawson called Gertie the 'brown-eyed girl that loved him in the latter end of spring'.[81] He told her in verse a few months later, though, that it was all over:

'Oh! my heart! for my heart lies dead in desolate Maoriland.'[82] However, long after Gertie married and moved to Australia, she was still writing to Lawson as late as 1920.

On 6 April 1894, the *Pahiatua Herald* informed readers that 'Mr Henry Lawson, the Australian poet ... left this morning for Wellington'. Lawson had written to a new friend there, Jack Louisson, who worked as a telegraph lineman and whose brother Bill was a telegraph line foreman in the Marlborough district in the South Island. Repairs were needed on a section of the line from Picton to Kekerengu and Lawson was hired. He called Bill 'a good-hearted old lunatic' and he became the model for 'Mitchell' in some of Lawson's more memorable short stories such as 'Our Pipes' and 'Shooting the Moon'.

Lawson left a £3 debt and some manuscripts as security at his accommodation, Lyme House in Molesworth Street, and wrote of paying a pound to cross Cook Strait to the South Island 'in one of those rusty little iron tanks' and going up Queen Charlotte Sound, 'a long crooked arm of the sea between big, rugged, black-looking hills'. There was a sort of lighthouse down near the entrance, and Lawson was told that an old Maori woman kept it.

After a four-hour run, the boat reached Picton, 'a small collection of twinkling lights in a dark pocket', and Lawson asked a policeman where he could find the telegraph office. He sent off a message to a friend in the North Island: 'Wire quid; stumped.'[83]

For the next three months, Lawson was engaged in hard physical work as a linesman and thoroughly enjoyed the adventure,[84] saying they were some of the most pleasant days of his life.[85] It was 'hard graft' at first, through rough country, in the depth of winter, and camping out all the time – humping poles sometimes where the horses couldn't go. The boss was a hard master but Lawson told himself it was better working in the great outdoors than to be 'brain-sweated in the city'.[86]

When he heard that New Zealand's leading poet Thomas Bracken was in a dire financial condition, he wrote to Tom Mills from beyond Blenheim about the ingratitude of New Zealanders generally, and editors particularly, in not supporting local poets.

He asked Mills to sell some of his works, including 'To Tom Bracken', to help pay the Wellington accommodation bill.

Lawson was happy and productive in New Zealand but on 30 June 1894 the trustees of *The Worker* announced plans to transform their newspaper from a weekly to a daily 'for the uplifting of humanity'. Their plan was to help the Labor candidates in the upcoming New South Wales election. Lawson received the news in the chilly coastal wilds of Kekerengu and was told that there was an important job for him on the expanded staff.

'Get behind me, Literature!' he said, 'but she didn't; so I threw up my billet and caught a steamer that touched the coast to deliver poles.'[87]

Lawson travelled steerage from Wellington to Sydney on the 2252-ton steamship *Tasmania*, via Napier and Auckland, with more than 200 other passengers including a circus troupe, and many fellow Australians whose work opportunities had not materialised.

He arrived home full of optimism and excitement about this bold new opportunity on 29 July 1894, or in his words, 'three days after *The Daily Worker* went bung'.[88]

Chapter 12

*Henry Lawson has a real streak of genius perhaps, as poet and
story teller united, a more luminous streak than any
other man in Australasia.*

THE BULLETIN'S LITERATURE CRITIC ALFRED STEPHENS[1]

AFTER A WEEK AT SEA Lawson arrived back in Sydney
to find that his full-time writing work had sunk to the
bottom of the harbour. The experiment of a *Daily Worker*
newspaper throughout July 1894 had imploded with losses of
£2000, and the newspaper was back as a weekly from 4 August,
when new editor J. Medway Day announced: 'Henry Lawson's
ghost was blown across from N.Z. to Sydney. Regarding the
rumor that he has been married to a Maori girl, H. L. gives it a
most emphatic denial.'[2]

Lawson was in no mood for banter, though.

The Australian Workers Union (AWU), which was bankrolling
the newspaper, was in financial distress. Wool prices had tanked
again and shearers, already demoralised by the arrest of their
union leaders, had been forced to accept even less pay and poorer
conditions. Not only did the union have to subsidise the heavy
losses of the *Daily Worker* but it had to find thousands of pounds
in strike relief to help its floundering members across Queensland
and New South Wales.

Lawson told Medway Day that he'd given up a job in New
Zealand on the promise of a position at his paper and recalled that

'after a deal of shuffling humbug, I was put on the weekly *Worker* as "provincial editor".[3]

Lawson became a sub-editor, working on news reports from other union branches throughout the colonies, while at the same time submitting his own poetry and prose almost every week. The paper ran a notice declaring: 'Henry Lawson has been engaged to write exclusively for the *Worker*. For the next few weeks the stories by this popular writer will have thousands of readers in the sheds and camps, and in every place where the *Worker* circulates.'[4]

That same day, *The Worker* ran 'Drifted Back', Lawson's short story about a swagman's return to a bush town, and the following week placed Lawson's political poem from Bourke, 'Martin Farrell', as well as the short story 'The Flour of Wheat: A Hard Case From The West Coast, N.Z', and the poem 'Rewi To Grey: The Old Maori Chief's Last Message'.

The following week, on 25 August, 'Remailed' showed Lawson's genius as a short story writer as he focused on bushmen recirculating newspapers among family and friends with marked paragraphs that touched the heart. In that same issue Lawson's poem 'Beautiful Maoriland; Or, Love And The Union' appealed to New Zealand shearers not to work in Australian sheds, telling the story of one, about to sign a non-union contract, who hears the voice of his dying sweetheart to be true to his mates, and then suddenly drops the pen as though it were a snake.[5]

The verses appeared as the situation in the Australian sheds grew worse.

The collapse of the Union Bank of Australia had forced the Reid family to sell their 400,000-hectare Tolarno Station on the Darling River at Menindee in western New South Wales. Union shearers greeted the new owner Benjamin Chaffey with blockades along the railway lines as part of their fight for better wages. Chaffey sent the £5000 paddle-steamer *Rodney*, one of the finest boats on the Darling, to collect fifty non-union shearers from Echuca, but just before 4 a.m. on 26 August 1894, armed men, their faces masked by smears of river mud, leapt onto the boat[6] while it was moored in the river at Moorara Station, forty-

five kilometres downstream from Tolarno. The invaders chased
the hired labourers into the water, looted the vessel, and then set
it alight.[7] The *Rodney* burnt for six hours and then sank as the
masked men hooted and gave three cheers.

The following night, police shot and wounded two union
shearers[8] as the men attacked imported labourers on Nettalie
Station near Wilcannia, east of Broken Hill.[9]

On 3 September, the AWU organised a meeting at the
Protestant Hall, opposite McNamaras' bookshop, and Medway
Day gravely told his audience that police in Queensland had been
given instructions 'to fire upon the leaders of riots or the assailants
of the police, and, if possible, *with effect'*.[10]

Reading from the police manual on dealing with protesters,
Day said: 'Firing over the heads of mobs or crowds engaged in
illegal pursuits is *not to be allowed*, as harmless firing, instead of
intimidating, would give confidence to the daring and guilty ...'

Day paused.

'For cold-blooded cruelty,' he asked, 'could anything be worse
than that?'[11]

There was sustained applause from the audience.

The public meeting in Castlereagh Street had taken place just
hours after a manhunt in central Queensland had ended with
the apparent suicide of unionist Samuel 'Frenchy' Hoffmeister.[12]
He had been accused of an arson attack that finished a gun
battle between union shearers and the law at Dagworth Station,
a property of more than 100,000 hectares on the Diamantina
River, 130 kilometres north-west of Winton. The property was
under the management of the four Macpherson brothers,[13] family
friends of Banjo Paterson's fiancée Sarah Riley.

At a magisterial inquiry, Hoffmeister's comrades said he always
carried firearms and always advocated violence in dealing with
'scabs'.[14] It was surmised that he had shot himself because he feared
imminent arrest, but his death was cloaked in mystery – a mystery
that Paterson would find intriguing when he visited Dagworth a
few months later.

FIVE DAYS AFTER that shootout, Lawson's paper announced that 'Henry Lawson intends to revise a selection of his poems for re-publication in the *Worker*. Friends outside the unions will greatly oblige by subscribing to this paper right off and at once.'[15]

Lawson provided his recycled 'radical songs' 'Spread the Truth' and 'Freedom on the Wallaby', the short story 'Meeting Old Mates' and a letter replying to the claims in the book *John Bull and Co.*[16] by the French visitor Paul Blouet, who was on a speaking tour. Blouet had referred to the workingman as a 'sham democrat who goes to Hyde Park to listen to the inanities of ragged wind-bags'. Lawson said the Frenchman's barbs were 'just near enough to the truth to be nasty – that's where the boot hurts'. Too many Australians, Lawson said, still toadied to the scrub aristocracy.[17]

Lawson spent only a month on the staff of *The Worker* before he received his notice 'alleged to come from the trustees, to the effect that, on account of the financial position of the Workers' Union, they were regretfully obliged to dispense with my services "for the present, at least"'.[18] Bitterly, he said no one took responsibility for the broken promises to him, nor for what he called the 'gross mismanagement' at the publication and the 'exorbitant' salaries paid to some of the staff.

Lawson agonised over what to do next. 'House-painting was dead,' he complained, 'clerical work was always out of the question – I couldn't add a column of figures without hanging on like grim death till I got to the top, and two trips with poor results utterly demoralised me. Deafness stood in the way of a possible Government billet.'[19]

Instead, Lawson brokered a deal with *The Worker* to provide prose at 12 shillings and sixpence a column and poems at a penny a line. On 15 September, the same day as *The Worker* ran Lawson's 'The Dying Anarchist', Medway Day repeated his notice from the previous month that Lawson was writing exclusively for the union publication.

'Board And Residence' drew on his experiences in shared accommodation and 'Thin Lips and False Teeth' later in the year invoked memories of lost love. Then, on 6 October, sick of what he saw as violent behaviour that was unworthy of the unions, he railed against 'The Cant and Dirt of Labor Literature', declaring 'it is a great pity that the word "scab" ever dirtied the pages of a workman's newspaper. It is a filthy term in its present meaning … a low, filthy, evil-working, ignorant, cowardly, and brutal term, and belongs to the slang of the brainless, apish larrikins and the drunken prostitutes of the city slums.'[20]

His article drew angry letters to the editor during a time when the newspaper needed every friend it could, and his sympathetic sketch of the squatter Baldy Thompson won him no friends among the working class either. Lawson tried to make amends with 'The City and the Bush'.[21] He was not 'ink-slinging' against bushmen, he argued, but fighting against bush-unionism and clannishness in the interests of a 'wider and truer Democracy'.[22]

AT THE SAME TIME, Paradise was being lost in Paraguay. After the arrival of the *Royal Tar*, 'Colonia Nueva Australia' had been officially founded on 28 September 1893 with 238 people. By the following June, though, the *Sydney Morning Herald* was reporting that some of the emigrants were calling it 'a hell upon earth'.[23]

The commune was lashed by torrential rain and then swarms of mosquitoes and ants. Drovers and shearers proved to be poor farmers. There was an oversupply of men in relation to the number of single women, and Lane's ban on alcohol sparked rebellion. Lane was furious that some of his followers had formed relationships with the local indigenous women, against his express orders about racial exclusivity. By the end of 1894 there were reports that seventy families were destitute and fleeing New Australia for the old Australia.[24] Lane and fifty-eight others then left the settlement to form Cosme, a new colony seventy-two kilometres further south.

Despite the reports, Mary Cameron, still teaching at Stanmore while writing her socialist essays, was saving all the money she could to join the pilgrims.

She was living at 46 Newtown Road, Darlington, in a terrace boarding house established in September 1894 by Billy Lane's wife Anne, who had returned to Sydney on the *Royal Tar* with two of their sons. Mary invited Lawson to tea with Mrs Lane and another of her friends, Jack Brereton,[25] the twenty-two-year-old-year-old editor of the Sydney University undergraduate magazine *Hermes*, and a young man who would eventually become the university's Professor of English. Mrs Lane thought Lawson was a waste of space and wondered why Mary even bothered with him. But Brereton was an unabashed fan of the young poet. As a child, Brereton had met Henry Kendall, and he was a disciple of Mungo MacCallum, who would become the university's chancellor. Brereton had been seduced by Lawson's work since clipping 'The Wreck of the "Derry Castle"' from *The Bulletin* seven years before.

The meal had started before Brereton arrived, as he had some difficulty in finding the house. But as he stepped into the dining room, Brereton saw facing him 'with head bent forward and eyes dark and deep and eloquent' looking up at him, a lanky 'shy, bearded young man'.[26] Lawson rose rather awkwardly, mumbled a brief greeting and sat once more, watchful and silent. Then Lawson bumped his tea, and already embarrassed by his deafness 'was filled with mute confusion'. The talking was maintained chiefly by the two women and Lawson spoke only with what Brereton called 'his appealing eyes'.[27] But after tea, the two young men went off to the nearest bar and toasted each other's health. Lubrication loosened Lawson's tongue and they walked down to Circular Quay, happy in what was the start of a lifelong friendship.

As they drank the night away, Brereton found Lawson full of experiences from the bush 'where his deafness, sensitiveness, diffidence and a melancholy tendency to dwell upon the pains of life had exposed him to misunderstanding and misery'.[28] As they turned the corner of George Street, near the Quay, Brereton was talking to him about democracy and the brighter future that the workers were about to win when Lawson stopped and stared at Brereton 'with all the grey wisdom of youthful disillusion'.

'Now listen,' Lawson replied, 'I know what I'm talking about. I couldn't say it in public because my living depends partly on what I'm writing for the *Worker*; but you can take it from me, Jack, the Australian worker is a brute and nothing else.'

Such was the bitterness in Lawson's heart, Brereton recalled, 'after association with the careless, rough company of the shearing-sheds. It was a mood, but one that was characteristic of his shrinking self-consciousness. His condemnation was harsh and unjust, but it was honest and heartfelt. Read his sketch of "A Rough Shed",[29] which is true in every detail, but shows only one side of the truth – and you will understand. He was to make full amends in many a tale and poem commemorating the courage, generosity and self-sacrifice of the Australian worker.'[30]

Brereton and Lawson saw a lot of each other over the next few years, 'wandering together into strange nooks and corners, cheerfully and irresponsibly'. 'We shared a common purse,' Brereton wrote, 'I mean that, when we were together, the one who happened to have money spent it, and the other accepted the arrangement as a matter of course.'[31]

Alfred Stephens remembered that it was generally Brereton who funded their conviviality, 'not because "Harry" objected to paying for the beer, but because "Jack" had usually more money than "Harry"'.[32] Lawson had much the stronger character, Stephens recalled, 'and liked to be admired ... Brereton had the weaker character: he liked admiring.' [33]

Often they drank from foaming tankards of beer at sixpence each that were perched upon a marble table in a 'broad, cool, low-ceiled bar' that offered the best free lunch in Sydney. They tipped their waiter liberally when they could afford it and he brought them free meals of choice dainties, as much as they could eat. They would then loll indolently in the adjoining winter-garden, smoking sixpenny cigars, and then stumble into the street, penniless and content. But ordinarily, three-penny beer and scraps of bread with little squares of cheese sufficed. One night they sat on a kerb and happily shared a dry tea-cake – the largest meal fourpence could buy. They had tried to charm a pretty shopgirl into adding a small pat of butter, 'not for cash but for love', but the eye of the owner was on her, and she rejected their pleas with a reluctance that Brereton found 'almost tearful'.[34] Once when Lawson was still lodging with his 'extremely tolerant' Aunt Emma, now living in East Crescent Street, McMahons Point, overlooking Lavender Bay, he and Brereton broke into her house in the small hours, and scoffed down what was intended for her family's breakfast.

To make a few shillings, the pair tried to replicate Lawson's Bulletin Debate with Banjo Paterson and eventually engaged in a short poetical sparring match in the *Elector*, a journal run by Labor politician Frank Cotton. Lawson's contribution was 'To The Advanced Idealist'.[35]

Lawson was well versed in literature from his rudimentary schooling and he would point out to Brereton various localities in Sydney which he fancifully associated with the scenes described by Charles Dickens. Brereton never considered Lawson an avid reader though and could remember his borrowing only one book from him in all the years of their friendship – Rudyard Kipling's *Barrack Room Ballads*.[36]

AS CHRISTMAS 1894 APPROACHED, Louisa Lawson devised a plan which she hoped would allow her and her son to capitalise on his growing fame. Lawson's younger brother Peter, who had journeyed with him to Western Australia three years before, had come to notice as a musical composer, publishing 'The Rosalind Waltz' to great acclaim at just twenty-two. While Lawson was encouraging the outback shearers to rally round the flag of rebellion, Peter was encouraging the big end of town to glide around polished floors.

He dedicated his waltz to the English-born actress Hilda Spong,[37] who had just had her portrait painted in Melbourne by Tom Roberts, and who had been appearing on stage in Sydney with such local stars as Bland Holt.[38] The waltz had received 'well-merited applause' when played at a benefit concert for Hilda at Sydney's Criterion Theatre[39] on 14 August as she prepared to embark on a career in London.

Louisa had started selling the sheet music to the waltz at 2 shillings a copy from *The Dawn*'s office and now planned to do the same for a book featuring Lawson's *Short Stories in Prose and Verse*.[40] The book would include 'The Drover's Wife', 'The Bush Undertaker' and 'The Union Buries Its Dead' and a note from Lawson that it was 'an attempt to publish, in Australia, a collection of sketches and stories at a time when everything Australian, in the shape of a book, must bear the imprint of a London publishing firm before our critics will condescend to notice it'.[41]

A month before the book appeared, Brereton pumped it up in *Hermes*, saying that Lawson had 'an intense power of sympathy that forces him to realise the struggling efforts of human nature upwards'. Within Lawson, Brereton said, were 'the elements of greatness'.[42]

The book – Lawson later dismissed it as a crude 'pamphlet' – was, however, badly timed and overpriced with an unattractive sickly-green cover. Among its ninety-six small pages, there were also a number of shoddy-looking advertisements that Louisa included from *The Dawn*. On the way to the binders in York Street, some of the sheets were blown into the street and while Lawson tried to retrieve them, a council water cart sprayed some, ruining them. *Short Stories in Prose and Verse* appeared just three days before Christmas, missing most of the gift-buyers. Louisa printed just 1000 copies. She kept 500 to sell through *The Dawn* at a hefty price of 1 shilling and threepence a copy, and gave her son 500 to sell through *The Worker* at a penny less.

Brereton recalled meeting Lawson one day in George Street as his friend was heading to the Public Library with two copies of his book to lodge in accordance with the Copyright Act. Lawson told him that he really only needed to lodge one copy, and that Brereton could have the spare. Lawson told Brereton that Louisa 'was the hardest businessman I ever met'.[43] He later claimed his mother had broken her word by including advertisements in the book and that she had been careless with the printing. He said all he had made from the deal was £5.

Under the headline 'Henry Lawson: An Australian Poet', Alfred Stephens wrote in *The Bulletin* that the book was 'a poor little, badly-printed volume' but that 'every Australian should invest a shilling in a copy – firstly, because the book is well worth it; secondly, because it is a characteristically Australian book, one of the few really original attempts towards an Australian literature; and, thirdly, because the author will be thereby encouraged to produce a bigger volume in better form – a form more worthy of his genius'.[44]

In an accompanying biography of Lawson, Stephens described him as 'slight, but tall and muscular, with prominent features and large, eloquent brown eyes' and called him 'the voice of the bush'; even though Lawson would base much of his writing in urban settings.[45]

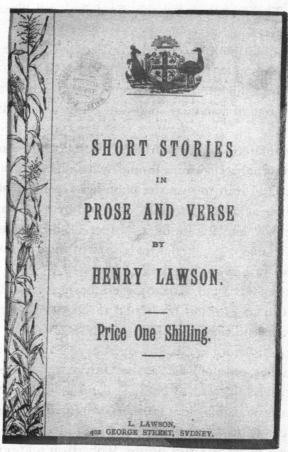

Lawson's first book was published by his mother.
University of Sydney, Lawson Collection

Lawson sold most of his books through *The Worker* which ran ads for it regularly, but Louisa struggled to make a penny through her campaign in *The Dawn*. Six years later she still had 200 unsold copies which she offered to Angus & Robertson for another £5.[46] In 1917 she admitted that the book was 'badly set and badly printed' but it did give her son 'a decided start'.[47]

LAWSON HAD HOPED TO SPEND Christmas back in Wellington, New Zealand, but a drinking spree left him broke. His exclusive deal with *The Worker* ended but he still wrote 'A Trick Of Memory – And Trick Of Mitchell's', and 'I'll Tell You What, You Wanderers' for the 5 January 1895 edition. *The Bulletin* published 'The Old Bark School: An Echo' and 'Steelman' that same month.

Lawson took time off to holiday in Bathurst and see old friends from his childhood. He was back in Sydney in April to farewell William Wood, his union mate from Bourke, who was ignoring the reports out of Paraguay and was going to join Billy Lane's experiment.

Lawson submitted 'Jones's Alley', a story of the slums, to *The Worker* and went back to Aunt Emma's where he found a letter from Brereton telling him to visit the publisher George Robertson[48] at his bookshop at 89 Castlereagh Street. Brereton assured Lawson that Robertson and his business partner David Angus[49] had just made 'The Banjo' a good offer for a book of verse and would likely do the same for Lawson if he pushed his case.

Robertson was a tall, dark-bearded, burly thirty-five year old. He was born in England but raised in Scotland after his father, a Unitarian minister, had died when Robertson was seven. Robertson left school in Glasgow aged twelve and was apprenticed to a bookseller and publisher at the University of Glasgow. Then at nineteen he migrated to New Zealand for three years of hard manual work with his older brothers, who had established a bush sawmill near Waimate, in the South Island.

Seeking a more lucrative future, Robertson sold potatoes from a barrow to earn his fare to Sydney and arrived in February 1882.

He worked in the George Street, Sydney branch of a Melbourne bookseller named George Robertson, who shared his name but was no relation. Another Scot, the red-bearded David Angus, was working there too, but he soon left to become his own boss. Robertson married and in January 1886 he paid £15 for a half-share in a bookselling business that Angus had started in Market Street. Angus's health was failing and he wanted a partner who was tireless.

In 1890, the company Angus & Robertson moved into much bigger premises in a former coach-building factory in Castlereagh Street down the road from William Kerridge's workshop where Lawson had toiled as a teenager.

While the bookselling business was going well, publishing in Sydney was still in its infancy with most of the stock coming from Melbourne or overseas. Angus & Robertson had published two books of verse[50] early in their partnership but Robertson knew his former boss had lost £100 trying to sell Henry Kendall's *Leaves from Australian Forests*.[51]

Still, compulsory Education Acts meant literacy rates in Australia had risen sharply by the mid-1890s and Robertson, now the driving force of the partnership, believed there was a pent-up demand for Australian stories about Australian people by Australian writers.

In April 1895 he invited Paterson to meet with him in Castlereagh Street and discuss publishing a volume of Banjo's work. Paterson immediately drew up his own contract. Angus & Robertson would pay all costs of printing and publishing and would split the profits with him. The book would be called *The Man from Snowy River and Other Verses*.

Lawson followed Brereton's advice and made haste to see Robertson as well. He even offered some suggestions for Paterson's work and Angus & Robertson wrote a memorandum to Banjo to say: 'Lawson suggests as "The Story of Conroy's Gap" is widely known as "Conroy's Gap", "The Story of" ought to be dropped. It would look better from a compositor's point of view I think too.' Banjo wrote across it: 'All right. This suits me. – A. B. Paterson.'[52]

On his next visit to Robertson, Lawson brought with him some of his poems, and the idea for two books was discussed — a book of verse and a book of short stories and sketches. But Robertson did not think Lawson's selection of poems was adequate and sent him on a hunt to supply only the very best that he had written. Lawson had not kept much of his own work, and so he searched through old newspapers and magazines and asked friends including Archibald and Brereton to help him dig up some of the gems that he had penned. Fortunately, Arthur Parker, Lawson's old mate from the Mountain Push, had kept a scrapbook with every bit of Lawson's work that he had read. Paterson then drafted a contract for Lawson to author two books, one of verse and one of prose, under the same terms Banjo had signed.

The book of verse was to be called *Faces In The Street and Other Poems*. Robertson approved Lawson an advance of £14. The book of short stories would be called *While the Billy Boils*. Lawson signed the deal on 26 July 1895 and *The Bulletin* announced it the following day.

With his future looking brighter, Lawson decided to upgrade his digs to a fine hotel. For a man besieged by the demons of drink, living in a hotel was not the best option, but Lawson felt on top of the world, and chose, as his new home, John McGrath's Edinburgh Castle Hotel on the corner of Pitt and Bathurst Streets. Brereton helped him move.

All Lawson's worldly goods were in a large sack, and Brereton was surprised at its weight. They took turns carrying the load on their backs. Everything in that bag, Brereton said, 'was in admired confusion — togs, scraps of copy, photographs, and a general miscellany'. Lawson promised to show Brereton a particular photograph, and dived into the sack. 'His head and shoulders were out of sight but the movements of the sack indicated that he was rummaging actively, and, somehow or other, he found at last what he was seeking as well as some manuscript which he had given up as irretrievably lost. He emerged, red, ruffled and triumphant.'[53]

Lawson tried to spend his £14 advance at the pub as quickly as possible with a variety of friends.

There was the lanky poet Rod Quinn,[54] an old actor Harry Teece and the teetotal whisky salesman Jack Moses,[55] who was a founding member of the Bondi Icebergs Club of year-round swimmers. Moses later adapted a teamsters song into the poem 'Nine Miles from Gundagai', about a dog on a tuckerbox, and he was a constant source of mirth as a practical joker, always telling Lawson he needed better hats and sometimes punching his fist through them to prove the point. Lawson recalled that once when his hat was just a little too good for such treatment, Jack made him swap it for the ragged headgear of a street beggar. Ten minutes later, Lawson remembered that he had hidden half-a-sovereign in the lining. But the beggar had vanished.[56]

Among other pranks, Moses was fond of taking Lawson's overcoat and pawning it.[57]

Lawson's £14 advance went so quickly that by October, as the book of verse was being prepared, he told Robertson that he wanted to sell the copyright. Lawson explained that since he wrote for *The Worker,* he feared anyone with money would shun his offering. Robertson tried to talk Lawson out of it, but in the end agreed to pay him another £40 in instalments whenever Lawson asked for it. The total payment amounted to almost a year's pay for a manual worker but Lawson had a lot of drinking buddies. Within two months of signing away the copyright, the additional £40 was gone too.

THE MAN FROM SNOWY RIVER AND OTHER VERSES was released to rave reviews on 19 October 1895 and galloped away from bookstores.

Robertson sent hundreds of review copies to newspapers throughout Australia and even to overseas literary figures such as Rudyard Kipling. The first edition sold out in the first week and within three months it had beaten the sales record for an Australian book of poetry with more than 4500 copies sold,[58] on its way to more than 100,000. Its cover price was 5 shillings, half a day's wages for most Australians, but Angus & Robertson had the presses working overtime to meet demand.

Lawson drafted a letter to friends in New Zealand urging them to buy his book when it appeared there, and took it for posting to Robertson's shy young secretary Rebecca Wiley, who was intimidated by his presence on their first meeting.

She remembered him as 'a very handsome young man … tall, dark, heavy prominent eyebrows and moustache, his eyes were not only beautiful brown ones [but] had a weird uncanny look in them as if you could read your innermost thoughts. Many people including George Robertson remarked on this. He would accost and address anyone; so when he came over and, as I thought then, glared at me, and spoke, I was scared.'[59]

The company secretary Hugh Maccallum came to the rescue and told her 'no use trying to answer him, he can only hear by shouting right in his ear, he is almost stone deaf. He is a young Australian poet for whom we are publishing a book, and promises to become famous … sometimes he's a little worse for drink: but he's always gentlemanly, and you needn't be afraid of him.'[60]

Publication was delayed by Lawson's drinking and his tardiness in supplying some final works. Robertson snapped up three new poems Lawson had written for *The Bulletin*: 'Peter Anderson and Co',[61] 'Since Then'[62] and 'The Vagabond',[63] which was one of Robertson's favourites. But Robertson was unhappy with the mishmash that was 'The Grand Mistake', which Lawson and Brereton had co-written while carousing at the Edinburgh Castle. Robertson let Lawson dry out in the back room of the Angus & Robertson headquarters, and get to work rewriting it. The poem became the militaristic 'The Star of Australasia'.[64] It was also in these new temporary digs that Lawson wrote the introductory poem 'To An Old Mate', dedicating the book to Jules Archibald.

The delays caused by Lawson's drinking stopped his book capturing the vital Christmas market which Paterson was dominating, but renamed as In *The Days When The World Was Wide*, Angus & Robertson saw it as part of a planned deluge of Australian literature, with following works to include a novel by

Lawson called *The Hero of Redclay*, a book of Banjo's short stories, and poetry books by Victor Daley and John Farrell.[65]

Lawson needed every penny he could scrounge. Seeing the enormous success of Paterson's book, Lawson began to rue the bad deal he had cut in selling his copyright, but Robertson was a benevolent man, who wanted to nurture Lawson's talent. He asked Paterson to draw up a new agreement in which Lawson was to have the same deal as 'The Banjo' with a half share of all profits.

It was something of a balm to the emotional wounds Lawson was feeling after Mary Cameron finally set sail for Cosme to meet up with her love Dave Stevenson. With the *Royal Tar* sold, she left Sydney on 15 November 1895 aboard the *Anglian* bound for New Zealand to meet the *Ruapehu* that would then carry her to South America. She recalled that Lawson and his mates Brereton and Jack Jones came to see her off and that 'Henry's sad face was the last face I saw, his voice the last I heard. He looked lost and hopeless.'[66]

But then Lawson found some wind in his own sails.

A 'very young and attractive woman' with a 'soft and rich voice' and eyes that were 'particularly fine'[67] fell in love with him.

It was the biggest mistake she ever made.

Chapter 13

I did not realise then the restlessness which always filled Harry's
heart and soul, a state which was entirely due to the blood
that ran in his veins – wanderer's blood.

BERTHA LAWSON ON MARRYING A FAMOUS BUT STRUGGLING WRITER[1]

AS HE WAITED ANXIOUSLY for the publication of *In The Days When The World Was Wide*, much of Lawson's life was centred around Sydney's Castlereagh Street, where, no longer able to afford lodgings at the Edinburgh Castle Hotel, he sometimes found a bed at Charlie Lofgren's Clyde Coffee Palace, or at the dosshouses near there. Angus & Robertson's headquarters were just along the road, and further down was McNamara's bookshop, where every radical thinker in Sydney congregated to talk about red flags and a white Australia.

One morning late in 1895, as Lawson rounded the corner of Bathurst Street into Castlereagh, he bumped into an old pal, Carl Lindquist,[2] who was also a friend of McNamara's wife, Bertha. Lindquist was walking with 'Mrs Mac's' daughter Bertha Bredt Jr,[3] and was keen for the 'People's Poet' to meet the pretty eighteen-year-old trainee nurse, who was on a holiday from Melbourne visiting her mother. Lawson introduced himself as 'Harry'.

The girl Lawson met that morning was 'a voluptuous little bundle',[4] short and dark, with big hazel eyes and a corseted, hour-glass figure that she maintained all her life.[5] Lawson was hooked and they immediately became, in Bertha's words, 'very great friends'. Lindquist had already shown her Lawson's first book of poetry published by Louisa, and they chatted about their mutual admiration for the stories of Mark Twain.[6] She recalled that the harshness of his early life 'doing a man's work with his father when he was only a boy' had taken its toll 'for he was frail and thin and very delicate looking – though full of eager enthusiasms'.[7]

Bertha had also known hard times. The death of her father, childhood poverty and her mother's remarriage and move to Sydney had rocked her equilibrium and she was not happy staying at McNamara's bookshop. The place smelled of beer and onions,[8] and the assortment of angry anarchists and subversive socialists was much rougher and more careless with their language than she was used to, especially as a self-styled young 'gentlewoman'.[9]

Lawson was substantially deaf but he pricked up his ears when Lindquist told him he was escorting Miss Bredt around the harbour city, showing her the most picturesque points. He readily joined them and together the three strolled through the Domain, savouring the warmth of the glorious parkland under a vivid blue sky, and they drank in the magnificent panorama at Mrs Macquarie's Chair. Lawson pointed out the beauties of Sydney Harbour, but he was more interested in the vision Bertha presented. Lawson would later explore his emotions aroused by that first meeting in a story about a young man, who for the first time 'got what you called properly gone on a girl'.

> … I think it was a case of love at first sight. They only knew each other for about six months, and were only 'courting' (as they called it then) for three or four months altogether, but she was that sort of girl that can love a man for six weeks and lose him forever, and yet go on loving him to the end of her life – and die with his name on her lips.[10]

Lawson asked if he could see Bertha again. She told him that she would be very busy all the next day, as she was going to see an old friend of the family. But Lawson arrived at eight o'clock the next morning, saying he had come to see Bertha's mother. Using this

Bertha Bredt Jr as a teenager in Melbourne at about the time she started training to be a nurse. State Library of NSW, FL3319414

pretext, he called every day for a week. Then Lawson arranged to take Bertha for a trip to the Hawkesbury River, accompanied by Aunt Emma as chaperone.

'My dear little mother did not approve of the match, nor did other members of my family,' Bertha wrote.[11] Mrs McNamara placed one obstacle after another to stop Bertha going with a man who had 'no worldly goods – nothing but his literary genius'.

'She thought Harry was seeing too much of me,' Bertha recalled. 'She could see he was fond of me and knew he had no prospects whatever. But I went. It was on this trip that he asked me to marry him.'[12]

Bertha refused the proposal. She told Lawson her mind was set on returning to work at the Melbourne Homeopathic Hospital.

MARY CAMERON knew rejection too. She had spent twenty-two days sailing from Wellington to Montevideo before the *Ruapehu* was battered by a severe storm off the coast of Argentina. Then there was the arduous 1600-kilometre voyage on the steamer *Olimpo* up the River Plate and into the Paraguay River, made even more gruelling by the extreme December humidity that left all the passengers lathered in greasy sweat. From Asuncion, Mary took an all-day train ride to the village of Sosa, where she expected to be wrapped in Dave Stevenson's muscular arms, but those arms were occupied elsewhere. Instead, there was only John Lane, mounted on a horse and with another for her to ride the twenty-five kilometres to Cosme. The date was 2 January 1896, and it was a deflating start to the new year and to Mary's new life on the other side of the world.[13] Stevenson had formed an attachment with a nurse named Clara Jones on the first voyage of the *Royal Tar*, and although Clara had married William Laurence in Paraguay, she and Dave remained close. Mary was now an imperious looking woman on the wrong side of thirty, an uncomfortable position for single women of the late nineteenth century when marriage and motherhood were the ideals. Tom Hall, the unionist Lawson had befriended in Bourke, wrote that Mary's 'old affair' was off, but that 'she is well liked by all of us'.[14]

Billy Wood described Mary as a 'great girl' and said he would like to see her wed one of Cosme's 'best fellows ... No sign of that as yet tho! Of course it's not every man would suit a girl of her description.'[15] Dave Stevenson apparently made no effort to resume the relationship and instead Mary devoted herself to teaching the twelve pupils enrolled in Cosme's one-room school, using Queensland State School readers and Spanish-language books from Argentina.

IN THE FIRST WEEKS OF JANUARY 1896, Lawson was, according to Bertha Bredt, devising strategies to make her change her mind about becoming Mrs Lawson, and also eagerly awaiting the delivery of his baby – *In The Days When The World Was Wide*. The artist Frank Mahony, whose work dominated Banjo Paterson's office, composed the artwork for the book's title page, featuring Lawson with swag, nosebag and billy can. George Robertson liked the illustration so much that the original graced the lounge in his holiday home at Blackheath for the rest of his life.

Robertson advertised on *The Bulletin*'s Red Page on 11 January 1896 that the book would be ready in four days, but it wasn't until 8 February that Archibald announced in *The Bulletin* that it would be released that week. Robertson was so confident with 1000 advance sales that another 3000 were being printed.

On 11 February, Robertson tallied the advance sales of Lawson's book at 1127. *The Bulletin* had ordered 200 copies, and booksellers around the country could see the merit in Lawson's work. Melbourne's George Robertson had ordered a hundred copies for his store there, seventy-five for his Sydney shop and twenty-five for the one in Brisbane. William Dymock had ordered seventy-five and Cole's in Melbourne wanted 125 too. Even though Bertha McNamara had a low opinion of Lawson as a suitor for her daughter, he persuaded her to take half a dozen books for her Castlereagh Street shop.[16]

Lawson called on young Bertha every day and took her on long walks with him, even though Mrs McNamara remained

Frank Mahoney's depiction of Lawson for the title page of *In The Days When The World Was Wide*. Angus & Robertson

staunchly opposed to their relationship. She was even said to have locked Bertha inside the bookstore only for her to scramble out of a window.[17]

Soon, though, she and Lawson were taking ferry rides from Circular Quay and sometimes they drifted about for hours on a rowboat through the wilds of Middle Harbour as Bertha sewed, and Lawson read Kendall and Byron and Gordon to her, or composed poems, chanting the lines over and over again to get the beat and rhythm.[18] Sometimes they talked about the cottage they planned to decorate, and how it would have a big garden full of rustic seats and arbours that he would make.[19]

Bertha's unhappiness at McNamara's bookshop forced her to move into lodgings with a plumber's wife, Mrs Emma Schaebel, at 3 Regent Street, Newtown.

Bertha's younger sister Hilda[20] was only seventeen but already about to marry the Labor zealot Jack Lang,[21] and Mrs McNamara was not about to lose her oldest daughter to a man who seemed to have no prospects and was already firmly wed to the bottle.

Mrs Mac had a reputation as 'a highly emotional German'[22] and there were bitter family rows about letting Lawson into their circle. Bertha claimed later that her mother 'blew him up', telling Lawson that her daughter was 'too young' and 'You've got no home, nothing settled. How can you provide for her?'

Mrs Schaebel's home became a sanctuary for the mismatched couple and Bertha would sometimes act as Lawson's secretary, taking pen and paper and writing down his verses as he paced to and fro, dictating.[23]

According to Bertha, Lawson was always asking her to marry him and after about six weeks of courting, Bertha finally said yes, believing that 'together we could overcome everything'.[24]

At least that was Bertha's story.

Others saw things differently.

Mary Cameron reckoned Bertha was in love with the notion of living with a literary genius; that she saw herself as his muse, and claimed Bertha chased Lawson relentlessly 'till she got him'. 'She threatened to commit suicide or something, and said her [step-] father was going to turn her out into the streets if he wouldn't marry her! It was what Henry himself told me once in a broken-hearted moment when his wife had been particularly cruel to him.'[25]

Regardless of who was wooing whom, though, George Robertson could see disaster.

Years later he told his secretary Rebecca Wiley that he was horrified 'when Henry brought in this beautiful young girl, only then in her 18th year'. Robertson said: 'She had great big hazel eyes, and shining with excitement; they were undoubtedly very much in love with each other.' Robertson said he knew 'that Henry even then was a confirmed drinker; had times a very nasty temper, and all the other things that go to make a genius very difficult to live with … I could see nothing but tragedy in it for both of them.' As Lawson was engaged elsewhere, Robertson spent a whole morning in his office pleading with Bertha 'not to take this irrevocable step. I told her I had three little girls of my own, and I'd rather see them dead, than to marry a temperamental genius, who was a drunkard as well. It was all in vain, she knew she could keep him straight, love would do it, and so on. I said, "Will you come up to Blackheath and spend the weekend with my wife, and talk it over; she'd love to have you." She refused. Well, as everyone knows, it turned out unhappiness for them both.'[26] When Lawson came back into Robertson's office, he asked Bertha what she and the publisher had been talking about for so long.

Bertha told Lawson she had promised not to get married yet, 'not till we got some money from his book which had just been published and was getting wonderfully favourable reviews'.[27]

IN THE DAYS WHEN THE WORLD WAS WIDE was released on 14 February 1896 at a stiff price of 5 shillings – way beyond the means of the battlers Lawson wrote about. It featured fifty-one of Lawson's finest poems and, among some reviewers, sparked favourable comparisons with the works of Kipling and Harte. Sydney's *Evening News* declared that while there was 'a good deal of rather crude speculation of a socialistic nature' where Lawson 'is strongest, most picturesque, and most poetical, he is unmistakably Australian – a man really influenced by his surroundings, and expressing himself in that natural way which is essential to the production of a true poetic note of any kind'.[28]

Alfred Stephens, in *The Bulletin*, said while Lawson was comparatively uncultured 'how graphic he is, how natural, how true, how strong',[29] while the *Sydney Morning Herald* added that Lawson's work 'may not be poetry of a high type, but it has strong stanzas and vivid lines of true feeling'. The writing, it said, was sometimes too rugged to please the ear 'but it has the voice of the bush in it'.[30]

Others, though, saw Lawson's glorification of those 'roaring days' as contrived and even his pal Jack Brereton, looking in vain to start a debate with Lawson in the manner of *The Bulletin* battle with Paterson, told Lawson that the 'golden days are vanished' and to 'Sing the present'.[31]

LAWSON AND BERTHA PLANNED a wedding for February at St Stephen's Church near Mrs Schaebel's in Newtown. Lawson promised Bertha that he'd stop drinking. He told her he'd only started when he was with his Mountain Push mates – 'wild young spirits of the bush' – and that in the bottle he forgot 'the sensitiveness and nervous diffident shyness that so oppressed him, forgot that he was deaf or tired or lonely or defeated. He felt confident and exhilarated, able to do anything, and to face the world.' He told Bertha that his dependence on booze would never trouble them again, though, and that she could give him the comradeship he had missed in those hard days of his youth.[32]

In later years, though, Lawson became fond of the line by another *Bulletin* contributor, David McKee Wright,[33] that 'beer makes a man feel as he ought to feel without beer'.[34]

Lawson's drinking was not the only threat to the marriage. Neither of them had any money as Lawson's book had not yet made a penny. After more heart-to-hearts they decided to postpone the nuptials for six months. Bertha would return to the

Melbourne hospital as planned, and Lawson would go back to New Zealand 'to try his fortune over there', and if all went well, he was to come for Bertha and they would live in New Zealand.[35]

Lawson drew up an agreement with Angus & Robertson, witnessed by Hugh Maccallum, that in the event of his death the company would use his profits to pay off people who had loaned him money – £3 to J.H. Simpson of Lyme House in Molesworth Street, Wellington; £3 to John Farrell; £1 to Tom Mills; the same to Edward Tregear; and 15 shillings to Jack Moses. Half of Lawson's money was then to go to 'Miss Bertha Bredt, daughter of Mrs MacNamara [sic] and step-daughter of MacNamara, bookseller, Castlereagh Street, Sydney'.

Lawson sailed to Wellington as a steerage passenger on the *Hauroto* on 15 February bound for Wellington. Bertha waved goodbye from the dock.

Lawson was distressed at the parting and they were both unhappy, but agreed it was the best thing for their long-term future. Bertha said she would wait in Sydney for a letter from him before heading south, but in her version, he arrived in New Zealand only to catch the first boat home. Lawson, perhaps already breaking his promise about drinking, failed to get off the ship in Wellington and arrived instead in Dunedin by mistake. He returned to Wellington and only spent an afternoon there with Tom Mills, despite the efforts by a girl Lawson knew to make him stay. Mills convinced his friend to get back on the boat on 28 February. Lawson arranged for Mills to send him the manuscript of Lawson's 'An Unfinished Love Story' that Mills had failed to place in the New Zealand press and which Lawson needed for the book of prose Angus & Robertson were planning.

Lawson told Mills all about Bertha and his Kiwi friend described him as being in 'womanly trouble'.[36] Lawson again returned as a steerage passenger to Sydney and, as his oscillating mood escalated heavenward, composed a love poem to Bertha: 'After All'.

Rest, for your eyes are weary, girl — you have driven the worst away —
The ghost of the man that I might have been is gone from my heart
    to-day;
We'll live for life and the best it brings till our twilight shadows fall;
My heart grows brave, and the world, my girl, is a good world after all.[37]

The *Hauroto* deposited Lawson back in Sydney on 4 March 1896 and according to Bertha, he immediately rushed out to Mrs Schaebel's and begged Bertha to marry him as soon as possible. But she remained determined to return to Victoria for six months until they had enough money behind them to tie the knot.

'Next morning,' she recalled, 'I received a letter. When I opened it it was the poem "After All". I wired him to come and see me, and we decided then that we would undertake the great adventure.'[38] That was provided Mrs Mac agreed and though Bertha had her doubts about Lawson swaying her opinion, he was confident of winning her over.

Lawson sold 'After All' to *The Bulletin* to start his wedding fund. Tom Mills sent Lawson the manuscript for 'An Unfinished Love Story'[39] and Lawson immediately sold it to *The Worker*, and put it on the list for inclusion in his prose book.

The wedding was set for April at St Stephen's in Newtown, but Lawson was growing moody and impatient.

He said he had received Mrs McNamara's consent but had not been able to convince some of Bertha's other relatives and friends that he was a desirable husband. Louisa was opposed to the union too, and Lawson was reminded of her poem seven years before in *The Dawn*, written perhaps as a warning to Mary Cameron.

Don't marry a man to reform him!
To God and your own self be true.
Don't link to his vices your virtue;
You'll rue it, dear girl, if you do.[40]

Lawson began receiving hate mail from Bertha's people over the impending wedding, and started to suspect there was a conspiracy against him. He feared that unless they were married soon, someone would force a permanent wedge between them. Then Lawson saw a newspaper advertisement for Weldon's Matrimonial Association at 57 Phillip Street, next to the tradesmen's entrance to the Hotel Metropole. Weddings were performed for £1, and 'legally solemnized by fully ordained Ministers of Recognized Churches'. Witnesses were provided for free.[41]

On the morning of 15 April 1896, Lawson decided he'd waited long enough. He had already taken out a loan for £10 from a financier in Pitt Street and borrowed another £1 off writer and Pacific adventurer Louis Becke[42] to pay for a wedding ceremony. In later years Lawson would say that he always regretted Becke giving him the money because of the trouble it unleashed.[43]

He called at Mrs Schaebel's house early that morning and told Bertha, 'I want you to look very, very nice, so put on your wedding dress to please me.'[44]

Bertha said she was horrified at the thought of wearing her wedding dress before the big day, so instead she donned her travelling dress, a green silk frock with a straw hat wreathed in red poppies.

Then Lawson took her to a house in Phillip Street where she understood they were to meet his friend Jack Moses. It proved, however, to be the headquarters of the Weldon's marriage agency and the Reverend W.T. Adams, a wandering minister of the American Methodist Episcopalian Church, was waiting to wed them. Two witnesses Lawson had never met were standing by.

Bertha protested about the change of their plans from a proper ceremony and a honeymoon in the Blue Mountains, and she told Lawson that he hadn't yet received her mother's consent. He drew a letter from his pocket to say it had been 'given in writing' and he also had a 'special licence'.

So it was that Henry Archibald Lawson, journalist, age twenty-eight, wed Bertha Marie Louise Bredt, gentlewoman, age nineteen.[45]

The newlyweds booked in for the night at a hotel near Saint Andrew's Cathedral and the next day they went to Darlinghurst, where they found a flat with a furnished sitting room and bedroom in Forbes Street for 25 shillings a week. The landlord asked for a deposit. Lawson asked if he had change for a £10 note. He didn't, but impressed with the young couple's prosperity he let them move in.

Lawson had been bluffing as all he and Bertha had in ready cash were a few shillings after the cost of the wedding, cab and hotel room had been settled.

Bertha said that not long after Lawson took her to meet *The Bulletin* staff. She said they thought the wedding news was another of Lawson's practical jokes. But she claimed that *The Bulletin*'s manager, William MacLeod,[46] then gave them hearty congratulations and advanced Lawson another £10. Archibald did the same. Alfred Stephens had taken to dressing like a bushman in town; an open-necked Crimean shirt with rolled-up sleeves and an old reefer jacket. He was always inflating his chest as though puffing himself up with pride. Bertha recalled that 'in his kindly, pompous way' Stephens stared right into Bertha's eyes and asked if the news of the wedding was really true.

'It is quite true,' Bertha answered. 'We were married yesterday. I'm going to try and make him happy.'

'I hope he is going to try and make *you* happy,' Stephens replied.[47]

LAWSON'S BOOK RECEIVED blanket publicity and mostly positive reviews, but by April 1896 Paterson's *The Man from Snowy River* was still lapping him in the sales race at a ratio of more than two to one.

It was also around this time that Paterson composed the verses for a song called 'Waltzing Matilda', an expression used by German settlers for a man tramping with a blanket or coat to sleep in.

From a slow start the poem would become an alternative national anthem. Paterson had based his verses on stories he had heard at Dagworth Station, when holidaying in Central Queensland with his fiancée Sarah Riley and her old schoolfriend

Christina (Chris) Macpherson,[48] whose brothers ran the vast property.

At a gathering at Dagworth one evening, Chris, a shy and bespectacled 31-year-old spinster, entertained the guests by plucking out a marching tune called 'Thou Bonnie Wood of Craigielea'[49] on a zither.[50] Banjo said he could write some lines to fit her tune and, inspired by the tale of the suicidal arsonist Frenchy Hoffmeister and other battlers fighting the wealthy squatters, he gradually worked up the verses about a swagman who steals a sheep and then, surrounded by policemen, dives into a billabong and drowns himself rather than surrender.

Maybe Paterson paid too much attention to Chris at Dagworth, though. Sarah Riley and the Macpherson brothers apparently thought so and his engagement ended abruptly. He took the parting in his stride, just as he did the enormous success of his first book.

Two years earlier in his *Bulletin* essay on 'Some Popular Australian Mistakes',[51] Lawson had scoffed at the 'waltzing Matilda' expression. 'A swag is not generally referred to as a "bluey" or "Matilda",' Lawson wrote, 'it is called a "swag" … No bushman thinks of "going on the wallaby" or "walking Matilda," or "padding the hoof," he goes on the track – when forced to.'

But Banjo liked the way the words 'Waltzing Matilda' rolled off the tongue and so did many others. Paterson was providing Australia with the horseman's voice 'and the genial humour of the comfortably off'. Lawson's work, though, represented the gritty voice of the swagman, shearer, spieler and slum dweller. His humour was the grim observation of the hard-up, and unfortunately his hard-up audience found spending 5 shillings for his book prohibitive.[52]

Lawson's mood was not helped when a reader's poll by *Cosmos* magazine picked Paterson as the preferred poet of the two. Lawson complained to Banjo that his fans simply didn't have the money of Banjo's audience. 'Do you know who's buying my book?' he asked Paterson, but before Banjo could reply, Lawson told him, 'Your friends of the capitalist class. The Labor people are not buying my book. They have declared me bogus for writing a story disclosing some good points in a squatter.'[53]

Not long after that, Medway Day sent a call out to give Lawson a hand, writing in *The Worker,* 'The volume of Henry Lawson's poems has had a good sale, upwards of 3000 copies having been disposed of. Amongst the bush workers, however, the sale has been comparatively small … cannot our members during the shearing season spend 5 shillings in purchasing a copy? By an arrangement with the publishers the funds of the *Worker* will be benefited by every copy sold through the secretaries or shed reps.'[54]

AS A NEW HUSBAND, Lawson settled down to work, as Bertha recalled, to 'amass the fortune he was so sure he would make for us'.[55] When they had money they lived comfortably; when they had none, they occasionally went without their breakfast and lived sparingly till Lawson could sell a poem or sketch.

Sometimes Lawson would work right through the night and into the morning, unaware of time or meals. He took the greatest pride in his writing and Bertha said it meant more to him than anything else in the world.[56] In the few weeks after the wedding his output was limited, though, perhaps because the pair would frequently go on picnics to Mosman, and scramble over the rocks to gather oysters and drink tea from a billy. During May, he submitted the sketch 'The Provincial School' and the poem 'Years After the War in Australia' to *The Bulletin,* and for *Truth* 'Write by Return' and 'When You're Bad in Your Inside'.

He and Bertha sometimes went to the theatre on press tickets. Their visitors were mostly Ted Brady, Jack Moses and Jack Brereton, who recalled:

His wife had sympathy, patience, humour, energy and resource, and she needed them all. She did her best for Lawson, encouraging him in his moods of depression, and guarding him against himself and others. And, in those old days, he understood and was grateful. No one who saw them in their home could doubt the love that bound them. He spoke to me with deep gratitude of her staunchness and self-sacrifice.[57]

The Darlinghurst flat represented the first time that Lawson had a home of his own, or a comfortable home life, and he had a childlike enthusiasm for his new surrounds. In Paraguay, Mary Cameron had also found love among the ruins of New Australia. He was Will Gilmore,[58] a rugged shearer and farm labourer from the Victorian bush, described as quiet and popular, 'a fine, sturdy, loveable man and mate ... with the sort of head that young girls rave about, clean cut features, nose somewhat aquiline and forehead crowned by a big bunch of bushy curls'.[59] Two days after she had arrived in Cosme, Mary began nursing Will, who had been badly injured saving some children in the village playground as their swings gave way. While Gilmore slowly recovered in bed, it was said that he became mesmerised by Mary's soothing voice as she read to him.

Mary still had a soft spot for Lawson though, unaware he had married Bertha.

From 'Colonia Cosme' Mary wrote, asking Lawson to send her his new book of verse. 'I'd give a lot to see you here,' Mary wrote, adding that the country was 'a constant wonder'. 'If you were only here, Henry. Don't let someone else snap your chances. Come while the field is new – as a visitor, I mean – though I'd like you to come for good ... Come if you can, dear old friend. You know I wouldn't ask you if I didn't think it worth it. PS I didn't get married.'[60]

THE PARAGUAYAN PARADISE was imploding all around Lane's followers, but other Australians were making haste to what they saw as a golden future in Western Australia, the recent gold strikes at Kalgoorlie adding to the earlier rush at Coolgardie.

Lawson had come home dejected from the west on his first visit to Albany, but this time he thought he might strike it rich on one of the goldfields. While *The Man from Snowy River* had found a market in England, Lawson's verses had struggled in the same stores, and he now had a notion that he could travel to London himself to make his name there. A visit to the goldfields could pay his fare.

Lawson again sold Robertson the copyright to his book of verse and then sold him the copyright to the upcoming book of prose *While the Billy Boils*. Robertson let Lawson keep the advances and gave him an extra £70. Lawson then made an extra guinea from *Truth* for 'The Man from Waterloo' and booked tickets for himself and Bertha on the 2524-ton *Marloo* leaving Sydney for Fremantle. He and Bertha planned to eventually sail from Fremantle to London. In the week before they left Sydney, Lawson earned another guinea by selling 'When You're Bad in Your Inside' to the *Bega Gazette* and he had another copy for the *Coolgardie Mining Review*.

Bertha told Lawson that before they left on their great trek, they should say goodbye to their mothers as they had seen neither since before the wedding. Lawson insisted they see Mrs McNamara first before his even more formidable mater.

Mrs Mac was ropeable about the marriage. 'You pair of lunatics,' she screamed. 'Henry Lawson get out of my house.'[61] Bertha recalled that Mrs Mac 'was naturally very hurt and angry at having been told nothing of our wedding. I explained that we had been afraid of being parted and had felt it was the only thing we could do. So we left her quite reconciled. She came to see our little home ... Harry was always very fond of her.'[62] Lawson often referred to Mrs Mac as 'the little mother-in-law' and joked to his socialist friends that they should learn the names of the Chicago martyrs — the men executed after an act of anarchy in Chicago's Haymarket in 1886 — as it guaranteed a meal and bed at her bookshop.[63]

After seeing Mrs Mac, Henry and Bertha went to *The Dawn* office to tackle Louisa. She had not seen her son for a long time. He explained matters and presented his new wife. Bertha had dreaded the meeting, and felt timid in the presence of this 'tall, commanding personality'.

'She was a very brilliant, intellectual woman – not at all domesticated in any sense,' Bertha recalled. 'Ambitious and high spirited, she was an intrepid and fearless battler in the cause of the advancement of women. I think the women of Australia do not realise their great and lasting debt of gratitude to her. She championed every cause that would improve their conditions, and worked tremendously hard in pioneer movements, against glaring abuses. Strong-minded, self-willed, and of exceptional intelligence, she was particularly fitted to carry the banner of progress in those early days, when a woman's interest in public affairs was looked upon with disapproval and suspicion.'[64]

But Bertha could well understand, as she grew to know Louisa, what was behind Lawson's 'attitude of obedient respect' towards her.

'He was rather afraid of the "Chieftainess" as he called her, while admiring her fine qualities,' Bertha wrote. 'She fostered and encouraged his literary abilities, but she could never have given him the sympathetic understanding or affection he most needed. I think this helped to increase his sense of loneliness and nervous diffidence as a boy. One had only to know her well, as I did, to realise that it would be impossible for her to settle down to any sort of domestic or family life, and to realise also that Harry's stories of his boyhood are not overdrawn.'[65]

In spite of Bertha's misgivings, Louisa gave her new daughter-in-law a box of twelve black cashmere stockings as a wedding present and she was on the dock beside Mrs Mac wishing the newlyweds bon voyage as they sailed on the *Marloo*.

They left Sydney Harbour on a glorious afternoon of brown, grey and blue shadows across the water. Bertha was excited about the voyage and the 'splendid future' she saw before them, 'one filled with happiness and prosperity'. She was sure that 'Harry was going to be the greatest writer Australia had ever known' even though he seemed more concerned about becoming 'a lucky digger' on the goldfields.[66]

As they swept through the Heads, Bertha felt a sudden rush as the ocean and the world beyond opened before her.

'I wanted to cry,' she recalled, 'and would have if Harry had not held me with one arm around me while we watched the shore sliding past.'

Lawson whispered in her ear: 'Don't cry, little woman, I'll look after you.'[67]

Lawson saw golden opportunities in the west but it would be Bertha's first taste of hell.

Years later Lawson would reflect on the turmoil surrounding their courtship and marriage:

> Cheap boarding house, pretty, but hysterical, daughter; mother, step-father, and sisters; rows and scenes more violent than at home. Tale of ill-treatment. Last big row. Cab, box, and hurried, mad marriage at a 'matrimonial bureau'. Seven years of it.[68]

Chapter 14

*He became shiftless, and drink got a firm hold of him. He had some
social ambitions and would like to have had a comfortable home for his
wife; but he was too careless and too selfish to make any sacrifice to
provide one. He had generous impulses but no steadfastness
of purpose in any direction.*
LAWSON'S DRINKING COMPANION BERTRAM STEVENS[1]

T HE *MARLOO'S* FIRST STOP on the voyage to the west
was on 2 June in Melbourne, where 'the principal industry
at that time was debts'.[2] Lawson had a week's business to do and a
small army of friends to see but speculated that maybe the captain
and crew owed money there, because the *Marloo* sailed on after
just a day.[3] He barely had time to meet some of Bertha's relatives
at Williamstown and to catch up with an admirer, John Steele
Robertson, who was the secretary and librarian of the University
of Melbourne's Medical School, and who wrote for *The Bulletin*
under the byline Steele Grey. A week before Lawson's arrival in
Melbourne, and without having met him, Robertson had written
a glowing report in the magazine *Free Lance*. Based on Lawson's
reputation, Robertson had declared that Lawson had 'a well-
shaped head, keen intellectual face, and peculiarly piercing eyes,
which he fixes on you with an intensity almost disconcerting.
This intense gaze is really due to the fact that he suffers from
deafness, and is to aid him in grasping the meaning of your
imperfectly-heard speech.'[4]

Lawson called in to the *Free Lance* office to meet the writer, but Robertson was not there. They finally met on the wharf in the shadow of the ship. Robertson described Bertha as 'a Gippsland girl, plump and pleasing of aspect, charming in conversation'. She looked upon her husband, Robertson observed, 'with large and deep brown eyes filled with worship of him and his works. And Lawson's eyes as he looks on his young wife, are also full of love and a kind of wonder that she ever thought enough of him to marry such a wanderer.'[5]

The ship sailed on and Lawson was having a high old time speculating on his prospects, and discussing the best places to find gold with a 'stout, elderly'[6] Polish scientist, Modest Maryanski, who was to have a huge influence in developing the Western Australian goldfields[7] at a time when the young mining engineer and future American president Herbert Hoover was also working there.

Lawson noted that Maryanski 'had about £500 worth of jewellery on his fingers and shirt' and that he had been used to the 'first hotels, and saloons, in the world', while Lawson was more used to workmen's boarding houses.[8] Maryanski had an assistant named Darrow, a 'slight, quiet, gentlemanly Yankee, from some big mineralogical college in the States, who collected everlasting flowers, sea-weed, and shells for his mother – a dear old lady by her portrait'.[9] It was a reminder to Lawson, who saw himself changing from 'a socialist' and 'red Republican' to 'a democrat', that he was 'constantly meeting bloated capitalists, and their agents, who turn out to be pleasant-faced, gentle-spoken, simple-hearted, good-natured men' – even cheerful, and jolly, and boyish. 'Tis a world of changing contradictions, and man will never get the hang of it.'[10]

The *Marloo* spent three days anchored in Port Adelaide, where Lawson was fascinated by the train running through the main street, with the stoker ringing a bullock bell 'to scare off furniture vans, etc'.[11]

Lawson left Bertha in the care of a young Pole named Litvinski,[12] who became a character in Lawson's story 'The Hero of Redclay'.[13]

On the trip across the Great Australian Bight, Lawson thought it 'glorious' to be up early when the decks had just been washed down, and everything was fresh and bright, and there was a stiff breeze blowing, and the blue sea was covered with whitecaps; and, sometimes, there was an island or a headland close by, with a line of breakers round the base. Sometimes 'on a sunny, bounding day' he and Bertha would lounge on deck chairs and watch the masthead moving constantly backward and forward across the pale blue sky, the fleecy clouds flying over, and every now and then a mighty white-capped wall of green rising beyond the bulwarks.

In the smoking room, he and Bertha played deck quoits, cards, dominoes and draughts; read magazines and yarned lazily.[14] He watched a mining man, who was returning west with some of his family, use a long-barrelled revolver to take pot shots at sea birds over the stern until Captain Allen 'interfered angrily, and suddenly', telling him that he could bring bad luck on the voyage if he killed one.[15]

There were a number of newly married couples like the Lawsons, and an old maid, who 'haunted them', beaming on their canoodling with moist eyes, as if she 'longed to adopt them, and take them to her lonely breast'. There was a theatrical agent too, 'with a great stock of very original anecdotes' for the smoking room, and a frank, fresh-faced boy, who couldn't understand why he couldn't raise a lather with soap in the hot salt water. Lawson told him he thought it was because 'the salt in the water killed the soapiness'. And there was a digger, who had been over to Sydney to farewell and bury the last of his family, a grown-up daughter. 'I'm glad I got over in time to see the last of her,' he told Lawson slowly and sadly one evening as they smoked their pipes by the rail. 'She was a good girl, Annie. The mother died when she was a child.' The digger turned his shoulder to Lawson abruptly, so that he did not show his tears. He folded his arms tightly on the rail, and gazed out over the darkening sea.[16]

The *Marloo* arrived at Albany while the passengers were breakfasting on 12 July, and after delays with the hauling of cargo, rounded Cape Leeuwin and Rottnest Island to reach Fremantle late on the evening of the 14th. Two other ships had arrived at the same time and accommodation was scarce, but Lawson and Bertha found a hotel before taking a small train the next day through the scrubby sand to Perth, which now had a population of about 40,000, with hundreds more arriving every week. Clearing of the land was taking place all along the rail line and small galvanised iron, weatherboard and brick suburbs were being built from Fremantle to Perth.

Lawson and Bertha tramped through Perth for most of the day in search of reasonable lodgings, but none were to be found. The balconies and verandas of second-class boarding houses were covered at night by the horizontal forms of single men, who picked up their swags next morning, took the train to the goldfields, or camped on the outskirts of the city to find work. Cottages were taken before they were built, and the tenants of existing cottages were often given bonuses of up to £25 to get out. They then camped in tents, hessian houses, or erected weatherboard boxes. The hordes flocking to the goldfields stirred bitter memories of Lawson's boyhood, and when he went into the city looking for work, journalists he met told him of broiling heat and rampant fever at Coolgardie. After that first day in Perth, Lawson realised that as a young man of limited cash who had brought his wife with him, he had made a monumental blunder. Work was plentiful, he wrote, wages were fair, but the price of meat and groceries was 'appalling, and a cottage not to be thought of'.[17] Now calling himself 'the foolish young husband', Lawson found that instead of going to the fields and making a pile, he would have to 'hustle for groceries in Perth'. With no lodgings to be found within their meagre budget, Lawson and Bertha had to splurge for a few days at Perth's Shamrock Hotel, with the intention of sailing home on the next available boat.[18]

Lawson went looking for his old mate from the Mountain Push, Jack Jones, 'a born comedian, with a quiet grin and an inexhaustible store of quaint and original lies' who was working as a plasterer in Perth.[19]

Jones had written to Lawson a couple of months previously, saying that 'things were grand in the building line in Perth' and that beer 'ran out the pub doors and down the gutter' and there were always plenty of people with money to shout the bar.

Lawson visited building sites all over Perth asking for 'Jones of New South Wales', and finally found him at 5 p.m. getting ready to knock off from his job at some new cottages. Jones had built a hessian house and had sent to Sydney for his wife. He had a small tent, and he placed his house at Lawson's disposal until he could 'run one up' for himself.

Despite Lawson's worries about having to pay customs duty on household items, Bertha had brought with them a set of flat-irons, 'enough crockery to start a hotel', and a full set of kitchen utensils. They set up home in a paddock beside the Swan River near St George's Terrace alongside the tents of Jack Jones, his brother Davy and Arthur Parker from the Mountain Push.

Lawson built his own bag-and-canvas-covered frame, with a tent inside. They used packing cases for furniture and a nail can with holes as a fireplace; the whole portable home cost £5, including a wire mattress, stretcher, bedding, etc.[20] The workers' camp mushroomed to more than a hundred homes and the residents even named their own streets there after the ones they'd left in Sydney – George Street was the main thoroughfare, connecting with Bathurst, Market and King Streets.

LAWSON BEGAN WORKING as a painter on building sites but six weeks after he and Bertha had erected their tent home, a mounted policeman came calling to move the squatters in accordance with new sanitation laws designed to combat typhoid fever and diphtheria. Bertha rushed into the city to obtain a licence that for 7 shillings and sixpence a month allowed them to erect their lodgings in a government camp at East Perth, below an old, neglected cemetery and with a water frontage beside a brook. Lawson wrote:

> The health inspector rode down one day, and casually
> mentioned that he wouldn't use the brook water for
> drinking or cooking … We found, soon enough, that the
> brook was one of the city's natural sewers – perhaps the
> main one.[21]

Lawson erected two 12 foot x 10 foot tents under a wooden framework; one was a bedroom and kitchen and the other a dining room that doubled as Lawson's study and where he wrote three sketches for the *West Australian*: 'The Shanty-keeper's Wife',[22] 'Mitchell's Jobs'[23] and 'Black Joe',[24] in which Lawson recalls a childhood friendship with an Aboriginal boy and his family. 'Black Joe' instructed Lawson, or 'White Joe', in Indigenous survival skills and he was 'very black', the colour coming, young Lawson surmised, from living off the land and the burning off of grasses to promote regeneration. White Joe's colour came from being a 'sickly town boy', but because he also had an interest in 'burning off' and a disinterest in 'cold water', especially in winter, 'the difference in our complexions was not so marked at times'.[25]

Within the family of his young Aboriginal friend, Lawson also found a balm for his familial and social alienation.[26]

Lawson thought 'Black Joe' was 'wiser and cleverer than any white boy in the world' but the white man's 'civilisation' was destroying both his culture and his family. When White Joe is in anguish at the early death of Black Joe, his family has a mistaken perception that the dead was one of their own, though 'cross-examination explained the mistake, and I retired to the rear of the pig-sty, as was my custom when things went wrong, with another cause for grief'.[27]

The workers' camp in East Perth also helped set the scene for Lawson's later piece 'A Case for the Oracle'.

Lawson wrote to the intrepid journalist 'Smiler' Hales[28] in Coolgardie, asking if it was wise to take Bertha to the diggings but 'Smiler' told him it would be 'madness'. To cheer up his teenage bride, Lawson made their home as comfortable as possible. The floor was pine, made from long wooden cases that had been used to pack galvanised iron, and which were turned face down, and there were kerosene lamps and rustic chairs that Lawson made from tea-tree growing near the brook. As the wife of a literary genius, though, this was not the comfortable life Bertha was expecting. She would have preferred to be back in Melbourne, or at Mrs Schaebel's, or even amid the smell of beer, onions and anarchy at Mrs Mac's; anywhere really rather than a tent beside a sewerage stream in the shadow of a cemetery. But the feisty young woman made the best of her situation. She took a wheelbarrow and collected discarded bricks from a nearby kiln, and Arthur Parker used them to make a fireplace and chimney for the Lawson home. Parker remembered that despite the privations, the Lawsons 'were very happy and very fond of each other'. Much of the trouble that followed, Parker said, was down to the 'readiness of Henry's friends to celebrate with him'.[29] As Lawson admitted, despite his promises to Bertha about beating the booze, in Perth 'there was a great deal of drinking'.[30]

Some of Lawson's friends at the workers' camp in East Perth in 1897. Jack Jones is on the left, Dave Jones standing in the middle. State Library of NSW, FL3319349

WHILE THE BILLY BOILS, Lawson's book of prose, edited by Arthur Jose, had advance orders of 1428 when Angus & Robertson published it on 29 August 1896. Robertson sent out 235 review copies too, which had an immediate effect. Writing in the *Review of Reviews*, Sydney barrister David Ferguson said Lawson's prose was 'finer and more certain' than his verse:

> The shearer's shed, the shepherd's humpy, the cockatoo selector, the station cook, the fossicker, the swagman, the bush shanty, the bush spieler – he has transferred them whole into his pages, and there they stand, with the full glare of the Australian sun on them, harsh and unlovely of aspect for the most part, yet never quite without a chastening touch of humour or pathos, and always and unmistakably alive ... What Mr Lawson leaves out, may be comprehensively exemplified in a sentence: There is not a horse in the book, from title page to imprint – not one horse![31]

The *Sydney Morning Herald* praised Lawson's moral courage in highlighting the struggles of country women in 'The Drover's Wife' and called the book of fifty-two stories 'an unsparing picture of the realistic, hard, unlovely side of life as lived in the Australian bush'.[32] This kind of praise was soon being repeated around Australia, and Medway Day gleefully told readers of *The Worker* that many of the book's sketches had first appeared in his newspaper.

Across the Tasman, in Wellington's *Evening News*, Gresley Lukin praised Lawson's 'undoubted artistic power', while the *West Australian*, now buying Lawson's newest work, lauded his 'power, pathos and humor'. 'Few men have so wide and so intimate an acquaintance with the more interesting phases of Australian social life as Mr. Lawson,' it noted. 'Fewer still have the penetration, literary endowment and artistic temperament enabling them to transfer to the printed page faithful pictures of the scenes they have visited ... He has caught the tone of bush life in particular more than anyone ...'[33]

The Irish-born writer Tighe Ryan[34] knew Lawson well and called him 'the greatest gift the gods have so far given to Australia ... a genius to the fingertips'. It was all the more remarkable, Ryan said, given that Lawson was an awkward youth, 'a true son of the Australian Bush', who existed in the slums of Sydney, spent his childhood in a tent and was 'known in the back blocks as a swagman'.[35]

Lawson wrote to Robertson on 3 September 1896 to say, unflatteringly, that he had seen the new book and 'it looks alright'.

'Have been living very quietly here,' he told his publisher. 'Rent and rates for board and lodging outrageously high, so I bought a camping kit and put up a place ... Have been working at my trade. I go to graft again this afternoon. Bertha is well and happy and we are very comfortable but we are only making expenses. I am saving copy for the East. Country is rather barren of material. I'm working up a couple of novels ...'

He couldn't help but whinge. 'WA is a fraud. The curse of the country is gold, as sheep are the curse of the east. A more sordid, vulgar condition of things would be impossible to conceive. There is a ridiculous land and building boom in Perth. The country will be in awful condition when the mining boom bursts ... It is madness for any man to bring his wife here unless he has money.'[36]

As the Lawsons' cash reserves dwindled despite his efforts with brush and pen, Bertha landed a job as a saleswoman in a Perth draper's. Lawson, however, wouldn't condone it, later writing that like many Australian men he was too proud to have his wife working for wages.[37]

The next day he came home from his painting job at lunchtime, spattered with paint and red with rage. He had been working on the outside of a pub when he and the landlord began a fierce quarrel and he was again unemployed.

He was drinking a lot too, with 'journalistic friends', but Bertha said she could never be too angry with him because he was always so 'penitent',[38] and she knew how much his drinking companions meant to him, 'deaf, and shy and lonely as he was'.[39]

By the end of September 1896, early sales were even better for *Billy Boils* than those for *The Man from Snowy River*. Yet Lawson knew he would not see royalties for some time. Bertha was left alone for long periods in the little camp beside the cemetery, and the approaching summer threatened epidemics of typhoid and cholera.[40] Although Lawson had dreamed of striking it rich on the goldfields and then taking his wife to London, Bertha claimed that she appealed to Lawson in one of his repentant moods and convinced him to return home and then think about London later on.

They sold their portable camp for £35,[41] and bought two steerage tickets to Sydney on the Adelaide Steamship Company's 1677-ton *Wollowra*. Lawson used the sale as material for his story 'Bill Will'[42] but it wasn't one of his best and Robertson only bought it because Lawson needed the money, and Angus & Robertson never published it. Lawson wrote to Robertson to say he had decided to 'go to the Auckland district in New Zealand in two or three months and might get round by Sydney'.

The Lawsons arrived in Melbourne on 8 October 1896 after a four-day voyage from Albany. Two days later as Lawson was drinking with some Melbourne friends, he was joined by Henry Hyde Champion,[43] an admirer, who published a number of titles at different times including the eponymous weekly *Champion*, which promoted socialism and women's suffrage. Lawson presented a frail image. Some of his fingers had been bandaged after he had jammed them in the ship's pump. He had fainted with the pain.

Champion was an Afghan War veteran and he described Lawson as 'a tall, slight man, delicate in appearance, and with an air of refinement and sensitiveness'. 'Lawson would give a first impression of femininity,' he wrote. 'This is deepened by his quiet, though decisive, style of speech. It is in the virility of his thoughts and the directness of his manner that his masculinity is manifested.'[44]

That afternoon, 10 October 1896, Lawson and Bertha continued their voyage to Sydney, now on the 1560-ton Huddart Parker steamship *Burrumbeet*. Even though Lawson was only a steerage passenger, Captain Walter Hipgrave was a fan and

allowed him to drink with the saloon passengers. By the time the
Burrumbeet docked in Sydney on 12 October, the Lawsons had just
2 shillings left.[45]

Bertha wrote later that they rented a furnished room at 43
Clarence Street, 'near the top end of Wynyard Square[46] ... and by
a strange coincidence the landlord's name was Henry Lawson'.[47]

THE COUPLE TRIED to keep up appearances. They still had
good clothes and did not let anyone know where they lived or
that they were desperately hard up. Lawson called on Robertson
and told him that he and Bertha had done well in the west but
found the climate disagreeable. Lawson wrote to Arthur Parker
asking him to organise photos of the camps for articles he planned
for *The Bulletin* and *Town and Country Journal*, though the photos
never came and the articles didn't appear until three years later in
the *Australian Star*.

Lawson and Bertha stayed in their furnished room for a month
before moving to 99 Regent St, Redfern, and then No. 91. Ted
Brady, who had just remarried, lived nearby with his second wife
after he had divorced the first on the grounds of adultery.

Also living nearby was Bertram Stevens,[48] a 24-year-old law
clerk with the well-known firm Allen, Allen & Hemsley. Stevens
wore an 'imperial' moustache with the corners turned up and
according to Lawson had 'a foolish longing for the somewhat
doubtful society of "men of letters"'.[49] He had long been a Lawson
devotee and the two new books confirmed the young man's lofty
opinion of his hero. A mutual friend, an ex-jockey, introduced
them at the jockey's home in Waterloo.

Stevens recalled:

On going to meet him I felt that I was to have the privilege
of shaking hands with a genius and, what was most
important to me – a fellow countryman who was putting
the spirit of Australia into print for the first time.[50]

I remember the first meeting very well. Lawson said
little in the house, Mrs Lawson did most of the talking and

repeated my remarks to Henry as he seemed very deaf. She was young and attractive … dressed neatly (she told me afterwards that it was her wedding dress she had on that night), and as we walked home afterwards she talked as one who was devoted to Henry, but had already discovered the inconvenience of having a genius for a husband.[51]

Bertha liked Stevens at that first meeting but said she wanted to keep her husband away from 'the breezy, careless, humorous comradeship that made up the Bohemian life of the writers and artists whom he met' and who encouraged him to drink.[52]

One day she met Stevens in the street and he told her he 'would like very much' to visit Lawson at their home.

'Do you drink?' Bertha asked.

'No,' Stevens said, 'I am a teetotaller.'

'Very well,' Bertha replied. 'But you must promise never to ask Harry to have a drink.'[53]

Stevens promised. Easier said than done.

He saw a great deal of Lawson for several months after their first meeting. Lawson would call for him two or three nights a week, and they would walk downtown, visiting various pubs and talking about poetry and the single-tax theories of Henry George.

Stevens said that deafness sometimes made Lawson suspicious and morose. It was difficult to talk with him and a third person, as Lawson seemed to think he was missing remarks about himself.[54]

At this time, Stevens recalled 'Lawson certainly had a good deal of respect for his wife and recognised that she was trying to keep him from drink for his own good'. Lawson amused himself by dodging Bertha's efforts, though, and the high praise for his books from around Australia inflated his ego.

As Stevens had more interest in Lawson's company than he did in booze, he generally got him home sober, at least early in their relationship. For a long time, when Lawson brought Stevens home for a drink and a yarn, they came with bottles marked as non-alcoholic 'Hop Beer'. By accident Bertha drank some and realised it was full strength, putting an angry end to the charade.

Lawson did not disclose to Bertha all that he earned from *The Bulletin* either, and sometimes he would hide his drinking money in his hat and boots. Sometimes he would secrete sixpences in the corners of their home and occasionally he would leave small deposits of cash with friendly barmaids as insurance against 'dry days'.[55]

He found many drinking partners including Ted Brady, whose wife, Annie, like Bertha, was fighting constantly with him to curtail his vice. Another who helped Lawson ease his constant thirst was Dick Holt, who wrote for *The Bulletin* under the pen-name '6 x 8'. Bertha claimed that after one night 'on the syrup', Lawson and Holt came staggering home together, announcing their arrival after midnight for all the neighbours to hear, having either missed the tram or having exhausted the last of their coins on booze. A horse and dog had followed them in an absurd procession.

Lawson seemed to derive a perverse amusement out of self-destruction, as though waving his alcoholism like a flag 'in defiance of the dull, respectable world that had no place for poets'.[56]

One man Lawson no longer drank with, though, was Jack Brereton. They fell out over Brereton's criticism in *The Bulletin* for Lawson to 'Sing the present' and Lawson, who could swing from deep depression to soaring egomania when the moods took him, resented Brereton's advice on what books to read to improve his poetic technique. Lawson unloaded on Brereton, and his fondness for Elizabethan writing, in 'The Uncultured Rhymer to his Cultured Critics'.[57]

> You grope for Truth in a language dead —
> In the dust 'neath tower and steeple!
> What know you of the tracks we tread?
> And what know you of our people?[58]

Lawson's opinion of himself and his writing had entered stratospheric territory, though he was stumped trying to write the novel *The Hero of Redclay* and instead offered Robertson a narrative poem of the same name.

'My line is writing short stories and sketches in prose and verse,' he told his publisher. 'I'm not a novelist. You will find a man to write you an Australian novel soon enough. If you were a builder, would you set the painters to do the carpentering? Probably if I published a novel now it would fall flat and squelch both of us, though I won't say that a decent one mightn't come to me yet.'[59]

He suggested to Robertson that the publisher should produce a second book of Lawson's prose, from material that didn't make *While the Billy Boils*. He castigated Robertson over a slowdown in book sales, a comment that made the publisher bristle. He told Robertson that it would be better to publish another prose book, since another of poetry 'would take more time for revision, and be the cause of more worry, advice, hope, despair, blue-lights, rows and consequently beer, than I could stand at present'.[60]

One day in November 1896, Lawson went into the city and began drinking on his own. With his thoughts jumbled and his mood low, he stormed into the offices of Angus & Robertson and hurled abuse at everyone there. Then, as abruptly as he arrived, he turned and stamped his feet back out onto Castlereagh Street. On his way home, he came to his senses. Embarrassed, he confessed to Bertha about what he had done, and she wrote an apology to Robertson, telling him she hoped to take Lawson to New Zealand soon, away from his drinking companions.

Robertson was non-committal about another book of prose and Lawson lambasted him, complaining about the publisher's 'black looks and short words'. Who did Robertson think he was dealing with after all? He told Robertson that he 'would not put aside my self-respect for the sake of a few shillings'.[61]

Robertson told Lawson that he was free to find another publisher if he wished and that: 'We do not intend to publish any new work of yours.'[62]

It was the first time a publisher had given Lawson his marching orders and Robertson was Lawson's biggest source of revenue.

The Worker had suspended publication for a few months but Archibald was snapping up all he could of Lawson's and there was always a little to be made from *Truth*, *Freeman's Journal* and the *Town and Country Journal*. Despite the huge output of work, though, most of Lawson's money was being spent in hotels.

Bertha saw Bert Stevens as a generally positive influence on Lawson, despite the 'Hop Beer' episode, but that changed on the night of 4 March 1897, following the election of the New South Wales delegates to the Federal Convention, among them Edmund Barton, who would become Australia's first prime minister.

'Henry called for me in the morning,' Stevens noted, 'and after I had voted ... we went to Manly. We bought some provisions and bottled ale, and carried them up into the bush near Curl Curl. The rest of the day was spent there in talking or paddling on the beach like two kids ... I mentioned to Lawson ... that one of the reviewers of his book had girded at "The Star of Australasia" as a hectic sort of shout for war for its own sake, and he went off into a passionate outburst as to the good war would do Australia. He was emphatic ... that military training would be the best thing for wiping out larrikinism – then at its worst.'[63] Legless with beer, Lawson was adamant that Australian youth needed discipline.

The sozzled pair returned to Redfern 'very late, after many drinks and a row at a coffee stall' after Lawson misheard a harmless remark from a cab driver. They made up a story that was to account for their lateness but as it was necessary for Stevens to speak loudly to Lawson, every word he uttered during rehearsal in the quietness of 1 a.m. reached the young ears of Bertha who met them 'like an avenging Fate'.[64]

Stevens complained in vain that Bertha had lost her sense of humour.

But the 'dead finish' of Stevens at the Lawsons' home came after another night out for the pair with journalist Herbert Low, of the *Sydney Morning Herald*. Stevens remembered a little Frenchman at the gathering singing 'The Marseillaise' which had an extraordinary effect on Lawson, but not nearly the same effect as Bertha had on her husband when he and Stevens stumbled along to her front door at 2 a.m.

Lawson's drinking wasn't the only problem that Bertha, now just twenty, faced. It was about this time that he met another twenty year old, Hannah Thornburn.

She was a 'plain, delicate girl',[65] about five feet four inches (163 centimetres) with grey eyes, reddish gold hair like her mother's, a fair complexion and lips that appeared to always be in a pout.[66]

She was thin, too, like a 'clinging vine',[67] and her ghostly image would haunt Lawson and Bertha for the rest of their lives.

Henry Lawson painted by
John Longstaff in Melbourne
in 1900. Jules Archibald,
who commissioned the
painting, was so impressed
he eventually instituted the
annual Archibald Prize.
Art Gallery of NSW

Lawson's grandfather Henry Albury, still
a big, imposing presence in 1895 aged 70.
State Library of NSW, FL9245508

Lawson's grandmother Harriet Albury
aged 60. *State Library of NSW, FL9245509*

The Lawson home at Eurunderee after additions had been built on. *State Library of NSW, FL9245590*

Lawson's parents, Louisa and Niels Larsen (aka Peter Lawson), after their marriage in 1866. *State Library of NSW, FL9245511*

Lawson always remembered his mother Louisa (pictured with her daughter Gertrude at the Henry Kendall memorial in 1882) as a cold, tough, woman. *State Library of NSW, FL9245514*

Henry Lawson at thirteen. *From T. D. Mutch, 'The Early Life of Henry Lawson', Royal Australian Historical Society Journal, Vol XVIII, Part VI, 1932.*

Louisa Lawson made *The Dawn* an important journal in the fight for women's rights and helped drive her young son's literary ambitions. *State Library of NSW, FL9245517*

Lawson photographed by John Baillie after arriving in Wellington, New Zealand late in 1893. *National Library of New Zealand, PAColl-8674*

Lawson's wife Bertha not long after their marriage. *State Library of NSW, FL3319439*

Bertha with the Lawson's new-born son Joseph Henry, who was known as 'Jim'. *Royal Australian Historical Society Journal, Vol LV, Part IV, 1969*

Jim Lawson as an infant. *State Library of NSW, FL3319368*

Lawson's daughter Bertha captured by artist Florence Rodway in 1915. *State Library of NSW, ML 956*

George Robertson
London, 1900

Above left: After a tough childhood in Scotland, George Robertson became a titan of Australian publishing, nurturing the talents of Lawson, Banjo Paterson and others. *State Library of NSW, FL3194942*

Above: Barta became a librarian and helped edit a collection of tributes to her father: *Henry Lawson by His Mates*. *State Library of NSW, FL3319459*

Left: Mary Gilmore, with son Billy, was an early flame, and a great supporter of Lawson throughout his life. *State Library of NSW, FL1113104*

Jules Archibald gave Lawson his start as a writer at *The Bulletin* and helped him throughout his life. *State Library of NSW, FL9245534*

Left: Jim Gordon (left) and Walter Jago, photographed in the 1920s. Gordon, who wrote as Jim Grahame, had an intensely close relationship with Lawson. Jago became the partner of Lawson's daughter Barta. *State Library of Victoria H28050/3b*

Above: Hannah Thornburn became the symbol of Lawson's ideal woman. *Colin Roderick Collection*

Above: Lawson on his small farm at Leeton, NSW in 1916. *State Library of NSW, FL9245536*

Left: Lawson as seen by artist David Low. *National Library of Australia, 8489660*

Lawson was photographed by Phillip Harris with children in North Sydney three weeks before Lawson's death. *State Library of NSW, FL214519*

Crowds line the Sydney streets for Lawson's funeral in 1922. *State Library of Victoria, H25847*

Chapter 15

So he sailed away from the Streets of Strife,
he travelled by land and sea,
In search of a people who lived a life as life in the world should be.

LAWSON ON TRYING TO BEAT THE BOOZE BY RESTARTING HIS LIFE AS
A COUNTRY SCHOOLTEACHER IN NEW ZEALAND[1]

A S LAWSON CONTINUED to make the social rounds of
Sydney without regard to his young wife, he made many
new friends and admirers including Nelson Illingworth,[2] a long-
haired, poncho-wearing sculptor. 'Buster' Illingworth, then
in his mid-thirties, was the son a Portsmouth plasterer and had
been in Australia for five years. One of his young models was
the curvaceous Rose Soady,[3] whose nude form in the paintings
of her future husband, Norman Lindsay, scandalised conservative
Australia. Rose remembered that Illingworth had a studio in a
lane behind a draper's shop on Brickfield Hill, not far from
Lawson's home in Regent Street.[4] The artist's studio 'was an
indescribable muddle of benches covered with clay, plaster-of-
Paris moulds and wet rags, from which Nelson would rise in a
white smock, beaming and tossing his great mane of hair'. He
was a stocky little man with an enormous head, which he shook
and tossed like a dog gnawing a bone all the time he worked. He
sculpted a nude of Rose, kneeling and looking to the heavens, and
she often stole a side glance at Mrs Illingworth when she brought
her knitting and sat through the afternoon.[5]

English-born Hannah Forrester Thornburn[6] may have been another of Illingworth's models and a reason for Lawson to spend even more time at the studio. Lawson gave a clue to this when he wrote a poem about Hannah and a 'sculptor friend' brushing the clay from the hem of her skirt,[7] though the incident may just have been a poetic image in Lawson's imagination. Bert Stevens remembered Hannah as nothing special to look at but said she was 'a romantic' and believed that 'a poet of any kind would appeal to her and Lawson – *the* Australian poet – was regarded with something like worshipful admiration'.[8]

Hannah's father John Thornburn had listed his occupation in England as a visiting Methodist minister, though Stevens called him 'a weak-natured man who drank and was often out of employment'.[9] The Thornburn family's first Australian home was in Melbourne but for two years from 1887 John Thornburn was a book importer and travelling salesman based at 62 Church Street, Balmain, before returning to Victoria. The Thornburns came back to Balmain in 1896, when Hannah was nineteen and Lawson was chafing at the periods of enforced temperance under Bertha's direction.

Just as there was in the Lawson home in Regent Street, Redfern, there was apparently a degree of marital friction between John Thornburn and his wife Betsy over his drinking.

Hannah taught Sunday school at the Balmain Congregational Church and became the family breadwinner as a bookkeeper and clerk at W. Ford's Memorial Engraving Company at 142 King Street.

Stevens said that like her poetic hero, Hannah also had a way with words and 'supplied the flattery and encouragement'[10] that Lawson was no longer getting from a disappointed wife. Lawson would later write that 'in the soul-striving days', Hannah came only 'to comfort and praise' and was 'the love of my life'.[11] She often spoke about Lawson to her friend Winifred Holford, defending him against Winifred's literary criticism, but she never revealed any relationship with the writer except an admiration for his work, and she never ever mentioned being a model for

Lawson with sculptor Nelson 'Buster' Illingworth in 1904. Photograph by Henry C. Drinkwater & Co. State Library of NSW, FL3313023

Illingworth. No matter how she and Lawson met, though, Hannah would become a model for Lawson's characters and would have a lifelong effect on his imagination and his heart.

'Sister Hannah' would soon feature in 'That Pretty Girl in the Army', 'a little girl, nineteen or twenty ... the prettiest girl I ever saw in the Army, and one of the prettiest I've ever seen out of it. She had the features of an angel, but her expression was wonderfully human, sweet and sympathetic. Her big grey eyes were sad with sympathy for sufferers and sinners, and her poke bonnet was full of bunchy, red–gold hair.'[12]

Hannah eventually became 'Ruth' in the poem and play of that name, and in the prose version, 'The Hero of Redclay'.[13]

When Lawson transposed Hannah into the Salvation Army at Bourke for 'That Pretty Girl in the Army', he made reference to her religious convictions, noting that 'The Pretty Girl was discussed from psychological points of view ... Religious mania was sexual passion dammed out of its course. Therefore he held that morbidly religious girls were the most easily seduced.'[14] Perhaps Bertha feared the same. Lawson's carousing was out of control, so she somehow found the money for two fares to New Zealand, where she hoped she could keep him away from his drinking friends and leave him 'free to write'.[15] She also procured a letter of introduction for her husband from Jules Archibald to the New Zealand premier Richard Seddon.

LAWSON AND BERTHA left Sydney on 31 March 1897 aboard the *Anglian*, which carried twenty-nine passengers in saloon, twenty-six including the Lawsons in steerage, as well as a load of timber, brandy and foodstuffs.

Lawson seethed about being taken away from the things he loved in Sydney and later claimed that 'when desperately hard up and with a wife to provide for, I was obliged to seek the means of earning bread and butter from the Govt, of a province (M.L.) [Maoriland] in whose people's interests I had never written a line'.[16] Sighting three pinnacles off North Cape, he wrote the ballad 'The Three Kings' about a man returning gleefully to his native land. His mood worsened, though, when the *New Zealand Times* reported on the couple's arrival in Wellington on 9 April that 'Mr Lawson intends to remain in New Zealand for several years'.[17]

Lawson and Bertha had just 12 shillings and sixpence in their pockets when they set foot on New Zealand soil, and 6 shillings of that went to rent a furnished room that Tom Mills found for them in Buckle Street, where he was also living. Lawson sold 'The Three Kings' to Charles Wilson, the editor of the *New Zealand Mail*, who ran it on 15 April.[18] The Lawsons next called on Labour Secretary Edward Tregear, who had found Lawson a job on the telegraph line four years earlier. Because Premier Seddon was busy organising a trip to London, Lawson showed Tregear the letter of introduction from Archibald. Tregear told him that the Native School for Maori at Mangamaunu, a remote coastal village 130 kilometres north of Christchurch, was in desperate need of a teacher. Education Secretary William James Habens had doubts about Lawson's suitability because of his deafness but Tregear told him: 'I know Mr Lawson well. He is a distinguished literary man, well known all over Australia for his pen work.' Tregear noted that Lawson was married now 'to a nice little woman who has been a hospital nurse and has got him in hand well so that I hope he won't go "baresark" any more but will settle to steady work. He intends to write up New Zealand and I think it good for the colony for a man of such rare literary ability to come here.'[19]

Education Minister W.C. Walker approved the appointment and the Mangamaunu school, which had been closed for almost five months, was about to reopen with a deaf Australian teacher. Bertha would be the school's new sewing mistress. On 29 April, the *New Zealand Mail* ran pieces of Lawson prose – 'On a Good-tucker Track: An Australian Sketch' and 'Drift from a Wreck: A New Zealand Sketch', written from his observations during the last days of his linesman work above Kekerengu, when he saw a wooden slab in the shape of a tombstone marking the grave of an unknown passenger from the wreck of the *Taiaroa* in 1886, which claimed thirty-six lives. Lawson earned a few guineas for the sketches and with a 30-shillings advance on his wages for fares and cartage,[20] he and Bertha loaded a mattress, a few pots and pans, and a handful of groceries into two cement casks that Lawson planned to transform into a pair of chairs for their new home.[21]

On the evening of 4 May 1897, they boarded the small coastal steamer *Wakatu* for the 250-kilometre journey south-east, and at seven the next morning woke to see snow on distant mountains and the whaling settlement of Kaikoura coming into view, nestled under a steep bluff. From there they rode with their baggage eighteen kilometres north in a coach; the snow-covered Kaikouras behind them, and the vivid blue ocean breaking on the rugged, rocky shore to the east. They rode along a ridge overlooking the boulders on the bed of the Hapuku River and past its junction with the Puhi Puhi until, in the afternoon, they reached the tiny village that was to be their new home beside the wild sea. There were just a few small houses on the riverbank and some more on a high hill beside a weatherboard church built by Catholic missionaries, but now used by the Presbyterians, the denomination the local people had adopted. Beneath the hill in a neglected, overgrown paddock was a large schoolroom and residence – a small, three-room wooden cottage with a veranda, wood floor and brick chimney.

All the able-bodied men were away whaling but the villagers left behind, about fifty of them ranging from babes in arms, to beautiful young women with lustrous eyes, and old, tattooed warriors in their eighties, came out to greet the new schoolmaster and his wife. One carried a tray of steaming sweet potatoes, another a plate of wild pig,[22] the smell of which made Bertha sick.

Lawson had high hopes for this new experience among impoverished but noble Maori. In the patronising tone of the time, Bertha called them 'affectionate kind, loving people – quite Europeanized',[23] and Lawson hoped meeting new people in a new culture in majestic surrounds would curtail his drinking and inspire the next step in his creative ambitions that would lead to a life among the literati in London. Here he was, a famous though poor Australian writer with a field of dreams for new material and the chance to make his name writing about another country as well.

The Lawsons explained to the Maori that most of their furniture was coming later. To avoid prying eyes, Bertha made blinds from their red-and-white mattress cover and Lawson cut bracken to place the mattress on a high pile of fern. They camped like that for days inside the cottage, cooking with a frypan and billy can.

Lawson opened the school the morning after he arrived; nine children attended the first day and eleven the next and soon there were fourteen. Having been without a teacher for so long they were 'backward' in their education. Lawson requested leave to gather enough firewood to last him and Bertha through a snowy winter, but instead the department sent him a pamphlet containing gardening tips after the local sheep had trampled all the vegetables.

Bertha had brought no supplies with her, thinking they would be staying in a town with stores, but she learned that a coach passed through Mangamaunu once a week on the run from Blenheim to Kaikoura, and she arranged for the coachman to deliver meat and provisions. Lawson made a corner wardrobe and two chairs from the cement casks and Bertha decorated the cottage with flax mats woven by the Maori and native flowers so that they eventually had 'quite a charming home'.[24] His story 'Water Them Geraniums' included a close description of the Mangamaunu home.[25]

As Mary Cameron took a break from teaching in Cosme to become Mrs Mary Gilmore, Lawson taught the children of Mangamaunu history, geography and drawing, and according to Bertha 'managed well in spite of his deafness'. Bertha taught them reading, arithmetic and sewing. Even in the depths of winter the children only had thin clothes, cheap flannelette and cotton, and rotten, sodden shoes. They could never pronounce 'Lawson' and instead called him a name that sounded like 'Mr Lawrence'.[26]

When school was over at four o'clock, Lawson and Bertha would wander into the forests and Lawson, 'a wonderful shot' with an old muzzle-loader, would bag a rabbit or two for dinner, since Bertha still could not stomach the wild pork. Sometimes they gathered large clams together, and on weekends fished for hours, usually without much success, but when they caught something, they grilled it on the rocks. When they didn't, they buried potatoes in the hot ashes and ate those instead. Bertha boiled watercress from the nearby creek.

She wrote that Lawson was 'thoroughly contented' in his remote home and that the pair of them were 'like two children in a Garden of Eden'.[27] But not for long.

Soon, Bertha complained that the village's 'Christian religion was a convenient outside show' and that the Maori still made people taboo (tapu). One woman became desperately ill after being cursed, and when Bertha nursed her and sent for a doctor in Kaikoura, 'I myself was taboo for entering her house'.[28] There were no children at school the next day and Lawson threatened to send for the police if the students did not return within the hour. He started ringing the school bell like he was trying to throttle it and presently the students came scampering down the hill.

Hardly anyone ever visited Mangamaunu except the local Presbyterian minister who came to preach in the church. One young farmer occasionally walked eight kilometres to the school to recite his own poetry to the Australian writer. He could never understand why no one would publish the verses but Lawson and Bertha knew exactly why.

After only a few weeks, Lawson was only putting up with Mangamaunu because he planned to use his circumstances for a book called *The Native School*. He felt that the isolation and cultural differences, and the lack of alcohol, was suffocating him. Lawson told Hugh Maccallum that his encouraging letters lifted him when 'I feel inclined to brood over mine own old folly … which only happens now on rainy days and in hours of enforced idleness [and which], increases the magnitude and the blackness of the world's apparent ingratitude and treachery towards myself to such an extent that I feel like a danger to vested interests and a menace to society at large'.[29]

Perhaps he missed Hannah Thornburn. In Lawson's story 'The Ghosts of Many Christmases'[30] he wrote of the wreck of the *Tasmania* off Table Cape, New Zealand, on 29 July 1897 and 'a letter from a sweetheart of mine amongst her mails when she went down'.[31]

There were stories about Lawson borrowing a white horse behind Bertha's back and riding into Kaikoura for drinking binges.[32] In an effort to thwart him – since there were still 'hard-drinking old whalers and shepherds' in town – Bertha told the Maori that her husband was a rich man and that they should drive hard bargains with him. From then, the Maori wanted £1 to rent a horse or £3 to rent a buggy. Lawson would come storming into the little house, swearing to Bertha about the greediness of the locals.[33]

MANGAMAUNU WAS FAR more remote and primitive than Lawson expected, but in the bustle of London, publishers Simpkin, Marshall and Co were securing the British rights to *While the Billy Boils*. It was not a huge publishing house, but it was a start for Lawson in the British market where he had always wanted to make his name. More influential publishers from Scotland, William Blackwood and Sons, and W. and R. Chambers, had also shown interest in his work, with Blackwood offering two guineas – about a week's average wage in Australia – per thousand words, and Chambers's editor saying they would welcome more short stories for *Chambers's Edinburgh Journal*, so long as they were as good as the ones in *Billy Boils* and did not deal with 'questionable subjects' as they produced a 'family magazine'.[34]

On 24 July 1897, the *Town and Country Journal* was one of many Australian publications to report on the glowing review for *Billy Boils* and comparisons with Kipling in the London *Spectator*, a review which was actually written by the book's editor Arthur Jose. The review called Lawson 'the greatest Australian writer ... biting into the very heart of the bushman's life, ruthless in truth. ... Mr. Lawson is a less experienced writer than Mr. Kipling ... but there are two or three sketches in this volume which for vigour and truth can hold their own with even so great a rival ... Here you get Australia, actual Australia, seen and put down as it is, and not as it is imagined.'[35]

Under the headline 'An Australian Humorist', the British literary review *Academy* compared Lawson's writing to Bret Harte's, but said that while both men were 'concerned with rough and ready pioneers ... the Californian writer thinks of the story before everything else, the Australian, of the human document'.[36]

LAWSON KNEW THAT BERTHA was 'a gem from the first' and he said their time together in New Zealand proved he was right in his first assessment of her as he was 'in most other things where drink did not madden my instinct'.[37]

He told Hugh Maccallum that Bertha was 'a favourite everywhere and worshipped here'. Being a good husband, he said, would 'show some of my kind relatives (who never assisted me or thought of me except perhaps as a soft idiotic fool to get money and work out of) who advised Bertha against me from the first, and kindly told her all my worst points – whilst, on the other hand, and in common with one or two good but mistaken friends, they persuaded me against being "trapped" and ruining my prospects when "I might marry money"'.[38]

Lawson spent a lot of time in his cottage writing and found the characters in Mangamaunu fascinating, especially one of his older pupils, Mary Jacob. Bertha reckoned Mary to be about thirteen or fourteen, 'always brooding alone ... wretchedly miserable'. The other children were afraid to play with Mary, Bertha said, because she was 'too cranky'.[39]

Lawson described Mary as sixteen, 'a pure-blooded aborigine – if there ever was one – of the heavy negro type, whose father killed her mother eleven years ago (fit of jealousy) and on whose family (three or four sisters) there seems to be a brooding cloud. This girl, they say, would take to the bush, if the last teacher punished her, and climb a tree and sit there and brood for hours – for days, if they didn't find her and get her home.' Mary's father had just been released from prison after eleven years but she had cut out a picture of another father figure, the Russian Czar, from an old copy of the *Illustrated London News* and pasted it on the wall of the home where she lived with an aunt. She told Bertha she loved the man in the picture and Lawson told Hugh Maccallum he could use that idea for a 'psychological sketch'.

Mary Jacob was, in fact, born Mere Ratima in Mangamaunu in 1876, making her nearly twenty-one when she met Lawson and Bertha. When Mary was seven, her father had killed her mother by stabbing her in the neck. The previous week the local Maori council had met to consider a charge of adultery involving Mary's mother and her father's brother. The father was found guilty of murder and though sentenced to hang, the sentence was commuted to life in prison.[40]

Mary grew attached to Bertha. Lawson said she followed his wife 'like a dog' and Bertha would take her into the Lawsons' cottage after school and give her cups of tea. Half in her own language and half in English, Mary told Bertha she would like to stay with her. Bertha asked Mary's aunt if that would be all right, and she had no objection. So Mary moved in. Then the Lawson groceries shipped from Wellington started to disappear. Mary said it was passing swagmen. Bertha suspected it was Mary, and told her she would have to go home. She was sure that Mary's aunt received the stolen goods and that was why she allowed Mary to stay in the first place.[41]

BERTHA AND LAWSON BEGAN to talk seriously about leaving Mangamaunu, and once Bertha discovered she was pregnant they made up their minds. There was 'no hope of proper nursing or medical aid' there and Lawson would not hear of Bertha going alone to Wellington and then bringing back the baby.[42]

Lawson's 'psychological sketch' of Mary Jacob instead became a rage against romanticism, a racist rant about poets putting idealism in front of reality.

In Mangamaunu, he had taken up the challenge of observing and interpreting a different culture, but instead chose to judge them by the values of the people who had dispossessed them. As a result, Lawson succumbed to bitterness and hostility when the values of his own culture were offended, referring to his students as 'the young heathen'.[43] His marriage was again under strain, his confidence was severely shaken and he took out his frustrations on the Maori and sentimental poets.

In 'A Daughter of Maoriland',[44] Mary Jacob became the character 'August' because that was the month in which he composed the sketch for the *Antipodean* magazine, which was edited by Banjo Paterson and George Essex Evans. His story centred on an altruistic new teacher – 'green, soft, and poetical' with 'a literary ambition'[45] – who arrives at a Maori school and takes pity on a lonely and apparently ill-treated pupil. He then discovers that his kindness has been exploited by the pupil and her relatives. Finally, he gives up his altruism and is at last respected for telling it like it really is.

Lawson had taken pride in his promotion of a human brotherhood but now he called the Maori girl a 'savage' and likened her in different passages to a cow, pig and dog. She brought a 'native smell' into the teacher's house, he wrote, and was 'fat, and lazy, and dirty'.[46]

Though he toned the sketch down for future versions, Lawson's original tale in *The Antipodean* finished with the warning to other writers: 'We rush off in imagination to coral isles and other places, and make heroes out of greasy, brown, loafing brutes, for no other reason, apparently, than that their fathers were even greasier and more brutal than their children, while thousands of brave, self-sacrificing white heroes, weeds for the most part, but heroic weeds, live, fight and die unnoticed in our own cities and bush, all the year round.'[47]

He said he hoped the sketch would do something towards 'knocking sentimental rot out of current literature'.[48] All it really did, though, was leave a stain on his reputation for future generations.

The moral of his story was that 'romanticism' was 'bosh' and it was useless to extend mateship to a people who didn't recognise the same values; his brotherhood of man, in fact, was a closed shop to anyone who didn't look like him or think like him, a point he hammered home again in 'The Writer's Dream' for *The Bulletin*,[49] when he wrote that he had woken up to all that idealistic 'nonsense'.[50]

He made light of his situation to Jack Brereton, with whom he was now back on good terms, in the poem 'Written Afterwards' in which he referenced entertaining Mary Jacob's aunt for the sake 'of a true little wife', but Lawson's 'The Ports of the Open Sea',[51] with all its fearful imagery of nature cursing his village, was a cry for help to escape from his desperate situation. 'The Jolly Dead March'[52] signalled the demise of this chapter of his life.

In 'The Lights of Cobb and Co'[53] and 'The Old Mile-Tree'[54] Lawson began to look back nostalgically on a life that he had never really known, fantasising about the glories of yesteryear in contrast to the mental pain he was feeling, with the approach of fatherhood and in an alien environment far from his drinking buddies in Sydney.

On 15 September 1897, with Bertha four months pregnant, he reported to the education department secretary William Habens that attendance at the school was down to seven or eight and not likely to improve. Four days later he wrote to Aunt Emma, to say that he and Bertha were getting out of Mangamaunu the next week and sailing back to Wellington. If he didn't get a good 'billet' there, he said, 'and the doctor thinks it's safe, I'll run across to Sydney'. He said work was pouring in from England.[55]

Archibald informed his readers, with all *The Bulletin*'s prejudices, that the Lawsons found Mangamaunu 'too unutterably lonely: there is neither butcher nor baker, and white faces are seen about once a month'.[56]

As they were preparing to leave their remote posting, Lawson and Bertha were stunned by the appearance of Aunt Emma, who had arrived in Wellington on 12 October and then made her way south as a surprise visit. Lawson was not in a good mood and swore when he saw Emma's buggy in the distance. That made Bertha laugh. Emma's announcement that she intended to stay for three months so overcame Lawson that he became speechless. However, he enjoyed her company, even though Emma told him 'fifty times a day' that he should be shot for taking Bertha to such a lonely place.[57]

Lawson, Bertha and Aunt Emma packed up their things and despite protests from the local chief, Pene Tahui, about the fate of the children, they took a coach ride to Kaikoura, where, on 6 November 1897, they climbed aboard a small, flat-bottomed coal and timber transport that was on its way to Wellington.

Thirteen years after that short voyage Lawson was contacted by Mrs Mary Moss, who had taken over the Mangamaunu school, and with a completely different mindset told him of the tiny garden 'now gay with flowers', the gorgeous sunsets and the mountains covered with snow. There had been forty recent earthquakes in the area, though, and ten children had lately died from consumption. The people of Mangamaunu had not forgotten Lawson and spoke of him often.[58] Lawson replied that he was 'sorry and ashamed' that he had left 'the poor little people' of Mangamaunu in rather 'a bitter mood'.[59]

WITH THE ENGLISH INTEREST IN HIS BOOK, Lawson wanted nothing more than to base his career in London, but for the time being he was stuck in Wellington with no money and no job. He found lodgings at Tom Mills's house and almost immediately Mills wrote a notice for the *Evening Post* that Lawson was in town after his stint as a country schoolteacher and that 'Maoriland will yield a rich harvest to one of Australia's most popular authors, and consequently New Zealand will reap a good advertisement ... by today's mail he received word from Mr A. P. Watt (who is Rudyard Kipling's literary agent) that Messrs. Methuen & Co., the English publishers, are anxious to secure the complete (English and colonial) rights of Mr Lawson's new book'.[60] Despite the optimistic tone, though, Lawson could still see the dark on the lightest of days, and later admitted that a 'paltry quarrel' broke out while staying with Mills because Lawson was 'worried and irritable and over-sensitive on account of my financial position, and quick to take offence at what I considered a slight'.[61]

Hugh Maccallum sent Lawson a telegram on 13 November asking if Angus & Robertson might see material for a new Lawson book, but Lawson was now playing hard to get, especially after the interest from Methuen, Kipling's publishers. He was not ready to make 'definite arrangements', he said. Scottish and English publishers wanted another book like *Billy Boils* and he wasn't sure whether to run his Maori series through an Australian or English journal first before publishing it in book form. Methuen and the others wanted English and colonial rights but if a deal with Angus & Robertson could be done for local rights, Lawson said he'd consider £150 plus royalties. Maybe, he suggested, A&R might like another book of poetry because he'd written a dozen or so poems lately and felt they were superior to those of *When the World Was Wide*.[62] He told Maccallum in a following letter that 'the chaps in the Govnt Buildings are looking up some temporary employment for me', though it appears that apart from a vague suggestion of more teaching work around Auckland, they didn't try too hard. In a sign that Lawson's ego was veering out of control, he told Maccallum from his high horse that he was not prepared to 'sacrifice' any more of his prose work in Australia.[63]

He and the now heavily pregnant Bertha moved into a room in a boarding house at 14 College Street, Wellington. Lawson had started writing a play for Bland Holt after the Australian actor advanced him £35. He called it *Ruth* and it was based on Lawson's idea for the story 'The Hero of Redclay'. Holt had arrived in Wellington in mid-November for a month-long season of his stirring war melodrama *For England* at the local opera house.

There was real-life drama on 8 December when an earthquake shook the Shaky Isles all the way from Auckland to Christchurch,[64] and in Wellington it devastated the reclamation area where Lawson had once slept in the water pipes. Aunt Emma headed home to North Sydney the next day, and after seeing her off at the dock, Lawson returned to Bertha 'with a broad, happy smile on his face'.[65] The fact Aunt Emma hardly featured in Lawson's life again suggests there was more than unstable earth rocking the once-solid relationship between the pair.

Bertha recalled the earthquake as 'a terrifying experience' but said she was fortunate because her kindly landlady at College Street 'proved herself a clever nurse and cared for me in a very motherly fashion'.[66]

Still, Bertha had 'a terrible time' delivering her son Jim on 10 February 1898.

Six days later Lawson wrote to Bertha's mother in Castlereagh Street to report the happy news and the ordeal that had preceded it. Mother and child were now 'doing well', Lawson said.

> It is a boy and a real little Bredt, as far as I can see. He is fat and healthy and very quiet now – does nothing but drink and sleep.
>
> To-day is a very anxious day for me on account of some work I have done for Bland Holt, and which must be decided about this afternoon, after the Sydney mail goes.
>
> Will write next week and let you know when we will be over. Remember me to Mac, Hilda and all.
>
> Love from Bertha.
>
> Your affectionate son
Harry.[67]

Chapter 16

*Seems to me that a good many men want to make angels of their
wives without first taking trouble of making saints of themselves. ...
Some men want to be considered gods in their own homes; you'll
generally find that sort of men very small potatoes outside.*

LAWSON, ON THE WAR OF THE SEXES[1]

BLAND HOLT'S EYES ALMOST BLED when he read
Lawson's convoluted, meandering muddle *Ruth* which he
would soon rename as *Pinter's Son Jim*. The actor was hoping
Lawson would pen a ripping drama that would make his audience
laugh, cry and cheer at the closing curtain. But instead of a
pulse-quickening thriller that tugged at the heartstrings, it was
an unworkable farce. Lawson presented Holt with four exercise
books – one for each handwritten act of the play – but the Poet
of the People, no stranger to the stage as a fan, had no idea about
writing for the theatre.

Holt estimated that Act One would take four hours to stage
and by the time he finished reading the first exercise book, he
must have been wishing that all the characters of this meandering
melodrama would just die and never be heard of again: Jim
Poynton, Pinter's son, 'a wild Colonial youth'; Ruth Wilson, 'a
girl as God made her'; Jack Drew, the editor of the *Cambaroora
Star*, 'clever but he drinks'; Dr Lebinski, his friend, a Pole and
'a black sheep'; Pinter: 'An Old Mate of our Father'; and the
optimistic Jack Mitchell, 'A Bush Micawber'.[2]

After ten hours of trying to get his head around Lawson's mess and still nowhere near the closing curtain, Holt's mind was spinning.

Lawson had spent three months working on what he thought was his masterpiece, but Holt told him it would take three weeks to watch just one performance.[3]

Lawson's story centred on a love affair between the saintly Ruth Wilson and the wayward journalist Jack Drew, whose hard drinking had seen him demoted from editor of the *Boomerang* to the lowly *Cambaroora Star*.

The set changes were impossible given the limitations of the stage in the 1890s and included, in Lawson's words:

Dusty main street of Cambaroora with Mitchell painting a weatherboard cottage in foreground, ragged blue-gum in middle of street, with the Royal Hotel in background.
Corner of King and another street in Sydney, Mitchell and Nipper selling newspapers.
The bank of Sheoak Creek.
Machine shearing shed in full operation.
The Great Plains at drought time with dry tank in foreground.
Bar of Overland Hotel.[4]

And in potentially dramatic scenes that required an economy of dialogue, Lawson wrote long unwieldy soliloquies such as near the finale when Jack Drew and Jim Poynton stagger through the desert; Jack blind, and both men dying of thirst. Instead of collapsing as his perilous, parched condition would suggest, Jack instead stumbles to centre stage and launches into a long and eloquent socialist tirade full of power and passion about the working man staggering through 'the roofs of hell' so that rich men can pay their wives' dressmakers in Paris.[5]

Holt thought the whole thing was gobbledygook. He told Lawson as politely as he could that it would require major surgery to ever have a life on the stage.

Actor and producer Bland Holt was a constant source of funds for the cash-strapped Lawson. State Library of Victoria, H2008.130/123

'But,' Bertha said, 'Henry would not hear of it being shortened or altered, so Bland Holt good humouredly handed it back to him.'[6]

The play would take almost a century to reach the stage in country New South Wales,[7] and while Lawson bristled at the rejection, he salvaged a feast of short stories from the wreckage including 'Out on the Roofs of Hell',[8] 'The Hero of Redclay',[9] 'Send Round the Hat',[10] 'The Blindness of One-eyed Bogan'[11] and 'Wanted by the Police'.[12]

He now complained that the bureaucrats in Wellington were a 'narrow, paltry-minded dog in the manger lot'[13] as there appeared to be no government work for him. While Lawson had been in New Zealand, *When the World Was Wide* had passed overall sales of 6000 copies, earning Lawson about £140 to date at a time when smart double-fronted brick cottages close to transport in the Sydney suburb of Leichhardt were going for £380.[14]

With his latest royalty cheque for £30, Lawson bought saloon passages to Sydney, informing the *Times* of his decision to both go, and to write a book about his most recent experiences in New Zealand over what was almost a year.[15] Lawson, Bertha and baby Jim set sail on the 2000-ton *Tarawera* for Sydney on 12 March 1898. Lawson had suffered many disappointments in New Zealand but the birth of his son more than made up for that, and he always retained a fondness for the country. He wrote the poem 'Sydney-Side'[16] on board, about his longing to see Bondi and Coogee, Woollahra and Balmain. Soon, though, writing for his character Mitchell, he ventured the opinion that when it came time to die, he'd prefer 'a cold place – where there's a glimpse of distant snow on the ranges across the tussock and black fern hills – where the mountain rivers run all Summer – down yonder – in – in Maoriland'.[17]

THE LAWSONS ARRIVED IN SYDNEY on 17 March and moved into rented accommodation at 1 Regent St, Newtown, next to Mrs Schaebel, who could help Bertha with Jim, since he was a difficult baby.

Lawson was now sporting a red beard and when Bert Stevens met him and Bertha in King Street a couple of days later, Lawson was carrying their child. Stevens guessed that the nickname 'Jim' was in honour of the 'Jims of the Bush' Lawson had written about.[18] For some time after Lawson's return to Sydney, Stevens wrote, 'he seemed fairly steady and sober', but despite the royalty cheques, his money was quickly evaporating without regular work, and he set off to find a steady income.

Lawson called in to *The Bulletin* office to keep that payment stream open. William Macleod, the business manager, was a close friend of the government statistician Timothy Coghlan, and Lawson landed a rort in that office making 10 shillings a day from 1 April to 30 June.[19]

Bertha recalled that 'Harry was to go to the office every morning at nine o'clock and leave at half-past four', but what he did in between those times was up to him.[20] Lawson was apparently free to write throughout his shift and before long was signing on at nine-thirty, with a humorous quip about a member of staff, before ducking out for the day and only returning for the four-thirty sign-off.

He wrote to George Robertson to tell him he had conquered the bottle and that there was 'no reason nor sense in letting the past or personal motives stand in the way of our material interests'.[21] He was hoping for some news about an English edition of *Billy Boils*, and was told that Simpkin & Marshall was publishing it there. He pitched a second book of verse for Robertson, full of sea sketches and outback ballads, and suggested that a third volume, chosen from the best of the two Australian books, might sell in England.[22]

Angus & Robertson sent Lawson a note pinned to a letter in which William Blackwood regretted that Robertson had declined his offer to publish *Billy Boils* and again asking for Lawson stories for his magazine. Lawson was angry, demanding to know why Blackwood's offer had been rejected in favour of a lesser publishing house and told Robertson he obviously did not know the publishing business.

Hugh Maccallum replied, telling Lawson that he wished for 'friendly business relations' and explaining that Robertson actually did know the publishing business very well. Methuen had made an offer after seeing the first edition of *Billy Boils* and Robertson had accepted before Blackwood's offer arrived. But the paper used in printing the first edition could not be obtained for the second, and when Methuen saw the inferior appearance of the shipment sent to them, withdrew the offer. That's when Robertson signed with Simpkin & Marshall.[23]

Lawson tried to keep busy writing, but even the discipline of having to sign on and sign off at a job that offered him the easiest of money played havoc with his moods and manic depression. The destruction of the Spanish fleet by the American China Squadron prompted him to write 'The Dons of Spain' in defence of the losers.[24] He started drinking again, and perhaps as a plea for redemption penned 'The Christ of the "Never"'[25] at around the same time as 'Out on the Roofs of Hell', which mirrored his personal despair.[26]

Lawson told Ted Brady, now living in Stanmore, that he had thoughts of suicide. He had become murder to live with as well, and Bertha was bearing the brunt.

Brady ventured to Lawson's Newtown home to reason with him on Bertha's behalf after a domestic incident.

'I found him in the front room, whither he had conveyed the mattress. He had made himself comfortable with a book, a candle, and a bottle of beer. When I ventured to enquire the reason for his queer behaviour, he informed me that he had been suffering untold restraint in an office, and wanted to feel that he was back in the bush again. I may say that greatly as I loved him, my sympathies were and have very much remained with his wife.'[27]

Bertha and the baby often went without necessities. Lawson was in charge of paying the rent but to him, drinking money came first and as a result at the end of June a stranger knocked at Bertha's door in Newtown, walked in, sat down in an easy chair and said he would wait for Lawson as he had plenty of time.

'When he explained that he was a bailiff, put in on account of the rent,' Bertha recalled, 'I was very distressed. Harry came home, sat down and had a yarn to him, took him out to have a drink, and I don't know what he ever did with him but he never came back.'[28] Still, the circumstances for mother and child remained dire and in the second week of July, Bertha's sister Hilda and her husband Jack Lang invited the Lawsons to stay at their house at 20 Dulwich Street, Dulwich Hill.

Living with Lawson was an eye-opener for the 22-year-old Lang, then a junior office assistant for an accounting practice.

Lang remembered that his wayward brother-in-law, now thirty-one, would 'go into the city and collect a few shillings at *The Bulletin* or get an advance from Angus & Robertson against future royalties. He would then forget all about writing, and start shouting for anyone who happened to come along. On one occasion he came home in a shocking condition. If he had been drinking spirits, he would become belligerent. If he had been on beer, he was morose and sentimental. On this occasion, it had been brandy. So we locked him in a room with a table and chair, and a candle.' Next morning Lawson emerged triumphant, Lang recalled. 'They always say that genius is erratic; well, Harry was a genius.'[29] As Lawson sobered up in his temporary prison, he completed the 2200-word short story for *The Bulletin* 'They Wait on the Wharf in Black'.[30]

It was the tale of a battler, working on the Western Australian diggings for two years for the sake of his family back east, and learning through the cold, hard, merciless words of a telegram that his wife had died suddenly 2000 miles away.

'Mor'n 20 year she stuck to me and struggled along by my side,' he tells his mates. 'She never give in. I'll swear she was on her feet till the last, with her sleeves tucked up – bustlin' round . . . And just when things was brightening and I saw a chance of giving her a bit of a rest and comfort for the end of her life. ... And she was dead and in her grave and I never knowed it.'[31]

'The world is damned rough on a man some times,' says Mitchell, one of the man's mates, 'most especially when he least deserves it.'[32]

Lang said the development of the story had also involved a Friday afternoon when Lawson had been drinking with friends and was very much the worse for wear. Lang had promised Bertha he would bring him home and had hailed a hansom cab.

'As we were travelling along George Street West,' Lang recalled, 'Harry decided that the driver was too slow. So he started to let him have it in good ripe Australian bush oaths. He became louder and louder. The driver pulled in at St Benedict's [on Broadway] and said he wouldn't go any further.' Lang was in 'a real quandary' but finally took out a 'huge bandanna handkerchief and gagged Harry for the rest of the journey. On arrival at Dulwich Hill he was completely helpless. We thought he was dead. He was only dead drunk.'[33]

George Robertson, who had warned Bertha she was marrying trouble, did his best to help her too, sending Lawson a bonus of

£22 6s 4d, which so impressed Lawson that he suggested another volume of short stories, even though not long before he had scoffed that he would no longer sacrifice his work in Australia. Banjo Paterson, who had now sold more than 25,000 copies of *The Man from Snowy River*, again acted as Lawson's solicitor and on 1 September 1898 Lawson received a £30 advance with another £20 to be paid upon publication. Most of the stories had already appeared in Australian publications but Lawson was also contracted to receive 4 guineas for each of six new stories as well as £25 for 'The Australian Cinematograph'.

The extra money only increased Lawson's drinking budget.

IN SEPTEMBER 1898, Lawson met the forty-year-old Irish-born poet Victor Daley, who had relocated to Sydney from Melbourne after the release of his book *At Dawn and Dusk*, which Angus & Robertson had published in July. Daley had been in Australia for twenty years and worked as a journalist and part-time poet, with his most notable contributions, before his own book, having been to Archibald's *A Golden Shanty* in 1890, which also introduced many Australian readers to the works of Lawson and 'The Banjo'.

Daley was being promoted as one of Australia's finest writers, with a lyrical, Celtic outlook and imagery as an alternative to the Australian tinge of Lawson, Paterson and the emerging Will Ogilvie, the Scottish-born stockman and drover whose book *Fair Girls and Gray Horses* was about to be published by *The Bulletin*.

Alfred Stephens recalled that Daley was a man of 'medium height, with a large head set on rather heavy shoulders. ... the eyes large, soft and dark in colour; the nose strong, the mouth and chin week. His hair and beard were brown, inclining to reddish.'[34]

The first week of Daley's stay in Sydney was spent on the yacht *Vesta* with Tom Durkin, a *Bulletin* artist, and Joe Brown, a theatrical agent.[35]

Daley was a man of considerable Irish charm and when Lawson was invited to join him and his friends on the *Vesta* 'he stayed there several days and returned home in a parlous state'.[36]

Not long after, Lawson and Daley as part of a 'representative push' headed out to a house at 51 Glenmore Road, Paddington, where Bert Stevens was living with his mother. He, Lawson and Daley had become drinking buddies, often going about town together after lunch at Chinnery's Fish Shop in Hunter Street. The group had heard Stevens was desperately ill but Lawson and friends found him 'alive and decidedly cheerful about it'.[37] With Lawson and Daley was 'Fred Broomfield, of the *Bulletin*, with fierce, pointed, dark moustache and beard, after the fashion of his beloved D'Artagnan of "The Three Musketeers"';[38] and Jim Philp,[39] a Scottish-born Australian journalist who had started his writing career in New Zealand covering the Maori Wars and who had founded Sydney's *Chinese Herald* in 1888 before joining the *Brisbane Courier*.[40]

Only a short time before, Stevens had been at Broomfield's home on the corner of Ice Road and Barcom Avenue, Darlinghurst, near St Vincent's Hospital, to form the Dawn and Dusk Club, named after Daley's new book.

The foundation members were Broomfield, Stevens, Philp, the journalist Herbert Low, William Bede Melville, a reporter for the Sydney newspaper *The Star*; Angus Sinclair, another writer; and Randolph Bedford, a former swagman and journalist, who having started his mining and literary journal, the *Clarion*, would eventually pursue other careers as a prospector, politician and novelist.

Daley was elected the club's 'symposiarch', or toastmaster, and Lawson one of the seven 'heptarchs', along with Philp, Stevens, Buster Illingworth, the artist Frank Mahony, journalist Con Lindsay, and George Augustine Taylor, who manufactured plaster, edited a journal called the *Builder*, and who, a decade later, would become the first man in Australia to fly a heavier-than-air craft when he piloted a glider off sandhills at Narrabeen, on Sydney's northern beaches.[41]

Philp drafted the club rules in Chinese, but since no one else could read them, Broomfield suspected they might have been an advertisement for garden seeds from the *Chinese Herald*. Lawson came up with the club's motto – to 'roost high and crow low'. Most of the members were broke but if they had money, they pooled whatever they could for a round of drinks and a free counter lunch.[42] It was a 'French menu and wine when the going was good, biscuits and beer' when it wasn't.[43]

The artist Tom Roberts sometimes joined the Duskers as did the future premier William Holman, but Jack Brereton wanted no part of the club, believing it was formed to facilitate drinking rather than intellectual discourse, and suspected it was named, not for Daley's book, but 'from its practice of meeting at dusk and parting at dawn'.[44]

Before long, Bertha felt the same. While she was left holding the baby, Lawson spent less and less time with her at the Langs' Dulwich Hill house, preferring moonlight trips to Manly with the Duskers and weekend trips to Gosford. Bert Stevens usually made up the shortage in the fares.[45]

One week, Lawson, Stevens, Daley, Illingworth and Philp headed to Gosford for a bout of revelry. Stevens, who was still working as a law clerk, also wrote for the *Gosford Times*, and convinced the publisher to provide them with a boat to explore Narara Creek and Fagan's Cottage, where Henry Kendall had lived. They all visited a dancing hall too, 'and became very merry … romping about the streets'.[46] Bertha said Lawson 'loved Victor Daley, and until Victor died they were the closest and dearest of friends'.[47]

Though Lawson had periods of melancholy, Broomfield remembered him at the time as having 'humour, quaint and twisted, and a rare gift of assuming a mask of quizzical ignorance in furtherance of a jest … Henry Lawson, at this period of his career, was no solitary and unhappy misanthrope … but he joyously took his place and his part among his fellows.'[48]

Lawson and Bertha clashed over his behaviour. She later described him as 'above all things, loyal, compassionate, warm-hearted and deeply sincere' and always 'greatly troubled by their marital difficulties'.[49] But he was also constantly drunk. By her family's admission, Bertha could be kind, loving, charming and enchanting but when the mood struck, domineering, volatile and bad-tempered.[50] The situation was not helped by the fact Lawson maintained contact with Hannah Thornburn after his return from New Zealand and in 1899 gave her signed copies of his two books as Christmas presents. Whatever the nature of their relationship, Lawson had started to idealise and idolise Hannah, imagining in his mind's eye what it was like to have a true soulmate. He also enjoyed the company of another woman he met at Buster Illingworth's studio and years later he wrote of her in the short story 'Lily of St Leonards'.[51]

In reply to an article by Daley in *The Bulletin* on the battle of the sexes, Lawson penned 'Joe Tries His Hand at a Sex-Problem Story',[52] which ran, not in *The Bulletin* but oddly in the Wool-growers' Co-operative Society journal, *Co-operator*, which was edited by Ada Kidgell, soon to marry William Holman. Kidgell moved in the same circles as Lawson's mother and she and Lawson were both friendly with the feminist Agnes Rose-Soley. Part of Lawson's own sex problem, he wrote, was that 'He loved her, and she loved him: but after they'd been married a while he found out that, although he understood her, she didn't and couldn't possibly ever understand him [and that] ... He saw that his life would be a hell with her ... But he couldn't leave her because he loved her, and because he knew that she loved him and would break her heart if he left her.'[53]

Lawson would rework the story for subsequent books but he spent most of October drinking. Bertha made repeated excuses for him, saying that 'the never-ending struggle against poverty and hard conditions had been too much for him' – despite the fact that for some years from 1897 Lawson was earning the equivalent of the price of an average Sydney house every year.[54] She said 'circumstance and temperament' played havoc with her husband, that 'he was acutely over-sensitive, and in some moods of dark depression he could feel hurt and very indignant'.[55]

AFTER ONE SPREE TOO MANY and for the sake of Bertha and baby Jim,[56] Lawson finally admitted himself into Rest Haven,

'Sydney's Temperance Sanatorium For Male Inebriates', on a farm at Echo Point in Roseville. The farm was leased by social campaigner Courtenay Smith and his wife Mary, the president of the Women's Christian Temperance Union. Patients undergoing their 'course of treatment' tended the hundred or so fruit trees on the property, worked in the vegetable garden, and fed the pigs and poultry, while they were weaned off the booze.[57]

A reporter for Sydney's *Evening News* noted Rest Haven was 'situated in one of the most picturesque and secluded recesses of Middle Harbor ... far from the madding crowd's ignoble strife. A walk round the premises and through the orchards and gardens gives one the impression of an English rural home. There is ample accommodation for from twenty-five to thirty patients.'[58] Courtenay Smith explained that 'in many instances the more nervously sensitive, and the more keenly intellectual the individual' the more liable he was to temporary, and even permanent collapse. Alcoholism is a nervous complaint, the paper explained, 'and often a concomitant of genius. It is rapidly coming to be recognised that the habitual abuse of stimulants is a disease, not a crime.'[59]

Lawson spent weeks at Rest Haven and later wrote 'The Boozers' Home'[60] about his stay, basing the character on himself, a sad wreck who couldn't start the day without a drink and who couldn't live for more than two hours without one.

'If a patient took a bad turn in the night at the Boozers' Home and got up to hunt the snakes out of his room, he wouldn't be sworn at, or laughed at, or held down; no, they'd help him shoo the snakes out and comfort him,' Lawson wrote. 'The institution didn't profess to cure anyone of drink, only to mend up shattered nerves and build up wrecked constitutions; give them back some will-power if they weren't too far gone.'[61]

When Lawson left Rest Haven, he said he was cured, and writing of himself in the third person noted: 'It was nice and novel to be looked after and watched and physicked and bossed by a pretty nurse in uniform – but I don't suppose he told his wife that.'[62]

He underwent a great deal of soul searching while he dried out. On 10 December, and saying that his stay in the rest home had set him 'on his feet all right', he took a room at 32 Castlereagh Street, Redfern, and tried to conceal his whereabouts from Bertha. In 'The Boozers' Home', Lawson admitted that his character was no longer the same man who won his wife's heart when she was a girl.

'Perhaps he'd killed the love in her before he reformed,' he wrote, 'and reformed too late. I wonder how a man feels when he finds out for the first time that his wife doesn't love him any longer?'[63]

Chapter 17

All his best writing was done in the years of his comparative sobriety.
Drunks do not create the basis of a national treasure
in prose and poetry.

LAWSON'S *BULLETIN* COLLEAGUE NORMAN LINDSAY[1]

AFTER HIS STAY IN REST HAVEN, Lawson feared that if he took just one drink now he'd be a lost man and he 'made a mania of that'.[2] He didn't flee temptation, but would still knock round the pubs on Saturday nights with his old mates, never drinking anything, though, but 'soft stuff' and he was always careful to smell his glass for fear of an accident or trick. He drank 'gallons of ginger beer, milk-and-soda, and lemonade; and he got very fond of sweets, too – he'd never liked them before'.[3]

His dry spell kicked off the most productive twelve months of his life, getting back with Bertha and writing, in the words of Bert Stevens, 'as strongly as ever and with more bite'.[4] 'The Boozers' Home' was too raw and close to the bone, though, and Lawson would have to wait three years for it to be published – and in England, at that – as none of his regular customers, not even George Robertson, would run it.

Lawson took his young family to Woonona, north of Wollongong, for a short beach holiday before moving them out of Jack Lang's home into rooms in the house 'Strathmere' in Lord Street, Lavender Bay. Then he called on Banjo Paterson to make final arrangements for his new book of prose, and set about finding the published works to be included, a tough task since he still kept no scrapbooks of his work.

He remained befuddled at times, and on New Year's Eve wrote to Angus & Robertson with a curt demand for a 'proper signed copy' of their last agreement, apparently unaware that Paterson had it securely locked away. Two weeks later he wrote to them about a poem called 'Past Carin' which he said had been quoted more than any of his other works and had 'been most favourably mentioned' in *The Bulletin*.[5] The poem would not actually be published for another five months, and not in *The Bulletin* but in the new *Australian Magazine*.

Lawson was clearly rattled, perhaps without alcohol to steady his nerves, and his frustration came to the fore. While he had been drying out, his rivals, Paterson, Daley, Quinn, Becke, Steele Rudd and even Mary Gilmore in Paraguay, had contributed to the bumper Christmas 1898 issue of *The Bulletin*.

Lawson's sour mood was reflected in 'Crime in the Bush', a dark essay about rural families living for generations in 'mental darkness' in remote pockets in the ranges, at the end of long, dark gullies. They were haggard or hard and vicious-faced '... if not born criminals' then trained 'in shady ways from childhood'. Lawson hinted at witchcraft and murder as a relief from the monotony of the scrub.[6]

His essay 'Pursuing Literature in Australia' was full of rancour. He lambasted *The Bulletin*, which ran the piece, for holding back 'some stories and sketches which were to complete the "Steelman" and "Mitchell" series' and thus causing 'the apparently haphazard appearance of the order of the stories and sketches' in *Billy Boils*. He feared they would again 'be responsible for the same thing' in his next book.

He cried poor even though he had already earned a small fortune as a writer, only to drink it away. He said he was so hard up that he was kept 'hanging about the office for weeks' at the Government Statistician's office, even though the only work he really did was to sign on, sign off and pick up 50 shillings a week. When he applied for a free railway pass to gather material in the bush for a month, he whined that he didn't even receive a reply. 'My advice to any young Australian writer whose talents have been recognised,' he wrote, 'would be to go steerage, stow away, swim, and seek London, Yankeeland, or Timbuctoo – rather than stay in Australia till his genius turned to gall, or beer. Or, failing this and still in the interests of human nature and literature – to study elementary anatomy, especially as applies to the cranium, and then shoot himself carefully with the aid of a looking-glass.'[7]

A firestorm of retorts followed. The playwright Bernard Espinasse refuted Lawson's claims about local writers not getting a go in their homeland and pointed out that he had done very well with the pen in Australia, even earning an astronomical 'three-figure' sum for one of his works. Ted Brady, who had seen Lawson shout the bar on all too many occasions after a payday, wrote that Lawson's biggest problem was 'a generous confiding temperament'.[8] And Alfred Stephens wrote in *The Bulletin* that while Lawson was a writer of 'undoubted genius', 'The Man with a Grievance' complained like 'the next-door dog, who doesn't look as if he got his tucker regular'.[9]

On 18 February 1899, Stephens rattled Lawson's fragile ego in *The Bulletin*'s literary journal *Bookfellow*, in his profile on the 'most characteristic literary product that Australia has yet achieved'. Lawson was, he said, a man with a 'good heart' and a 'capacity for keen feeling – the root of his literary power', who he had never known 'to say or do a mean thing'. Lawson, though, had uttered 'many foolish things' and had 'no head for business'.

'His grammar is shaky and he has small sense of literary proportion,' Stephens wrote, 'yet I believe he feels an editorial cut in his copy as keenly as if it were a cut in his flesh. He reckons loosely in money matters; he is sociable to excess; and so on ... He lives on a see-saw of emotion – is by sudden turns cheerful and morose, confiding and suspicious, well and ill. But no one can know him or read his books without seeing the sterling metal of the man.'[10]

As a writer, Stephens said, 'Lawson is always too close to his subject. It results that his work is minutely vivid, but also scrappy, detached, solitary.' Lawson might have complained about the order of the sketches in *Billy Boils*, but Stephens said 'were the whole of the Mitchell or Steelman sketches printed together, they would still remain flat silhouettes'.

Stephens was particularly riled by Lawson's complaints about his earnings and his claim that writers had to flee to London to earn their due, critically and financially.

'In proportion to its population,' Stephens argued, 'Australia buys verse more liberally than any country in the world.' He pointed out that British writers William Watson, John Davidson and Arthur Symons might have a print run of just 500 to a 40-million population, and do not always sell the 500.

'Yet Lawson can sell 6,000 copies of his verses at 5s in little more than two years – and grumbles! He has sold 7,000 volumes of his prose contemporaneously – and gives Australian authors the alternative of London or suicide! Plainly, this young man does not know when he is well off ... Nobody expects a poet to be a man of business. But for his failure to make poetry pay, whether Lawson blames himself or others, he should not blame Australia, which admires and loves and liberally encourages him.'[11]

Lawson did not take Stephens's words as encouragement but instead, despite needing to find material for his new book, wasted his time mocking Stephens in a trite satire, 'The Australian Writer',[12] which would not be published in Lawson's lifetime. Much more worthwhile was 'The Song of the Darling River'[13] for *The Bulletin* which carried Lawson back to his memories of Bourke, though memories of drought and flood reflected the emotional pain he was enduring without the crutch of alcohol. A week later there was 'The Sliprails and the Spur',[14] a ballad of love and loss inspired by a tombstone at the crossroads of the Bathurst and Bowenfels roads that recalled the life of a 'mad girl' who had committed suicide. His pain was evident again when 'Past Carin'[15] finally appeared. A woman who could be The Drover's Wife moans:

Through Death and Trouble, turn about,
Through hopeless desolation,
Through flood and fever, fire and drought,
And slavery and starvation;
Through childbirth, sickness, hurt, and blight,
And nervousness an' scarin',
Through bein' left alone at night
I've got to be past carin'.[16]

Perhaps spurred by Stephens's claims that he was a poor businessman, Lawson wanted 6 to 8 guineas from Angus & Robertson for 'The Ironbark Chip', even though he'd agreed to 4. The company's new secretary Fred Shenstone sent him 10 guineas to cover that story and 'Mitchell on the "Sex" and Other "Problems"'.

Lawson wrote to his friend the writer Ethel Turner to say that things were chaotic at home. Jim was 'troublesome' and Bertha 'has all the housework to do, and seldom gets a minute to spare'.[17] Saying he couldn't cope with the domestic situation, Lawson hired an office in the Exchange Alley building, off Pitt Street, near Circular Quay on 7 May so that he could earn £50 for six articles about Australian life for the *Review of Reviews*. Banjo Paterson had been collecting old bush songs for preservation by Angus & Robertson,[18] and Lawson asked Robertson for the manuscript to work some into his sketch 'The Songs They Used to Sing',[19] recalling some of the tunes his grandfather taught him when they worked together. Robertson gave him a bonus of 2 guineas for the sketch but rejected Lawson's *Bulletin* article 'If I Could Paint'[20] for the new book, though it was one of Bertha's favourites.

Lawson then gave Robertson his story 'The Hero of Redclay' and hinted that he had sacrificed a novel for it and should be compensated with £20.

Robertson couldn't be persuaded and Lawson had to give up his office after just three weeks but without consulting Paterson, Lawson wrote to Robertson demanding a pay rise from £75 to

£100 for the prose book plus royalties. Instead, Robertson asked Paterson to create a new agreement for another book of Lawson's verse and it was signed on 18 July 1899, giving the provision that Robertson would find an English publisher to sell the book there as well.

Lawson couldn't wait to tell Alfred Stephens and watch him stew as the critic told *Bulletin* readers: 'Lawson's star is waxing: his famous soul-unburdening on this page has unlocked critics' hearts and publishers' purses. Which shows that fame is synonymous with advertisement; since his recent work is no better than that of five years ago: it is only better known. A new volume of his prose, and another of verse, are preparing for publication; and a selection from the mass is to appear in England ... Then the author may go and be an Antipodean lion – for a little while: fancy him with frock coat, silk hat, crutch-cane, and patent-leather shoes, picturesquing Piccadilly!'[21]

Lawson wrote to Bland Holt, apologising that he was not yet able to repay a 'twenty quid' loan but promised him that with new book deals 'I'll be rich again in a month or two ... have been a teetotaller ever since you left and mean to stick to it. There was no other way – either all or nothing for me.'[22]

Lawson told Holt that the new governor, the Eton-educated twenty-six-year-old Earl Beauchamp,[23] was 'much struck' with his writing, which 'proves beyond a doubt that he is an intelligent, promising young fellow, and I'll drop in, when I have five minutes to spare, and have a chat with him and see what I can do for him'.[24]

It was Lawson who needed all the help he could get. Bertha was pregnant again and he had moved the family to North Sydney after meeting Mrs Isabel Byers, a budding poet who ran the North Sydney Coffee Palace at 145 Miller Street. Mrs Byers's husband had shot through years earlier and she supported herself with her cafe and by taking in boarders. She recalled their first meeting one Sunday afternoon, when Lawson, Bertha and Jim, not yet eighteen months old, came in for afternoon tea.

When they had gone out my little niece, who had waited on them, told me they had asked if we had furnished apartments to let. So, my little niece run after them and they came back and took a flat ... But for the smartness of my niece and telling me and running after them and saying I would like to speak to them, I might never have known Henry Lawson. ... I did not see very much of him except when he went in and out of the coffee palace and when he came to pay me at the end of the week for the flat. ... He was very much wrapped up in the works he was composing and was mostly writing.[25]

LAWSON WAS ALSO WRAPPED UP in a desperate search for published articles to include in the new book, and was having a battle to find 'The Selector's Daughter' which had appeared over two weeks in *Truth* in 1893. Sydney's Public Library had only saved issues of the publication from 1895 to 1898 but Lawson had written to a former sub-editor of the paper in Queensland hoping he had kept past issues. He told Shenstone of his fruitless search and pointed out that 'The Selector's Daughter' was not on the list he'd promised Robertson.[26] Shenstone had been advertising for copies of Lawson's published poems and paying 10 shillings to those who could deliver them. He suspected Lawson was fishing for more money, and told Lawson, 'Surely you are not serious when you allege the difficulty of procuring the copy, and the expense it has put us to obtain it, as a reason for making us pay again.'[27]

Lawson protested too much, scrawling a reply on the letter: 'Who the hell is asking you to pay again? For God's sake put prejudice aside and try to understand me!' Later that day he called on Arthur Jose, who would again edit his work. Jose told him that Robertson was sick with influenza which prevented him from sailing to London and planned meetings with British publishers over future deals. Shamefaced, Lawson wrote Robertson an apology expressing 'regret at certain hasty expressions ... which, had I known the state of your health, would not have been written'.[28]

Despite Robertson's ill health, it was he who took pity on Lawson and sent him the £25 advance for completion of the prose book that was not due until the following year. Lawson told him that the money was a godsend because the work he was now doing required the freedom from financial worry and that the bulk of his last cheque 'went to settle old wild oats debts of which the total was heavy. ... there is a new edition of the Henry Lawson family in the press, so your cheque was doubly welcome. I will work in as many free ads. for the books as I can.'[29]

He kept working on his 'Golden Nineties' series that was to begin in the *Australian Star* in October.

Lawson told readers that his purpose in publishing those articles, was 'to write of Australia as I have seen it, and do my share towards preserving Australian history ... and if – as some editors think, but I do not believe, the Australian reader only wants sex problem, sensation, or local news and scandal, then it is part of my duty to try and cure him. It might cure him of me, but I'll take my chance.'[30]

Lawson wrote that he had been analysing his 'strong and enduring sympathy for those black countrymen-o'-mine', and came to the conclusion that it was partly on account of the time he was at King George Sound in Western Australia, 'sitting at the door of the loneliest hut in the most desolate waste of bush, watching about the saddest Australian sunset that I think I had ever seen burn to ashes'. He had nothing to read, and no one to talk to, and was feeling so lonely and desolate when 'King Billy' – usually a patronising name of the time for Aboriginal people – arrived seemingly out of the dust, with a broad grin and a bundle of newspapers and letters from home, 'which he had brought 10 miles from the nearest point on the railway line'. Lawson said he would never get a cheaper stick of tobacco worth of joy as long as he lived.[31]

Lawson also started writing about the Second Boer War which broke out on 11 October 1899, though while Lawson stayed at home, Banjo Paterson sailed on the *Kent* for Cape Town, where one of Sydney's most fearless sportsmen would report for the *Sydney Morning Herald* on what he came to regard as the most sickening of all blood sports – the hunting of men. Breaker Morant, who had played polo against Paterson and ridden with him at the Sydney Hunt Club, would soon follow, hoping that the war in South Africa would provide a free passage home to England.

The Bulletin, with all its nationalistic bite, was opposed to Australian colonists fighting for British control of South African mines, and Lawson said the local race to enlist was born from 'the mad longing for change, intensified in Australia by the hopeless flat monotony of the country and its history – some of us are willing – wilfully, blindly eager, mad! – to cross the sea and shoot men whom we never saw and whose quarrel we do not and cannot understand'.[32] He made a similar point for Archibald again in 'Ballad of the Cornstalk'.[33]

He changed his tune for a different audience in the *Australian Star*, though, telling the soldiers: 'I trust that our chaps will do the work that is put into their hands to do, and kill the foe that comes within their range to kill, and take as many prisoners as they can lay their hands on – for the worldly honour of New South Wales.'[34]

And not only could Lawson change tune, but he could turn on his friends for a byline too.

After William Holman stood up in Parliament House 'to tell the truth about the Transvaal Contingent business', Lawson wrote in *The Bulletin* that 'he stood practically alone ... They howled at him because Unionism was dead; they sneered at him because his truth was old and threadbare and out of fashion.' George Black, Lawson's old pal who had just lost his seat in the House, came in for special attention for referring to the 'Red Rose of Socialism', with Lawson claiming that Black 'never had the pluck to wear a red ribbon or rosette in daylight in a public place'.[35] Black bit back like a terrier, calling his accuser '[t]he incoherent and emotional Lawson, who once hurried back to Sydney from New Zealand to join a Labor paper which died while he was on the way' and claiming he was unable 'to glorify W. A. Holman sufficiently without dispraising, either directly or by comparison, several other Labor men. It is difficult to know exactly what he aims at – a common fault of his unless rigorously edited.'[36]

LAWSON HAD WORK POURING IN and with Bertha now six months into her pregnancy, he moved his family out of Mrs Byers's Coffee Palace to Mrs Harry Humphries's furnished rooms in the modest Chaplin Cottage in Charles Street, not far from the Miller Street post office. To pay the rent, Lawson took a loan of £15 from the Pitt Street financier Joseph Booker – on condition he would repay him with £20 from his next Angus & Robertson cheque. Lawson was one of Booker's regular customers and knew he was not slow to bankrupt his debtors. Angus & Robertson came to the party and soon paid him £16 10s for four new stories for the book[37] and he was able to repay the loan three months later.[38]

Lawson was laid up at Chaplin Cottage with influenza in mid-November when he received a letter from an admirer, written from 'Bangalore, Goulburn' and addressed to Henry Lawson, Esq., Sydney.[39]

Dear Sir

This is written to ask if you will help me. I will explain. For some years I have been scribbling & have written a book. My trouble is I have lived such a secluded life in the bush that I am unacquainted with any literary people of note and am to [sic] hard up to incur the expense of travelling to Sydney to personally interview a publisher on the matter. As for posting a story to them in the hope of it being read, unless one has swell influence one might as well try to sell an elderly cow for a young racehorse – thus I have conceived the idea of beseeching your aid. Perhaps it is a foolish notion as probably you will have neither time nor inclination to extend a hand to me but if you would be good natured enough to read my yarn you would be helping me out of a deep hole. I merely ask you to run through it & state whether you think it twaddle, interesting or trash & allow me to use yr opinion ...

> Awaiting reply
> Sir
> Faithfully yrs
> Miles Franklin[40]

Lawson had never heard of Franklin and was constantly busy with the new books, his pregnant wife and small son. It took weeks and Bertha's prodding before he replied to 'Mr M Franklin' four days after Christmas.

> Dear Sir
> Send your yarn and I'll read it and tell you what I think of it; but you must give me, say a month, to get through it and see what I can do for you.
> Wishing you a lucky new year.
>
> Yours truly
> Henry Lawson[41]

The manuscript arrived post haste and Lawson was impressed, but as it seemed to contain a good deal of a girl's lived experience, he began to suspect that 'Mr Franklin' could possibly be a woman. His puritanical upbringing caused him to blush at a few of the passages but Lawson quickly wrote back to say: 'I believe that you have done a big thing. I've been through the life you write of.' George Robertson was now finally heading to England but Lawson said he would keep the book until the publisher returned. He would like some details about the author, though, 'who and what you really are? man or woman? and something about yourself?'[42]

Miles Franklin was in fact Stella Maria Sarah Miles Franklin,[43] a precocious twenty year old who had been raised on a station near Goulburn in a family whose fortune was downwardly mobile, but

Lawson's protégé, Miles Franklin, in 1902. State Library of NSW, FL3250523

whose writing talents were encouraged, and who transformed her experiences as a teenage governess in Yass into a novel.

Norman Lindsay, who was about to start work as an artist at *The Bulletin*, had a keen eye for the female form, and wrote of the young author that she was 'very short but pleasingly plump ... Her mass of dark hair reached her pert rump, which matched her pert nose. She had fine eyes, arched eyebrows and an alluring pair of lips.'[44]

AFTER NEW YEAR'S REVELLERS surged into Sydney on 'steamers, bus, train, and tram in thousands'[45] to usher in the 1900s, Lawson began to make plans to fulfil his long-held dream of making his name in London. He laughed at Bertha's fears about travelling across the globe with a newborn baby.[46]

He had no qualms about crying poor to raise the money for fares, either.

Lawson wrote to the new governor, enclosing his *Bulletin* plea 'Pursuing Literature' and a scrapbook containing English reviews of his work.

'I heard that you had spoken kindly of my books,' he wrote, 'and as you take an interest in art and literature I thought ... I would confide in you and ask you to help me.'[47]

He complained that he had been forced to 'sacrifice two more books in Australia' and pointed out that he had been contributing to a Sydney daily selling copy for £1 per column 'that is honestly worth five'.

'In short, I am wasting my work, wasting my life, spoiling the reputation I have gained, and wearing out my brains and heart here in Australia. If I were single I would find my way to England somehow; but I am married, have one child, and another one due this month, so I am tied hopelessly. We live comfortably on £2 per week, and it takes me all my time to make that with my pen. Will you help me out of the miserable hole I am in? I heard you are rich, all my friends are as poor as myself. ... If you cannot help me, kindly destroy this. It is the first letter of this kind I have ever written in my life, and will be the last.'

It wasn't. A day after he had received a favourable reply from Beauchamp, Lawson wrote to the wealthy book collector and philanthropist David Scott Mitchell, on 4 February 1900,[48] complaining that he had been working for the *Australian Star* at £1 per column but his work had been 'crowded out by the war'.

'Now I've made up my mind to go to England in April by the *Medic* (all second-class line) and, as I am taking Mrs Lawson and two youngsters, it will be a tight squeeze financially'. 'Mrs L' would be confined any day and Lawson figured he would have about £50 clear by the beginning of April. 'Now £50 is not enough,' he told Mitchell, 'as I may want to hold out a month or so in London … If I had £100 clear I'd be alright … Another thing is I think I can get something done for my hearing in London – and – well, to look the thing square in the face, this is a begging letter – and I'd be the last man in Australia to write one if I didn't believe the whole future of my work depended on it.'[49] Mitchell 'lent' Lawson £25 and his cousin, the feminist Rose Scott, a friend of Bertha's, also helped out.

At the same time Miles Franklin had come to Sydney to train as a probationer nurse and Lawson wrote to her to say that given Bertha's experience in hospitals 'you will be "put upon" considerably by the head and other nurses until you know the ropes … Anyway don't "buck" till you know where you are. Past experience should aid you now. The paltry tyrants of my life seem so very very small to me now that I can scarcely remember them. Write when you'll get a day off an[d] come on that day – says Mrs Lawson.'[50]

On 31 January 1900, Lawson's mother was alighting from a tram at Circular Quay when it shunted forward, throwing her face down on the roadway. The accident put her under medical care for five months but eventually she received £450 in compensation.

On the same day, Lawson wrote to his friend Walter Head, Mary Cameron's former editor at *The Hummer* and *New Australia* journals, and one of Lawson's many creditors. Head was now living in Hobart under the alias Walter Alan Ashe Woods, lest he be brought to trial for embezzling the New Australia funds.

With his wife and seven children, Head had intended to follow Billy Lane to Paraguay, but his plan was tragically ended in 1893 when Head's son Rowland disappeared in the Gippsland bush, never to be seen again. Head's eldest son Walter left for Paraguay on the *Royal Tar* and never returned. Head was probably guilty of mismanaging the New Australia funds rather than embezzling but he was not willing to face a trial to defend himself.

Lawson told Head that Billy Lane was back in Sydney from Paraguay and going to edit the Sydney *Worker*. He had done his bit 'by way of barracking for Holman', he said, but the New Australia movement in Cosme was a mess and 'I wish Wood, Hall, Mrs – (Miss Cameron – she has a son) were out of their hole. Who's to ask after them or help them now.' Lawson's ego was running wild and he said that Robertson was in England 'on my account, I think'.[51]

BERTHA MARIE LOUISA LAWSON was born in Chaplin Cottage on 11 February 1900, and inherited her father's dark, searching eyes. Lawson gave her the nickname 'Barta' but spent little time at home helping the new mother. Bert Stevens said the 'strain of sobriety' was telling on his friend. 'He found domestic affairs a burden and welcomed me as one upon whom he could unload his troubles.' Stevens also said at this time Lawson found 'solace' again with Hannah Thornburn.[52] He made trips to Mudgee and Gulgong for a refresher on the Australian bush, but rather than editing the proofs of his upcoming books for Shenstone, he spent time reading a play by Ethel Turner, advising her that there was too much dialogue 'but plenty of room for cutting out'.[53] Without mentioning the debacle of *Pinter's Son Jim*, he told her Bland Holt had 'been at me for a long time' to write a 'genuine Australian drama'.

Lawson's tardiness in checking and returning page proofs delayed the release of the prose book and Shenstone decided to spread it over two volumes, *On the Track*, to be published on 17 April 1900 and *Over the Sliprails*, to be published on 9 June.

One afternoon while Lawson was out, Bertha had a strange

visit from a 'tall, rugged, and striking looking man, with very bushy eyebrows'. He introduced himself, inspected the new baby with interest, and chatted to the mother in friendly fashion for a while. Bertha went to make tea but when the kettle had boiled and she came back into the room, the visitor had left without a word. The visitor was Henry Albury, Lawson's grandfather, rising seventy-five and now a widower.[54] It was the first and last time Bertha ever saw him, but Lawson said it was typical of 'the old man' who 'would always rather camp alone in the bush and split palings and shingles for tucker and an occasional spree than live in comfort with one of his married daughters'.[55]

IN SOUTH AFRICA, Banjo Paterson was in the thick of the fighting, reporting on the Battle of Paardeberg near Kimberley, on 27 February, when Britain's Lord Roberts forced the surrender of Boer general Piet Cronje and more than 4000 men.

Two weeks later Banjo was at the taking of Bloemfontein on 13 March, reaching the town before the British troops, galloping into enemy territory on his black racehorse for an exclusive on the Boer retreat.[56]

Two weeks later, Banjo met Rudyard Kipling, who was making a hurried visit to the war. Banjo found it hard to believe that this small 'square figured man with the thick black eyebrows and the round glasses' was the creator of Mowgli. 'His talk is a gabble, a chatter, a constant jumping from one point to another.' Kipling seemed more like a fast-talking businessman 'than a literary celebrity'.[57]

Three days later, on 28 March 1900, Banjo sat next to Kipling at a war correspondents' dinner in honour of Lord Roberts. Around the same time, Banjo also met the stony-faced Lord Kitchener, and the mercurial Winston Churchill, who was covering the war for London's *Morning Post*.[58] Churchill had 'such a strong personality', Banjo explained, 'that the army were prepared to bet that he would either get into jail or become Prime Minister'.[59]

MILES FRANKLIN QUICKLY gave up her nursing ambition and returned to Bangalore. Bertha wrote to her there explaining that she had been 'very ill for a long time, and things have been all upside down'. Robertson was not yet back from England and 'Mr Lawson' had not been able to do anything with her book yet. Australia was 'a hopeless place for Art or Letters', Bertha said, but Lawson's advice was for Miles to try 'some short sketches for the *Town and Country* or *Sydney Mail*'. She and Harry were heading for England 'next month', and she was sure Harry would meet with success there.[60]

Lawson would soon write to Robertson that 'the truth and vividness' of Franklin's work 'was startling even to me ... In my opinion it is the Australian *African Farm* and immeasurably ahead of *Jane Eyre* ... I think the work goes deeper, is more vividly realistic and more perfect than my own.'[61]

Robertson arrived home in early April 1900 but Lawson had still not read the proofs of four of his stories and had lost part of the fifth. He had also lost some of the proofs of the verse book. He seemed more interested in his 'banquet', a lavish send-off the 'Duskers' were planning for Lawson and the Sydney newspaper artist Harry Fullwood, who had auctioned all his possessions for his fare to London.

About forty writers, musicians and artists assembled in an upstairs room in Sydney's Hotel Victoria on 5 April, 'sprawling round the dinner-tables in an atmosphere of wine and cigars'.[62] Despite his criticisms of Lawson, Alfred Stephens proposed a toast to 'still the man who has best represented Australia in literature'. Rod Quinn recited a poem and Lawson stood to make a speech, 'those great dark eyes,' Stephens wrote, 'woman's eyes, dogs' eyes – full of sympathy and emotion'.[63]

The night ended with 'terrific midnight yells' at the ferry wharf where the revellers were joined by latecomer Jack Brereton, who having gone to bed after forgetting the date, arrived with a raincoat over his pyjamas. Together Lawson's friends formed a double file and under an arch of 'walking sticks, umbrellas, temporarily purloined palings, make-believe rapiers of ravished scantling, and arms raised skyward' they cheered him onto the boat taking him home to Bertha and the children.[64] When Lawson got there, Bertha knew he had broken his promise about not drinking.[65]

Lawson took his family on a train journey to the Bulli cliffs just south of Sydney and patched things up with Shenstone by saying he had found the lost proofs and would return them. He claimed his 'servant' had mislaid them, which must have made Shenstone guffaw, knowing the state of Lawson's finances.

When Lawson returned to Sydney on 9 April, he found there were no cabins available on the *Medic* and his family would have to travel on the 3700-ton *Damascus* of the Aberdeen White Star Line. It was 'a clipper-built sailing ship' with masts, sails and engines[66] and it was leaving for London via Cape Town on 20 April. The ship carried only saloon and third-class passengers. Since Lawson did not have two £50 saloon adult fares, he took a two-berth third-class cabin for £40 instead.

Robertson had not been able to read Miles Franklin's book yet and Lawson asked her if she would like him to take the manuscript to London with him. There was a 'margin for compromising with publishers prejudices,' he said, but 'all the same I'd fight to have every line published as written'.[67]

She replied at once: 'Please take my MS. story entitled "My Brilliant (?) Career" to England with you. I trust you to do yr. best for me in the matter and desire you to use your own discretion in the choice of a publisher & in the style of publishing.'[68]

LAWSON WAS ABLE to read some of the reviews for advance copies of *On the Track* before leaving. They were mostly positive, occasionally rapturous. The *Town and Country Journal* said Lawson's 'two philosophers, Mitchell and Steelman, reappear entertainingly'.[69] The *Bendigo Independent* said Lawson's stories were 'artistically and graphically told, and are thoroughly Australian in colour and setting'.[70] Sydney's *Evening News*, though, said while the book was full of Lawson's 'well-known descriptive power' they'd had enough of his sordid side of the bush. His 'unlovely swaggie' had become 'wearisome'.[71]

The *Sydney Morning Herald* called him a 'gifted young Australian' and declared that his insight into bush life was 'hardly equalled'. 'Mr. Lawson has a quick eye for the pathetically humorous and for the humorously pathetic,' it said. His visit to 'the old country' would only expand his view.[72]

On the morning of 20 April, fourteen of the Duskers trooped aboard the ship at Dalgety's Wharf at Millers Point to farewell Lawson and his family. They couldn't find him but Daley sat down inside someone's cabin and wrote a poem 'On the Departure of Henry Lawson' before stuffing it into the breast-pocket of the skipper Robert McKilliam,[73] a good-humoured Scot with a big sandy moustache.[74]

The Duskers then adjourned to the Lord Nelson Hotel for 'five to ten minutes', but their tipple stretched into four and a half hours, and none of them heard the ship's farewell siren at 3 p.m.

As the crew was about to raise the gangway, though, George Robertson raced down in a cab and pressed a roll of sovereigns into a grateful Lawson's hand.[75]

Perhaps Hannah Thornburn was there to see Lawson off too, perhaps not. Maybe the intense bond of love between them that Lawson would write about existed only in his mind. Lawson was chasing a dream in London, and leaving a fantasy behind.

Years later Lawson would write about looking out from the ship to the crowd in Sydney that was waving goodbye:

They cheered from cargo ways and ballast heap and pile,
To last him all his days – they sent him off in style.
(He only took his book.) He only turned his head
In one last hopeless look towards a cargo shed
Where one stood brimming eyed in silence by the wall –
No jealous eyes espied that last farewell of all.[76]

Chapter 18

... poor Mrs Lawson has gone mad – driven so, I have no hesitation
in saying, by her brutal husband. He has been drinking heavily and
I quite expect the shock of him taking to drink again
has completely turned her brain ...

BERTHA'S FRIEND EDITH DEAN[1]

CAPTAIN MCKILLIAM glided the *Damascus* south and the Lawsons arrived in Melbourne on 22 April. Lawson had taken 'the last possible rag'[2] of their soiled linen ashore to the laundry, and bought eggs, fruit, medicine and jam, and was about to make some minor renovations to the family's cramped cabin when he received a message from the renowned artist John Longstaff. At the last minute, Archibald had commissioned Longstaff to paint a portrait of his literary star.[3]

Bertha took the baby to see relatives, while Lawson donned a white shirt with fancy cuffs, a crimson tie and his new suit, bought at David Jones[4] for £2 10s. He took two-year-old Jim with him to Longstaff's studio in Grosvenor Chambers, at No. 9 Collins Street, to meet the burly artist.

Lawson was already one of Longstaff's most ardent admirers. Archibald owned the artist's celebrated painting 'Breaking the News', which had hung in William Macleod's *Bulletin* office, showing the plight of a woman as she learns of her husband's death in a mining accident. Lawson wrote in his story 'If I Could Paint' that he would be 'prouder of a picture like

"Breaking the News" than of a hundred exquisite alleged studies in "the nood"'.[5]

In his best clothes, Lawson sat all day as Jim amused himself in a corner covering himself with paint.[6] Lawson and Jim were also in Longstaff's studio the following day and a photographer took shots of the writer from all angles to help Longstaff with the detail after Lawson had sailed.

Longstaff and Lawson decided to leave out the fancy shirt cuffs from the finished portrait, but the painter left in the firm gaze and expressive eyes that are still illuminating more than a century later. Bertha called it 'the truest and most living portrait of Harry ever made',[7] yet Lawson claimed he only saw the portrait twice, once when it was wet and again in 1902, because it was 'in a way, connected with the tragedy of my life'.[8]

Archibald was so impressed with the final work that he left a bequest for an annual portrait prize that still bears his name. Longstaff won the Archibald Prize five times.

As the *Damascus* was about to leave Melbourne, Lawson sent a card to Shenstone asking him to send 'Brilliant Career to me in London. Author wired to me to take it home. But if you want it you might write her first.'[9] Captain McKilliam sailed for Albany on 25 April with thirty-nine saloon passengers and 165 in third class, including Lawson and family. Rough cabins had been built around the lower forward hatch to cater for a rush of passengers who failed to appear. Lawson had initially purchased a two-berth, but was now hoping for an upgrade. The ship was a 'pretty sight whether under steam or sail', and McKilliam was 'always working the sails and coaxing a breath of wind'.[10]

The ride across the Bight was 'beastly rough'[11] but at Albany, Lawson moved his family into a four-berth cabin. He posted a quick apology for not seeing David Scott Mitchell before he left, explaining that in the whirr of departure, he had spent the whole afternoon on business that should have taken a few minutes,[12] and he dashed off a letter to the *Australian Star* to say he and the family were 'now very comfortable' and that there were a good many readers of his work on board, including the ship's doctor.[13]

Lawson 'chummed up' with the ship's carpenter, who knew the Norwegian ports where Lawson's father had worked. After giving the carpenter an 'overdose of rum', Lawson borrowed his tools, knocked out the two porthole berths in his cabin, widened the lower berth for the baby and Bertha, and made a little bunk for Jim. He made a seat so that Bertha could sit while bathing the children with warm water, which came from the cook's galley, and he built lockers for the family's private store of eggs, tea, sugar and preserved milk.[14]

Lawson also built a hinged, one-legged seat in the cabin, in which he would sit and 'half dream' in solitude but admitted that 'a freelance writer can't write when well at sea. His mind gets too contented and restful and healthy.'

Sometimes Lawson would sit aft with a mate or two and, in the moonlight, watch the ship's shimmering wake stretch back over the long swell of the Indian Ocean.[15]

The saloon passengers staged a concert including a warbled rendition of 'Advance Australia Fair', and Lawson led a deputation to McKilliam for the steerage passengers to return the favour. McKilliam let them heave a piano upstairs.[16]

After three weeks in the Indian Ocean the *Damascus* was 'within ten or twelve miles of Africa' before Lawson could see 'that dark and troubled continent with the naked eye'. Then the outline of what he'd thought was a bank of blue-black cloud behind the haze came into focus as the line of hills behind Durban.[17]

Lawson wanted to hear of news about the war in South Africa, having left Albany three weeks earlier with reports that a 'great engagement was imminent ... a decisive movement pending'.[18]

All the 'lumping' in Natal was done by Zulu men. Lawson observed that 'the Natal [stevedores] struck me as being the happiest people on earth'. They boarded the *Damascus* 'halloing, laughing, singing and dancing', and before going below deck to haul up the refrigerated beef and mutton carcasses they 'danced a war dance on deck'.[19]

Five of the young Australians who went ashore enlisted for the war, and Lawson took a rickshaw ride with a Melbourne man,

Albert Lee-Archer. The Zulu who pulled them 'was the dandy of the rickshaw stand' with bands of red ribbon round the ends of his 'knickers', with loose ribbon-ends free, to act as streamers. He had strings of shells and feathers down his back with little bells, such as those fastened to the harness of London cab horses. He wore, fastened to his closely curled woolly pate, a pair of short, black, polished horns.

Lee-Archer told Lawson later that when he got into that rickshaw, he felt sort of ashamed to be pulled along by a 'human being' in the place of a horse. Lawson put quote marks around the word 'human being' when he related the tale, but added looking back, 'I should have felt [ashamed] too; but – ah well! I'd knocked round and roughed it too much; and besides, I taught a Maori school once. I've an immense admiration for Kipling's "White Man's Burden".'[20]

From Durban the *Damascus* continued on to Cape Town, where some of Lawson's mates went ashore, became blind drunk in 'a Dutch spree', and brought more refreshments on board after it. One of the Australians suddenly remembered that another had insulted him the last time they'd been drunk together in Australia, so they had to go behind the end of the washhouse, out of sight of the crew, and have a scrap.[21]

There was fighting far more intense and deadly in South Africa, and as the *Damascus* rounded the Cape of Good Hope and headed north towards London, the British took Johannesburg on 31 May 1900 and Pretoria on 6 June.

Lawson wrote to George Robertson to say his 'wife and youngsters' were all right, but confessed that they all had endured a 'hard time' on the voyage.[22]

From Spain, Lawson spent hours peering into a 'fog, thick, heavy and wet'. Captain McKilliam had the siren going the whole time, and through the night, sirens from many other ships pierced the darkness. Somewhere, coming out of the Bay of Biscay, the *Damascus* just 'shaved a big four-masted sailing ship that suddenly developed out of a smudge in the fog'. Visibility was poor all the way past Plymouth, but Lawson finally saw the white cliffs of

Dover on a fine, bright morning. When they entered the Thames, Lawson likened the river to Melbourne's Yarra, but on a larger scale, and without the smell.[23]

THE *DAMASCUS* REACHED the Tilbury docks on 13 June 1900, ending a voyage that Bertha summed up as 'weary'. Buster Illingworth's father Tom met them, and took them into his home, a terrace built in a half-circle on The City Road in the heart of London. After dinner, Lawson sat by the window and watched the buses and horse-trams go by, painted pink and blue and yellow, according to their routes, and covered with advertisements.

On a Sunday morning 'the Buster's Dad' and a couple of friends took Lawson round to show him the great city. He looked along the narrow alleyways and imagined Dickensian characters there, but while his London friends seemed to expect him to drop his jaw in astonishment at the grandeur of the buildings, the only thing that surprised Lawson 'was to see St. Paul's and those places reduced to about half the size I expected them to be, and very black and dirty'.[24]

The drizzle made Bertha despondent and while Lawson would often go sightseeing in the grey rain, she quickly became exasperated by the 'endless streets, the noise, the bleakness, poverty and misery of the East End'.[25]

Three weeks after the Lawsons arrived in London, Queen Victoria gave her Royal Assent to the Commonwealth of Australia Constitution Act,[26] and more than ever Bertha and Lawson were longing for clean air and sunshine like they remembered at home. An Australian woman, Edith Dean,[27] reading of their arrival in the newspapers, invited the Lawsons to her home in the village of Harpenden, in leafy Hertfordshire, so she could help look after them. Bertha found Edith 'a very lovely and charming woman', though the eminent man of letters George Bernard Shaw called the former actress and nurse a 'vulgar liar and rapscallion'.[28]

Edith was the widow of the poet Francis Adams, the former *Brisbane Courier* journalist, whose work had once overshadowed Banjo's 'Clancy of the Overflow' when they appeared together on the same *Bulletin* page in 1889. Adams had returned to England after the death of his wife in childbirth, and their newborn son soon after. In 1893, at the age of just thirty, he was in a boarding house at Margate suffering a severe tubercular haemorrhage when he asked Edith, his second wife, to hand him the revolver he carried for just such an emergency. She did, and he placed the barrel in his mouth. When Edith was later asked by the coroner if she could have prevented her husband's suicide, she replied that she would have considered herself a 'contemptible coward' had she done so. She was not convicted of assisting his suicide, though, and, instead, by the time of the Lawsons' arrival in London was something of a public figure because of the scandal and her new marriage to the painter Frankland Dean.

The Lawsons stayed with Edith Dean for a few days, but then found a furnished cottage, 'Spring Villa' in Cowper Road, near her home, that they could rent for just 7s 6d a week, and which was only a short run into London on the train.

The rich beauty of the countryside and the 'wonderful English summer'[29] with its long twilight was a refreshing change from the city. Harpenden seemed like a 'haven of peace and comfort' and the view from the kitchen was indescribably lovely ... beautiful hayfields bordered with tall English trees' .[30] There was a common, an old inn with thatch two feet thick, neat cottages and sedate lanes shadowed by majestic elms.

At night, Lawson would sit in his charming cottage and listen to the clattering hooves on the road outside as farm wagons took their produce to the Covent Garden markets.

But was it all an illusion? The populace was well-to-do, with some of the grander homes having butlers and footmen, but there were a few shopkeepers and labourers as neighbours too, and England's class structure was confronting. Bertha could not afford a maid, but she had a visit from some local ladies who told her if she continued to do her own housework 'the best people would not call'.[31] She was advised to get a girl from the local orphanage for 5 shillings a week.

THE ENGLISH SUMMERS might have looked spectacular to Bertha, but on 30 July she informed her mother that the baby had been 'seriously ill with colic, and for four days and nights I did not know what sleep meant ... Jim is a shadow of himself, a poor miserable whining child. It is his teeth again, he is cutting his 2-year-old teeth together ... We get very little time to feel lonely – but seldom talk of Sydney – for tears and lumps in my throat are my trouble and Harry is as miserable as a bandicoot for days. Oh I shall be glad when we can get back again.'

They wouldn't be coming back hard up, though, she said, because Harry was certain of success.

'If Harry makes a splash we'll go to Italy or the South of France ... I do hope Hilda is over her trouble alright and that the newcomer is a son.' (Her sister actually gave birth to a daughter, Eirene Grace Lang.) Appearances were everything and Bertha asked her mother to tell all their friends 'we are getting on famously and Harry will write to all as soon as he gets this rush of work off ... Australia seems a dead world to the people here. There is no news in English papers of it worth reading so if you can spare a paper occasionally we would be so thankful.'[32]

In London, Lawson befriended a Dubbo-born journalist, Arthur Maquarie Mullens,[33] a Sydney University graduate who, writing as Arthur Maquarie, devoted two large articles in the magazine *Argosy* to the arrival in England of this great antipodean literary talent. Lawson would return the favour by writing of Maquarie in his 'Letters to Jack Cornstalk'. Lawson also met two important members of William Blackwood's staff, David Storrar Meldrum,[34] the company's London manager, and Ted Garnett,[35] who had worked closely with Joseph Conrad and would later help D.H. Lawrence with the publication of *Sons and Lovers*. Garnett was the son of Richard Garnett, a key figure at the British Museum, and he had a reputation for nurturing literary talent. Together with his wife Constance acting as translator, Garnett had introduced Russian writers such as Tolstoy, Chekhov and Dostoevsky to the English reading public, and he saw in *While the Billy Boils* a strident voice of democracy.

Meldrum and Garnett recommended Lawson hire the agent James B. Pinker,[36] a Londoner, who during his career represented James Joyce, Stephen Crane and Henry James, and who had just sold Joseph Conrad's novella *Typhoon* to the *Pall Mall Magazine*.

Pinker sold Blackwood a story based on Lawson's 1889 *Town and Country Journal* ballad 'Brighten's Sister-in-Law' for £21 5s. The publisher told Lawson it 'was a good and strong piece of work' for *Blackwood's Magazine*, known by its abbreviated title *Maga*, and suggested that since *Billy Boils* had not enjoyed a big circulation in Britain with Simpkin & Marshall, they were interested in publishing it 'afresh'.[37]

Lawson sent Robertson a copy of Blackwood's letter, urging him to make a deal and asking that if the story 'Thin Lips and

Lawson and his British agent James Pinker in London.
Royal Australian Historical Society Journal, Vol LV, Part IV, 1969

False Teeth' had not been used, could he have it back to sell in England. But Robertson and Shenstone had used it in place of a section of advertisements in a special edition of *Over the Sliprails* that was published a week before Lawson arrived in London.

Lawson instead gave Pinker the story 'A Double Buggy at Lahey's Creek' and showed the manuscript of *My Brilliant Career* to David Meldrum, who thought parts of it were powerful and asked Lawson to revise it. Lawson wrote to Miles Franklin on 6 September 1900, telling her that he was leaving the negotiations to 'Mr. Pinker, who has set me on my feet … He'll get more money than we can', and enclosing an agreement with Pinker for her to sign.[38] Franklin sent Lawson and Bertha her 'great thanks' and some green leaves and a sprig of wattle as a reminder of their home so far away.

Lawson suggested a series of stories for Blackwood based around a bush battler named 'Joe Wilson', who is ruined by drought. The protagonist, based loosely on Lawson's uncle Job Falconer, would not have the nonchalant air of Clancy of the Overflow, nor the boldness of the man from Snowy River; he would not be the 'strong, energetic, tough, optimistic nation-builder' in the way that 'pioneers' had traditionally been portrayed.[39] Joe Wilson would, rather, have a 'natural sentimental selfishness, good-nature, "softness" or weakness – call it which you like'.[40] In Joe Wilson, Lawson was incorporating insights into his own nature and that of his father.

Wilson would be another isolated man, more often finding an answer to loneliness in male mateship than in marriage. Lawson's celebration of mateship became a key part of the Australian self-image; 'sitting comfortably alongside a commitment to White Australia'.[41]

The final story in the Joe Wilson series, 'The Luck that Came Too Late', revolved around Wilson being saved from ruin, only to see his wife become insane. Lawson told Blackwood he had not yet decided whether the wife 'recovers or dies'. The dilemma was close to home.

Despite Bertha's apparent joy after arriving in England, life with Lawson had become tumultuous. Lawson turned to carpentry to soothe his nerves, relating years later that 'there's a dinner wagon of my make in Harpenden Hertfordshire England, also a new kind of wardrobe, a hat rack, and other things, polished, stained, and varnished, and not a nail in 'em and likely to last longer than any of my other works'.[42]

But Bertha claimed that Lawson's 'entry into the Bohemian life of London caused a backsliding into the arms of his old weakness'.[43]

Lawson's drinking, his frequent absences from home on trips to London, loneliness, the difficulties of looking after small children in a foreign land without a support network, and Bertha's growing homesickness played havoc with the fragile emotions of a young woman of just twenty-four. The loneliness had been too much for her in Mangamaunu and so it was in Harpenden.

A year earlier Lawson had written a story about 'Ratty Howell', a man suffering hallucinations over his long-dead wife in 'No Place for a Woman'.[44] Lawson had witnessed Bertha's mental deterioration in the wilds of New Zealand, and had experienced his own mother's melancholia, her hysteria, and his grandfather's eccentricities. His brother Charlie, finally out of prison after his latest long lag, had suffered from instability all his life, and would soon become a patient at Sydney's Callan Park asylum. Now Bertha's violence and threats about what she could do to the children became terrifying.

AS THE LEAVES FELL off the trees in her garden, Bertha began to fall apart. On 11 September 1900 she wrote to her mother to say that England now seemed like a 'grey, cold place … and the weeks of grey sky are so depressing'. She signed off by telling Mrs Mac, 'I'm afraid I have the Blues tonight'.[45] From what Bert Stevens heard back in Australia, Lawson was neglecting his wife and children and Bertha was 'out of her mind … He was temperamentally unfit for domestic life and she was not capable of managing a nervy egoist.'[46]

Bertha began suffering with insomnia, and became frantic at the lack of sleep and a feeling of hopelessness, so far from family and friends. Her dream existence in an English country garden was replaced with hallucinations. On 10 October 1900, she was admitted to Bethnal House, what was then termed a 'private madhouse' at Bethnal Green in London. Licensed to hold 300 patients, its rates were 'from 25s to £3 3s per week according to the nature of the case and the accommodation wished for'.[47] Doctors told Lawson it might take months for Bertha to recover.[48]

Edith Dean wrote a damning letter to Archibald, telling him that 'poor Mrs Lawson' had been driven mad by the heavy drinking of her 'brutal husband'.

> Three weeks ago my husband and I left home for a holiday leaving a servant here. On our return we find Mrs Lawson in the county lunatic asylum and Lawson in lodgings with <u>my</u> servant and the children in London ... I am troubled as to what Mrs Lawson is to do when she comes out. ... Lawson is such an unmitigated liar that I don't trust him ...[49]

THREE MONTHS LATER, on 1 January 1901 in Sydney's Centennial Park, 60,000 people gathered to witness the proclamation of Australia's new Federal Constitution, uniting six formerly independent colonies as the Commonwealth of Australia. A choir of 10,000 public-school children performed, and Queen Victoria's official proclamation was read by Australia's first Governor-General, Lord Hopetoun. Federal ministers including Prime Minister Edmund Barton and Attorney-General Alfred Deakin were sworn in.

Lawson could not give this historic news much attention, though, during his winter of unprecedented discontent. Even the death of Queen Victoria on 22 January 1901, after a reign of sixty-three years, failed to inspire him to pick up his pen.

The Dawn and Duskers were still having a good time back in Sydney. Victor Daley and Louise Mack,[50] who penned a column called 'A Woman's Letter' for *The Bulletin*, organised a farewell dinner – with drinks, of course – for the bush balladeer Will Ogilvie at the Hotel Australia. Ogilvie was returning to Edinburgh after eleven years.[51]

There were no toasts in the Lawson household, though. He was forced to give up the Harpenden cottage when Bertha was admitted. Needing money quickly to pay for her treatment, Lawson took emergency measures. He moved into a three-roomed flat at Clovelly Mansions on London's Gray's Inn Road with baby Barta and with Arthur Maquarie as a flatmate. Mrs Dean's servant Lizzie Humphrey moved in to help with the baby, now eight months of age. Jim, now almost three, was sent to live with a family friend, Mrs Brandt, in the Surrey village of Shepperton thirty kilometres up the Thames. If there was a sexual relationship between Lawson and Lizzie, she did not have the same residual effect on Lawson's heart as Bertha or Hannah Thornburn because he did not mention her in his writing except in his three-part story 'The Triangles of Life',[52] in which a domestic servant, 'Lizzie Higgins', appears in a crucial role, at Clovelly Mansions.

News travelled fast and as Mrs Mac wondered why she was not receiving letters from her daughter, the *Truth* newspaper gave her some bad news through its column 'The Lights of London':

> Pessimistic Lawson is here, buried in a dull, London flat, all alone. His wife craved and longed for the sunshine of her native Australia and is now in a mad-house, while her husband wanders about London and lives, nobody knows how.[53]

Madness haunted Lawson's frantic writing. In the immediate aftermath of Bertha's hospitalisation, he wrote 'The Babies in the Bush', as a poem for Archibald[54] and as a short story for Blackwood.[55] It dealt with the breakdown of Walter Head's wife Carrie after the disappearance of their son in the Gippsland bush. Lawson's next two pieces, 'The House that was Never Built'[56] and 'Telling Mrs Baker',[57] explored hallucinations and delusions.

Blackwood felt for Lawson and sent him a cheque for £22 10s for 'A Double Buggy'. He told Lawson that he would pay for future stories in advance on acceptance.

Angus & Robertson published its second book of Lawson poetry, *Verses Popular and Humorous*, to mixed reviews. Alfred Stephens told *Bulletin* readers that Lawson's 'second vintage' was 'inferior to the first' and while many of the works had found homes in 'ephemeral newspaper columns', they had 'no claim to be set on permanent record'.[58]

Blackwood agreed to publish *My Brilliant Career* and Robertson would later lament that his company had passed on the opportunity while he was overseas. The publisher sent another £39 to Lawson for 'The Babies in the Bush' and 'Past Carin' but more than half of that went on Bertha's fees at the asylum and board for the children, who were now together with Mrs Brandt.

Blackwood suggested Lawson write some amusing sketches for his magazine as his recent output had been maudlin, and he encouraged him to send him a long story that Lawson was hoping to turn into a novel. Bertha's recovery took much longer than Lawson imagined, though, and the novel never eventuated; only the haunting story 'A Child in the Dark'.[59]

Given his domestic turmoil, Lawson's moods were even more unpredictable than usual. Realising the bills would only keep mounting, he began recycling a lot of his old poems into short stories for other British magazines such as *Argosy*. In May 1901 he wrote to Robertson to say he had been an 'invalid for the last six months' – perhaps a euphemism for heavy drinking – and told him that Blackwood's edition of his prose, *The Country I Come From*, was going ahead; he was angry about Robertson's English agent Young J. Pentland and complained about poor distribution of his books, though he said he was thrilled by a seeming multitude of positive reviews in the English press, not mentioning that *The Scotsman* had called his work 'horse poetry' or that the *Daily Chronicle* said he was no Kipling. Lawson thumped his chest, pointing out that even though Angus & Robertson had rejected *My Brilliant Career*, Blackwood was publishing it on Lawson's recommendation after he had edited it and written the preface. The children were well, he said, and 'Mrs Lawson's health improving'.[60]

It wasn't.

On 14 May 1901, Bertha was transferred to the Bethlem Royal Hospital, better known as 'Bedlam', in the London borough of Southwark.

She was registered as patient 2616. 'Mr H. Lawson', who sent a deposit of £10, was noted as the person 'by whom authority sent'. Bertha's disorder was attributed to 'lactation' and the admission notes recorded: 'Melancholia with ideas of unworthiness. Hallucination of hearing & suicidal tendencies'.[61]

The certifying doctor reported:

She sat hiding her face in her hands and was most taciturn. She said 'I did it' over and over again, but would not state what. Stated she had no feeling anywhere, said she had killed both her children. Testimony by Florence Pope, a mental nurse at 123 Bond St, London: tells me Mrs Lawson hears voices. Supposed nurse to be the devil.[62]

Lawson told the doctor that his wife had tried to climb out of an upstairs window, and that Bertha had desperately begged him to kill her, or give her the means to kill herself.[63]

Chapter 19

Do not blame Harry, whatever you do. He has been the
best and most considerate Husband that ever lived.

<small>BERTHA DURING HER CONVALESCENCE AFTER BEING CONFINED
TO THE BETHLEM ROYAL ASYLUM[1]</small>

EARL BEAUCHAMP HELPED pay half of Bertha's medical
bills but as the winter snow and sleet eroded Lawson's own
mental wellbeing, he began to think about getting her out of
Bethlem and back to her family in Sydney.

Bertha decided to do it without his help. According to Mary
Gilmore, Bertha climbed a twenty-foot wall at the hospital 'by
means of a gas pipe, and reaching the Thames, started to swim
across'. A policeman, not knowing Bertha was a good swimmer,
jumped in to save her. The policeman could not swim and Bertha
nearly drowned him. Mary related that 'he contracted pneumonia
and Henry had to pay his expenses besides having to give him £5
for saving his wife'.[2]

Bertha was taken back to Bethlem, and with tender care and
sleeping draughts, her hallucinations became less frequent. The
voices in her head were silenced. Rumours of her husband's
drinking and cruelty gathered pace in Sydney, though, and she
rose from her sickbed to his defence. She apologised to Mrs Mac
for not writing sooner:

Dearest Mother,

… How sorry I am you have been kept in such suspense. Believe me, Harry did it out of kindness to your feelings. Mother, I've been dreadfully ill, or else you would have had a letter from me, it is only within the last month that I've been able to write at all, and as you see I'm a little shaky still.

Lawson was not to blame for her ills, she insisted, and she only wished that she could be half the person he was.

No, the fault was entirely mine. I have had too much responsibility for my years. You know what high pressure we had in Sydney, especially when Harry drank so heavily and then moving about so much, and the birth of the two little ones and the journey home [to England] finished me. An engine will only go a certain time and then will want repairing, and we mortals are the same. Never mind, I fought the drink fiend successfully and have done other things that people twice my age would not attempt and I mean to fight this, the voices and all the other frightful nightmare of this disease, have vanished and I hope soon to be able to sleep naturally – I'm sick of sleeping draughts. Now for something pleasant. Harry will make a big hit here, if only he keeps well physically. Oh, he has got so thin with the worry and trouble of this unfortunate illness. I expect to be soon home now and I'll fatten him up. Bertha has cut her teeth and Jim is in knickers though I have not seen him. Poor little mites, Harry has a kind, motherly old woman looking after everything but all the same it is not like a mother. If Harry had been wise, he would have sent me to a Government institution instead of keeping me in a private place and paying three guineas a week for me … Mother they drove me mad where I was before, well you understand more than I can tell you. … I expect to be home very shortly.[3]

A view of Bethlem Royal Hospital, London, from Lambeth Road, at the time Bertha Lawson was a patient. Wikipedia

Lawson planned to take his family home and then return to London by himself to continue writing.

While visiting the children at Mrs Brandt's at Shepperton, he found half a house for rent in the neighbouring hamlet of Charlton, which meant he could visit Jim and Barta more often. It was here that Lawson worked on the rest of his stories for the book *Joe Wilson and his Mates*, and where he hoped to house Bertha when she was finally allowed home. He would also use Charlton as the setting for his three-part story 'The Triangles of Life'.

Charlton was a farm labourers' village much poorer than Harpenden and next to the Lawson home were six two-storey cottages, or 'hutches' as Lawson called them, of 'dirty, smoky-looking brown brick tiles', for which the labourers paid 3 shillings a week. The cottages had steep little stairs more like ladders. Labourers' wages were from 15 to 20 shillings a week, women half that. Many of the girls, seeking better conditions, had gone either into service or into factories.

In his observation entitled 'Chawlton',[4] Lawson said the local peasants, much like his English ancestors, were 'slaves, and treated as slaves, and seemed invulnerable in their position as willing slaves'.

> I'd often fill the pewter, and be just getting comfortable with them and getting copy when one would spoil it with, 'We 'ope we ain't intrudin', sir? We 'ope we ain't makin' too free, sir?' They'd carry a 'gent' home beastly drunk and call him 'sir' all the time. 'Excuse us, sir, but you're bein' sick, sir! Hadn't we better stand yer up agen the wall, sir? Till yer right, sir?' Once I said, 'For Heaven's sake don't call me sir,' which only embarrassed and struck them dumb! It was no use trying to treat them as equals. 'He's a gent, and Gol darn it! Why don't he let us treat him like a gent?'[5]

Lawson sent Blackwood the story 'Joe Wilson's Courtship', the first of two humorous sketches that the publisher wanted for his magazine.

'I think that the happiest time in a man's life', Lawson wrote in the tale, 'is when he's courting a girl and finds out for sure that she loves him and hasn't a thought for anyone else. ... Make the most of your courting days, you young chaps, for they will never come again.'[6]

The *Joe Wilson* book was a hastily assembled collection of stories by a man under enormous stress, who was doing his best to regain balance in his life as everything seemed to be turned on its head. One of the stories, 'The Loaded Dog', about three easy-going goldminers, two dogs of different temperaments, and the chaos that ensues when the dogs treat a bomb cartridge like a bone, remains a Lawson classic. His desperation for money saw him constantly badgering Pinker for payment, though, and within a week of Lawson submitting the *Joe Wilson* collection, Blackwood posted two cheques of £50 each as an advance on royalties for the new book with a note saying: 'We trust this sum will help Mr Lawson in his present difficulty.'

Lawson's requests for more money began to grate. On 23 July, Lawson was in Pinker's office at Arundel Street off London's Strand, trying to find a buyer for his story 'Send Round the Hat'. Pinker sent it to Blackwood, telling him it was, as requested, in the humorous vein. And if he could send a cheque, it would be of great service to Lawson. At the same time Lawson sent a letter to Blackwood from Charlton, telling the publisher 'I wish to take you into my confidence', and letting him know that Bertha was in 'Bedlam' and would be released in a week or two. Lawson told the publisher he wanted a comfortable abode for his wife when she came home as well as a nurse for her and the babies. Could Blackwood send £50? 'Help me if you can.'[7]

The response was slow and confronting.

IN JULY 1901, LOUISE MACK arrived in London hoping to make her name as a writer on the world stage. She told Lawson and Maquarie that rumours of Lawson's drinking and Bertha's breakdown had caused a scandal in Sydney.

Maquarie was living with Lawson and the children while Bertha remained hospitalised. Edith Dean labelled Maquarie a 'ne'er do well', but he wrote to Archibald to assure him that malice was Mrs Dean's motive for her attacks and the talk of Lawson being abusive to Bertha was all 'rampant and criminal lies'. From what Lawson had told him, Maquarie had formed the opinion that Bertha's family had a history of instability and 'were all shut up from time to time. There's fancy names for the malady but only one word for it – hereditary.' While Lawson's good name was being blackened, Maquarie declared that he knew Lawson 'and his life' better than anyone in England and despite talk of drunkenness and abuse, he and his mate were actually 'living quietly by the Thames'.[8]

Archibald was also moved to defend his star protege, and eventually published the note: 'From one of Henry Lawson's friends in England: Lawson has had a terrible time (wife ill, &c.) and has come out of it like a strong man. He is doing well and has paid off the £200 advanced him by his literary agent during his wife's illness.'[9]

But Lawson wasn't doing anywhere near as well as he'd hoped.

Bertha came out of Bethlem on 14 August 1901 into the Charlton home as Maquarie moved out. A week later, Blackwood sent Lawson the final page proofs for the *Joe Wilson* book, but Lawson's enthusiasm for the project had waned as Blackwood's money had dried up. Blackwood had written to Lawson to tell him he was 'very distressed' by the writer's misfortune and glad to hear that Mrs Lawson was out of hospital, but sent Lawson only £15 for his story 'Telling Mrs Baker'. Blackwood said he hoped it would help, but he rejected Lawson's story about Peter McLaughlan, the bush missionary, and others because even though they were 'excellent', he had 'other engagements' for his magazine and he did not want to make it top heavy with Australian content.[10] He hoped Pinker would find buyers for the stories elsewhere. The publisher's explanation seemed fair enough, but Lawson's pride was hurt and their correspondence became more strained and formal. Then one of Blackwood's staff told Pinker that they would not be accepting the story 'Buckolt's Gate' because it was 'not up to the level of Mr Lawson's previous work'. Finally, in November, Blackwood sent Lawson another £100 for final payment in advance royalties for *Joe Wilson*, with a note saying he doubted sales would cover the advances.

Back in Sydney, Alfred Stephens was putting in the boot, telling *Bulletin* readers that 'Lawson is not relishing the winter, and talks of returning to Australia. Some of his recent work in Blackwood would hardly pass muster here.'[11]

Bertha recalled that 'Harry had been frantically distressed' about her illness and 'worked manfully' helping to nurse her 'back to convalescence'.

As I grew stronger we were very happy again. For, save in those dark moods for which he was not really responsible, Harry was a wonderful companion – sensitive, keenly appreciative, and very kindly. I know how grateful he always was, how firmly determined never to fail me again, and how he battled, through all the years, against the almost insurmountable difficulties of deafness, nervousness, poverty, discouragement, and ever-present temptation. That highly nervous temperament of his, which caused his moods, had also endowed him with a great vitality and a power of feeling and understanding which carried him through the dark places of his life, leaving the bitterness behind.[12]

Bertha, meanwhile, found the approaching English winter 'cold and trying'. Long, quiet evenings in the country, with the grey rain and the wind, and the snow falling, threatened a relapse. Lawson was frequenting Shepperton's Harrow Inn. Sometimes he would see old gypsy women warming their pints of ale over the pub's coal fire. Occasionally he would wander up to the camp called the 'Medder', on a triangular patch of ground off the Charlton Road, and stare at the painted wagons and the swarthy groups around the campfire, and he would recall the stories that his mother had told him about their supposed gypsy blood. The freedom of these travellers appealed to Lawson, unfettered as they were by the class system that bound the farm labourers; a system

The Harrow Inn on Charlton Road at Shepperton was one of Lawson's favourite places to drink. Alamy

that to Lawson was the curse of English man and woman. Lawson hinted at a sexual encounter with one of the women at the camp in his poem 'Gipsy Too'.[13]

Bertha put on a brave face and told her mother on 2 November 1901:

I'm writing by a blazing fire and have a thick jacket on and I'm still not warm. The fog is thick, you cannot see a dozen yards ahead. I do so sincerely hope this will be our last winter in England ...

Bertha and Jim are fat and roly. You would love the kiddies, they are so good. Jim is a very tall boy full of life and fun and Bertha is a pretty child. We'll get our photos taken as soon as we can afford it and I'll send one out ...

Harry's new book will be out on the fifteenth. The country is looking desolate, all the leaves are falling and everything is bare ... I've had both children vaccinated last Thursday, small pox is raging ...

Harry is truly fond of the children. He's been at it this afternoon making a train for Jim ...

How I wish we were spending Christmas together – we are lonely. I haven't a single friend. We never have a visitor, so unlike Sydney times ...

Harry is fortunate in having a splendid agent, he charges ten percent but when I was ill he advanced Harry sixty pounds so he must feel confident of him and his work.

As far as the slander you heard was concerned, there was not a shade of truth in them – Harry is, and is doing all in his power to make me happy and to atone for the drinking days ...

Dear Mother I shall have to say good night. Harry is waiting for the pen – again wishing you every joy and blessing for the New Year ...[14]

THE LAWSONS LEFT the loneliness of Charlton and took a tiny fifth-floor attic flat in Highbury – two small rooms and a kitchenette – for which they paid 7s 6d a week 'in Paradise Lane, off James Street and Holloway Road'.[15] On warm afternoons, as Bertha returned to health, they would take their children into Highbury Park, putting them in the pram, which they kept in a little shop around the corner, as there were ninety stone steps to the flat. Bertha said they would walk for miles all over London, with Harry roaming 'up and down the endless streets at all hours of the day and night gathering impressions, colour and experiences'.[16] Lawson worked by lamplight in the kitchenette, scribbling away long into the evening.

By January 1902, he thought he had enough stories to fill another book. He had five that Blackwood had rejected – 'Buckolt's Gate', 'Send Round the Hat', and three other stories he had taken from the 'Peter McLaughlan, Bush Missionary' idea: 'Shall We Gather at the River', 'His Brother's Keeper' and 'The Story of "Gentleman Once"'. He also had stories he had brought from Sydney such as 'The Boozers' Home' and 'On The Tucker Track: A Steelman Story', and still others written while Bertha was at Bethlem, including 'The House that was Never Built'.

Some of these stories, such as 'The Romance of the Swag', painted a stark contrast to the claustrophobic, Dickensian world of a small London flat in a cold, grey winter.

Lawson's collection of stories, prose and poems was a homage to the Australian bush and the characters who survived it – 'shearers, rouseabouts, drovers, bush union secretaries, swagmen, hatters, bush philosophers, bush missionaries, dipsomaniacs, remittance men, and shanty keepers'.[17] Lawson wanted to call the new book *The Heart of Australia*.

He wrote 'Barney, Take Me Home Again' for Bertha and ribbed her with the opening lines: 'This is a sketch of one of the many ways in which a young married woman, who is naturally thick-skinned and selfish – as most women are – and who thinks she loves her husband, can spoil his life because he happens to be good-natured, generous, sensitive, weak or soft, whichever you like to call it.'[18]

But as the narrator of the story, Lawson was longing for his island home too.

> I could stand the flat no longer. I had to go out and walk.
> I was sun-sick – I was heart-sick for the sun, for the sunny
> South – for grassy plains, blue mountains, sweeps of
> mountain bush and sunny ocean beaches. I walked hard …
> I walked through the squalid, maddening sameness of miles
> of dingy, grimy-walled blocks and rows of four-storied
> houses till I felt smothered – jailed, hopelessly.[19]

Bertha and Lawson would walk together through the English greyness, talking about the sunniest spots they could think of. 'Harry picked North Sydney and I picked Manly,' she wrote. 'When very blue, we'd pretend we were back in Sydney – walking up George Street and meeting our friends. Then we'd look out into the drizzle and fog, and pine and pine for blue skies and yellow beaches. I'll never forget walking up the Strand and hearing someone call, "Mimosa! Mimosa!" It was a flower-seller with a basket of wattle. We bought the lot and decorated our little flat. We were both feeling miserably lonely.'[20]

Lawson wrote to David Scott Mitchell to tell him that 'Mrs Lawson has had a very long and severe illness – however, things look bright again. … I have three or four publishers after me now and would have been in a comfortable position but for the heavy expenses of Mrs Lawson's illness. … Of course I've heard all about the countless stories that were circulated concerning me in Sydney. The origin of those lies is too paltry and contemptible for me to explain. I dare say Miss [Rose] Scott knows the truth by this time … I heard she was one of the few friends who remained true to me.'[21]

In Sydney, Louisa Lawson was fighting her own battles, in her case with the bureaucracy, led by Postmaster General William Patrick Crick. Louisa's experience running the bush post office at Eurunderee thirty years earlier had led her to develop a new type of fastener for mailbags. She supplied them to the New South Wales Government for four years and was negotiating with the governments of Victoria and New Zealand for the sale of the patent to them. Crick came up with a pirated design, but on 12 February 1902 Louisa was granted a permanent injunction restraining its manufacture and eventually awarded £300 compensation, reduced on appeal to £60. Still, she was left with 7000 surplus fasteners that cost her '£300 for brass alone'.[22]

LAWSON HAD AN IDEA to mock pompous literary critics such as Alfred Stephens with a book of his own criticism called *As Far As I'm Concerned: A Book on Pretty Prattle, Cackle, Fiddle Faddle and Diddle Daddle in Art and Literature.* He hoped Garnett, who was reading for several major publishing houses, would be able to place it. Garnett thought little of that project, but was much more impressed with Lawson's other work, declaring in the magazine *Academy and Literature* that 'I have never read anything in modern English literature that is so absolutely Democratic in tone, so much the real thing, as "Joe Wilson's Courtship"'.[23] Garnett wrote of 'The Drover's Wife' that 'given its significance in ten short pages, even Tolstoi has never done better'. Garnett said that Lawson would outshine all other writers in the Australian constellation, which made Lawson certain Blackwood would buy his new book, especially when Earl Beauchamp agreed to write a preface. But Blackwood was disappointed with sales of *Joe Wilson* and returned the new manuscript. At the same time Garnett told Lawson that the 'sarcastic' book of criticism was a waste of time. Lawson not only felt the harsh sting of rejection, but he was broke again and Bertha was desperate to get home with the children.

Big, burly Randolph Bedford paid the Lawsons a visit in London, rushing up the ninety stairs with the enthusiasm of a schoolboy only to find Lawson living in squalor and 'crying to be delivered from this death and to be set down in an Australian sun again'.[24]

Then there was a flash of light in the fog. Garnett and a colleague, E.V. Lucas,[25] recommended *Heart of Australia* to the publishers Methuen, whose list of writers included Arthur Conan Doyle, H.G. Wells and Henry James. They accepted it, with an advance of £100 that went to pay Lawson's many debts – and decided to publish it under the title *Children of the Bush*.

Still, Bertha remained fixed on taking the children home and her escape route was opened by the arrival in Liverpool in March 1902 of Mary Gilmore, her husband Will, and their two-year-old son Billy, who were making their way home to Sydney. The Gilmores had left Paraguay when Billy Lane had given up the ghost of his socialist utopia, and had spent time in southern Patagonia, where Mary taught English and Will laboured on sheep farms to earn their passage home. Mary obtained the Lawsons' London address from the New South Wales Agent General and invited them to visit her in Liverpool.[26] Bertha asked the Gilmores to come to London instead, and when Mary wrote to say that it was not possible because Billy was too ill, Bertha sent a telegram asking them to come immediately, with Lawson adding 'Mad for Australian face; come at once, bed's made, cot's ready'. The Gilmores arrived in London in late April and turned up at the flat earlier than planned. Lawson was out and a dishevelled Bertha was caught unprepared. Mary had never met Bertha, and in an age when some still gave credence to the pseudo-science of phrenology as being able to reveal insanity or criminality traits, said she was dismayed at the structure of Bertha's neck and skull. All of Lawson's money had gone on Bertha's medical fees and there was only one good chair in the flat. There was no bathroom and the Gilmores washed themselves in a tub in the communal laundry.

The kitchenette was so small that Mary had to sit wedged against a wall by Lawson's small writing table as Bertha prepared lunch lest she be scorched by the stove. That wasn't the most alarming thing. Bertha might have praised Lawson in her letters home, but within half an hour of meeting the Gilmores for the first time, she presented a very different picture. She told Mary the marriage was over, that she couldn't wait to get away from

London and from Lawson, and that she would never live with him again. 'Again and again' she said she hated her husband.

Then Lawson came home, and to the Gilmores he seemed a much different man to the monster Bertha had been describing.

'He was clean, bright and kind and affectionate in his manner to his wife and children,' Mary remarked.

Over dinner Lawson told the Gilmores that Bertha wanted to go home to see Mrs Mac. He planned to follow after finishing the proofs for *Children of the Bush*.

Mary wasn't too sure about being Bertha's escort and her fears were soon compounded.

After dinner Lawson and Will Gilmore went for a walk, and Mary and Bertha stayed with the children. Bertha had been waiting all evening to fire a second volley at Lawson and Mary would later write: 'I never met anyone express hatred so vindictively as she did.'[27]

The Lawsons gave the Gilmores their tiny bedroom, and Mary spent the night jabbing an umbrella at bugs that fell from the ceiling.

The following morning, Lawson and Will Gilmore went walking again and Lawson revealed that Bertha had spent ten months in London's asylums and told him about what he called 'the false charges against him, in regard to the servant'. Lawson said Bertha wasn't mad but bad.

Back at the flat Bertha fixed Mary with a forceful gaze and told her Lawson was 'guilty of unnameable immorality' and that he was extremely violent and had tried to kill her with a carving knife. Mary said she could see 'no visible scars' of such an attack and from what she'd observed Lawson seemed fond of her and the children.

'That is his cunning,' Bertha spat. 'That is all put on.'

Almost in the same breath she claimed that Lawson was afraid of her, and would do whatever she wanted because if he didn't, she would 'threaten to throw the children out of the window'.[28]

The Gilmores stayed in the flat for ten days and all the time, Mary said, Lawson looked 'fagged and ill'.[29]

Will Gilmore later told Mary that he didn't believe anything that Bertha said, and that he suspected that she had only married Lawson for his fame as a writer, and that since he had not made it big in London she wanted to get back to Sydney and be a 'somebody' again. Will was furious when he heard Bertha whispering to little Jim that his father was 'a bad man' when she knew Lawson couldn't hear.

Mary was understandably hesitant about travelling to Sydney with Bertha and had Lawson take her to Bethlem to interview the doctor who had treated Bertha there. The doctor told Mary that if she didn't take Bertha away from Lawson, she would turn him as mad as herself. Bertha was quite safe to be around, the doctor told Mary, so long as she got her own way. Mary then called on Nelson Illingworth's parents and Buster's father said that Bertha had made Lawson's life hell.

When Mary took young Billy to Bertha's personal physician to make sure he was fit to travel on a long voyage, the doctor told her a different story about Lawson. He lamented that Bertha had a lot to put up with, being married to a drunk.

LAWSON WAS NOW JUST nine stone (fifty-seven kilograms) of sparse flesh on his skeletal six-foot (183 centimetre) frame. In a letter to *The Bulletin*, he wrote that he would be coming home soon and that while he had been 'wonderfully successful from a literary point of view', his health had 'completely broken down' in London, and he would have to spend a year or so in Australia recuperating. He now knew England as well as he knew the bush and had a wealth of material for Australian publications.[30] Alfred Stephens ran Lawson's letter in full on the Red Page that he edited, with his own stinging commentary: '"I know London" – a bit of a delusion that!'[31]

Bertha, the children, and the Gilmores were booked in steerage below deck on the 5057-ton Norddeutscher-Lloyd steamship *Karlsruhe* that on 30 April 1902 was to begin the seven-week route to Sydney from Antwerp via Genoa, Naples, Cairo, Port Said, Aden, Bombay and Colombo.

Bertha borrowed some money from Mary to buy clothes for the voyage and Lawson borrowed £40 from Pinker to cover the loan and to pay for the fares.

The Lawsons fought viciously over whether he should go to see Pinker alone or with Bertha. On the day of departure Lawson was 'anxious beyond belief for the children … afraid of insanity', and worried that he had burdened the Gilmores with too much worry. Bertha told Lawson that she hated him, and that even if he was dying, she would not come to his deathbed. He had wanted to go with Bertha and the children to Harwich where they would catch the ferry for Antwerp, but Bertha wanted to be rid of him as soon as possible and threatened worse trouble if he did not leave them at Liverpool Street Station. She refused to kiss him goodbye or even shake his hand.

Mary recalled: 'She crossed to the side of the carriage farthest from him, turned her back on him and drew the children's attention from their father to the scenery. He stood sad and humiliated at the other window.'

Lawson mumbled, 'Aren't you going to say goodbye Bertha? You are going to the other side of the world and we may never see each other again.' But Mary wrote that Bertha 'even prevented Jim from saying goodbye to his father'.[32]

Mary had tears in her eyes at the sight of it, and Will Gilmore said it was the most callous thing he'd ever seen.

The Gilmores' shock continued in Genoa when Mary claimed Bertha flirted with staff, and at the Campo Santo fountain hit Jim in the eye with his own fist, blackening it as punishment. Back in his dingy flat, Lawson quickly became frantic worrying about his children, and decided to head home immediately too.

There may have been another pressing matter as well. At the end of 1901, Hannah Thornburn, the ideal woman Lawson fantasised over, had moved back to Melbourne where her parents were running a music shop. She was in difficult circumstances. Perhaps she had told him in a siren call, as one of his poems dedicated to Hannah suggests:

She was mine on return from succeeding
In a struggle that no one shall know;
She only knew my heart was bleeding,
She only knew what dealt the blow.
I had fought back the friends that were clutching,
I had forced back the heart-scalding tears
Just to lay my hot head to her touching
And to weep for Two Terrible Years.[33]

Despite pleas from Pinker and Earl Beauchamp to see *Children of the Bush* through to completion, Lawson decided to end his two years in England by catching a ferry to Antwerp to sail on the *Karlsruhe*'s sister ship *Gera*, just three weeks after Bertha's departure. He planned to send the proofs for the new book, complete with the dedication to Bertha, back to London from every port of call as he completed each set. But even before he climbed on board the *Gera*, Lawson began drowning his sorrows and 'A Foggy Night in Antwerp'[34] was born from his hazy recollections of the town where he spent much of his time at the bar. When the *Gera* sailed on to Italy, Lawson's poem 'Genoa' suggested he was finding love on the run and doing everything he could to forget about Bertha.[35]

Most of his memories from his two years in London were so bitter that he would write sombrely of days there 'like a nightmare',[36] and ...

That wild run to London
That wrecked and ruined me.[37]

Chapter 20

*[It was] a little message of love – her unforgettable love and
understanding. I think Ruth must have been a second Mrs Byers
only young, and fresh with the sweetness of youth. Lawson had told
me all about Ruth. Once she said to him, 'I would like to have a
child to you Harry ... I would like to be the mother of your child.
How wonderful he would be.'*

<small>DAME MARY GILMORE RELATING THE GREAT LOVE OF LAWSON'S LIFE[1]</small>

LAWSON ARRANGED with Mary Gilmore to write to him
from each port with updates on the voyage and especially
on the safety of the children, because Lawson 'was afraid of the
insanity, and terribly anxious' for their welfare. Mary said he was
'fearful for the children's mental inheritance ... lest it should be
unstable and asked me to write a full account of them and my
opinion of them'.[2]

The German ship had a voyage that mirrored the violent storm
between Bertha and her husband, and Lawson said his wife made
the *Karlsruhe* 'a miserable boat for more than one aboard'.[3]

In the Red Sea, two days after leaving the Suez Canal,
the *Karlsruhe* lost a propeller blade 'believed to be due to an
uncharted rock on the track to Aden'.[4] Once the ship reached
Aden, Mary composed a report for Lawson, saying exactly
what she thought of Jim and Barta 'as to appearance, capacity,
and futures'. Mary posted her letter with the ship's mail, but
Bertha, apparently suspicious that Lawson and his old flame

may have rekindled a romance, retrieved the envelope and read its contents.

'About an hour later I went up on deck,' Mary wrote, 'I noticed a crowd of people and Mrs Lawson amongst them. As soon as she saw me she rushed at me and struck me, shrieking, "I'll teach you to write to my husband behind my back!" and indulged in a series of accusations and charges in the most vulgar and violent language ... As I saw that she had my letter in her hand I said, "since you have stolen my letter, and since you have made accusations before all these people, I insist on you reading that letter aloud so that the people who have heard you will know just what I have written ..."

'The passengers turned away saying "well there is nothing in that letter to make a fuss over!"' Mary, though, was so upset that she took the letter from Bertha, tore it up and threw it into the sea.[5] She believed that a lack of news from her about the children had accelerated Lawson's dash from London on the *Gera*. Lawson had sailed from Genoa to Port Said, Aden and Colombo without incident, but the *Karlsruhe* continued to hit misfortune.

A day after leaving Colombo, a second blade came off and with bad weather on the horizon, Captain Koenemann turned around. There was no suitable dock in Colombo when he returned there, though, so he sailed the *Karlsruhe* back to Bombay, where guests were sent on shore and put up at hotels for five days.[6] When Lawson arrived in the cloying heat of Colombo on the *Gera*, he expected the *Karlsruhe* to already be at Fremantle, but instead, despite three weeks' head start, Bertha and the children were now four days behind him at Bombay. He sent Bertha a telegram saying that he would wait for them.

When the *Karlsruhe* reached Colombo again, Mary was 'too thankful for words' that Lawson was relieving her of the responsibility for Bertha, suggesting that she should still be in a psychiatric ward. Bertha watched with a menacing scowl as her husband approached from across the water. 'I saw a catamaran making for our ship, in it a figure, white-clad from hat to shoes, standing in the bow, while the crew salaamed to him as if he were a prince. Piled on the outrigger were heaps of oranges, pineapples, guavas, durians and other kinds of fruit, all belonging to Harry.' She was angry that the 'tall, gaunt figure in white' had obviously 'celebrated well'. Next morning, he was repentant, but Bertha still felt hurt and could not forgive him for his drinking.[7] Lawson described the change of vessel as going from 'heaven to hell',[8] and kept out of the shared cabin with Bertha as often as he could, yarning, instead, with the ship's crew and Will Gilmore. He saw three burials at sea.[9]

When the *Karlsruhe* docked at Fremantle on 6 July, Mary dashed off a letter to *The Bulletin*, telling the magazine 'Henry Lawson is with us' and that 'While in London I saw the manager of Blackwood's. He told me it would be madness for Lawson to leave London for a year or so. "He has the ball at his feet, and there's nothing to stop him," he said. A big publishing-agent told me the same thing.'[10]

Four days later, when the *Karlsruhe* reached Adelaide, Lawson fled the unhappy environment on board and caught a train to Melbourne. Bertha said it was 'in order to interview my brother and ask him to arrange a reconciliation between us. Eventually this was done there, at a family dinner at my brother's home in Williamstown.'[11]

Reconciliation with Bertha, though, was not Lawson's priority. Instead, he went looking for Hannah Thornburn.

Mary Gilmore always referred to Hannah as 'Ruth', Lawson's name for the character he had long ago fashioned from Hannah's image, and she wrote later that Lawson had dashed off to meet the girl, with a love letter from her by his heart.

Mary would later tell George Robertson: 'As long as I live I shall never forget that little bit of soiled and crumpled paper, which had never left that man's pocket – the breast pocket – and which held a hope that kept him able to endure. ... he came back to me with the light quenched and his life in ashes.'[12]

Lawson learned that Hannah had died in agony at Melbourne Hospital six weeks earlier on 1 June 1902. She was only twenty-five.

In mid–May Hannah had taken ill at a railway station. Three or four days later she suffered a large discharge of blood and on 25 May she had begun douching herself. Her hospital admittance record four days later listed Hannah's occupation as a 'domestic' and her address as 'Balaclava', though her parents lived at 19 Railway Avenue, Malvern. She was of the Congregational faith and single. She was also four months pregnant.

Within twenty-four hours of admittance Hannah's temperature had soared alarmingly, and a curette was needed to scrape the lining of her uterus, producing a mass of infected blood. Hannah became gravely ill during the night and died at two-thirty the next morning. Her friends believed that she had suffered an internal injury from lifting a piano in her parents' music shop,[13] but Dr H.I. Holmes listed the cause of Hannah's death as 'endometritis', a common condition after botched abortions.

When Hannah's mother Betsy was informed of her daughter's passing, she could not locate Hannah's father John, and so in desperation she sought the assistance for the funeral from the YWCA in Spring Street. Hannah was buried on 3 June in a YWCA communal plot assigned for the use of six bodies.[14]

The last time Lawson had been in Melbourne was when he had sat for his portrait in Longstaff's studio two years earlier, confident and excited with his eyes alight for success in London.

Now he was a broken man, and in a sense he never really recovered. Part of him was buried with his muse and he wrote of mourning beside her grave. He soon wrote 'Ruth'[15] in Hannah's honour, borrowing the character from his play and 'The Hero of Redclay' story.

Hannah would feature in some of Lawson's most personal and emotional work, and her memory probably kept him alive in the many dark hours he was about to endure. With his marriage in tatters, and Bertha seemingly an enemy rather than a friend, Lawson's embodiment of feminine perfection became the 'Spirit Girl' in 'To Hannah',[16] a moral guide and companion who Lawson hoped would protect him through the rough passages of life:

Through the world that I inherit,
Where I loved her ere she died,
I am walking with the spirit
Of a dead girl by my side ...'[17]

He perpetuated the fantasy later with the poem 'Hannah Thornburn' in which he embellished the details of the voyage on the *Karlsruhe* as a dash to meet his ailing goddess.

And in 'Do They Think That I Do Not Know' he answered critics who claimed he did not write deeply enough of love, or of passion:

She lives in the Marriage that Might Have Been
do you think that I do not know?[18]

LAWSON REJOINED HIS FAMILY and the Gilmores at Port Melbourne, but he was not keen on travelling with Bertha any longer.

Before going in search of Hannah, he had told Mary, 'If I can only find Ruth and lay my head in her lap I will be cured of all my trouble.'[19] He had told Will Gilmore about Hannah too. When Lawson returned crestfallen from the search, Mary felt so sorry for him that 'I could have told him to lay his head in my lap; only that when you are married to someone else you do not do these things'.[20]

Monte Grover, the brilliant young reporter for *The Argus* newspaper, arrived at the dock while Lawson was still there and he interviewed him and Will Gilmore over the failure of New Australia.

'He's had six years of the brotherhood of man,' explained Mr. Lawson, 'and he's full up.'[21]

'I told my mates I was sorry,' Gilmore revealed, 'but I wasn't communist enough to sacrifice my family for my principles.'[22]

Lawson and Bertha had twenty-four hours together in Melbourne but remained at loggerheads, and he returned to Sydney by train, depressed and disheartened about Hannah's death and his marital mess, the rattle of the carriage on the tracks playing a background tune to the racing staccato of his mind. His marriage had become a battlefield and now, broke, unstable and drinking heavily, he preferred the memory of a dead woman's love to the company of his wife.

Bertha and the children continued home to Sydney on the *Karlsruhe*, and all the way, as the steamer crashed through the waves, Bertha's worries grew worse. On arrival on 19 July, she chose to stay with her mother[23] while Lawson found 'a little snuggery edging on to the ocean beach at Manly'.[24]

Lawson (right) and fellow writer Albert Dorrington at Sydney's Circular Quay after Lawson's return from England. State Library of NSW, FL867110

On 2 August, *The Bulletin* let readers know that 'Lawson arrived in Sydney last week, having hastened his departure from London on account of illness. Lawson is suffering much from nerve trouble, and is now under medical treatment; but the bright skies of sunny Sydney should soon set him up again.'[25]

The *Daily Telegraph* interviewed Lawson not long after he arrived at Manly and said his memories of London were 'still fresh and rapturous'. Lawson revealed that 'for the first few months the monotony and loneliness of London was worse than the monotony and loneliness of the bush', but he had 'grown fond of the grimy old Babylon'. He planned to return during the next northern summer.[26]

He had high hopes for *Children of the Bush* and had arranged for the publication in Australia of 'a short series of articles dealing with the chances of Australian writers in England'.[27]

Lawson submitted a manuscript to Archibald entitled 'Succeeding: A Sequel to Pursuing Literature' in which he now advised writers to still 'Go to London – don't bother about Eternity or Timbuctoo'. The article did not appear for another year and then in an abbreviated form and with Alfred Stephens adding caustic comments about Lawson shunning editors and using an agent.[28]

Lawson wrote to Bland Holt, who had just opened his production of *With Flying Colours* at the Lyceum Theatre on Pitt Street, telling him he had promised 'Mr Archibald to go to Nurse Keys' Private Hospital[29] tomorrow morning and I s'pose I must stay there, for three days he says: I think for three weeks'.[30]

Bertha reluctantly decided to give Lawson another chance for the sake of the children and found them a home called 'Marlow' at 3 Beauchamp Terrace off Whistler Street, Manly. She was trying to coax Lawson into an inebriates' home, such as Rest Haven, for six months.[31]

His time in the private hospital was a start, and although Bertha had no writing paper, she scrounged around the seaside cottage and found a business letterhead.[32] She wrote to Lawson on a Friday in early August:

Dearie,

I wont come in tomorrow, it is such an expense it cost me 2/6 last night. I'll bring the children in early on Monday. And we will spend the day with you. I'm so glad you are getting on so well. We will be very happy yet. You must just let your own good nature overcome the evil one. Six months [in the inebriates' home] won't be long skipping past. And I'll come and spend one day a week with you. You must make great resolutions for the future and you will keep them, I know. Above all get to work and work hard. By so doing, you will forget the past and you will also forget yourself in your work. And I want you to make the most of your chances. You know you are a long way ahead of all Australian writers. But every week you let go by is so much lost. And it makes way for others, get ahead with your novel. It will be a big success and you must sell your work now, because your name is now before the public on account of [Children of the Bush]. You know dearie, in the past you have always let your opportunities slip past. Be like Kipling now, and make the most of it … Jim is not very well. He is troubled so with worms. I'm giving him a treatment for them. I think I'll take him to the Dr tonight. These bills have been worrying me greatly they keep asking me for them. So Dearie I'll be glad if you can fix them up. We have a good name here as far as debts are concerned. I've paid the rent and 7/6 for vegetables. And I really can't pay any more. There is a bill for bread for 9/- to Harper. I've paid the other bread bill myself. Good bye till Monday. With love from the youngsters and your wife.

Bertha[33]

The stay in hospital and sunny days beside the seaside with Bertha and the children did Lawson's mood a world of good and he was positively euphoric when he next wrote to Holt on 12 August 1902, to say that he had been in the private hospital for a spell 'where there were six (6) pretty nurses and I the only good-looking patient. Was getting very contented when Mrs Lawson called and fetched me home … Mrs Lawson sends kind regards. She is blossoming into an authoress.'[34]

Lawson captured the sheer joy of living in a place that would soon be promoted as being 'seven miles from Sydney and a million miles from care'.[35]

> Oh ! moonlit nights at Manly,
> When all the world was fair!
> In shirts and turned-up trousers
> We larked like big boys there.[36]

Lawson sent his article 'From Highbury Crescent to Chancery Lane' to A.C. Rowlandson for his 1902 *Commonwealth Annual*.[37] It was a travel piece about a walk through London, but Rowlandson rejected it and so Lawson gave him 'Joe Wilson in England', in which Lawson visits his friend Joe in Harpenden and hears a list

Lawson briefly found happiness with the sun, sand and surf of Manly Beach. National Library of Australia, 13294757

of grievances from him and his wife. Lawson had become an efficient recycler, and he sold the rejected sketch to *The Bulletin* as 'A Stroll to the Strand'.[38] *The Bulletin* also ran 'The Lost Souls' Hotel'[39] set on the Hungerford Road.[40] Lawson also sent three stories from *Children of the Bush* to the *Australian Star*, but still he and Bertha struggled to pay the rent at Marlow. They found a cheaper home a few doors away called 'Ladywood' at the end of August. It was from there that Lawson wrote to Miles Franklin, who was now living in Jersey Road, Woollahra, with Rose Scott. Franklin was also corresponding, flirtatiously, with Banjo Paterson who was giving her legal advice on her publishing contract and suggesting she sail away with him to a tropical paradise in the New Hebrides.[41] Following his daring stint as a war correspondent, Paterson had given a series of lectures in New South Wales and Queensland on his experiences, including the British atrocities in South Africa, and he had written about the execution of Breaker Morant, for murder in Pretoria, suggesting his old riding partner had become 'drunk with power' and had deserved his punishment.[42]

Lawson recommended that Franklin remain with Blackwood for the publication of a planned second book, *The Outside Track*, about a frustrated country girl who wants to be a singer. Despite Lawson's endorsement, sales of *My Brilliant Career* had been painfully slow in the first year: just 387 copies in England, and 1012 in Australia and New Zealand, and Franklin thought about signing with Angus & Robertson instead. Lawson's advice was that it would be a mistake to leave 'a leading British publisher' for an Australian house.[43] He had his concerns with A&R, too, he said, and claimed his books had to pay for the losses incurred by the failure of 'Dyson and others'.[44]

Lawson also sold *The Bulletin* 'A Child in the Dark' for its 1902 Christmas special. The disturbing tale was based around his childhood in the bush with an unpredictable, neurotic mother and coloured by his own marital trauma with a wife he characterised as hysterical, a son who was prone to convulsions and a baby who always seemed to be crying.

Manly was a far different environment to the grey and wet loneliness of London but Lawson was still drinking and the troubles with Bertha worsened. Her fragile emotional state cracked once more and Lawson had her admitted to a private hospital against her will. He dashed off a frantic note to Bland Holt, who was again helping him financially. 'Doctors consulting by telephone,' Lawson wrote. 'Specialist will be down in Manly tomorrow morning. It will be a long illness, but, they say, there is nothing to fear. Quiet and rest and trained attention is necessary … Old trouble, gastric ulcer. It would be as dangerous to carry her to Public Hospital as to carry her home. At home (and she wants to come home) the noise of the children would worry her. Kiddies alright. Little Jim told the Senior Sergeant that he had worms and his daddy had rats.'[45]

Bertha eventually returned to Whistler Street but Lawson feared it would not be long until she had a breakdown like the one she had suffered in London. The bills were mounting and he was out of prose and poetry to sell. The family's furniture was taken in lieu of unpaid rent.

Mary Gilmore, now living in Woodstock Street in Waverley, feared for Lawson, and said Bertha was constantly looking for revenge or to humiliate him. Lawson told her that so long as his children were 'fixed up' in life, he wanted to die, the sooner the better.[46]

Bertha then asked Lawson for a legal separation and he went with her to see the barrister David Ferguson at his chambers in Elizabeth Street, Sydney, to talk about it. Ferguson couldn't decide which of them was at fault – perhaps 'both of them' – but surmised Lawson had 'been at the whisky a fair bit since he returned'. Not only was Lawson now skint but he remembered he still owed Walter Woods £5 after borrowing it five years earlier. He said he would send it to Tasmania as soon as his next cheque came from Methuen in London, not realising there would be no cheque as *Children of the Bush* had not earned even half the royalties Lawson had been advanced.[47]

Lawson also consulted Dr Frank Bennet[48] about Bertha's prospects. Dr Bennet had been the Bredts' doctor in Bairnsdale before coming to Sydney, but soon it was Lawson who needed help for anxiety after Bertha took the children and moved back in with her mother. Drinking even more, Lawson became frenzied. He scrawled a rambling, unsigned note to Holt on four sheets of newspaper copy-paper using an artist's thick 4H pencil:

> I have to see Dr Bennet tonight about getting my wife into an asylum. I have just left her in care of friends. Trouble is I want to borrow £1. 1s. She wants to come home with me, but it is impossible. She is now at her mother's in Castlereagh Street, next the fire station. Her mother is also insane. I want to get her away from there. Ring up a Dr Bennet in College Street and he will tell you the truth ...

It was a factor in Lawson's manic personality that he never took responsibility for his behaviour or for its repercussions. His problems were always someone else's fault.[49] Now Bertha and her mother had become 'insane Prussanized Germans'.[50]

Lawson quickly wore out his welcome at McNamara's bookshop, pleading with Bertha to come home. Instead, on 4 December 1902, he learned that she had signed a sworn statement claiming she had to flee him out of fear. Lawson went back to Manly with the weight of the world on his skinny shoulders.

On 6 December, the Metropolitan Police District in the State of New South Wales summoned Lawson to the Water Police Office, Sydney, with Bertha alleging that she

> was compelled under reasonable apprehension of danger to her person, to leave the residence of you, her husband, and she therefor [sic] prays that she may be deemed to have been deserted by you without reasonable cause. That she is now at Manly aforesaid without means of support. That you are well able to support her but neglect to do. These are therefore to command you, in His Majesty's name, to be

and appear, on Wednesday the TENTH day of December 1902 at Ten O'clock in the forenoon at the Water Police Office, Sydney, in the said state, before such [Stipendiary] Magistrate or [Stipendiary] Magistrates for the Metropolitan Police District in the said state as may then be there, to answer to the complaint and to be further dealt with according to law.

On that same day, 6 December, Lawson was dazed, confused and desperate, as he stood on the top of the Manly cliffs and looked at the dizzying drop to the rocks thirty metres below.

Shortly after 10 a.m. a fisherman found Lawson's crumpled form near the water's edge.[51]

Chapter 21

For my ways are strange ways and new ways and old ways,
And deep ways and steep ways and high ways and low;
I'm at home and at ease on a track that I know not,
And restless and lost on a road that I know.

HENRY LAWSON, 'THE WANDER-LIGHT'[1]

O N 25 MARCH 1903 the British journal *To-day* ran the news that 'Henry Lawson is dead' along with a lengthy tribute saying that Australian literature had its origins with him, and with the observations of a unique land and people through Australian, rather than British, eyes. Had Lawson lived, the obituary lamented, 'He might some day have realised the glowing promise of his first book. But he is dead.'[2] The writer of the piece was Ballarat-born journalist E.C. Buley,[3] who was in London after serving sixteen months in Melbourne's Pentridge Prison for theft when employed at the city's Royal Mint.

Buley had broken the first rule of the obituary writer's code, though, because Lawson, though badly hurt, was still very much alive.

The fisherman who found Lawson crumpled at the bottom of the Manly cliffs helped him back to the track at the top, where Dr George Hall,[4] who had attended Bertha earlier in the year, reported that Lawson had a broken ankle and lacerations over the right eye, among other injuries.[5] Lawson was taken to the city and remanded from the Central Police Office as being of unsound mind before being admitted to Sydney Hospital, where his broken ankle was put in a cast.[6]

Eight days after Lawson was admitted to hospital Bertha wrote to say she had agreed to postpone a hearing for maintenance payments and told him 'eat all you can, and you will soon be well'. It was a struggle for her to feed herself and the children, though. She pawned some of their belongings for £10 and sent him a summary of the bills including her legal fees, his doctor's account, rent, laundry, cab to the hospital, lunch, stationery and stamps so they could correspond with each other, childminding charges, and the cost of some chicken and eggs she'd prepared for him. Bertha thought she would rent out a room at the Manly cottage or 'if all else should fail, I can still go out and work by the day. I answered an advertisement for an assistant in a draper shop, but they didnt want me.' She had tried to sell a story of her own to *The Bulletin* but had heard nothing back 'so they apparently wish to treat me with silent contempt'. She sent Lawson two sketches based on their domestic warfare to see what he thought of her writing. She was so desperate for food and rent money that she thought of asking Bland Holt for a part in one of his productions, but was adamant she would not take charity from Buster Illingworth or any of Lawson's other bohemian friends.[7]

As he slowly recovered from his physical and, more troubling, mental wounds, Lawson made light of the incident, writing to Robertson from Sydney Hospital's G Ward: 'I wasn't a success as a flying machine, was I.'[8] Robertson, believing the fall was an accident, annotated the message for his archives with: 'H. L. fell over a cliff at Manly – drunk of course.'

Lawson was overcoming his depression but as 'a temporary Wreck' submitted his 1200-word sketch 'In Hospital'[9] to *The Bulletin*. Despite hopes of a reconciliation with Bertha, he hinted that his predicament was all her fault. 'You see the majority of the accidents come about through drink, ... and the drink the result of woman's work.'[10]

Newspaper reporters suspected that Lawson's injuries may not have been accidental, with one declaring that Lawson had been 'under a mental cloud'[11] and another observing that he had said that he was living beside the ocean at Manly because 'the swells of the sea assuage sorrow'.[12] When commenting on an English newspaper's report on the incident, Alfred Stephens used inverted commas to describe Lawson's 'fall'.[13]

Lawson made light of it all, with a short explanation for *The Bulletin*: 'Fell sheer, as far as I remember, and the condition of my clothes bears this out – coat and waistcoat all right, pants torn a little at knee and foot of one leg, one boot "bust." Landed between jagged rocks on bed of sand – or sand and rubble. Broke ankle and lost an eyebrow. (Pipe, tobacco and matches safe.) ... Had whisky on board.'[14] Years later Lawson came clean, though, and admitted the fall was 'a mad attempt at suicide'.[15]

He confirmed that in verse too:

Twas the white clouds flying over, or the crawling sea below, –
Or the torture of the present or the dreams of long ago,
Or the horror of the future born of black-days, fate – or all –
Never mind! the gods who saw it know the cause of Lawson's fall.[16]

Mrs Byers, Lawson's old landlady from the Coffee Palace, visited him in hospital.

'What a wreck he looked,' she said. 'He was thin as a skeleton but how pleased he was to see us. A niece of mine was with me and he held onto us as if he feared we would leave him too soon ... We called to see his mother in Phillip St. She spoke kindly of him but said that Harry should never have left her, and that his proper place was with her.'[17]

Mrs Byers recalled that a doctor had taken a revolver from Lawson and returned it with great reluctance since it was the writer's personal property. As soon as Lawson got it back, he sold it.[18]

Bert Stevens visited Lawson on 20 December, the day *The Bulletin* published 'Ruth', and by then Lawson was recovering well 'as proud as a boy with a broken arm' to use a line from his 'The Star of Australasia'.[19]

With Bertha's encouragement – she called him 'Dearie' – and news that Barta was telling 'everyone her daddy has his legge in a cradle',[20] Lawson left Sydney Hospital after a month, still on crutches. On his way out, he shook hands with a boy who'd had some toes cut off, 'a manly little fellow – and he said: "Good-bye, Mr. Lawson, better luck next time!"'[21] Lawson thought that was funny, but not quite as funny as the reports of his death which had been greatly exaggerated.

Banjo Paterson recalled that 'Henry read with great interest and enthusiasm' his 'very flattering obituary notices'. 'The Banjo' asked Lawson what he thought of 'these final "reviews," and he said that, after reading them, he was puzzled to think how he had managed to be so hard up all his life!'[22]

LAWSON ENTERED a 'convalescent home' in Marrickville for treatment of alcoholism and sent Bertha a plea in verse:

And let us pray for happy days –
Like those of long ago.
Ah! had we knelt together then
We'd not have parted so.[23]

Husband and wife reunited in February just long enough for her to fall pregnant again.

The Critic newspaper reported that 'Henry Lawson has now quite recovered … but is usually accompanied in his walks abroad by Mrs. Lawson – in case he should slip again, as it were. He is brighter and cheerier than he has been for years.' Lawson wanted to go back to England, the paper noted, 'but Mrs. Lawson says that she would want £1,000 a week to live in Bourke (N.S.W.) and would sooner live in Bourke than in London'.[24]

Lawson could not stop drinking and the fighting started again.

Norman Lindsay remembered that Lawson was such an obnoxious drunk that even his idolators would 'have dived for cover' to escape him. 'Henry must've been an impossible man to live with,' Lindsay said. 'I knew Mrs Lawson fairly well, and liked her.'[25]

Lawson found a bed where he could, sometimes even paying 5 shillings a week to stay in the Castlereagh Street dosshouse run by Bertha's mother, though he always demanded a receipt. George Robertson loaned Lawson £5 but Bertha saw none of it. He stayed with his mother and brother Peter for a time, and wrote to Bertha asking to see her.

'My Dear Harry,' she replied:

… Why did you ask me to go to day. You can never know what an awful struggle I had with myself to come & see you. You know dear, if you would rather we were parted, *I am willing.* And it would be best to part now, we have made the break, and you did not seem a bit pleased to see me. Would you rather we separated?

I must know this. I have suffered. God alone knows. You never understood me and never will. Now through your family, I have to fight for my reputation. I have scarcely a friend … Of course when you are drunk, you are not responsible for what you say … If you wish us to come together again it is on the understanding not a relative of yours darkens our door. I will never speak to Peter or your Mother so long as I live. She can go where people can see her and shed her crocodile tears and make a blessed fuss, but she would not put her hand in her pocket and give your children a sixpence. I hate her. Now Harry I want to impress on your mind. I'll have no deceit. It must be all or nothing with me. I have forgiven you. And I never thought I could do it … I have stopped all law proceedings, and I hope you will soon be well and strong again. You have plenty of sympathizers, plenty who will shield you, behind the slanders of your wife. I think I have the courage to live it all down. If I wanted to love another man, or go wrong, it was not for lack of opportunity. You know my ideas of life, and you also know you are the only man I ever cared for. It is cruel the report should be round I forced you in to a marriage. Any way. My own heart & conscience is the only comfort I have.

Love from the children & your wife
Bertha[26]

Before long, Bertha suffered another breakdown, and called on Dr Hall, who despite Lawson's furious and foul-mouthed protestations, had him admitted to Prince Alfred Hospital as an alcoholic.

Bertha wrote to Lawson there, still hoping for the best:

Darling,

... Dr. Hall has just called in to ask after you, he told me to tell you he'll be up to see you the first day he can get away. Harry he is your truest and staunchest friend, dont you let your delusions carry you away in this matter ... I'm a woman and I know men, think of all he did for you. And he has shielded you, all through Manly. And he will take a great interest in you still. You be your true self to him, tell him you never meant what you said when you were drunk – you know you were so cruel to him that morning, when he came to get you into Prince Alfred Hospital. Tell him also I'm not the black woman I'm painted. I would feel it if he believed me bad because he is one of the few men I have any respect for. I respect about five men in the world, and I hope they also respect me. I love one – does he love me.

I will bring the children to see you on Wednesday. Dearie I owe Dr. Hall my reason and my life. If it had not been for him, I should certainly have gone mad, and I'd have taken my own life to [sic]. So that is why I want you to be nice to him and thank him for all he has done.

Why dont you write to me I'm so lonely. I get very miserable at times. Do you think of me. Ah, dearie, do let us forget the past. And we'll try and make the future bright for each other, hurry up and get well. And we will commence a new life here by the sea. We wont have any relatives, and only those who have proved themselves friends. —… Harry do you love me as much as I love you.

love from the children and your lonely wife

Bertha

Dont you be influenced by anything your Mother or brother says.[27]

Bert Stevens recalled that 'it was clear to me at the time that Lawson was very fond of his wife and loath to lose her, yet it was impossible for them to be happy together'.[28]

Bertha, pregnant and fretful, agonised over her next move but eventually decided that Lawson was unable to reform.

Since Stevens was still working in a legal office, Lawson and Bertha asked him to fix the matter privately. 'Lawson, however, came to me afterwards,' Stevens wrote, 'and wanted me to bluff his wife and prevent her from completing the separation. I advised Mrs Lawson to go to a solicitor and apply for a judicial separation, which she did. From that time Lawson went downhill steadily.'[29]

Bertha contacted her solicitor Thomas Henderson, who filed a petition in the Supreme Court for judicial separation, claiming that 'My husband has during three years and upwards been an habitual drunkard and habitually been guilty of cruelty towards me'. Bertha claimed that Lawson struck her 'in the face and about the body and blacked my eye and hit me with a bottle and attempted to stab me and pulled me out of bed when I was ill and purposely made a noise in my room when I was ill and pulled my hair and repeatedly used abusive and insulting language to me' as well as 'other acts of cruelty to me whereby my health and safety are endangered'.[30]

Writing to Lawson in hospital three weeks later on 23 April 1903, from her solicitor's office:

Harry,

If you do not send Mr. Henderson, some money for the children at once, I shall be forced to place them in the Benevolent Asylum.[31]

Bertha had a reputation for being overly dramatic, her daughter admitted in later years. She made the asylum claim even though Bertha's mother and sister Hilda lived only a few miles away. But she continued:

I have 1/6 left and have to pawn my ring to day. I dont care about myself, but I cannot see my children starve. I have had to place them with strangers, while I tried to earn a living. The people have sent me word, to come and take them away to-morrow because I could not pay them for their support this week. I think it is most dreadfully cruel for any Mother, to have to part with her children let alone be placed in the position that I am in.[32]

Lawson was convinced he could charm his way back into Bertha's heart, and told Robertson three days later that he was in Prince Alfred Hospital 'remanded for medical treatment – drunk. She (Mrs L.) has taken out a legal separation, but will forgive me.'[33]

Not likely. Robertson was on Bertha's side, too, and had just given Rose Scott £5 to help Lawson's family.

Lawson heard about the money and in Prince Alfred Hospital asked young doctor Charles Bickerton Blackburn[34] for a loan of 2 shillings so he could go downstairs to buy tobacco. That was the last time the doctor ever saw him.[35] Lawson turned up at Rose Scott's house in Woollahra wanting to take charge of Robertson's £5, but that was not going to happen and Bertha later sent Robertson a letter of thanks to say she could now pay a woman to look after the children while she went into hospital for an operation on her jawbone following a tooth extraction that had gone horribly wrong.

Lawson appealed to Bertha for mercy.

Girlie, Do try to forgive and forget. My heart is breaking and I can't live without you. Remember I was ill, very ill, and not responsible for what I said. It was all my fault. If I make you suffer, think how I have suffered … Dearie I love you with all my heart and soul and will never say an unkind word to you again. Don't listen to friends and neighbours – listen to me … Remember the happy days we had once. Only think of me as the man I was and will be again … Forgive me and come to me and we'll be happy in spite of it all.[36]

At another time he apologised for speaking harshly 'knowing the state of your nerves' but that she should consider the state of his health and not repeat or believe 'vile slanders' about him.[37]

Begging didn't work, and so Lawson hired James Elphinstone as his lawyer. He was advised that he had no hope for custody of the children given his record of alcoholism, and on 28 May 1903 agreed to the separation, on the undertaking that Bertha would drop all charges, and that while she would have sole custody, Lawson would be granted access to Jim and Barta for one afternoon a week. Lawson was to pay Bertha's legal fees of 20 guineas as well as 30 shillings a week – a little more than £6 a month – in child support.[38] Bertha's claims of his cruelty were never tested in court and only she and Lawson ever knew what had really happened between them; how he really behaved when he was too drunk to remember, or how much of Bertha's story was hard fact or embellished emotion.

The Critic newspaper reported: 'A certain Australian writer has been lately gravitating from the lock-up to the hospital with surprising swiftness. Some folks have been writing sympathetically about the strain of overwork which drives so many Australasian literary men astray. It is not overwork, but over drink which is to blame.'[39]

Mr Justice Simpson accepted the terms of separation in the case of Lawson v Lawson on 4 June 1903[40] and thus the 'author and journalist' was spared a public hearing over Bertha's claims of his violence, cruelty and drunkenness.

LAWSON SOUGHT REFUGE in the Thomas Walker Convalescent Hospital on the Parramatta River at Concord, an institution funded by a wealthy family which had just welcomed Banjo Paterson into their fold as the new husband of the lovely Alice Walker, a station owner's daughter from Tenterfield. Banjo's book *The Man from Snowy River* continued to be a bestseller and the success of a follow-up collection, *Rio Grande's Last Race and Other Verses*,[41] ensured Paterson had sold more books than any other Australian. He had also just been appointed the editor of the major Sydney newspaper the *Evening News*. The contrast with Lawson's lot in life could not have been starker.

Lawson was taken with one of his nurses, Alma Clarke, who reminded him of Hannah Thornburn, and he wrote the poem 'New Life, New Love',[42] telling himself that in Hannah's memory he 'found a light in my long dark night, Brighter than stars or moon'. He came back to reality with the lines in another poem that he had 'sacrificed all for drink/And the nights of Leicester Square.'[43]

To feed the children, Bertha was now working as a saleswoman for a firm of booksellers, Stuart and Co in Elizabeth Street,[44] while struggling through the pregnancy, the pain of her fractured jaw, and the emotional and physical scars she said Lawson had left on her.

Now four months' pregnant, she responded to her estranged husband's pleas for another reconciliation with a letter on 15 June 1903, from her small rented flat at 397½ Dowling Street, Moore Park, that she shared with the children.

Harry
… Re the children. I will not consent to let them go. Not through any paltry feelings of revenge, but as a matter of duty. You see, you left me, with these two little children. I was turned into the world, with 1/6 and not a shelter or food for them. I had to pawn my wedding ring to pay for a room. And then had to leave the little children shut up in the room, while I sought for work. And when I got

work to do I had to leave them all day, rush home to give
them their meals. And back to work again. And mind
you, I was suffering torture all the time with toothache,
and had to tramp the cold wet streets all day, knowing
unless I earnt some money that day the children would
go hungry to bed. (I was a fortnight working before
Robertson gave Miss Scott that money.) I had no money
to pay a dentist. (I wrote to you at P.A. Hospital telling
you, you were forcing me to place the children in the
Benevolent Asylum and you took no notice of the letter.)
I went to the Dental Hospital and had a tooth extracted.
They have broken part of the jaw bone. And I go into
hospital on Wednesday and go under an operation to have
the dead bone removed. The children will be well looked
after. While I am away I have to pay a pound where they
are going. So I trust you will endeavour to send Mr.
Henderson some more again this week …

God alone knows how often I have forgiven you and
how hard I struggled for you. And how have you treated
me. Harry there is no power on the earth will ever reunite
us. You are dead to me as far as affection goes. The
suffering I have been through lately has killed any thought
of feeling I may have had for you.

When you have proved yourself a better man and not
a low drunkard you shall see your children as often as
you like. Until then, I will not let you see them. They
have nearly forgotten the home scenes when you were
drinking – and I will not let them see you drinking again.
I train them to have the same love for you as they have for
me. And if baby's prayers are heard in heaven, you should
surely be different, to what you have been. They will have
to decide the right and wrong between us, when they are
old enough to understand. I think you are very cruel to
make the statements you do about me. You know Harry as
well I do they are absolutely false. Why dont you be a man.
And if you want to talk to people of your troubles, tell

them *drink is the sole cause* … I am so weary of struggling against pain and sorrow that I do not give a tinkers curse for anything – or anybody.

Bertha[45]

Lawson extracted another £5 from Robertson and paid £3 to the police department on 22 June as part of his maintenance settlement. Through her solicitor, Bertha wrote to Lawson again on 25 July to tell him she would be 'laid up either the end of October or first week in November' with the birth of their third child. It was only for the sake of Jim and Bertha, she said, or she would either have had an abortion or committed suicide.

I cannot walk far or stand long, and it is not a very cheerful prospect to look forward to, knowing as you know well, I will very likely die. I cannot save anything out of the thirty shillings a week. I have seven shillings rent to pay. 10 [shillings] every week to pay off the dentist bill … You promised I should have every comfort. I am not asking you for that but for bare necessary's.

Your wife
Bertha Lawson[46]

Lawson told friends and family that Bertha was lying over the rumours that he mistreated her, but those who had seen him drinking suspected she was telling the truth. In his defence, Lawson wrote 'The Men Who Live It Down', declaring that he and Christ knew 'the truth!'[47]

In 'The Alleys', which earned Lawson a few shillings from *The Bulletin* and £3 for future use by Robertson, Lawson wrote of 'a madness I inherit, and a blind and reckless spirit'.[48]

When Lawson found a bed at his mother's house again, she was still hoping the Federal Government would buy her huge store of excess mailbag fasteners, but it wasn't to be. The stress was disturbing her mind and, like Bertha, she was having to offload furniture to meet debts. The tensions between her and

Lawson escalated again, and in his manic feelings of superiority, Lawson would accuse his mother of being lazy and jealous of his reputation as a writer.[49] But Lawson found a sheaf of her poems that he thought might interest Robertson, including 'To a Libertine' about a man who destroys the love that a young woman had for him. Robertson liked some of the poems 'very much' but was unsure whether they could turn a profit, so Louisa published them herself in *The Lonely Crossing and Other Poems*.[50]

Jack Brereton reacted with concern to Lawson's dark writing in 'The Alleys' and wrote a poem, 'To Joe Swallow',[51] for *The Bulletin* which was designed as a 'kick in the backside' to wake up his 'friend of ten years' for all his 'blustering' and whining. Lawson, though, was much more interested in Robertson's offer to help him ensure his maintenance payments to Bertha by writing a 35,000-word autobiography, a project that would give Lawson full vent to his longing for nostalgia and introspection. Lawson was to deliver the manuscript by 7 April 1904, with a £100 advance, comprising £20 down and £4 a week for twenty weeks. Lawson signed an agreement on 1 October with Castlereagh Street solicitor Bert Davies that the book money would go to Bertha, while Robertson paid for Lawson's food and shelter.[52]

Bertha's confinement approached but her baby was stillborn, and the wedge between her and Lawson grew ever wider. With the loss of the baby's life, and the unravelling of his own, Lawson's autobiography stalled as a loose series of superficial sketches, often fictionalised.

Instead, Lawson found shelter with Mrs Byers, who took him under her protective wing at the Coffee Palace in North Sydney at the end of 1903.

LAWSON WAS NOW thirty-six and Mrs Byers was fifty-five, the same age as Lawson's mother, having been born to a Scottish family on a farm in the Hawkesbury region way back in 1848 as Isabella Ann Ward.[53]

After Lawson's marriage break-up, she had written to him, saying: 'I feel very much troubled about you. I can't bear to see you looking so thin and miserable, so cheer up and make the best of things.'[54] Mrs Byers had a reputation for taking in every stray cat and dog that wandered by the Coffee Palace and she was able to provide sympathy for Lawson's battered psyche. She turned a little tearoom into a bedroom for him. On his first day back with Mrs Byers, Lawson sat at one of the tables, buried his head in his arms and cried.[55] Bert Stevens said Mrs Byers became 'a devoted admirer, wife, mother, nurse, champion, and business agent combined – but she could not keep [Lawson] straight and perhaps did not try'.[56]

Lawson affectionately called her the 'little woman'. They may have been lovers but more likely it was a mother-and-son relationship. Lawson complained about her multitude of cats, but would regularly bring home stray dogs and kittens. Sometimes she would forgetfully leave eggs on his bed, which he would accidentally sit on, spreading yolk over his pants.[57]

At the end of 1903, *The Bulletin* ran Lawson's 'The Wander-Light' in which he blamed his restless, erratic nature on gypsy blood and the nomadic existence of his parents during his early years. Christmas 1903 would be his first apart from his children and he wrote the poem 'Barta':

I dreamed, when I was good, that when
The snow showed in my hair,
A household angel in her teens
Would flit about my chair,
To comfort me as I grow old,
But that shall never be –
Ah! baby girl, you don't know how
You break the heart in me.[58]

Despite the expressions of love for his children, though, Lawson could not, or would not, settle down to a steady job to provide for them. Bertha wanted him to go back to house painting and write in his spare time, but he had become too feeble for manual work and too erratic to work in an office. In his poem 'The Passing of

Scotty',[59] Lawson empathised with the nomadic Phil Mowbray, the Scottish-born swagman, who wrote for *The Bulletin* as 'Scotty the Wrinkler', and whose obituary appeared in the magazine on 5 November 1903. Jules Archibald, now fighting his own battles with depression, had handed over the editorship of *The Bulletin* to James Edmond,[60] a Glaswegian who started his impressive career in journalism in Rockhampton and whose large head and wise visage recalled a portrait of Socrates.[61] Lawson sold Edmond the story 'A Romance of Three Huts'. Then he sent him an exploration of his alcoholism in the form of a letter to run in the magazine's first issue of 1904:

> Dear Bulletin,
> I'm awfully surprised to find myself sober ... Why does a man get drunk? There seems to be no excuse for it. I get drunk because I'm in trouble, and I get drunk because I've got out of it. I get drunk because I am sick, or have corns, or the toothache: and I get drunk because I'm feeling well and grand. I got drunk because I was rejected; and I got awfully drunk the night I was accepted. And, mind you, I don't like to get drunk at all, because I don't enjoy it much, and suffer hell afterwards. I'm always far better and happier when I'm sober, and tea tastes better than beer. But I get drunk.[62]

Lawson's poem 'The Afterglow'[63] reflected his depressed mood as he looked back on the blunders of his life 'from the loneliness/ And depth of my disgrace'.[64]

Robertson bought the copyright for seven Lawson poems to help Bertha, as Bert Davies now made monthly requests for £10 for her. Among the poems Robertson bought was 'The Secret Whisky Cure',[65] satirical verses about a nagging wife, a theme Lawson pursued again in 'The She-Devil', about women and their false charges.[66] Despite Robertson's generosity, Lawson fell behind in his monthly payments to Bertha and went into hiding from the law. As he dodged the police he pumped out 'The Last

Review',[67] in which he pictured himself on his deathbed looking back at his life.

Using Mrs Byers's collection of Charles Dickens's novels as his reference, he turned an unfinished poem called 'Dick Swiveller' into 'With Dickens',[68] which Banjo Paterson ran in the *Evening News*, which was now boasting 100,000 sales a day.[69]

Lawson sold the Biblical 'The Good Samaritan'[70] to Robertson for £5 and received £7 for a batch of five others including 'The Heart of Australia',[71] written in England for *Children of the Bush*, and 'The Ballad of the Elder Son',[72] which referenced the 'shame' caused to the family by Charlie's life of crime. Robertson decided to publish a new book of Lawson's poetry including those from his time in England. Lawson was excited to again be in demand, and penned a series of new poems including 'Joseph's Dream and Reuben's Brethren' and 'When I was King', a rant against the world's mean and paltry things. Paterson also ran Lawson's poem 'The Crucifixion'.[73]

AS LAWSON HUSTLED AROUND Sydney chasing buyers for his work, he was at Circular Quay's North Shore Wharf just before noon on 27 December 1904. He watched as a diminutive young woman named Ettie Thrush of 14 Glenmore Road, Paddington, placed her five-month-old baby gently on the pontoon and then jumped into the water to drown herself. Without a moment's hesitation, Lawson leapt into the water and with another man, James Sabbach of Chatswood, hauled Mrs Thrush to safety. The crowd cheered and newspapers around Australia topped their reports with such headlines as 'Brave Rescue by Henry Lawson',[74] though *The Bulletin* reported that after saving the woman from drowning, Lawson 'didn't pose for any laurels ... but went quietly home to dry his only suit of clothes'.[75]

Mrs Thrush was taken to the Sydney Hospital. When asked why she jumped into the water she replied, 'I have got my troubles.' The Circular Quay police charged her with attempted suicide and took her baby to the Benevolent Asylum.[76]

Lawson tore a report from the *Australian Star* the next day and on the back of a bank deposit form wrote a quick note to accompany it for Bland Holt: 'They told me she would be alright. They had yanked her out of the hospital and taken her to the police station. She wanted to see me. I can't help her. You might telephone. Are we savages?'[77]

Mrs Thrush appeared at the Water Police Court on 4 January 1905, and admitted that while drunk and depressed she had tried to end her life. Her husband told the court that he had forgiven her a hundred times, even though she had done 'very bad things' and she drank a lot. On the judge's prompting, Mr Thrush said, yes, he was willing to give his wife one more chance, but would prefer to do it only on a 'three-month trial' to see whether she 'behaved herself'. Ettie asked the judge if she could get her baby back. The judge said that would be 'seen about' later on.[78]

Such was the way courts treated depression in 1905.

The law would have little mercy for Lawson, too, as his war with Bertha escalated. Mrs Byers offered him a comfortable bed, but Lawson was about to find prison accommodation soul-destroying.

Chapter 22

You are a child of field and flood,
But with the gipsy strains
A strong Norwegian sailor's blood
Is running through your veins.

LAWSON WRITING TO HIS SON IN THE POEM 'TO JIM'[1]

FACING HIS SECOND CHRISTMAS without Jim and Barta, Lawson's mind was flummoxed. Mrs Byers said that Henry 'often hoped and wished' that the estrangement with Bertha would be bridged and that they could all settle down together in the country.[2]

Bertha remained living in Manly 'with a very kind woman, Mrs. Ellison, who took care of the children' when she went to work. 'Harry', she said, 'often came to see us but it was useless taking up house again as he was quite penniless and the children had to be provided for. He undoubtedly had some resentment about the situation, but I told him he would always be welcome to come and see us. And so the years passed on.'[3]

Lawson came to see the children one afternoon every week as the conditions of the separation allowed.

'At heart he was a good husband and father,' Bertha remarked, 'except when the temptation to drink was too strong.'[4]

Barta's first memory of her father was meeting him 'on the back of an old Spit tram' near Mosman. 'At least, that's when I first clearly remember him. He seemed very tall, and was dressed

Jim and Barta Lawson (indicated with crosses) at Enmore State School not long after their parents' separation. State Library of NSW, FL3319372

in comfortable old clothes, and he got on a stop or two after we did. He had a large cane picnic hamper, the square sort with the skewered lid. He sat this on the floor and took me on his knee … We were making for the tiny beach on the other side of Middle Harbour, a little rocky curve long buried under the highway. He had brought chicken, and some other treat for Jim and I. He loved to be responsible for the day's outing. I remember I was busily exploring some rocks, while Mother bathed and Jim went wandering off, and I fell in. My wails brought Dad flying. I had cut my foot, not badly, but I remember how upset he was, tearing a handkerchief into strips and binding it firmly while he comforted and quieted me.'[5]

Barta remembered, too, how carefully Lawson would brush his moustache aside when he stooped to kiss her.

Every parting with the children was bitter but at the Coffee Palace, Mrs Byers mothered Lawson. He became a local curiosity. Coffee was not his favourite drink in a city of 300,000 people and more than 3000 pubs.

Lawson often ended up legless from long boozing sessions and described a pub in the Blues Point area of North Sydney as his local, 'frequented – haunted – by ancient mariners, wharf and water side characters, carters, casual smugglers and such like – and, strange to say, by a few ghosts of retired and forgotten bushmen'. There were also 'a disbarred solicitor – an artist ... a very cheerful professor of something or other'. They were all mostly separated from their wives, Lawson noted, 'and anything else (except beer) that makes life interesting'.[6]

Lawson's moods could change dramatically from hilarity to sombre self-recrimination. His first poem of 1905 for *The Bulletin* was 'Australian Engineers',[7] in which he thundered against a people who sent steamers to England 'with our timber and wool and gold' and had them return with shoddy goods 'for stunted and white-faced Australians to sell in our sordid shops'.[8]

His writing reflected his bipolarity. His jingoism was offset by his republican socialism; his bohemianism by a puritan hangover from childhood; his sympathy for downtrodden women, particularly bush-women, by occasional virulent anti-feminism forged by the bitterness of his separation; his notions of a brotherhood of man by rampant xenophobia and racism. He confessed a hatred for the dry, harsh landscape of dirty brown rivers and an ill-disciplined people at the same time as he became a hopelessly ill-disciplined addict.

On the afternoon of 30 January 1905, Lawson stood among a crowd of thousands in pouring rain at the Domain to watch Earl Beauchamp's replacement as Governor of New South Wales, the beefy British naval officer Sir Harry Rawson,[9] unveil a statue of the bard Robert Burns which had cost the Highland Society of New South Wales more than £1600; a multi-million-dollar amount in twenty-first century currency. Prime Minister George Reid was to speak as well, but had begged off in the foul weather, saving his tribute for a concert in Burns's honour that night in Sydney Town Hall.[10]

Lawson sold *The Bulletin* his take on 'Robbie's Statue', in which he hears the ghost of the swagman Scotty the Wrinkler telling him not to worry about his critics who were mere 'fly-dirt on the pages'.[11]

Robertson bought the poem too, for inclusion in Lawson's new book, and Lawson also gave him 'The King, The Queen and I' in which the narrator tells Scotty the Wrinkler that the Longstaff portrait of Lawson hangs beside those of the King and Queen in Sydney's National Art Gallery.[12] He may have been looking down upon those who had mocked his current station in life, when he declared in 'The Soul of a Poet':

> But wronged, and cast out, drink-sodden,
> But shunned, and 'insane' and unclean,
> I have dared where few others have trodden,
> I have seen what few others have seen.[13]

Banjo Paterson was seeing and daring what few others had tried as well. One of the perks of being editor of the *Evening News* was that he could give himself plum assignments, and in early February 1905 he covered the Dunlop Motor Reliability Trial from Sydney to Melbourne, the first such event for automobiles. Banjo had long been lauded as one of the country's premier horsemen but he knew the days of the steed were numbered.

At the same time Lawson became intrigued by the ideas of a Mosman doctor, Richard Arthur,[14] who had just been elected to the Legislative Assembly for Middle Harbour. Dr Arthur was forever warning Australia that they must be prepared for a Japanese attack, and he was also a strident campaigner against alcohol, advocating hypnosis as a cure–all for many nervous complaints.

Lawson gave Dr Arthur's treatment a try, but with little success. Instead, Lawson was arrested for drunkenness and presented with a summons for maintenance arrears of £6 12s 2d. He did not have the money and despite his output of poems and the promise of a new book, had little means of collecting it. Instead, he went into hiding, bottle by his side, but not before leaving a note for Robertson on 15 February: 'Dear R., How will you take me – hypnotized or tight? [H.L.].'[15]

'Neither', most likely. Lawson 'tight' with drink was bad enough but under the influence of hypnosis who knew what could happen?

For Lawson, Robertson had become a 'money lender, financial advisor, private secretary, father confessor, legal expert, literary consultant, elder brother, bondsman, and general milch cow ...'[16]

For Robertson, Lawson had become a pest, albeit a gifted one. The proud and noble figure who had sat with dignity for John Longstaff was now a shambling, rambling wreck and Lawson began to arrive staggering into the Angus & Robertson building, reeking of stale beer, sweaty clothes and tobacco juice. Occasionally he would interrupt the publisher's business meetings, silently holding up three fingers – for threepence, the price of a beer – and then when it was placed in his palm, elaborately bow as he shuffled off to the nearest bar. Sometimes Lawson would arrive unexpectedly off the street and simply leave scribbled notes bearing cryptic messages for his publisher in an almost indecipherable scrawl.

Owing to misunderstandings caused by his deafness, and the distortion made by copious refreshments, Lawson could turn an innocent remark into the opening bell of a fistfight. On one occasion, he took it into his head to challenge Robertson, pacing up and down through his bookstore and bellowing: 'Where's Robertson? Where is the chief?' before eventually sobering up.

Lawson became so obnoxious that Robertson would scurry up a steep flight of stairs into a hidden hutch to work unobserved if he had warning that Lawson was on his way. But Lawson rarely left the publisher's office empty-handed.

The bookseller Jim Tyrrell[17] remarked that when he was working for Angus & Robertson, Lawson's IOUs – most of them for 2 shillings – made quite a heap on the desk of 'kindly old Dan Angus', the elder brother of Robertson's business partner.

At *The Bulletin* office, editor James Edmond tried to dodge Lawson too. Edmond would patiently go about his work while still pretending to listen to Lawson's frequent ruminations.

The novelist Vance Palmer[18] recalled that only once was the little Scotsman's patience exhausted. Lawson had brought in some verses and insisted on Edmond reading them.

'Not now, Henry,' Edmond protested. 'Leave them here for half an hour and I'll look them over when I have a minute to spare.'

Still, Lawson insisted, waggling the verses in front of Edmond's eye until the editor 'laid down his pen, slowly lit a cigar, and then applied a match to the drooping manuscript in front of him'.[19]

Lawson still worked at his various hideouts, trying to find the maintenance money.

After calls in the press to harness the Murrumbidgee River, Lawson wrote 'The Water',[20] a poem he called 'a song of irrigation'. He sold it to the *Amateur Gardener* magazine along with others such as 'Waratah and Wattle',[21] 'The Stringybark Tree' and the autobiographical 'Tomorrow'. The *Amateur Gardener* was edited by ginger-haired John Lockley,[22] who also wrote garden columns for the *Sydney Morning Herald* as 'Redgum'. Lockley had started his working life in George Robertson's packing room and he had planted many of the roses at Halstead, his boss's holiday home at Blackheath. Robertson also bought these poems for Lawson's new book to be called *When I Was King*, while Lockley would collect others for his own, subsequent, book of Lawson's work.[23] 'He is so human,' Lockley wrote. 'Indeed, he has too much heart. What Lawson suffers through that poetic temperament of his no one but himself can ever fully know. He sees and feels more keenly than you or I can ever hope to do, and through his eyes and his heart he has added materially to the literature of his native land.'[24]

Lawson's 'poetic temperament' was being shaken further by news that his drinking pal Victor Daley was dying of consumption. Daley had been persuaded to take a trip to the country for his health but wrote to a friend complaining 'I have tried the nature cure too late'.[25]

LAWSON'S LOW MOODS and heavy drinking were becoming known around the new nation, with even a small newspaper in country Western Australia reporting on 1 April: 'Henry Lawson is breaking up fast and is now more than ever given to futile tears over the "slings and arrows of outrageous fortune". Victor Daley, whose constitution is also rebelling against Bohemian habits, faces his troubles with a fine poetical philosophy and whatever his private grumbles may be he doesn't blame anyone in print save himself.'[26]

Lawson was too busy drinking to heed the advice.

On 2 April 1905, police finally arrested Lawson over unpaid maintenance and the next day he appeared in the North Sydney Police Court charged with wife desertion. He was taken inside the foreboding sandstone walls of Darlinghurst Gaol's Lunatic Reception House and told he would stay there until he found the £6 12s 2d. Mary Gilmore claimed that Bertha was really punishing Lawson because he was now living with Mrs Byers, and in later years Lawson told Mary that while he loved his son and daughter dearly, he would never have had children with Bertha if he suspected she was 'insane'.[27]

While Lawson's brother Charlie was no stranger to prison life, Darlinghurst Gaol poleaxed Lawson, who was in such poor physical and emotional condition that it seemed he might disintegrate at any time. For someone who had always taken pride in personal freedom and a nomadic existence, he felt trapped like a rat in a prison built by convict labour as a place of terror, torment and shock.

Less than two years earlier inside the thick prison walls, the state's official hangman, Nosey Bob Howard – so named after a horse kick to the face left him frighteningly disfigured – had broken the necks of two men convicted of killing a policeman,[28] and the execution of the Aboriginal bushranger Jimmy Governor at Darlinghurst was still fresh in the public's mind.[29] Some of the prisoners feared their ghosts, and Darlinghurst was also beset with problems of drainage, security, disease, bad air circulation and overcrowding.

Prisoners serving time for failing to pay welfare to their families were known as 'wife-starvers'.[30] The Lunatic Reception House was designed for the temporary detention of prisoners believed to be insane, pending a full diagnosis. It helped prevent people who were not insane being sent to asylums and also protected the public from 'those whose insanity was not sufficiently pronounced to be certifiable, but who may, perhaps, be dangerous'. It processed many with 'acute alcoholic insanity'.[31]

Lawson was placed in a communal dormitory. A day later, terrified, he wrote another begging letter to Bland Holt.

> Darlinghurst Gaol.
> 4th April 1905.
>
> Dear Bland Holt
> I'm in very deep trouble and beg of you to help me once again. You will never regret it. The amount is only £6 12s. for maintenance. I am also very ill.
>
> Yours truly,
> HENRY LAWSON
> Have a pound or two coming to me but can't get them just yet.[32]

Holt came to the rescue, but Lawson only made it through Darlinghurst's heavy iron gates into the outside world the next morning to face another summons for arrears. This time he pleaded to David Scott Mitchell. 'Can you help me to meet it? I have been working. I have been drinking lately, but I *never* ill-treated my wife, and I kept her in comfort. This is the fourth separation and it is a most shameful and cruel case for all parties concerned. *I intend to defend the next action.*'[33]

As soon as Lawson was released, he again sought refuge in the bottle but the artist in him observed the wreckage of his own making in 'The Drunkard's Vision'[34] for *The Bulletin*:

> He sees his bright-eyed little wife;
> He sees the cottage neat and clean —
> He sees the wrecking of his life
> And all the things that might have been!

WHILE HIS BATTLE WITH BERTHA would only escalate, a far greater war was taking place between Russia and Japan. The Japanese had formed an alliance with Britain, but Lawson sided with the hypnotic Dr Arthur, who argued that the Japanese were

One of Lawson's letters from prison begging Bland Holt for assistance with his maintenance payments for Bertha. State Library of NSW, MLMSS 8105

the people most likely to attack Australia. Jack Lang said Lawson 'had visions of a great yellow horde descending on this country' and writing in *The Bulletin* again, Lawson said an alliance with the Russians was Australia's best defence.

Hold them, Ivan! staggering bravely underneath your gloomy sky;
Hold them, Ivan! we shall want you pretty badly by-and-by![35]

A few days later, in a poem dripping with racism and fear-mongering, Lawson told readers of *The Worker* that Australia needed to get rid of all non-European foreigners – 'the Calico Jimmy, the nigger, the Chow, and his pals' – and the country should stop relying on England and her fleet. Australia should keep its wealth in Australia by making everything it needed within its borders,[36] he said. Too bad for all those relying on trade to feed their families. As the mood took him, Lawson would descend into what Billy Lane called his 'blue fits' of literary rage.

Lawson managed to sell a few poems in the militaristic vein and he squeezed another £25 advance out of Robertson for the autobiography that was going nowhere. But on 24 July he was back at North Sydney Police Court and again charged over maintenance arrears totalling eight weeks.

Lawson wrote of 'The same dingy court room, deep and dim, like a well, with the clock high up on the wall, and the doors low down in it; with the bench, which, with some gilding, might be likened to a gingerbread imitation of a throne; the royal arms above it and the little witness box to one side, where so many honest poor people are bullied, insulted and laughed at by third-rate blackguardly little "lawyers" ...'.[37]

This time magistrate Francis Isaacs[38] hit Lawson with £12 5s 10d or two months in prison, and again, Lawson immediately found himself behind bars meditating on the wrong turns he'd taken in life.

He was taken to Darlinghurst in a Black Maria prison van, along with some other sad, desperate characters, looking through a grate on the floor to see whether they were over tramlines or road to judge their location.

Silence falls ... Time for a last smoke. Some put last bits of tobacco between their teeth, for soon they'll take everything of us except our skin and hair – and in one or two cases they'll take off our hair too, later on. We feel the van swing and go upwards; and we *feel* the cold shadow of the great gateway, with its iron gates and its great black head of the British lion overhead (with the great black British key in its mouth) and presently we feel Black Maria swing, with a sort of contemptuous fling, or jerk – as having done her part – to lay her rotten eggs.[39]

The first feeling of inmates was an overwhelming 'mixture of awe and loneliness'.[40] In the heart of the city, with its bustle and its turmoil outside, prisoners felt completely isolated and shut away.

During their exercise time, they 'walked to and fro, and up and down, and backwards and forwards incessantly, as caged men have always done'.[41]

At four-thirty in the afternoon Lawson found there was a general assembly, when everyone answered to their number, as names were forgotten and prisoners became 'a human numerical unit'. After the roll call prisoners marched to their tea of bread and hominy. Then they marched to the cells, where by the touching of a lever, every door was closed simultaneously. From then until six the next morning, Lawson and the hundreds of others were locked up with their thoughts and regrets.[42]

This time Lawson spent twenty-four days behind bars until supporters could find the arrears. He wrote the 'Rising of the Court'[43] and 'Going In' about his experiences, though 'Going In', with references to his own maintenance case and others 'very common in Sydney', was deemed far too personal and vindictive towards Bertha to be published in his lifetime. Released from jail on 17 August, Lawson tried to stay busy selling the euphoric 'As Good as New' to *The Bulletin* and the depressing commentary on what was left of his marriage in 'The Pink Carnation' to Lockley.

He managed to keep his estranged wife satisfied with payments but made an enemy of Rose Scott and her feminist supporters with 'The Cliques of the Who'll-Get-In'.[44]

Despite a steady output of work, Lawson's debts continued mounting. By September he was not only a month in arrears to Bertha but he owed Mrs Byers £5 for board and lodging at the Coffee Palace. His behaviour was so erratic that she shut up shop and headed off to seek refuge with a brother at Windsor. Soon Lawson owed Ellis's Coffee Palace at 50 King Street in Sydney £1 15s for board and a small loan, and he owed the Farmer's department store in Pitt Street £3 17s 11d for new clothes. Robertson and Shenstone settled the debts, including yet another month's alimony, with purchases for Lawson's new book and his promises for more work on the autobiography.

Positive reviews for *When I Was King* and Louisa's self-published *Lonely Crossing* began appearing in November 1905, but *The Bulletin* was slow offering its opinion and Lawson called into the office to see what could be done. He was told a positive review would appear soon and with a touch of glee he informed Robertson:

> From the *Bulletin* assurance that we shall have no need to complain and they will give a good review. And [Alfred Stephens] will have no hand in it.
>
> Fight through,
HENRY LAWSON
And you were quite right in that fight.
We have Stephens down …

Stephens thought otherwise. In his *Bulletin* review four days before Christmas 1905, beside Lawson's sketch about his now eighty-year-old grandfather Henry Albury,[45] Stephens declared that *When I Was King* was 'below Lawson's reputation, and below his merit', despite containing works such as 'The Shearer's Dream' and 'The Wander-Light'.

> These are not the best of Lawson, but the worst; and he has written so much that is good, and strong, and brave, that one cannot be satisfied with dismal doggerel of the alleys and the pubs. It is necessary to say this, for Lawson is regarded as a representative Australian author: he is possibly the most original and characteristic author that this country has produced.

Stephens advised Lawson to cheer up, to 'leave himself and his troubles right out of his writing, and use his good eyes and his good heart to write the joys and sorrows of other people – especially the joys'.[46]

Perhaps, most painfully for Lawson though, was the critic's statement that 'Henry Lawson is aged 38, Mrs Peter Lawson is 57; yet her verses are less gloomy than his, less self-conscious, less querulous …'[47] Stephens wrote that Lawson's 'sympathy, his sincerity, his power of keen observation: Lawson inherits them all from his mother ... she was revoltress as he is revolter from the smug conventional order – espousing the cause of downtrodden women as he has defended the attitude of luckless, striving men'.[48]

Lawson responded with 'And What Have You To Say?', telling Stephens and the other detractors that he would continue to write the truth until he found 'a drunken pauper grave'.[49]

One of the few things in life that shook Lawson from his gloom during this barren time was his visits with his children. Barta remembered: 'Dad was tall, tense, straight. He had marvellous eyes. You could go on looking down and down in them. He liked to dress in a slightly old fashioned way. He wore dignified high collars and he was never without his stick. He was a far more powerful personality than any sentimental dreaming could make of him. He was a law unto himself, and often difficult, but just as often warm and friendly, full of laughter, kindness and quick understanding, as he always was with us. He had a gleeful sense of the absurd ... He spoke softly. He was quiet and he could be very gentle. He could be restless, nervously impatient, rearing as a thoroughbred, very angry at anything he thought was blind unfairness, but just as ready with sorrow and apology.'[50]

Lawson often despaired at the mess he'd made of his family life, but he hoped that his children would always think of him with fondness. Though Stephens had ridiculed *When I Was King* as being below par for Lawson, it contained a heartfelt message for Lawson's son which had first appeared in *The Bulletin*.

'To Jim':

These lines I write with bitter tears,
And failing heart and hand.
But you will read in after years,
And you will understand:
You'll hear the slander of the crowd;
They'll whisper tales of shame,
But days will come when you'll be proud
To bear your father's name.[51]

Chapter 23

They shut a man in the four-by-eight, with a four inch slit for air,
Twenty-three hours of the twenty-four, to brood on his virtues there.
LAWSON IN DARLINGHURST GAOL[1]

THE DEATH OF VICTOR DALEY at his Waitara home four days after Christmas 1905 should have served as a wake-up call for Lawson. Daley was just forty-seven, and left behind a wife and four children, who within a year would be poor orphans. Lawson said that with Daley's death 'the old bohemian days in Sydney died' and that he seemed to also be making 'a strenuous attempt to get up a funeral on my own behalf'.[2] The Duskers talked about erecting a monument to Daley. John Norton thought otherwise. Norton's long-suffering wife would eventually be granted a judicial separation because of his habitual drunkenness, cruelty and adultery, but, back running the *Truth*, Norton told his readers: 'Victor Daley practically drank himself to death. ... He played all sorts of paltry tricks on his family and friends in order to obtain drink. At one time he represented that one of his children had died, and he hadn't the means of giving the body [a] decent burial.' Norton said that like Lawson, Daley 'could have had plenty of literary work, both in prose and verse, on the daily and weekly press, but he was so seldom sober for long that no editor cared to have him about the premises, where he was little better than a drunken nuisance'.[3]

Norton described the Duskers as 'men who don't, or won't, pay their tradesmen's debts [and] who have to be summoned in police courts for the maintenance of their wives and children ...' To Norton, Lawson and his pals were a 'band of bad-breathed, bardic bounders', and he said that at Daley's funeral in the Catholic section of Waverley Cemetery, 'two or three of these boozy bards were so drunk as to be in danger of falling into the grave'.[4]

Lawson paid tribute in *The Bulletin* to his friend, and to the other poets 'resting, one by one, in graveyards by the sea',[5] and he later wrote 'The Empty Glass' for Elizabeth Daley, the 'widow that weeps by the Hornsby line ... she stood by him long and true'.[6] After a meeting with the Duskers and others at Sydney Town Hall in the week after the funeral, Lawson organised a fund for Mrs Daley. He had promised to escort her home after the meeting but needed a loan of £1 from Robertson, telling him they had seen Daley home 'near Kendall's old grave ... We are getting a bit crowded at Waverley – only three graves left. I am following shortly.'[7]

Lawson was able to make an arrangement with Angus & Robertson to cover his maintenance payments to Bertha throughout 1906 while he supported himself with freelance work, and he moved back to Miller Street as Mrs Byers returned to North Sydney hoping to reopen the Coffee Palace. Lawson barred no one when it came to asking for a loan and he wrote to Francis Isaacs, the judge who had sent him to prison six months earlier, to tell him he had a new book out 'since I saw you last'; had the 'kids'' maintenance fixed for the next twelve months, and was now free of the drink.

'In the meantime I am very hard up,' he told the judge. 'I am trying to gather a few pounds to help me on my feet and to tide over. You might help with a little today if you can. I would be very grateful, and it means a lot to me ... a pound would help. I could pay back.'[8] He told Isaacs that 'The wife is thoroughly bad' and claimed she had travelled saloon passage to Western Australia and was working in a bar there, a rumour repeated by the Kalgoorlie *Sun*.[9]

Isaacs was unimpressed, and Lawson sent Mrs Byers to Robertson instead, with a note asking for 'a pound or two until I get some more work in'.[10]

Lawson wrote a few poems around a constant theme: 'Divorced', 'My Wife's Second Husband', 'Keeping His First Wife Now', 'Before We Were Married' and 'The Peace Maker', an olive branch for Rose Scott. Then he wrote 'Victor' for the opening page of a booklet accompanying a tribute matinee for Daley's family at the Theatre Royal on 30 March 1906.[11] He produced the poem 'Mrs Muscovy Duck' for John Lockley, but had to admit to him that he had slipped with the bottle again, and had not been 'presentable' for a scheduled meeting. Lawson's drinking and cadging became such an annoyance that Robertson barred him from his office, but soon after the order to stay away, Lawson stumbled into 89 Castlereagh Street again, unwashed, unshaven, bleary eyed and 'bad-breathed'. The writer who had once won favourable comparisons with Tolstoy arrived just in time to stagger into the path of Sydney's Archbishop Saumerez Smith, who had just joined Robertson's Sydney Book Club.

Lawson threw his arm around the city's chief Anglican and kissed him before Robertson, aghast, had him thrown out.[12] Lawson wrote a belligerent apology saying Shenstone had wanted some information about *My Brilliant Career* or he wouldn't have 'come near the shop again'.[13]

Lawson lacked both the physical and mental stamina to fight his relentless demons.[14]

He went back to the Walker Convalescent Hospital and spent a month drying out. Barta and Jim visited him there, and Barta recalled that 'Dad showed us all over the place, and we sat in the grounds and wandered about by the water'.[15] Mrs Byers told him that the reopening of the Coffee Palace was not feasible, and instead she decided to rent a cottage in leafy Market Street, Naremburn, a few kilometres to the north. It wasn't that far from Robertson's family home in Ellimatta Road, Mosman, and now pretending that he owned the Coffee Palace, Lawson wrote to Robertson with the unwelcome news that he was being 'bought out' and am 'just taking a little place up near where you live ... poultry and ducks and a little kitchen garden'.[16] The prospect of Lawson on Robertson's doorstep at all hours must have terrified the big Scot, even though Lawson had Mrs Byers to run his errands, telling his publisher: 'A mistress will do a hundred times more for a man than a wife will do ... A mistress is my last chance.'[17]

Lawson's move north coincided with Bland Holt's revival of *For England* at the Theatre Royal.[18] The production was winning rave reviews and Holt was always good for petty cash. Lawson sent Holt a note, written in the large unwieldy scrawl to suggest the writing was well lubricated, asking if Holt wanted him to 'dramatize any story or character or quotation of mine' or to use any of his poems. Holt did not respond. Lawson sent another note, this time to 'Dear Mr Holt ... about that matter mentioned in my note of the other day'. Still no reply. Lawson's frustrations, fuelled by alcohol, erupted and he wrote again, telling Holt that the actor's silence 'hurt me a lot. I want to borrow £1 ... I am trying to act like a man. I will not drink it! ... You hurt me, old man .... Been good ever since, HENRY LAWSON.'[19]

Still nothing.

And then:

'Dear Bland, I want that quid – pound ... tonight. I will wait.' He assured Holt again that he wasn't drinking and signed the letter 'Yours *faithlessly* HENRY LAWSON'.

On 30 June, Holt finally replied: 'My dear Lawson, your note last night. Enclose the quid. Of course I know you'll knock it down, but I suppose you can't help it.'[20]

FROM THE NAREMBURN COTTAGE, Lawson now gazed west and imagined 'The Horseman on the Skyline'[21] and 'Above Crow's Nest',[22] with a mysterious rider galloping along the ranges warning a decadent generation of the doom ahead, a doom which Lawson previewed for *The Bulletin* in his poem 'Cypher Seven'.[23] Lawson's interest in Norse mysticism was growing as a carryover from the fireside chats with his father. Apocalyptic visions weren't the currency needed to pay Bertha, though, and Lawson scoured newspapers for topics to write about. He wrote the poem 'The Stranded Ship'[24] after the French barque *Vincennes* was beached at Manly on 24 May 1906, but it would take years to sell it. *The Bulletin* instead bought a poem about his thirty-ninth birthday, 'With scarce a sign of crows' feet, In spite of all my sins'.[25]

Lawson was way behind on his autobiography but with the ever-present threat of jail hanging over his head for maintenance arrears he suggested selling the copyright of his English book *Children of the Bush* to Robertson, unaware that it had failed to dent the market in Britain. Lawson went to see Robertson on 24 July but Shenstone intervened and told him that they would take no new work from him until the autobiography was complete, and that they would consider *Children of the Bush*.

Lawson was momentarily exhilarated over the chance to make some more money from the stories he'd already written, and scribbled a note: 'Dear Robertson. You are a man.'[26]

Three days later, though, with his pockets empty and Mrs Byers needing rent money and groceries, Lawson wrote to Robertson again, saying he would expand the autobiography to a hundred thousand words. He also wished 'to borrow £5'.[27]

Robertson agreed to publish *Children of the Bush*, using leftover unbound sheets from the British publishers. He planned to also use the prose in two separate small volumes, *Send Round the Hat* and *Romance of the Swag*. He gave Lawson a few guineas for some token revisions.

DEPRESSED AT HANDING away control of *The Bulletin*, Jules Archibald launched himself into a new monthly magazine called *The Lone Hand* – the title he originally planned for *The Bulletin* two and a half decades earlier. He went on a manic spending frenzy, paying contributors unheard-of sums. Lawson was disappointed to miss the largesse, though Archibald did write to him from Medlow Bath to say 'Keep up your pecker, old man ... I am going to see that you are born again.' Archibald's behaviour became so erratic that his business partner William Macleod finally convinced Archibald's wife Rosa to sign the paperwork for him to be forcibly removed to the Callan Park Asylum. Archibald never truly forgave Macleod, even though he eventually recovered his faculties.

In October 1906, with Robertson's year-long plan to pay the alimony coming to an end, and with Bertha often travelling for her bookselling work, she was determined that Lawson pay his fair share to support Jim, now almost eight, and Barta, six. There were none of the previous greetings of 'Dear Harry' or 'Darling', when Bertha next wrote.

> Sydney.
> 6/10/06
> Dear Lawson,
> Re the amount to be paid by you for the children. ... It is impossible for me to keep them at Boarding School unless you pay the amount. I only ask you to pay for their Board as I manage their clothes, education, etc. Angus & Robertson's term will be up next week, and I have to look to you for the weekly amount, and do not wish to have any more unpleasantness or court proceedings over the matter. ... I have struggled hard enough the last three years and have kept the children well ... I have enough Business worries without the incessant anxiety of providing the necessary amount for the children's weekly account.[28]

Lawson, though, had started to revel in his reputation as a drunk, regularly writing to Bland Holt asking for 'a bob' (a shilling) and calling himself 'Vice President of the Ancient Order of Sinners'.[29] His drinking earned him a brief appearance at the Reception House in December 1906 and unpaid rent caused Mrs Byers to lose much of her furniture. They had to move again. Robertson wanted to publish Lawson's work but from a safe distance, so he offered Mrs Byers £2 a week to keep Lawson fed and housed – and away from his premises.

When Mrs Byers told Lawson the terms of the deal, Lawson railed at Robertson's generosity, telling him that while he had 'slipped' with booze the last time that he had invaded Robertson's office, he wasn't drinking anymore. 'You seem to have left Mrs B. under the impression that I have been kicking up in the shop every day since.' Still Lawson, with his ego again running wild, said he forgave Robertson and wished him 'a Merry Xmas & a better New Year, old chap'.[30]

Lawson composed the poem 'Lily of St Leonards',[31] hinting that if he'd stayed with Hannah and not Bertha, he would never have come home from London a wreck. He then chanced his luck and paid a visit to Robertson's office, only for Fred Shenstone to intercept him, again. Lawson managed to pocket a sheet of the company's letterhead and wrote to Robertson on it on 3 January 1907, pitching more books.

A month later Lawson visited Jim Tyrrell's bookstore in William Street, to find Tyrrell in conversation with the young Melbourne publisher Thomas Lothian.[32] Together they told Lothian a sob story about Lawson's plight and Robertson's refusal to take new work. Lothian felt 'trapped' into helping out the famous writer.[33]

On 16 February, the 25-year-old Lothian gave Lawson a £10 advance and signed an agreement to publish two new books – one of verse and one of prose – including Lawson's 'Jack Cornstalk' stories. Lawson would get a 10 per cent royalty and half of any foreign rights.

Having now moved with Mrs Byers to William Street, off Blues Point Road, North Sydney, Lawson began rummaging around for copies of his work, rifling through tattered manuscripts and torn clippings. His papers were in such disarray that he bundled everything he could find together and gave them to Lothian the next morning. Included in the bundle were statements from J.B. Pinker, invoices, maintenance receipts, and most surprisingly of all, Bertha's painful, heartbreaking correspondence to her husband since the marriage had started to break down.

Also there was a journalistic essay called 'King Billy',[34] in which Lawson wrote of the hypocrisy of white settlers and their treatment of the Aboriginal people. He described an old

Aboriginal man cadging for a drink, though the character might just as easily have been a self-portrait. One difference between the two races, Lawson wrote, was the absence of greed, and that 'if King Billy has sufficient for the day, he will not cadge for the morrow'.[35]

Later he wrote of the way Aboriginal people had become curiosities in their own country and how one knowingly posed as 'the last of his tribe' for tourists; and he hinted at the atrocities committed against Australia's first people – rapes and murders – and how such things are 'veiled in obscurity'. He ended his piece by insisting that 'Australia will never forget the wonderful kindness of those blacks, who wept over the bodies of dead Burke and Wills, and saved King – and who would have saved the other two had they stayed with them'.[36]

Lothian painstakingly went through the mass of crumpled poems and stories and found that Angus & Robertson had already published most of it. So Lawson sent him 'The Ridiculous Family', which centred on his brother Charlie's life of crime and Lawson's attempts to help him. He told Lothian that his 'Child in the Dark, and a Foreign Father', which had run five years earlier in *The Bulletin*, was what was left of a novel he had started in England. His story 'The Triangles of Life' gave a rundown in point form of his life with his current situation summed up as: 'Police court. Desertion. "Judicial separation." Maintenance order. Reconciliation – court – reconciliation – court. Summons for desertion, and maintenance. Summons, summons, summons, Darlinghurst. And the full knowledge of what sort of woman she was.'[37]

Though Lawson had already been to prison three times for missing alimony payments, and was begging his friends for food money, he grandiosely told Lothian that he might have to take another trip to England for research. The addict inside him spurred Lawson to sell Lothian rights to works he had already sold to Robertson and Lockley. He scrawled a note to Robertson: 'Dear George, I am forced to do the only dishonest action I ever did in my life (for a woman's sake). You will forgive me after it is done.'[38]

Lawson received a letter from Lothian's Melbourne office on 22 April 1907, including proofs for the prose book and a request for the verses. In his confused, rambling state, Lawson left some money for Mrs Byers and took off to solve the crisis. A week later, upon opening Lothian's premises in Elizabeth Street, Melbourne, the office boy found what he assumed was a dishevelled vagrant asleep at the front door.[39] It was, in fact, the company's star literary signing, very much in need of a bath, but clutching a bundle of manuscripts after a steamer journey south.

Once he had sobered up, Lawson said he was ready to cut a new publishing deal. With his dark, sensitive, appealing eyes working overtime, Lawson proposed selling Lothian everything he still had the rights to, throwing in some more titles that were actually owned by Robertson. Lawson was adamant that he needed money right away to base himself in London again.

Lothian agreed to give Lawson £50 for the material he already had and the new manuscripts Lawson had carried with him. He handed Lawson £5 and said with the £10 he'd already given Lawson, there would be only £35 more coming.[40]

Lawson was desperate, and among the works he sold was 'A Bluff that Failed', a story Bertha had transcribed for Lawson and which he had sold to Robertson in 1899. Lothian found Lawson a room at the Victoria Coffee Palace, a temperance hotel, and two weeks later saw him set sail for Sydney in steerage. Soon after Lawson wrote to Robertson again with a degree of guilt, that he had sold 'a thing that belonged to you ... I didn't do it for drink.'[41] But Lawson was working hard to double-sell everything he could. He told Lothian that *Review of Reviews* would pay £2 10s to run one of the stories, but the publisher later found that Lawson had already tried to sell it there for a guinea – less than half that – something Lothian told Lawson 'was not very pleasant to me'.[42]

Bertha was again demanding maintenance arrears, and Lawson convinced Robertson to give him £35 and get it off Lothian when the new books appeared.

That would take a lot longer than planned.

By September 1907, Lawson had not returned the proofs of the story 'The Stranger's Friend', and had an idea that he would take it back, along with a story called 'Mateship'. He offered Lothian a substitute yarn called 'The Editor of the Comet' which *The Lone Hand* had rejected. Lawson wanted to visit Lothian in Melbourne again to talk it over but the publisher couldn't tell him quickly enough to stay right where he was. Instead, Lawson soon bumped into Lothian in Sydney and this time demanded that the deal be changed and that his two stories be returned. Lothian told him to honour his word. Lawson flew into a rage.

When Lothian returned to Melbourne, he found a letter from Lawson again demanding he return the two stories. 'You went out of your way to insult me,' Lawson said. 'You gave me £50 for what was worth £150. You acted like a consummate little cad.'[43]

Lothian immediately replied: 'If you can truly think that there has been the slightest pleasure in my doing business with you, that my former experiences should make me anxious or pleased to meet you, then I will apologize. After destroying three Agreements, and preparing new ones … after obliging you by paying for books that were guaranteed to be ready for publication three months from acceptance, (and it will be over twelve months according to your last cool advice, before any start can be made on them): after other interviews that I remember well, I regret that I fail to see why I should desire any fresh interviews. From my point of view, your letter is just about "the last straw".'[44]

Lawson continued to stall with Lothian's proofs and tried to bargain for the return of the two stories for sale elsewhere. Lothian had other business to attend to and with Lawson such a difficulty, it would take six years to publish the prose book as *The Triangles of Life* and the verse book as *For Australia*.

In a nod to his difficulties with the writer, Lothian hung an intimidating life-size caricature of Lawson at the entrance of his office. It was drawn by the poet Ted Dyson's younger brother Will,[45] and in solid black, it showed Lawson long, lean and angry, twirling his elaborate moustache while clutching his walking stick behind him as though poised to strike.

After years of battles with Lawson, publisher Thomas Lothian came to treasure Will Dyson's menacing caricature of the writer. State Library of Victoria, H30828

LAWSON CONTINUED TO BITE the hands that fed him. He complained bitterly to *Lone Hand* editor Frank Fox[46] over the treatment of his story 'The Rising of the Court' that had been passed on to *The Bulletin*. Lawson said the story had been mutilated in the editing process and that these 'unnecessary' changes jarred, irritated and maddened him. 'You seem to cut out the very guts of the thing ... God, man! ... Do you want my readers to think that the Salvation Army has got hold of Henry Lawson?'[47] He had been angry with *The Bulletin* for a long time, he said, despite Archibald giving him his start as a writer. Alfred Stephens was at the heart of his fury.

'There were many flagrant cases of my style being crippled and mutilated in the *Bulletin*, right back to George Black's time, and especially through Stephens's reign ... Stephens didn't hesitate to alter whole verses, rhymes and all.'[48] Lawson said that even the new editor 'Jimmy Edmond' was guilty of changing copy to suit his editorial policy.

Fox wrote back to Lawson, tersely, to say that everyone made mistakes, and they would forget about all the times Lawson stumbled into their office drunk. While they would send him proofs for revision in future, it was often difficult to publish his work without last-minute corrections, Edmond said, given that Lawson was so often late with submission.

Lawson drank most of the money Lothian and Robertson advanced him and by December 1907 was drying out again in the Charlemount[49] private hospital in Darlinghurst, a building now occupied by the Bourbon & Beefsteak Hotel. On New Year's Eve the Children's Court at Ormond House in Oxford Street, Paddington, heard two more charges of child desertion against him, each of £4 10s for arrears in maintenance with 17 shillings in costs. The judge was not so much interested in Lawson's psychological problems, only that he had again broken the law. Lawson went to jail that day as Mrs Byers scurried around to find the money for his release. He left the Reception House on 3 January 1908, a psychological mess.

Robertson and Shenstone were so sick of Lawson causing a ruckus at their offices that they next gave him £5 to stay away, making him write a promise that he would not enter their Castlereagh Street premises again until it was repaid.[50]

On 24 February he turned up at *The Bulletin* office demanding to see Edmond. He was barred from entering and replied by smashing the editorial glass door with his walking stick. Lawson was arrested and Edmond had him charged with malicious damage. By coincidence, Lawson's 'The Song of the Back to Front' that includes a description of a drunken brute and the line 'Now-I'm-going-quietly-don't-you-lay-a-hand-on-me … All right, constable!' appeared in *The Bulletin* just three days later.[51] Lawson fronted court, but Edmond, seeking only to teach Lawson a lesson, withdrew the charge.[52] Soon after, Lawson sent Mrs Byers to *The Bulletin* office to collect money from his recent work, and reimbursed Edmond 12 shillings and sixpence for the shattered door.[53]

Showing there were no hard feelings, *The Bulletin* ran three of Lawson's poems with a medieval theme, including 'As It Is In The Days of Now',[54] exploring adultery, even though the setting did not really fit a magazine about Australian life in the early twentieth century.

Bert Stevens edited a condensed version of Lawson's unfinished autobiography for Robertson, and ran it across nine pages of *The Lone Hand* on 2 March with Longstaff's portrait.[55]

In his few sober, reflective moments, Lawson peered deeply into his flawed character in the story 'The Man Who Was

Drowned', calling himself John Lawrence – after the way the children in Mangamaunu pronounced Lawson's name.

> John Lawrence drank deep at times, and was a maudlin idiot and a raving lunatic by turns when he drank deep. And he'd go very low. Black eye (and a blood-shot one), battered hat, ragged dirty clothes and burst boots with no socks. ... He managed to hang onto his soul, but he pawned everything else.[56]

Keenly aware that he needed help for his addiction, Lawson had his request accepted for admission into the new facility, officially known as Sydney's Mental Hospital, on 18 May 1908. It was situated at the Reception House next to Darlinghurst Gaol, and designed as a place to treat those with severe nervous disorders, borderline insanity and those whose mental instability was caused by alcohol.[57] The Mental Hospital would admit anyone sent by a doctor, or those deemed suitable patients by the sister in charge, Alberta de Villiers MacCallum. There were two dormitories, one with six beds, the other eighteen. Lawson stayed until 3 June but found Sister MacCallum so kind and the hospital routine such a salve for his boozing and depression that he booked a second stay from 27 June to 13 July.

Bertha said his trips to the Mental Hospital were no excuse for his tardiness in payments, though, and Lawson was summoned to court again on 4 August 1908.

Bertha's sister Hilda Lang was also preparing a petition for a judicial separation from her husband Jack, on the grounds of his adultery with 'Nellie (Louisa) Anderson, of Iceton Street, Burwood'. Hilda's petition claimed that Jack had 'lived continuously' with Nellie 'as her husband', rather than with Hilda and their children.[58] The application was cancelled,[59] but Lang, who would soon be elected Mayor of Auburn, continued to live with his mistress.

Lawson was ordered to pay two amounts in arrears totalling £24 16s. He ran away, hiding out with friends for four days until

The foreboding entrance to Darlinghurst Gaol, which Lawson called 'Starvinghurst' because of the meagre rations for prisoners. State Library of NSW, FL1231374

he surrendered to again face imprisonment. Mrs Byers wrote to Bland Holt for help but he was travelling and it would be almost a month before Holt produced a cheque for £25 from Auckland. In the meantime, Lawson became more and more detached from reality in prison, writing to Robertson that it was 'almost *finis* as far as my brain is concerned'. He could only pace a few steps in his cage and was not allowed to smoke. He was only allowed to write an occasional letter and said it was 'refined torture to have a brain teeming with ideas and not be able to write them down … imagine the effect of such confinement on a temperament like mine'.[60]

While the 'clever scoundrels' were all outside, Lawson complained, 'moneyless mugs' like him were in jail, all because of 'a mad wife's lies'.[61]

Lawson was letting his beard grow and it was white underneath.

While he was in Darlinghurst Gaol, his grandfather Henry Albury died on 17 August at the age of eighty-three, and was buried beside his wife Harriet the next day at Rookwood Cemetery in western Sydney. Lawson began to think more and more of his own

mortality. Released from Darlinghurst Gaol on 31 August, he tried
to be readmitted to the Mental Hospital but was sent home to Mrs
Byers at William Street. He drew up a will and made his way to
Angus & Robertson's office where he had Fred Shenstone witness
it on 3 September, leaving instructions that Archibald, Robertson
and Mrs Byers were his friends, and asking that his mourners 'lay
out the body decently … for the soul was great'.[62]

By the end of 1908 Lawson was again in arrears to the tune
of £25 and had nothing that could generate that amount of
money. He was terrified of going back to the prison he called
'Starvinghurst'[63] because of its meagre rations. His fear was laid
bare in another *Bulletin* poem, 'One Hundred and Three', the
number he wore on his drab prison uniform, and the number the
guards would shout.

> One Hundred and Three, it is hard to believe that you saddled your
>   horse at dawn;
> There were girls that rode through the bush at eve, and girls who
>   lolled on the lawn.
> There were picnic parties in sunny bays, and ships on the shining
>   sea;
> There were foreign ports in the glorious days —
> (Hold up, One Hundred and Three!)[64]

Chapter 24

When Lawson got out of jail his bones almost rattled. This is no
exaggeration. He was a skeleton. I am not one who is inclined
ordinarily to show great emotion but this time I cried when I saw him.

LAWSON'S LONG–TIME COMPANION ISABEL BYERS1

O N BOXING DAY 1908, Sydney played host to a
monumental sporting event that would change the world
forever, and Lawson was disgusted by the spectacle.

In a specially built wooden arena at Rushcutters Bay, more
than 20,000 people packed into Sydney Stadium to see Jack
Johnson, a black Texan, and the son of former slaves, fight for the
world heavyweight boxing championship against the titleholder, a
white Canadian named Tommy Burns.

No black man had ever been allowed to compete for the
championship, but the enterprising Sydney promoter Hugh D.
McIntosh correctly predicted that a legally sanctioned 'race war'
could generate a huge profit.

To Lawson and the white establishment, Jack Johnson was a
dark menace. At a time when black Americans could be lynched
for whistling at white women, Johnson flaunted his sexual,
intellectual and fighting prowess, battering the best white boxers
in the world and trampling over society's taboos, living with a
succession of white women, dressing in furs and diamonds, and
roaring about in the most expensive automobiles.

Leading into the fight, Australian newspapers used every racial slur imaginable in their attacks on the African-American. Some implored readers to pray for a white victory,[2] but Johnson chopped Burns's face apart with his flashing fists, laughing at the smaller white man's feeble efforts. The victory by a sneering black man over the symbol of white supremacy turned social norms on their head. For the first time on a global stage, a black man had proved his superiority over the white world in emphatic fashion. The Sydney-based *Fairplay* newspaper derided Johnson as a 'huge, primordial ape', while Randolph Bedford, writing in the Melbourne *Herald*, said Johnson's victory was like clean sunlight being snuffed out by ugly darkness.[3] Lawson's commentary on the fight – and on Johnson – was the most racially vicious of all, so much so that even in the days when a White Australia was the government's official policy, no one would print his poem 'The Great Fight'[4] for decades.

Lawson wrote it as though demented.

His mental health, in fact, remained precarious and he spent time back at the Charlemount private hospital in February, reading Shakespeare's *Hamlet*, *Macbeth* and *Julius Caesar*. On the subject of Hamlet's madness, Lawson told Robertson that he believed the Prince of Denmark was 'ratty alright',[5] and Lawson's friends feared the same about him. When his spirits lifted, he wrote half a dozen short pieces which Lockley bought for just 7s 6d each.

The money, though, was never enough for Lawson to meet his daily expenses and pay his maintenance.

His life now involved constantly trying to stay one step ahead of Bertha and the bailiffs. In her mind, she was working to keep their children clothed, fed and schooled, while Lawson spent a good part of his time on his back, resting at convalescent homes and hospitals.

Lawson wrote three comic stories for Robertson – 'The Hypnotised Township', 'The Exciseman' and 'Instinct Gone Wrong' – and to further help his finances Robertson agreed on 19 December to publish another Lawson book of prose and verse, even though Lawson had little material for it. Robertson gave Lawson £30 and the book eventually appeared as *The Rising of the Court*.

Within weeks though, Lawson was skint again and on 6 April 1909, and now living with Mrs Byers at 143 Miller Street, North Sydney, Lawson was summonsed to appear on two more charges of failing to make maintenance payments. He went into hiding for ten days until arrested. He was sent directly to Darlinghurst Gaol until he could find £5 6s for the key. On 20 April, Mrs Byers visited him and was shocked by his appearance, writing to Robertson: 'I went to see Henry Lawson today. He looks a terable wrick it nearly broke my Heart to see Him. He looks nothing but skin & bone ... Poor fellow ... I'm sure He is ill and Heart broken to be there. He would not be there if I could help Him, but I am not able to do anything. I am very badly off myself just now ...'[6]

Mrs Byers did a whip-round, visiting Jack Brereton and Hugh Langwell, the unionist who Lawson had befriended in Bourke. She hoped that if she raised money from Lawson's friends, Robertson would match their contributions. So it was that Lawson went free on 28 April and wrote a tribute to the woman who stuck by him:

> There's a thing that sends a lump to my throat,
> And cuts my heart like a knife:
> 'Tis the woman that waits at the prison gate,
> And the woman is not his wife.[7]

Mrs Byers said she cried when Lawson got out of jail, such was his parlous physical condition. He had been on No. 1 ration 'or in plain "Australian" starved'.[8]

'Yes, this was done to Henry Lawson,' she said, 'the most childlike and kindest heart that ever breathed ... I have seen Henry Lawson bring a starved kitten or a dog in and feed it many a time.'[9]

Lawson's frame of mind was lifted by an article on 1 June 1909 in *The Lone Hand*, now under the stewardship of former war correspondent Arthur Adams.[10] The article was by a Frenchman, Emile Saillens, who taught English to high school students in Toulouse, and who had read *While the Billy Boils* while on a train in Australia. Saillens was struck by Lawson's originality. His story 'Telling Mrs Baker' had already been translated into German and *The Lone Hand* told readers that this article by Saillens would be the preface for an edition of Lawson's work translated into French.

'Of course his great natural talent is incontestable,' Saillens wrote. 'Great London critics, disdainful enough, as a rule, of "colonial literature," have not hesitated to compare Lawson in the short story to Bret Harte, to Gorki, or even to our own Maupassant.'[11]

Saillens claimed Lawson's name might become more widely known than that of many Australian statesmen, 'but are Australians as grateful to him as they should be? Do they realise that in coming years when the sons of their sons will desire to live again the heroic period of Australia-in-the-making, when they will want to know about the old bush and the early efforts of Socialism, and the bringing into the world of their Commonwealth, they will find no documents more inspiring and pathetic, more full of the dream and the suffering of the past than the poems and stories of this ill-fated Bushman.'[12]

Lawson was sure that Jim and Barta would be proud of him one day, but accolades and even international recognition did not satisfy the legal debts.[13] He wrote a poem about hollow 'Success',[14] but could raise only 5 shillings for it from Lockley, which he spent on another visit to the Mental Hospital before moving back with Mrs Byers. Bland Holt offered him some writing work but complained that Lawson was too 'irresponsible' to do it.[15] Lawson saved money on travelling costs by taking the 'Horse-and-Cart Ferry' across the harbour from North Sydney rather than the sleek passenger vessels, and wrote about a battling boozer on board for *The Bulletin*.[16]

LAWSON WAS SUMMONSED AGAIN to the Children's Court on 20 July 1909, and once again became a fugitive, this time for two months, though still selling material to Lockley and *The Bulletin*. He emerged from seclusion to cause a drunken ruckus in a North Sydney pub and was arrested, and then appeared in court on 21 September, charged with being drunk in a public place. He was handed a fine of 10 shillings or four days' imprisonment. Lawson was then taken to the Children's Court, and then to Darlinghurst Gaol where he was to stay until he, or his supporters, could find £7 16s for Bertha.

Now known as Prisoner No. 32, Lawson wrote 'The Song of a Prison',[17] furtively scribbled with the stolen stump of a pencil in an institution where inmates were allowed to write only two letters a week. The paper was smuggled to him from the prison printery by the jail pantryman, wife-killer George Love,[18] who had so far done twelve years of a life sentence, after an appeal spared him an appointment with Nosey Bob the hangman.[19]

In Darlinghurst Lawson noted the:

Staircase and doors of iron, no sign of a plank or brick,
Ceilings and floors of sandstone, and the cell walls two feet thick;
Cell like a large-sized coffin, or a small-sized tomb, and white,
And it strikes a chill to the backbone on the warmest summer night.[20]

Alongside other inmates Lawson worked in the prison factory, plaiting mats, and he met many desperate characters, and many like him who claimed that circumstance, bad laws, even the whole world, were against them. There was a prisoner he called 'Previous *Conwictions*' who claimed that past offences always counted against him and there was an old burglar who swept the jail religiously, muttering that the place was going to rack and ruin. Lawson walked for hours in the corridor of the jail hospital with the Paddington wife-killer David Hanna, who 'was suffering from an old bullet wound in the head'. Hanna told Lawson he was sorry his wife died. 'He told me all about it: cackling, mischief making women neighbours and relatives invading his home – and all. I sympathised with that man – his trouble had been in some respects so like my own.' One newspaper garishly reported that Hanna had 'pumped lead into his wife, and then made a bad attempt to blow his brains out'.[21] His death sentence had been commuted. There was also 'a big dark man, heavy in every way', who'd shot and wounded a man at Broken Hill for "lustin'" after another man's wife'[22] and there was Charlie Ah Sun, a middle-aged Chinese gardener, who was doing five years for trying to kill a love rival.[23]

Lawson gave *Bulletin* readers a rundown, with real 'gallows humour', of 'A Pleasant Balcony',[24] the platform erected between the corners of two wings of the prison, where the condemned were hanged. He saw the morgue every day, and felt he was being driven insane by a 'mad woman's lies'. The prison made Lawson recall the low bark homestead he grew up in, 'a pigsty compared with gaol'.[25]

It wasn't only the prisoners going through hell, though. Sometimes Lawson's jailers would pour out their hearts to him during their long lonely walks along the rows of cells. One warder would cling to the door of his cell as long as he possibly could before lights out, not to sympathise with Lawson, but to get sympathy for his own domestic miseries.[26]

In exchange for tobacco, Lawson wrote verse on order for some of the other inmates, risking time in solitary confinement if caught. One inmate named 'Kelly' slipped him a note that he was in 'for asult in company on a blocke in balmain'; while another instructed him to: 'write down tonight a poam about me and my girl while I am in gail I will get it off you in the morning when we come down for a wash Harry old boy don't forget'.[27]

Another told him 'well Harry old chap I want you to write me out a nice piece of poetry not too Sentimental, I want it for my girl, I will always give you a bit of weed, I must tell you I am doing six months for being a rogue and vagabond being in the company of prostitutes … 6 months for being alive … it was my previous convictions, I have been here so many times … so don't forget to give me one of your best about love *I won't forget you cheer up*'.[28] Lawson gave him the poem 'For Being Alive'.[29]

'Bound Over (To Lydia)'[30] was for a prisoner who promised

to take back a girl who he said continually lied to him and was a 'snake inside'; the kind of woman who in Lawson's mind could have joined Bertha in 'The Female Ward', Lawson's vitriolic poem about a hateful, scowling liar who could get men hanged with her treachery.[31] In a similarly vitriolic vein he later penned the 'Song Of What Do You Think'.[32]

Lawson's writing for other prisoners was finally uncovered and he was placed in a solitary cell.

With a heavy cold and head 'not clear', he used his first letter to ask Robertson for help again, and told him that when he got out, he'd try 'one last chance' to make it to London, though at forty-two he felt he was getting past the writing age. Prison was 'very cruel', he said. 'This is simply murder – it is killing my mind. There seems nothing for it in Sydney but suicide or a drunkard's grave ... You know I was trying to keep straight.'[33]

His second letter went to 'Dear Mrs Byers', who had moved yet again, this time to Bellevue Street, Cammeray. He told her he would soon go out of his mind, that this was 'real gaol this time' and the loneliness was terrible. He asked her to ferret a pound or two from Lockley on the promise of 'some good work for him' and to try to get some money out of Lockley's printers. She could tap Walter Hegarty, an occasional *Bulletin* writer, as well. 'Do anything to raise the money, and I'll take care this business will never happen again,' he said, repeating a regular promise. Louisa Lawson, now sixty-one, had retired *The Dawn* and was living at 'Old Stone House' near the Tempe Railway Station, south of the city. Lawson told Mrs Byers she could take the Cooks River tram to see Louisa and assured her that his mother had 'plenty'. If she wouldn't open her purse, maybe some of her friends would.[34]

Mrs Byers was taunted by neighbours for going out of her way to help a hopeless case who they said would 'never mend'.[35] But she was touched by the sign-off in his letter – 'Yours in trouble' – and she remembered the lines of one of his recent poems:

Who knows what Dame Fortune may turn in the end,
And smile, at the last, on that 'vagabond friend'.[36]

A FEW DAYS LATER LAWSON wrote to Bland Holt to say that Bertha and the children were in 'no want', yet he was in 'grim gaol'. He was 'ashamed' to have to write another begging letter but quite willing to blame others for his money woes, telling Holt 'but you know what publishers and editors are. Just a couple of pounds would help so much'.[37]

Over the next two weeks Mrs Byers tried everyone Lawson suggested. He told her to go after Lockley and stick to him since he'd got a book out of Lawson 'for next to nothing'. She could even try solicitor Bert Davies. He told her to put the hard word on Dr Frank Bennet. He could lend a pound or two; he was Bertha's doctor 'and knows all about it'. There was Dr Thomas at Manly, the partner of Dr Hall who had treated Lawson after his thirty-metre 'fall' seven years before. They had 'bled him dry' over there and could give some of his money back. She had done well already, and with money she'd saved herself, told Lawson the £7 16s was within reach. 'I have no fear of the future,' Lawson assured her.[38]

Through the tireless efforts of his poor and weary surrogate mother, Lawson was released on 14 October 1909. Robertson thought he could placate Bertha and stop her pursuing the alimony so relentlessly by offering her a job running an art gallery on his Book Club premises, next door to his office in Castlereagh Street. Bertha took the job but, to Robertson's astonishment, refused to back down on Lawson's 30 shillings a week. She later claimed that Lawson stalked her at the gallery, pretending he was only looking at the art but keeping one eye on her all the time.

But Lawson had hardly seen the sunshine outside the gates of Darlinghurst when he was hit with another summons, this time for £15 12s, arrears he had chalked up while in jail, plus legal costs. He had no way of paying and he donned the prison uniform again on 28 October as the metal gates clanged behind him. His name was changed to Prisoner 117 but he was still alone in a 'small and rather dark cell in a fit of great depression'.[39]

Mrs Byers said the 'persecution' Lawson underwent was 'terrible and it went on for years. The cruelty of it was bad but the ignorance of his persecutors was worse. Here was a poor, underpaid writer, expected to write poetry, stories and verse as if he was a printing machine. What were his brother-writers doing? Did they fully realise the torture such a proud and sensitive man as Henry Lawson had to undergo? Did any of them busy round as I had to? ... I do not blame them all though as a body, they seemed to lack the spirit of camaraderie and good fellowship.'[40]

Lawson told Bland Holt, who was now back in Sydney, that he had given everything he could to raise Bertha's money. 'I went straight, wrote hard, and did my best, but it was no use.' *The Bulletin* had only paid him £2 6s for 'The Song of a Prison'. He begged Holt not to desert him, and despite having made the same promise many times before, promised that this time it would be the last he ever begged him for help.[41] He complained that while he was destitute, Bertha was now earning good money from *his* publishers.

Mrs Byers feared that the flesh was being 'starved' off Lawson's bones and 'it really looked as if they would rattle'.[42] She dashed about all over Sydney begging on his behalf, and when she saw how emaciated he was she started bringing hot dinners into the jail, cradled in her lap on the journey across the harbour. Robertson gave Mrs Byers tobacco to take to him and suggested that perhaps he could pay for Lawson's food from a local arcade. He once again promised Mrs Byers that he would rekindle their previous arrangement of paying Lawson's weekly alimony so long as he stayed away from his office.

Mrs Byers told Lawson of the arrangement and on 11 November he wrote to her again, imploring her to 'Keep [Robertson] up to his promise about keeping me, even if you have to go to his private house – it is only at Mosman – or even to Blackheath ...'.[43] Lawson cajoled his elderly lifesaver to write letters around Australia. There was his Uncle Joe Albury in Goulburn – he hadn't seen him for years but he might be good for a pound or two. She could also hunt up Randolph Bedford's address and there were some journalists in Western Australia – he hardly knew them, but it couldn't hurt to try.

Mrs Byers called on Bert Stevens and Fred Brown, an artist who had illustrated Lawson's writing for *The Worker*. Stevens was still working as a law clerk but had built an impressive resume as a freelance journalist and editor, and had now replaced Alfred Stephens in charge of *The Bulletin*'s Red Page. Mrs Byers told him that prison had driven Lawson 'nearly mad'. Stevens had a plan. He rounded up some of Lawson's friends for a meeting at the Edinburgh Castle Hotel and together they started a fund to pay his debts. It was no good, they agreed, to raise money for Lawson if he was only going to drink it, but they planned to send him out of Sydney to get help. Stevens was voted chairman of the 'Henry Lawson Fund', Jack Brereton was made secretary, and Hector Lamond from *The Worker* was treasurer. Tom Mutch had just organised the Australian Writers' and Artists' Union, and got busy rounding up donations from colleagues. Mutch told everyone that he felt privileged to have been 'enrolled' as one of Lawson's friends years earlier at seventeen, when 'a tall, lean, dark man came to the counter at the old *Worker* office in Kent Street, Sydney, stood, smiled, saluted (recognising in me a new employee), and then impulsively came round the counter, placed his hands on my shoulders, looked long with the deepest eyes I have seen in a man, and said, "You'll do"'.[44]

THE 'HENRY LAWSON FUND' COMMITTEE took time to gather donations but soon they were on their way to a total of £22 8s 6d. Mrs Byers bought him clean clothes and underwear, and told Lawson that moves were afoot to spring him from his cell.

He planned 'a pleasant surprise' for the children on Christmas morning. But the fundraising moved more slowly than he hoped. Stevens went to see Bertha to see if she could drop the claim on the proviso that Lawson got out of Sydney and received help for his drinking. She told Stevens that Lawson's debt was now £29 and that the legal process worked automatically, and that he went to jail whether Bertha liked it or not. She agreed to Stevens's proposal but Lawson still spent Christmas and

New Year behind bars. When Stevens came to Darlinghurst to tell Lawson that Bertha had agreed to drop her claims for the money, Lawson was furious rather than elated. He was ropeable that Stevens had negotiated anything with her, stressing that he had not spoken or written to Bertha for years. Despite Stevens's charity on his behalf, Lawson labelled Stevens's visit to Bertha 'a sort of indignation meeting to sympathise with Mrs Lawson (he has always been a sort of knock-kneed friend of both)'.[45] He thought the whole project was just 'to glorify Bertram Stevens, and sustain his reputation of Old Woman, mischief-maker, and scandal-monger and carrier, and General Worm amongst the writers and artists in Sydney'.[46] Lawson said the proviso to ensure he got out of town was a 'conspiracy' to suggest he had been harassing his wife and that it would only poison the minds of Jim and Barta against him. Lawson worked himself into depression and was soon taken to the Mental Hospital, again under the care of Sister MacCallum, a woman Lawson called 'an angel'.

Brereton was angry at Lawson snubbing the hard work and generosity of the committee. He told Lawson that all his friends had seen him 'dazed, and maudlin, and ridiculous' and did not want to see him gibbering. Would he accept the terms laid down or would the committee return the donations and let Lawson stay where he was?[47]

Lawson accepted the terms and eventually agreed to a stay in Melbourne's Caulfield Hospital. Stevens negotiated his release with Bertha and John Garland, who had just been appointed the NSW Minister of Justice.

Sister MacCallum advised Lawson to remain at the Mental Hospital after his release before going to Melbourne, an invitation he readily accepted. Mrs Byers was a constant visitor and she reminded Sister MacCallum of a little bird 'as she fluttered, brisk and alert, up the garden to the Hospital, or perched on the edge of a chair … chirping happily of some new and wonderful plan for Henry, or of some recognition he had received, or flopping up her plumage in indignation at some criticism or slight'. Sister

MacCallum told Lawson biographer Colin Roderick many years later that Mrs Byers 'had rescued Lawson, not once but many times from actual destitution. ... She had found him after agonising hours of search lying in the street or under a bench in the park, helpless and filthy ... gathered him up, took him to her home, washed him, fed him and nursed him.'[48]

Within a week of entering the hospital, Lawson was experiencing a sense of exultation, even sending Robertson letters written with a mock Scottish accent about the 'graund' massages he was receiving from Florence Alexander, a 'Scottish lassie, big as a hoose'.[49]

He had a brief time on the outside, boarding at 95 Bathurst Street in the city, but paying his landlady, Mrs Coleman, only the first week's rent. Mrs Coleman wanted to know who was going to pay her for the rest of his board and Lawson replied 'Damfino'. She told the committee she wasn't keeping a 'benevolent asylum', but Hector Lamond gave her the 30 shillings owing. Lawson moved back to the Mental Hospital and wrote to friends thanking them for their support, telling Lamond that everything was 'O.k. O.K.er than you might think'. Full of excitement like a dog off its chain, his arrogance spilled over and he mocked the committee members for interfering in his personal affairs, making fun of Brereton's concern and calling Bert Stevens 'a purposeless dam'd article' and suggesting that the committee might now be able to supply him with five weeks of tucker and cheap beer.[50]

LAWSON HAD SPENT A TOTAL OF 159 days in jail over the past five years but on 29 January 1910, Bertha wrote to 'Dear Harry' from her home in Cammeray, saying she could speak to him 'now because you are yourself. And I sincerely congratulate you and hope that you will continue and win back your health and self-respect.' She had a sense of the dramatic but told him that Jim had been very delicate 'ever since he had pneumonia in Manly about six years ago' and had a cavity in the lung ... 'it only has been ceaseless care that has kept the boy alive'.

If you will help me to save Jim it will be a great comfort to you as well as to me. The child is already asking for you and begging me to take him to you. Will you see him. There is no need for you to see me at all. ... If I did not think you were going to keep yourself I would not ask you to do this. As the sorrow of you falling back would only [cause] more misery to the little fellow. The child dearly loves you and gave a boy a thrashing at school because the boy spoke slightingly of you ... Re yourself. No one is more pleased to see you yourself again than I am. Not from any personal feelings at all. Because we both realise our Position and both know that the only bond existing between us is the children. ... Don't let an idea that you are being shoved out of Sydney or that you are being influenced by your friends or indirectly by me. If so you are quite wrong ... If I were your sister I should beg of you for your own sake to leave Sydney for a little while to recover your health and strength and when you return settle down to some real good work. Re the Court. If you will pay into Court whatever you can afford to help with Jim that will do ...

PS I want you to quite understand that there is no personal reason for me writing ... as far as any personal feeling is concerned I might as well be dead. So don't be afraid that I am trying to influence you on my own behalf.[51]

That day Lawson called in to *The Bulletin* and drew up a document on the warped assumption that the money collected for the 'Henry Lawson Fund' was his. He declared that all the money should go to Jim's care but it seems Jim was recovering well enough. He and Barta visited Lawson in the Mental Hospital and Sister MacCallum then took Jim for a holiday on her family's sheep station at Yass where he fell off a horse and broke his arm. It was still a grand adventure.[52]

When Sister MacCallum returned, Lawson sent her to *The Bulletin* with his poem 'The Song of Broken English' which he

Lawson photographed by Sister Alberta de Villiers MacCallum upon leaving the Mental Hospital in 1910. State Library of NSW, FL867110

signed Henry Hertzberg Lawson. He asked Shenstone to give a fair price for it and to give Sister MacCallum a 'good copy of "Great Expectations" for my boy Jim'. He also sent *The Bulletin* the topical 'When Kitchener Shed Tears', a mocking piece of doggerel about Sydney's Lord Mayor giving the English general a banquet on 5 January.[53]

Lawson had recovered his health so much so that he was essentially evicted from the hospital on 5 February and he went back to Mrs Byers at Cammeray.

Lawson wrote to Bertha asking that she be reasonable over her new terms for support since he was 'pretty hard up' and thumping his chest to ram home the point that he had never authorised Stevens or anyone else to plead with her.

He told Robertson that from what he'd heard, Mrs Byers had been insulted at most of the meetings for the Henry Lawson Fund. Despite being a physical wreck, he declared that he had been hunting 'for that crawler Stevens' for three days and intended 'to give him the father, grandfather, and maiden aunt of a hiding on the first opportunity'.[54] Stevens wasn't hard to find because he had worked in the law office of Allen, Allen & Hemsley since Lawson first met him. 'Dear George,' Lawson wrote soon after. 'I have thrashed Stevens in his own office and I feel more contented. The clerks held the door while I did it.'[55] Stevens had a different take: 'As a reward for my trouble,' he wrote, 'Lawson made an attack upon me in a comic opera fashion. He walked into my room at Allen's and, without warning, struck me with his stick on the leg. I was infuriated at this and grabbed him by the collar, kicked him vigorously and ran him out.'[56]

Some time after, Lawson contacted him to apologise. Stevens could not retain any animosity towards Lawson, he said, because it was impossible to measure him by 'conventional standards of conduct'.[57]

Lawson was unique and had many more surprises in store.

Chapter 25

Harry was always fond of children ... perhaps the habit he had of hiding threepenny pieces in the band of his hat, to toss out to the kids had something to do with that. Anyway, all children took to him as an intimate friend.

LAWSON'S ESTRANGED WIFE BERTHA ON HIS GENEROSITY EVEN WHEN HE WAS BROKE[1]

FROM HIS CASTLE IN THE AIR inside Mrs Byers's cottage Lawson still saw himself as master of all he surveyed, and he was still fuming at his friends who he said had gone to Bertha behind his back. He told Jack Brereton that while he could go to hell, he now wanted the Henry Lawson Fund to pay for his fare to London and for the rest of the money to be given to his son Jim. However, the fund committee saw Lawson as a danger to himself and were not about to let him out of their remit.

Tom Mutch thought a trip to the country would do Lawson the world of good, especially if it was to see his old mate Ted Brady, who had taken his wife and three children to the coastal village of Mallacoota, twenty kilometres south of the Victoria–New South Wales border.[2] Brady hoped the remote setting would help him overcome his own alcoholism.

In the twenty years since Brady had befriended Lawson after lifting his poem 'The Cambaroora Star', he had forged his own reputation as a poet, though he made little money from his talent. He had spent many years in Grafton, working for the *Daily Examiner* and buying a share in an ill-fated newspaper there, *The Grip*.

Mutch called Mallacoota 'probably the most beautiful place in Australia',[3] and Brady said he was willing to help with Lawson's recovery, so long as separate accommodation was found for him as the pregnant 'Mrs B' wasn't up to looking after two alcoholics. Life with just one had 'been very much of a fight'. He thought locking Lawson up was a 'national disgrace' but admitted he was rather in 'dread' of him coming to Mallacoota.

'The truth about Lawson is that he was the life-long victim of sordid circumstances,' Brady wrote years later. 'With greater leisure and better payment for his output he would have gone further. Outsiders have said that he liked the life of the hard-up and the drinker, which is a damned lie. He enjoyed it no more than a skylark enjoys a cage.'[4]

Hector Lamond, the Henry Lawson Fund treasurer, gave Mutch £5 from the kitty for expenses on the trip. When their ship, the *Sydney*, was preparing to leave, though, Lawson was nowhere to be found. Mutch chased around his old haunts and found him at the Bathurst Hotel. There was no time to get his luggage, as Mutch 'shanghaied' him onto the vessel not long before she set sail at 6.30 p.m. on Friday 25 February 1910.[5]

They disembarked in the whaling port of Eden the following day and booked into the Commercial Hotel. Lawson befriended the hotel manager Arthur Cooper, but Mutch insisted that Lawson, who was feeling seedy from the voyage, drink only lemonade. Lawson sent a postcard 'To Mrs Byers, My best friend'.

They were up before dawn the next day after Mutch hired a coach for £2 to take them on a bumpy seventy-kilometre drive along a rough bush track and across the border to the Victorian village of Genoa, where Brady was waiting. Clean-shaven, sober and suntanned, Brady looked so well that Lawson and Mutch did not recognise him at first. Brady was with his six-year-old son Hugh and he told them that free of the booze he was in such rude health he would row them the whole twenty kilometres down the river and through a choppy saltwater lake to Mallacoota.

They arrived there at 9 p.m. and although the plan was for Mutch to camp with Brady and his family, he wasn't about to let Lawson out of his sight, and instead stayed with him at Allan's accommodation house.

Lawson wrote to Robertson to say there was the possibility of a new book in these new bush surrounds and as part payment he badly needed new clothes:

1 soft shirt, with collar, 15 or 15½ round neck,
1 soft shirt without collar (same size),
2 common workman's flannel undershirts and drawers,
1 "sweater",
Some handkerchiefs and socks.

He told Robertson that Shenstone could get them from Farmer's store and send them at once. He'd also like a strong pair of pants for bush wear, too.

His measurements were chest 37, collar 15½, waist 33, from fork to instep 32. He said the fund committee had left him with no money and Robertson might like to advance him a couple of pounds as well.[6]

The clothes eventually arrived and even without alcohol as a crutch Lawson was able to stand tall again. Heavy weather set in around Mallacoota but Lawson 'swam, fished, shot ducks, rabbits and jam tins'.[7] He and Mutch ate snapper and wild duck until they couldn't eat any more.

The Allans towed their boat across the bar and Brady, Lawson and Mutch rowed to remote Harrison Creek where Lawson kept telling ghost stories and playing pranks until Mutch protested and Lawson lost his temper, spoiling the excursion.

Lamond approved the financing of a third week of holidays and Lawson and Mutch rolled their swags, filled their pipes and tucker bags, and took off for a four-day tramp through rugged bushland leading to Cape Howe. They had their old pack mare and 'Darky' the kangaroo dog swimming behind their boat when they crossed the lower end of the lake.

Ted Brady's bush camp at Mallacoota in February 1910: (left to right) David Allan, Lawson, Tom Mutch, Brady and Brady's son Hugh. University of Sydney, Rare Books and Special Collections

At Cape Howe they built a structure from wreckage and the bleached bones of a beached whale. Mutch noted that Lawson had a dread of snakes and perhaps that coloured his writing in 'The Drover's Wife'.

But he was right at home camping; pitching the tent, making the fire, and cooking johnny cakes. He would tolerate no interference. Not with making the fire, and especially in his personal life. He still seethed over his friends negotiating with Bertha, and told Mutch that Brereton was no more than 'an animated hat-rack' and that Bert Stevens was a 'dirty, bloody, stinking, crawling cow!' He eventually calmed down and when night descended the campers coiled up on the sand and drifted off to sleep to the sound of the ocean's rhythm and the songs of the wild birds.

Lawson's son Jim was now eleven and still under Sister MacCallum's supervision after breaking his arm. Lawson wrote Jim a long letter about his adventures, promising to bring him down next summer and insisting that Jim learn to ride, swim and shoot. He wanted the boy not to be weighed down by the violent rows that had haunted his childhood and told Jim, 'Give my love to your Mother and little Bertha, and say I'm in grand form and have a lot of good work on hand ... Good luck from your Dad.'[8]

Mutch was confident that the Bradys would take care of Lawson and he paid his friend's board for another month when he headed home to Sydney. Lawson accompanied him as far as Eden and again they stayed at the Commercial Hotel, where Lawson met Margaret Midson, a thirty-year-old single schoolteacher from nearby Green Cape. She claimed that Lawson wrote 'Ben Boyd's Tower'[9] to commemorate their meeting, and that he referred to her in a letter to the *Twofold Times* as 'my lover'. In his next work, after he and the eldest Allan boy sailed past Green Cape to Twofold Bay, Lawson wrote:

Did you see us sailing past?
Syd. Allan sat by the little toy wheel
And your lover by the mast.[10]

Lawson was inspired to write 'Mallacoota Bar'[11] and 'Mallacoota West'[12] and wrote of his 'new love' in 'The Bar',[13] which Robertson bought to use in Lawson's new book *The Rising of the Court*. But Lawson started drinking again and was most likely under the influence when he turned up at Eden at the end of March 1910 hoping to find Margaret before heading back to Sydney. He caused a disturbance and wrote to apologise three months later, telling her that he had been in 'a semi insane state' and that he now realised that the residents of Eden were not those of Sydney 'who take little notice of the wild things I do, both sober and otherwise'.[14] Margaret forgave him and a year later arrived at Mrs Byers's rented home in William Street, North Sydney, only to find that Lawson had virtually forgotten her. Margaret wrote to him two years later from a remote posting on the Queensland–New South Wales border, but it took him six months to reply, as he had just come to his senses 'after a lengthy bad time punctuated by spasmodic writing for rent and tucker ... you poor lonely girl! You must forgive. I've had a lot of trouble and was worried and dulled with that and drink when I first read your letter and put it by.'[15]

Not long after Lawson's return from Mallacoota, one of his drinking buddies, the journalist Herbert Low, died from cancer at his Newtown home aged just forty-four,[16] and Lawson wrote 'Bohemia Buries Her Dead'[17] in his honour. Despite their physical altercation, Bert Stevens always tried to help Lawson and asked him to write about his favourite authors for a *Bulletin* series on prominent writers and their influences. Stevens offered him 30 shillings but Lawson forced up the price to £2 10s, only to take so long writing 'Men Who Did Their Work, or The Books I Like'[18] that he missed the deadline by seven years.

Lawson tried to sell a story about the Longstaff portrait and another about his time in Mangamaunu but no one was buying. He told Robertson he was 'losing heart' and that all he was selling was 'a bit of "comic" rubbish to the Bully'. He needed £1 10s that day or he and Mrs Byers would lose their furniture.[19]

Soon after, Lawson was again arrested for drunkenness, but this time the police took him to Sydney Hospital where he was treated as an outpatient. Robertson yet again came to the rescue with money. Lawson called him 'a grand fellow' and said the cash had arrived 'just in time'.[20]

LAWSON'S TWO NEW BOOKS, *The Skyline Riders* and *The Rising of the Court*, both appeared late in 1910 to indifferent responses. Lawson claimed in the preface to *The Rising of the Court* that his work was published exactly as he wrote it, but in his *Bulletin* review, John Bede Dalley said, 'Some of them would be all the better for a little pruning.' '"Mateship in Shakespeare's Rome" was interesting', Dalley said. 'The other prose sketches are poor. The poem "The Army of the Rear", though, written so far back as 1888 ... is a companion song to "Faces in the Street" of the same period, and has fire in it.'[21]

Lawson still had fire inside too.

He used mock Scottish in 'The Auld Shop and the New', which was formed as a letter to Dan Angus and 'written specially for "The Chief", George Robertson'. Nothing Lawson ever wrote made Robertson laugh so hard,[22] yet he and Lawson soon had a bitter fallout as Christmas 1910 approached.

Lawson came into the Angus & Robertson offices, sober for a change, but a dispute erupted and Lawson hit his publisher. Robertson grappled with Lawson but the belligerent bard broke free and ran towards Shenstone's office. Shenstone came out and tried to quietly placate Lawson, who responded by punching Shenstone on the nose and knocking his glasses off before escaping out the door.

Lawson wrote to Robertson soon after, saying grandiosely, 'You are the first man that Henry Lawson ever sent an apology or explanation to, and perhaps you may be proud of it.'[23] Robertson wasn't.

Lawson had ideas of setting up his own getaway like Brady's Mallacoota camp, but much closer to town, among the sandhills of Kurnell, telling Mutch that he could go down there for the summer with two tents and Mrs Byers as housekeeper and cook. He invited Mutch to come down as well and Mutch made plans to go there in November. But the money Lawson planned to use for camp equipment went on refreshments, and he told Mutch that the camp was just a pipe dream. 'I'm sorry you took the thing so seriously. It was really my fault (or the drink's). I should have called. Things are generally unsettled as long as I am as I am.'[24]

BY EARLY 1911, LAWSON AND MRS BYERS were weeks behind in their rent. Sister MacCallum and Archibald tried unsuccessfully to tap into the Commonwealth Literary Fund that had been established by Alfred Deakin's Federal Government three years earlier to assist needy Australian writers and their families.

The fund provided a maximum of £1 a week for adults and 10 shillings for children but usually only for the families of writers who had died poor. Lawson had exhausted and exasperated the generosity of his friends, but Archibald donated another £10 to the cause. When Sister MacCallum delivered the money to Lawson and Mrs Byers at North Sydney she was appalled at their poverty. By July 1911 Lawson was so dishevelled and grubby that Sister MacCallum called on Robertson to buy him some more new clothes. He had lost his hat and one of his shoes was missing its laces.

Lawson was drinking regularly with any of the Duskers still alive, often in the studio of Mrs Lala Fisher,[25] a Rockhampton-born journalist and poet who owned and edited *Theatre Magazine*. She tolerated Lawson even though he was a nuisance. She would hide her whisky and try to quell his constant thirst with ginger ale and soda, but in the end, it took beer before he'd go home.[26] He would write notes for her autograph collection in return for shillings. Early in their friendship he wrote a note to her explaining that he had wanted to be an actor but became deaf. *The Silver King* with George Titheradge in the lead was his favourite play and he said Bland Holt 'was the biggest hearted of them all: loved for his personality'.[27]

Mrs Fisher had Lawson photographed in her studio along with his colleagues Arthur Bayldon, Rod Quinn and Louis Becke, and their likenesses were used for endorsements in *The Lone Hand*, with Lawson, not exactly a picture of health, recommending Dr Jones's Australian Oil for rheumatism, advising readers that 'At the first sign of stiffness I rub the pungent, penetrating oil into the sore muscles. This invariably gets rid of the evil.'[28]

Dr Jones claimed his oil was 'the world's greatest remedy for rheumatism, gout, chest colds, sore throat, neuralgia, sprains, sciatica, malarial stiffness, and enlarged joints',[29] but it didn't help Lawson's alcoholism.

He admitted to Mrs Fisher that he had lost what he called 'the sledgehammer force of simplicity',[30] but he penned a tribute to the union leader 'Donald Macdonell' who died in 1911.

Much of Lawson's writing at the time was reflective, tinged with both nostalgia and regret, such as the poem 'Said Grenfell to My Spirit',[31] in which he hinted that his wrong turns in

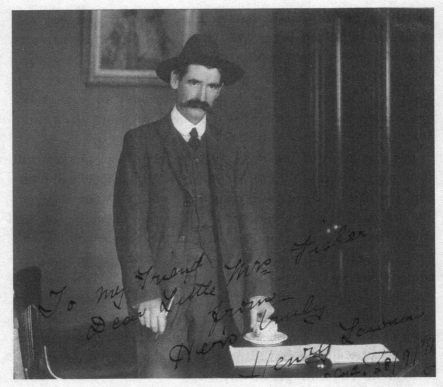

A 1911 autographed photograph of Lawson to his friend Lala Fisher. University of Sydney, Lawson Collection

life were dictated by fate rather than conscious decision, and 'Recollections',[32] which described his childhood on the old diggings and the 'sins of dark Leicester Square' when he became an adult.

He punished himself more in 'A Riddle in Remorse or, the Ruined Writer' over 'the rotten stuff he wrote for drink, and published to his shame!'[33]

He became even too much for Mrs Byers, and constantly drunk he stayed for three months in a city flophouse, always promising to have the rent money 'next week'. He sent cryptic notes to Robertson, promising two new stories that had been 'drafted in England' – 'Exit Mitchell' and 'Steelman Good-night', a carryover from his glory days when he had created the characters almost fifteen years earlier.[34] In one he called himself Henrick

Hertzberg Larsen, as though regressing to his childhood as the son of a foreign father. He pestered *The Bulletin* staff so much that on another occasion Jimmy Edmond ran him downstairs and gave him a shilling to go away. As he went off to buy a drink with the shilling, Lawson told *The Bulletin* editor in a slur 'you're touchy Jimmy – too sensitive and emotional'.[35]

Lawson was able to earn a little money from – of all places – the undertakers Coffill & Co, who commissioned him to fill their illustrated booklet, *Coronation Ode and Retrospect*, marking the coronation of King George V, on 22 June 1911. It contained Lawson's 'England' and 'The King', in which in a 180-degree turn from the republican cries of his youth, he now prayed the monarch would have a 'long, great glorious reign'.

BERTHA WAS MAKING A LIFE OF HER OWN, enjoying affectionate letters from Edward Tregear and the occasional day on the beach with him. Tregear, who had twice found work for Lawson in New Zealand, was an occasional visitor to Sydney.

Lawson, by contrast, was again putrid and paralytic by November 1911. He spent a night in the Mental Hospital, before being admitted to the Coast Hospital at Little Bay 'for a rest until after Christmas'.[36] He sent the landlady from the city flophouse to Robertson with a note saying she was owed about £10 in rent and could he pay it because she was hard up too.

The stay in the Coast Hospital restored Lawson's vigour for a while and he explored the unsettling depths of 'Jim-Jam Land',[37] his verses about the monsters of a drink-addled mind that followed a theme he had explored four years earlier.[38] He sold the work to both *The Bulletin* and Lockley and summoned the ghosts of his time in The Rocks with 'The Old Push and The New'.[39]

When the *Titanic* sank in the North Atlantic on 15 April 1912, Lawson wrote 'A Song of Brave Men',[40] and equated the disaster with the shipwreck of his own life. He sold his poem 'The Old Unionist', written in the voice of a veteran from the picket line, but it was pirated by the *Westralian Worker* and became 'Too Old to Rat',[41] with its emphasis changed so that it seemed as though

Lawson had been a union man for thirty years rather than the character he'd created for the verses.

At the end of July 1912, Lawson was working on his series of sketches called 'Elder Man's Lane' set around the horse ferry on Blues Point Road and a degenerate named Johnson who tried to maintain some sense of decorum as the demon drink eroded everything in his life.[42] Over the next eight years his three planned sketches stretched to fifteen, as Lawson traced his own life and failings and a marriage in which there were 'frequent and violent wrangles, and much unhappiness'.[43]

The second sketch in the series introduced 'Benno, the bottle-o' and the character Ah Sam,[44] a blundering opium dealer, and relative of another of Lawson's characters, 'Ah Soon'. It continued *The Bulletin*'s tradition of portraying the Chinese as criminals, but in opposition to the anti-Asian sentiment that appeared in Lawson's work, especially early in his career, was a warmth for individual Chinese that he had known.

In the ninth sketch, Lawson wrote of 'Johnson's Reformation', of the character he brought to life from his own shortcomings, and a marriage that mirrored his own. 'He was a weak man,' he wrote of Johnson, 'and in the end went down on his knees to her and begged her not to make a Public Scandal.' Lawson peppered the sketch with Bertha's evidence in her deposition against him, reciting a wife's tale of her husband's threats and violence.[45]

Lawson disappeared for two weeks on another drinking spree in July 1912 but around that time wrote 'Grandfather's Courtship' for *The Lone Hand*,[46] with Henry Albury as the central character.

In August *The Lone Hand* ran his short story titled 'Ah Soon: A Chinese-Australian Story',[47] as Lawson told a story of reciprocal kindness across two families and two generations. The first kindness was from Lawson's parents to Ah Soon, a Chinese gardener, when they lived at Lawson's Creek near Mudgee many years earlier. They helped Ah Soon to hospital when his cart tipped over near their home. The second kindness was from Ah Soon's son, Ah See, who sold vegetables to Lawson the narrator, and gave the struggling writer £6 when he had fallen on hard times. Lawson wrote:

I am anti-Chinese as far as Australia is concerned; in fact, I am all for a White Australia. But one may dislike, or even hate, a nation without hating or disliking an individual of that nation. One may be on friendly terms; even pals in a way. I had a good deal of experience with the Chinese in the old years, and I never knew or heard of a Chinaman who neglected to pay his debts, who did a dishonest action, or who forgot a kindness to him or his, or was not charitable when he had the opportunity.[48]

This was in the 'Dry Districts many years ago', Lawson wrote, 'when saints and sinners, Christian and heathen, European and Asiatic were fighting a long and cruel drought side by side ... If men couldn't be brothers, or at least charitable and kind and courteous to each other and forgetful of nationality and creed under such conditions – when could they?'[49]

On 12 August he let Robertson know that everything now was 'All serene, but it was a rather strenuous drunk while it lasted'.[50] Robertson eventually bought the rights to some of Lawson's recent work for a book he was planning called *Ah Soon and Other Australian Stories and Verses* but eventually decided the work was not Lawson's best and dropped the idea.

On 13 December 1912, after drinking at the Edinburgh Castle Hotel, Lawson climbed aboard a tram at Bathurst Street but did not have a single penny to buy a ticket. He gave his name and address as 'Bulletin Office' to the conductor and agreed to send the penny to the Tramways Office. A letter of demand came, so once again he went begging.[51]

Lawson must have felt like a complete heel when he received a letter from his son three days before Christmas telling him about his school camp; of how he was learning to swim in the surf, and how he would be going to grammar school soon. 'Mother has had to work very hard to send me there,' Jim said.[52] Barta sent

Lawson a poem for the first time; she told Lawson that she now had a canary, and thanked him for some money for art lessons 'as without it Mother could not afford to help me learn what I most wish to ... we are all very well but Mother is tired'.[53]

Lawson contemplated his own mortality again in February 1913, penning his *Bulletin* tribute 'Louis Becke'[54] after his fellow carouser died alone of throat cancer at the Hotel York in King Street. Becke's heavy drinking and infidelities had blighted his life and a housemaid found him slumped in a chair at a table with the manuscript of his latest work before him.[55] Becke was buried in the Waverley Cemetery near Kendall, and Lawson's friends feared that he would soon be joining them.

The publication by Lothian of *Triangles of Life* coincided with Archibald commissioning Florence Rodway to paint what he thought would be the last portrait of his protégé. Rodway depicted Lawson in half-profile as a hollow, almost ethereal character. Lawson told Robertson that he would still haunt his office after he had gone to the hereafter.[56]

LAWSON TRIED TO MAINTAIN a close relationship with his children despite his drinking. In February 1914 he promised to take a chicken for them to eat at Bertha's house at 140 Walker Street, North Sydney, but instead he started drinking and forgot. His delusions of grandeur overcame him as he told Barta: 'I could get no one to take that fowl up in time. (My little messengers were out and I couldn't "ketch a boy".) My foreman was away too.'

He was broke again, he explained, 'and Robertson and I are unusually antagonistic'. But there was some joy.

That old fool cat of mine, Dooly, came back after four or five months, in a deplorable condition, manged, half blind and nearly starved. He yowled like a child when I spoke to him. I pulled him through with hot milk, cooked liver, sulphur, grease and soap. I'm afraid he'll never get back his good looks. ... He looks like I do sometimes ... you'll see the finger marks of one of my infernal cats on the back of this, if you look close.[57]

Lawson and Bertha regained a sort of cautious regard for each other and she recalled that despite his poverty 'he had his happy times and I think those periods were usually associated with absolute freedom from responsibility and full expression of his genius. He hated to be tied down. Sometimes, I used to think he liked to be penniless; even money seemed to suggest bonds to him. At any rate, he got rid of it as quickly as he could.'[58]

Two weeks after writing his letter to Barta, Lawson was charged with being drunk and using bad language to two ladies in a North Sydney street. The *Truth* reported on the 'humiliation' of this 'Prodigal Poet'.[59] Lawson said he pleaded guilty to the drunkenness 'to save time' but denied using bad language. He said the 'boy' policemen in the area had it in for him, but he was fined 5 shillings for being drunk and ordered to pay 10 shillings for the bad language or serve three days' jail. A retired policeman, sympathetic to Lawson's struggles, paid the fines on the spot.

Lawson tried to sell his version of the incident and his poem 'A Sordid Tale' to *The Bulletin* but they were sick of his excuses.[60]

Tom Mutch, now a member of the New South Wales Labor central executive, thought the time was right for Lawson to revisit his old home. So in April 1914, with a helping hand from Mutch, Lawson caught the train to Mudgee and stayed at Flanagan's Victoria Hotel for two days before moving on to Eurunderee. Lawson repaid the hospitality by writing 'Flanagan's Hotel', later called 'Callaghan's Hotel' when it appeared in *The Bulletin*.[61] Henry O'Brien, now an elderly prospector, was still living in Lawson's childhood house but had added skillions to it. Ivy snaked across the front porch. As Lawson bedded down there, he put his hand out for some warmth, writing to Mutch for 'a spare undervest and drawers if you have them – or cheap common workman's flannels would do as well'.[62] The new pants and vest arrived just ahead of the first frosts, and the country looked glorious on Good Friday morning. The fish weren't biting but there were foxes and hares to shoot and while the local papers paid Lawson next to nothing for some mediocre poems,[63] he heard a whisper that there was going to be a whip-round to raise £50 'for past services to [the] district in writing'.[64]

On 20 April, Lawson visited his old school where James Elliott was now the master, and he wrote in the visitors' book: 'I cannot express my delight at the well kept appearance of the Old School which my Father built, and at which I worked and studied as a boy and in the trees that have grown up round it since then.'[65] In the visitors' book, he also penned a few humorous verses about the absence of his name from the punishment book.[66] Lawson sold those verses to a struggling local paper and wrote to Mrs Byers asking if she could chase up some money for him in Sydney, but she was skint too, and instead asked Lawson if *he* could send a shilling or two her way. Maybe he could sell some more verses in Mudgee.

Lawson sent her a poem for *The Bulletin* about an Aboriginal man who bravely met all obstacles in life with the expression 'Trouble Belongit Mine'.[67] It didn't fit *The Bulletin*'s White Australia theme, though Mary Gilmore called it 'surely the most pathetic elegy ever written of any people'.[68] She had once tried to interest Lawson in writing more about Australia's Indigenous people 'and their extermination ... [but] he said the subject could wait for later comers: that in any case anyone writing of the Aboriginal as heroic or romantic would only be laughed at and ridiculed, and very hotly'.[69]

As rain set in, Lawson drank cheap wine with 'madness in it' and it took 'three days and several gallons of bottled ale to repair the damage'.[70] Lawson wrote a second version of 'Eurunderee',[71] as he contemplated the world of his childhood and the changes to both it and himself. He wrote that he was still haunted by his sister Nettie's passing, still craving for the familial affection that he missed growing up.

Lawson hacked off the first six verses to sell to the *Western Post* as a separate poem called 'The Flour Bin', and he also composed a long sketch called 'Amongst My Own People', describing it as his search for the solution to a universal brotherhood, an old writer 'timbering up the walls of his ruined life and sinking through the mullock of the present'.[72]

The sketch was divided into three parts and showed Lawson's split personality, writing as both his alter ego John Lawrence and as Henrik Hertzberg Larsen.[73]

He moved out of the home Niels had built and into a spare bedroom at 'Weinsberg', the home of the widowed Mrs Gottlieb Wurth and her son Jim. Mrs Wurth was an old schoolmate of Lawson's mother. His hopes for a testimonial and the rumoured £50 came to nothing, though, and soon he was back in North Sydney and broke. His mood was blackened by a change at the helm of *The Bulletin* with Samuel Prior[74] replacing Jimmy Edmond for the start of an almost twenty-year tenure.

Lawson wrote to schoolmaster Elliott saying he'd like to come back to the Mudgee district and put in a day or two with him. He was 'awfully stuck for a few pounds', Lawson explained, 'and if you know one or two friends you might see them quietly … Even a modest fiver would be a great help till I get in some solid work.'[75]

Elliott couldn't help with the money but Lawson wrote again to say that he would soon be back with Tom Mutch, who was going to take photos of Lawson's boyhood haunts for an article in the *Sydney Mail*. He told Elliott to forget about the 'ugly awkward business' of the fiver and not to worry about him drinking because 'Tom hates drink, and any nip must be taken with the greatest secrecy. Otherwise there is likely to be a breach between me and my mate.'[76]

Lawson and Mutch availed themselves of Elliott's hospitality and Lawson showed Mutch the house Niels built, the diggings, even, Lawson claimed, a mound made from the gravel and clay from the shaft where Thomas Aspinall had died.[77]

Back in Sydney, Lawson was soon desperate for money again and appealed to Jack Lang, who had been elected the State Member for Granville following his return to Hilda. Lang had still been living with Nellie Anderson when their son Chris was born on 25 March 1910, but Nellie died in 1911, and Lang went back home to his wife and children, taking Chris with him.

They made their home in Auburn, and when he and Hilda had their sixth and last child in 1913, Jack named the new daughter Nellie Louise after his recently deceased mistress.[78]

Lang sent Lawson 2 guineas on the same day that *The Bulletin* sent him £5 for 'Amongst My Own People', but Lawson earned little else over the next few months.

Australia had bigger concerns than Lawson's money woes, after the assassination of Austria's Archduke Franz Ferdinand and his wife Sophie in Sarajevo on 28 June 1914 ignited the powder-keg of European tension.

More than 400,000 Australians enlisted to fight in the resulting world war, and 62,000 would die on foreign fields.

Lawson saw the Russians as the bears to devour the Germans in 'The March of Ivan',[79] while the rape of Belgium fuelled his rage against the beastly Hun in whom he saw echoes of the 'Prussianised' Bertha. Lawson's 'Dawgs of War',[80] defining the fighting characteristics of each Allied country's most popular canine, included the 'Kangaroo Dog', 'leaping high to gain his view', while in 'A Slight Misunderstanding at the Jasper Gate',[81] Lawson imagined Drake and Wellington coming out of heaven to lead the Allied fightback. 'Antwerp',[82] written after the Germans had all but destroyed that city, was a grim commentary on 'the terrible silence of children', twelve years after Lawson had spent a wonderfully sodden summer night there. Before long, though, Lawson was writing 'A Mixed Battle Song',[83] explaining that despite jingoism, good men were dying on both sides.

While *The Bulletin* bought all of Lawson's military verses, Lawson and Mrs Byers were still broke and forced to move home with their growing collection of cats, this time to a semi-detached cottage at 31 Euroka Street, North Sydney.

Despite his distressed and hungry state, Lawson wrote cheerily to Barta on her fifteenth birthday, congratulating her on her schoolwork, sending her 'fondest love' and offering her another 'Katt' ... 'I've got a beauty just now – a young Thomas.

Tabby, beautifully marked, very clean and affectionate, and a good ratter ...'[84]

At around the same time Lawson had a kind of out-of-body experience, and wrote the revolutionary 'My Army, O, My Army',[85] with echoes of 'Faces in the Street' stirred by the peasants' revolt during the French Revolution. He could never remember writing it, but it became the basis for another book of verse under the same name which Tyrrell published in 1915. The book featured a stirring Norman Lindsay painting of a march by revolutionaries led by Lawson, Alfred Stephens, Rod Quinn and Henry Boote, the editor of *The Worker*. Rose Soady, bare breasted as usual, dominated the painting as the Goddess of Liberty.

Lawson wrote 'The Vanguard',[86] claiming that he had tried to enlist for the war but had been turned back because of his age and deafness. Robertson asked him to sit for a bust by Illingworth and while Lawson agreed, he told his publisher he was now having 'suicidal tendencies',[87] a feeling that was barely assuaged by news that the British publishers Harrap's would publish *My Army, O, My Army* as a book there with Lawson's poem 'The Song of the Dardanelles',[88] about the Anzacs fighting on Gallipoli, as its opening work.

Lawson remained depressed and revealed nightmare visions in 'Lawson's Dream'[89] and 'A Dirge of Gloom',[90] while another stay in the Thomas Walker Hospital produced 'The Unknown Patient'.[91] *The Bulletin* deleted a stanza in which Lawson speculated that an inscription on a sandstone ledge there proclaiming 'God Bless Thomas Walker' may have been made by 'a drunkard parted from his children and his wife'.

He explored his unconscious mind for Bert Stevens at *The Lone Hand* with 'About Dreams',[92] in which his sexual aggression, repression, exhibitionism, insecurities and fear of death were all revealed. But staying sober for long periods had also become just a dream and Lawson's friends hatched another plan to help him dry out in a place fighting the drought.

ON 24 NOVEMBER 1915, Archibald led a delegation of journalists[93] to Premier Arthur Holman, explaining that the 48-year-old Lawson's drinking had left him destitute. They said he could be reformed by getting him away from temptation and, given his talent, could the government come up with some form of grant?

It was decided that Lawson could be sponsored by the government to visit and write about the recently developed Murrumbidgee Irrigation Area (MIA) in the Riverina district of the state's south-west, with a view to attracting farmers to settle there. The MIA had been created to control and divert the flow of local rivers and creeks for agriculture. It also had a prohibition on alcohol. Lawson accepted his new opportunity with 'no hesitation', telling George Evatt, the Secretary of the NSW Water Conservation and Irrigation Commission, that he had farmed at Mudgee in the drought and that his articles would not be as dry as that, but rather 'probably ... something novel and readable'.[94]

Lawson was given a six-month contract providing him with 2 guineas a week and a rent-free home with about a hectare of land in return for his journalism. His railway fares and furniture removal were also covered.

Early in the New Year of 1916, he called in to the irrigation commissioner's office asking for a £5 advance on his contract.

He also paid a visit to Lala Fisher and was 'uproariously drunk'. In making a deep curtsey to himself, he rolled over and broke two things she valued very much. She felt vexed but didn't say anything to him.

She thought he was 'so cute'.[95]

Chapter 26

I don't know what's come over the poor little lady, but she seems to be
developing into a regular Harpy with the tongue of a hell-hag ...
and always raving about food for the animals and
after money she knows I haven't got.

<small>LAWSON AFTER FALLING OUT WITH HIS GREATEST SUPPORTER[1]</small>

LAWSON AND MRS BYERS left Sydney by train on 10
January 1916 bound for the railway station of Yanco and their
new home in the nearby town of Leeton. The water commission
advised Lawson that dogs were not allowed on its property, but
they still took with them a bad-tempered, rough-haired cattle dog
named Charley, which had been left behind by a young soldier
heading to the front. Mrs Byers insisted that Lawson secure
a bullock's heart which she could cook and cut into slices for
Charley on the journey south.

Soon Lawson would be at war with both the elderly lady and
the dog, but for now he helped himself to a few refreshing ales
and enjoyed the first-class treatment in the sleeper carriage.

The American architect Walter Burley Griffin, who had
designed the town of Griffith and what would become the new
national capital, Canberra, had transformed Leeton from a tent
village in 1913 into a promising agricultural centre with a leafy
avenue of kurrajong trees. It became part of a network of farm
towns supported by the construction of canals, weirs, holding
ponds and the mighty Burrinjuck Dam.

Lawson had quickly spent his £5 advance from the water commission and then borrowed another £10 from it, agreeing to repay the money at 30 shillings a fortnight.[2]

Lawson and Mrs Byers arrived in Leeton on 11 January and were taken to their new temporary home in Pine Avenue. Although their furniture had not arrived, Lawson fixed up the place with a table and borrowed crockery.

The *Murrumbidgee Irrigator* reported the arrival of the literary celebrity, writing of 'his big brown eyes, backed by a hearty handclasp, telling of sincerity and manliness'.[3]

Lawson informed George Evatt at the water commission that Charley had made friends with every dog in Leeton bar one 'and he fought him to a draw – they'll meet again'.[4]

Lawson was also making new friends and reacquainting himself with old ones. Before long he would run into his old jail mates. George Love, the wife-killer, was the character he now called 'Previous Convictions'. Jim Gordon, who had tramped the outback with Lawson, was farming in Leeton and working on road maintenance. Despite the closeness of their relationship a quarter of a century earlier, Lawson now wrote to him as 'Dear Mr Gordon'. Alex (Leslie) McGill, another friend from Bourke, was now Leeton's cordial manufacturer and he began supplying Lawson with non-alcoholic hop beer. Another Leeton man, Jack McCausland, wrote to say he was a fan. Lawson told McCausland that he was getting around the booze ban in Leeton with a special delivery jar from Narrandera and that his three pet aversions in life were 'nagging women, boils, and sub-editors'.[5]

Lawson's first report to *The Bulletin* covered the journey south, watching the ghost bush sail past in the half moonlight and in the morning moving through a sea of wheat on both sides of the line to the irrigation towns bringing 'new life to an old dead land that is being made to live again'.[6]

After two weeks, Lawson moved to a more permanent home in a four-roomed weatherboard cottage on two acres at Farm 418 on Palm Avenue, surrounded by fruit trees, grapevines and fowls.

Lawson's first report on Leeton was not the flattering publicity the water commission had expected. He said it was 'unnatural' for a town not to have a pub and that the place was like a 'bad nightmare' as though 'he had been dropped into a disguised hell'.[7]

Soon, though, he remembered the script and said Leeton was one of the 'most cosmopolitan places I have ever been in, and perhaps the most naturally intellectual, and democratic'.[8] His opinion could change quickly. In '"Bonnie" of the Area' (named after Jim Gordon's three-year-old girl) Lawson wrote of the infertile 'clayband' around Leeton, but was more interested in praising the town's women – 'the settlers' wives, the tradespeople's wives, etc. – for their friendly and kindly nods and smiles' in contrast to the wives of the minor officials who acted like 'Darling Point ladies coming out of an Hotel Australia four o'clock tea … with a barrel-organ playing just across the street, and two low persons pushing a barrow load of blackened bananas past'.[9]

'Leeton Town'[10] was a homage to a country idyll with fruit trees either side of canals like English brooks.

PREMIER WILLIAM HOLMAN had started making moves for Lawson to receive a £1-a-week pension from the Commonwealth Government as a literary man unable to work because of poverty and Lawson was advised to submit the appropriate form to Dr Frederick Watson, the editor of the Historical Records of New South Wales. It seemed a mere matter of having the form rubber-stamped but Lawson made a hash of it, insisting that he was entitled to the money and going into a long harangue to Watson over his boyhood, his literary success and how his personal life had been 'one bitter black struggle' after that 'mad attempt at suicide near North Head, Manly'. He stressed that 'any stories' Watson may have heard 're my conduct and my treatment of my wife and children while in England were probably lies, and viciously insane or cowardly, envious, and cruel lies at that'. He told Watson that at some later date he might publish the truth about his private life for the sake of the 'thousands of my readers who believe in me and were pained by the evil reports, and for the sake of my work for Australia and humanity'.[11] Watson put up with Lawson's grandstanding in further correspondence and told Lawson that the application would be favourably considered. Between 1916 and 1917 Lawson actually earned about £600 from his writing, enough to buy a house in Marrickville or Woolloomooloo if he had saved the pennies.[12]

LAWSON'S REUNION WITH JIM GORDON after the closeness of their youth meant there was 'a certain shyness about the matter'.[13] In twenty-five years they had changed greatly. Gordon had worked as a drover and outback station manager before settling in Yanco in 1912. Now Lawson became 'Uncle Harry' to Gordon's children, though he taught the younger ones to pronounce it as 'Wuncle'.[14]

Lawson took Gordon home to meet Mrs Byers and Charley, who displayed a sharp row of fangs as Gordon stroked him. During the evening Lawson offered Gordon some hop beer, but Gordon declined, remarking that he had just had some whisky with an auctioneer.

'I must meet that auctioneer,' Lawson replied slyly.[15]

Gordon thought Lawson's nerves were shot as he rushed from room to room 'feverishly' showing off the furniture he had made. When it came time to part, Lawson walked home three kilometres with Gordon and when they were almost at his friend's front gate, Lawson broke down in tears, almost wringing Gordon's hand off as an old mateship had been reborn, telling him: 'God bless you – We are Jim and Harry again now.'[16]

The next day Lawson again walked to Gordon's four-hectare Farm 130. Gordon was away, so his wife Celia put him in the lounge room with half a bottle of wine.

'I seldom drink wine,' Lawson replied, but when Gordon arrived about an hour later, 'the half bottle was gone, and another had been taken from a shelf, and broached'.

Sometimes Gordon would find Lawson 'hilarious as a child', the next day 'down in the depths'.[17] But Lawson became a regular at Gordon's, helping him pick pumpkins and plough, and sitting with him by the fire yarning. Sometimes Lawson and Gordon travelled thirty kilometres to Narrandera, and Lawson repaid the gifts of beer from a hotel there with his story 'The Unknown God of Narrandera'.[18]

Lawson and Gordon camped and fished in the bush too, and when Lawson wrote about their trips,[19] he called Gordon 'Jim Grahame', the name Gordon would adopt for his own work. 'Jim Grahame' featured in more of Lawson's pieces including 'Women's Hearts and Women's Tongues'[20] and 'Yistiddee's Bread',[21] as Lawson remembered the Gulgong goldfield and a poor pigtailed girl with a pinched, freckled face, a print frock and a pair of old laceless boots asking for 'Yistiddee's bread please' for her struggling family because it was a penny cheaper.

Lawson had the idea for a series of sketches and skits in a *Book of Yanko* and he drew up an outline of twenty-one chapters. He boasted to Bert Stevens that *My Army* was 'selling like hot cakes'.[22]

Stevens commissioned Lawson to write a prose piece and a poem for *The Australian Soldiers' Gift Book*, a patriotic fundraiser which would also feature works by Mary Gilmore, Dorothea Mackellar, Norman Lindsay, May Gibbs and others.

Lawson's story 'A Letter from Leeton' was addressed 'To Corporal Ernest Watt ("Benno"), late of the Dardanelles', who was recovering from wounds in England, and it told him of nights in Leeton 'like the Breath of Paradise'.

Lawson wrote of his own desire to serve in the war as a doctor's orderly, 'mascot, or Regimental Goat, or something' and even wrote to Labor MP Campbell Carmichael offering his services as a medic, having had experience, he said, in broken noses and cracked skulls. His poem for the *Soldiers' Gift Book*, 'A Leeton Marching Song', was at odds with the other contributions, mostly, again, lamenting the lack of a pub in his town. He was back on point, though, telling *Bulletin* readers that 'Conscription',[23] a fire-charged issue that was dividing the nation, would 'make men of weeds', who could benefit from the sort of rigid discipline he claimed to be experiencing.

FIVE MONTHS OF SUNSHINE and regular sobriety transformed Lawson's appearance and he looked little like the haggard, 'tragic-eyed man' that journalist Isabel Ramsay remembered from Sydney when she visited Leeton to interview him for Sydney's *Sunday Times*.[24] She wrote of a contented man living in sunshine with his beloved landlady and his old mates. Lawson told her jokingly that he was 'the Government Irrigation Poet' and had been sentenced to six months there. Ramsay wrote that he was as irreverent as ever, frightening local authorities who were inclined to look askance at him, fearing attacks on their snobbery, and neighbours revealed that Lawson could often be heard chanting 'The Marseillaise'.

Mrs Byers, Ramsay wrote, was 'very diminutive, and she spends all the energies of her small body fussing round Lawson, keeping the little cottage spick and span'. When the mood was on him, Ramsay wrote, Lawson would work through the night, and 'this voluble little woman' would exert herself to refrain from conversation and instead 'keep the spirit of the writer stimulated with jugs of hot tea … If there exists another poet who glorifies the name of Australia, the Little Landlady has certainly never heard of him.'[25]

The article appeared on 4 June 1916, and it sent Mrs Byers ballistic. She read it just as Jim Gordon arrived at their cottage with a horse and cart to collect firewood. Gordon found Lawson 'with his face clawed from brow to chin, and bleeding, his shirt torn from him'.[26]

Mrs Byers screamed: 'You ridiculed your mother and belittled Mrs Lawson and now you and that bold hussy have ridiculed me.'

Gordon wrote that Lawson was saying wildly, 'Shut up woman, I want to write – evidently his stock weapon in such cases, as at that time he had no idea of writing, but was waiting for me. I poured what oil I could on the troubled mud and the old lady asked me, "now, Mr Gordon, am I a diminutive little lady? Do I look like a woman who would follow him or any other man round with jugs of tea?" Then she went for him again.'[27]

Lawson was 'very upset … not inclined to start out', and as he and Gordon got going, Lawson attempted several times to jump out in order to return and finish the argument. Each time Lawson tried, Gordon would 'whack the horse, which responded so freely, that Henry had to cling on to prevent himself from being thrown out'.[28]

After Mrs Byers made a trip back to Sydney and had been away three weeks, Lawson told Robertson he was at last getting some peace. Once again, he said, his trouble with women was all their fault. 'Damn the date' he wrote at the top of his correspondence and then opened fire.

… I've been having a similar time with Mrs B. to that which I had with Mrs Lawson the last year or so of our conjugal life … It seems strange that three of the four women I was closely connected with should develop into the Brute, so to speak. I may be meself – or because I am, and was always soft and yielding or good-natured and generous. Added to the Mater's natural bent as a selfish, indolent, mad-tempered woman, she was insanely jealous on account of my 'literary success'. Mrs L. was, of course, an insane Prussianized German, by birth on both sides, by breeding, and by nature. Mrs B. seems to have been developing into a combination of the two; and the horror of it was that there was no get-away from her here – unless I went to Narrandera (an ungodly town just outside the Area) and got drunk … Mrs B's pet insanity is dogs, cats, and fowls. I don't mind the fowls. But I've known her to have a clutch of chickens come out, her favourite cat eat them one after another, and then she set another hen – the tragedy to be repeated. The dog she brought up here is a fowl-killer and a man-killer – a horse-and-sulky chaser, and, all together, a dangerous dog. At least he was, but he isn't now. I lost him with the aid of two mates and a two-gallon jar of beer from Narrandera.[29]

Lawson was in no hurry to find Charley either, sending Jim Gordon a mock public notice that announced: 'Lost, a Dorg named "Charley": That Man wot finds that Dorg and Brings him back to me, will get the Biggest Hidin' a Man ever got'.[30] Lawson feared Mrs Byers would go 'raving mad ... just like Mrs L., or worse', when she returned and found out about Charley's disappearance. 'You don't know what disadvantages we Australian writers labour under ... I also lost one of Mrs B's four cats.'[31]

Lawson's spirits were lifted though not long after Ramsay's article appeared, when Jim Tyrrell, acting as his agent, brokered a deal with theatrical producer Frank Beaumont Smith[32] to adapt some of Lawson's stories for a stage production called *While the Billy Boils*. George Robertson sent Lawson £200 under their copyright agreement and Lawson was to receive £1 10s for each performance in Sydney, Melbourne, Brisbane and Adelaide and £1 for every performance elsewhere. English-born comic actor George Willoughby would oversee the production and George Hyam would provide the music. The premiere was scheduled for Sydney's Theatre Royal on 30 September 1916, and Smith also took out an option on motion picture rights.

The production centred around Lawson's story 'The Hero of Redclay' and began with a prologue featuring men sitting around a campfire while the billy boils. One of them bursts into song, outlining the story ahead.

Despite the royalties coming his way, Lawson applied for a free railway pass 'to transact urgent business' in Sydney though it was really to attend rehearsals.

Lawson missed the opening night but at the close of the premiere 'there were repeated cheers and calls for the author' and beside a report on the great Australian boxer Les Darcy beating American George Chip, the *Sunday Times* said that 'Henry Lawson, on his farm at Leeton, should be one of the proudest Australians to-day'.[33]

Billy Boils played in Sydney for a month before moving to Melbourne and it played to good houses for five more years.

THE SUCCESS OF LAWSON'S NEW project raised eyebrows over his sponsorship by the water commission and the fact that he had produced very little copy for them about Leeton. Another request for a free railway pass for Mrs Byers was rejected. The New South Wales Auditor-General F.A. Coghlan complained that the value of Lawson's 'alleged services' to the state was 'infinitesimal' compared with the cost, and that the whole exercise was 'wastefulness'.

Lawson heard of Coghlan's assessment when he was briefly back in Sydney in November 1916. He flew off the handle and handed a letter of resignation in person to George Evatt, demanding 'first class (and sleeper) passes' for himself and Mrs Byers for the return trip to Sydney from Leeton.[34] Evatt gave Lawson a pass to get back there to arrange his things but Lawson promptly lost it, and soon wrote to Evatt in an entirely different tone: 'Sorry to trouble you again, but …' before obtaining another.

Premier Holman wanted Lawson to stay in Leeton, though, because even without producing much work for the state, he saw his presence there as a ringing endorsement for the region. As government departments argued over who should pay for the 'Laurette of Leeton', Lawson and Mrs Byers remained in their cottage until August 1917, ten months after he resigned, drawing his 2 guineas a week, and writing nothing about the area for the last ten months of his stay. He was mostly preoccupied with revising some of his verses for a new book for Robertson called *Selected Poems*, which would be edited by David McKee Wright, *The Bulletin*'s verse editor. Instead of fulfilling his contract writing about the Murrumbidgee Irrigation Area, Lawson instead wrote explanations for Robertson on the characters and circumstances behind each of the poems being chosen for the book, such as 'Dan, the Wreck', based on Harry Teece, his old drinking pal at the Edinburgh Castle. He told Robertson of his regret at having not written more to 'repudiate' Bertha's 'lies', and that he had kept his tongue between his teeth at the time for the children's sake and because he 'still loved the brute'.[35] Robertson paid Lawson £5 per poem to slightly amend some of them and Lawson began

downing large amounts of Glenlivet whisky and Reschs Dinner
Ale as he worked. He went on more sprees, but he helped Tom
Mutch win the seat of Botany in the New South Wales Legislative
Assembly in March 1917 after telling voters that Mutch was 'the
straightest mate I ever had' – even if he did take 'pyjamas in his
swag' at Mallacoota.[36]

By August 1917, Lawson was hankering for a permanent move
back to the big smoke, telling Jim Gordon that he was now
'Commander of the Army of the Fed-ups in Leeton'.[37] Mrs Byers
was already back in Sydney with dental issues and Lawson secured
his own first-class pass back to the city. Now fifty and grey, he was
in such a hurry to get out of Leeton that he left all his personal
belongings behind. Robertson gave Lawson £50 towards the new
book for the copyright of the revised poems but a few days later
Lawson still asked his publisher to lend Mrs Byers 'a couple of
quid' to get her teeth fixed. Lawson said he was sick of lending
her money and that she was now 'no better than a harpy'.[38] His
twenty months in Leeton had cost New South Wales £338.

MRS BYERS, NOW CLOSING in on her seventieth birthday,
found a new home for them at 26 Euroka Street, North Sydney,
and recalled that Lawson made a great pet of a neighbour's dog.
It was always on the lookout for him and his bark was a signal for
Mrs Byers to prepare his dinner. 'When his simple supper ended
[Lawson] was happy as a king,' she recalled. Lawson would ask her
to sing him some old ditty as he sat down to his tea. Sometimes
when he was pleased with the ditty, he would say he had not heard
it properly and ask her to sing it again into his 'hearing ear'.[39]

The comforts of home could not appease Lawson's restlessness
for long, though. He still took no responsibility for anything
except his writing. Joe Noonan, the company secretary at *The
Worker*, now looked after Lawson's bankbook and the deposits for
him from Robertson, Beau Smith and others. Lawson was hardly
back in Sydney when he went on another bender. By the middle
of October, he was back at the Thomas Walker Hospital. Another
spree saw him in the Mental Hospital for Christmas 1917.

Throughout 1918 Lawson lived a transient existence with no fixed address. He had more battles with Mrs Byers and while she went to live at a boarding house in Lavender Bay, he found a bed anywhere he could while he worked on ten indifferent poems for *The Bulletin*, the revisions to his new book, and, although Jules Archibald called it 'demeaning', an endorsement for the popular Heenzo's Cough Cure, along with an accompanying verse called 'The Tragedy',[40] which ran in multiple publications and lamented the theft of his vital bottle of Heenzo by a trusted friend.

But as the Allies marched to victory in Europe, Lawson and Mrs Byers agreed to a truce and they moved into another house in Euroka Street, No. 28. Lawson commemorated the end of the war with 'The Belfries of Strasbourg'[41] but in 'Peace?'[42] he argued that a war was needed at home to clean up the country of 'racecourse scum', 'touts', and flappers 'flinging their modesty away'. This from a man who seemed to spend more days drunk than sober. A week after the German surrender Lawson had told Robertson that he would come into the city to autograph some limited edition copies of *Selected Poems* but he had been drinking heavily again 'due to the most exasperating domestic annoyance'.[43] At Mrs Byers's request, Robertson began paying Lawson a £2 pension each week, though Robertson insisted that Mrs Byers collect it. In the thirty years since he had railed against the monarchy, Lawson had become an arch-Imperialist and his new work, 'England Yet', fired the opening salvo in his collection of forty-six pieces for *Selected Poems*. The book appeared in stores in November 1918 and the *Sydney Morning Herald* said it showed 'Lawson in all his range and power'.

There is a critical preface by Mr. David McKee Wright, which analyses Mr. Lawson's work, and very fairly estimates his place in Australian literature ... Lawson remains the poet who for the past thirty years has most surely interpreted the spirit of Australia. 'He is,' claims Mr. Wright, 'the first articulate voice of the real Australia ... its rugged strength, its impatience of old restraints, its hopes and fears and despairs, its irreverence and grim humour and the tenderness and courage that underlie them all.'[44]

BERTHA HAD WORKED HARD to keep Jim and Barta safe and give them a good education. From 1910 she had earned at least £5 a week working for Robertson, and then in social services. By 1919 Jim, now twenty, was completing a course in milk and cream testing at the Hawkesbury Agricultural College, while Barta was studying for a Bachelor of Arts under the guidance of Jack Brereton at Sydney University. Lawson's responsibility for maintenance payments came to an end in December that year, but he was reminded of them when he wrote the preface for Vance Marshall's book *The World of the Living Dead*, about the brutality of the state's prison system. It was another opportunity for Lawson to vent his spleen about 'The Great Australian Nag' who, he said, put men behind bars because of their 'morbid craving for police court notoriety'.[45] Lawson was prompted to write a series of eight sketches for *The Bulletin* over the next three years about the adventures of 'Previous Convictions' and his mate Dotty. The final sketch in the series, 'The Last Rose of Winter', was Lawson's tribute to the women such as Mary Gilmore who had shaped his life.[46]

Lawson also wrote 'The League of Nations', a sceptical take on its aims to end war. It appeared in a new tabloid newspaper called *Smith's Weekly*, which had been founded by the former Sydney Lord Mayor Sir James Joynton Smith and his partners, theatrical publicist Claude McKay and journalist Clyde Packer. The literary editor was the rejuvenated Jules Archibald, who having sold his interest in *The Bulletin* and despite his poor health and considerable fortune, wanted to be a working journalist until his dying day. Archibald had bought two motor cars and although Lawson decried them as symbols of degenerate capitalism, he sometimes rode in them to Archibald's cottage at Port Hacking. Lawson would sometimes seek solace in a fisherman's shack on the Woronora River side of Como and he was photographed at the official opening of the ocean wharf at Port Hacking on 26 January 1919.[47]

But Archibald became ill in August that year and died in St Vincent's Hospital on 10 September 1919. He left an estate of £90,000 that included bequests for an annual prize for portraiture, and for a fountain in Hyde Park commemorating the service of Australian and French troops. He also left substantial bequests to charities including a fund for distressed journalists.

Lawson wrote the poem 'Archibald's Monument' as a tribute to the 'Old Chief'.[48] He always thought that Archibald had been a bulky and broad-shouldered man in his younger days and 'rather formidable for obvious reasons'. So, when the 'plain little coffin' was carried out past Lawson at Wood Coffill's chapel in George Street on its way to Waverley Cemetery, he felt a cold shiver and a sudden catch in his throat.

'It looked so small. How small and frail the body must have been to hold and feed so great a literary mind. It looked like the coffin of a child.'[49]

Chapter 27

Have you seen the bush by moonlight, from the train, go running by?
Blackened log and stump and sapling, ghostly trees all dead and dry;
Here a patch of glassy water; there a glimpse of mystic sky?
Have you heard the still voice calling — yet so warm, and yet so cold:
'I'm the Mother-Bush that bore you! Come to me when you are old'?
FROM LAWSON'S 'THE NIGHT TRAIN'[1]

B Y THE END OF 1919 Lawson's brother Charlie was living with their mother at the Old Stone Cottage in Tempe. Louisa was losing her mind and both were suffering from hallucinations. Lawson saw little of them except on the anniversary of his father's death.

The tram accident Louisa had suffered at Circular Quay twenty years earlier had caused lasting damage to her head and spine, and despite her ceaseless fight for women's rights she felt that other, more charismatic, feminists such as Rose Scott had received greater credit. When she closed *The Dawn* in 1905 Louisa told readers that the stress of the legal wrangle over her mailbag fastener had made her 'existence almost unendurable'.[2] She trusted no one else to run the paper since 'the independent woman journalist [is] almost as scarce as the good man politician', and in retirement brooded over the unfairness of life. Her nerves were so frayed that she banned clocks and their infernal ticking from her untidy home. She had once embraced seances and spiritualism, and now the voices in her head became constant. She and Charlie, who had spent much of his life behind bars, complained that the screams and wails of convicts being flogged kept them awake and terrified at night.

Louisa's youngest son Peter finally had Louisa committed to the Gladesville Mental Hospital.

Lawson wasn't faring much better. His trips to Como and Cronulla were replaced by stumbles through the city begging for drinks, spending his money from Robertson and Beau Smith as quickly as it arrived. Only the fact that Joe Noonan gave Robertson's £2 a week to Mrs Byers for safekeeping kept a roof over Lawson's head. Like the worn-out bush-women of his writing, it now seemed Lawson was also *past carin'*. His cryptic notes to Robertson included 'How about drawing up a will?', with several rambling afterthoughts about leaving all manuscripts and private correspondence to Angus & Robertson, and future royalties (if any) going to Mrs Byers and his son Jim.[3]

Lawson tried to remain close to his children. His lifestyle and unreliability often made them distant, though according to Barta, Jim, now twenty-two, remained his 'comrade'. Father and son would sometimes meet at Mrs Mac's.

'Nobody could possibly blame Mother for separating,' Barta wrote years later. 'They could never be happy again ... all that picture of our continuing devotion simply is not true. Mother, with great determination and ability, carved out her own successful life ... a life of high fulfilment. Dad did not figure in our scheme of things. Only Jim, without a thought, cut through it all to stand beside him.'[4]

When discussing his autobiographical poem 'Black Bonnet'[5] with Robertson, Lawson told him: '... my son Jim – 6 foot 2 ... has, or had, the same affection for and faith in his grandmother I had for and in mine. I must tell you about Mudder-in-Law some other time. She's got a sense of humour anyhow – can laugh even at herself as socialist and woman league-er. Had Mrs L. possessed the slightest sense of humour, things might have been very different between us, in spite of all the rest. But it is years too late for a reconciliation between us now – even if such a thing were barely possible?'[6]

Bert Stevens had remarked in 1917 that despite Lawson's drinking he was 'all wire and whipcord ... and as strong as a horse' but by 1920 Lawson was looking much older than his fifty-three years and had become increasingly frail and unstable, both physically and mentally.

Noonan and a sub-editor on *The Worker*, Robert Cassidy, were concerned about his rapid decline, and after prompting from Cassidy's future wife, a young nurse named Lucy Sullivan, decided Lawson needed another long break from the temptations of Sydney. Cassidy had a friend named Alick McManus, a storekeeper in the village of Coolac, near Gundagai about 350 kilometres south-west of Sydney. McManus was an 'old-time shearer and Union battler'[7] and they arranged for Lawson to stay with him for six months. On 16 March 1920, with a £25 advance from Robertson against Beau Smith's monthly payments, Lawson began his journey south. He wrote 'The Night Train' as a result, dedicating it to Lucy.[8]

A few days after arriving, Lawson wrote to Jim Gordon to say that he had been 'shanghaied' to Coolac, 'sentenced to six months' Bush again ... but I'm satisfied with my fate'. He admitted he had been drinking for the last two years with 'less than enough to live on'.[9] He wrote to fellow poet C.J. Dennis, the author of such works as 'The Songs of a Sentimental Bloke', praising him for his 'tremendous success' and asking for a 'small loan' because he was ashamed of his clothes.[10] McManus's twenty-three-year-old daughter Grace adopted Lawson as 'Uncle Harry' and waited on him, but within a week Lawson had spent his £25 at 'the pub next door' and soon headed back to Sydney under his own steam, leaving behind his new walking stick and dictionary. He disembarked at Strathfield and stayed for a while with another friend, Ethel Brown, at her boarding house at 16 Thomas Street, Ashfield.

Lawson went on a bender with a French soldier he met and left another of his bizarre notes for Robertson asking for a franc 'to have anozzer drink wiz my French soldier friend'.[11]

Robertson, meanwhile, was working with Banjo Paterson on a book of his collected verse. Paterson had lowered his age to below fifty so he could enlist for the front in World War One, serving first as an ambulance driver in France, where his wife worked as a nurse, and then as a major, overseeing the supply of mounts for the Australian light-horsemen in Palestine. Back in Sydney, Paterson was now starting a tenure as editor of the racing newspaper the *Sydney Sportsman*, a publication owned by the heirs of John Norton's estate.

At the same time, Charlie Lawson, eager to associate himself with his brother's fame, claimed to have recalled Henry's earliest poems, one about William the Conqueror and the other about Charlie coming a cropper on his mare. Their sister Gertrude, now living with two of her sons at Rozelle, sent them to Robertson, who remarked that future generations would be grateful for saving them from oblivion. Charlie also sold Robertson four drawings for 8 guineas, which he claimed included Lawson's first home, Niels's original hut, and Lawson's old bark school. Charlie sent the poems to *The Bulletin* and one was published along with his explanation of its composition.[12] When Lawson heard about it, he laughed and said that Charlie had written the poems himself. He didn't recognise any of the places in the drawings.

Lawson's focus wasn't that sharp, though, as he drank heavily, but he still wrote a touching poem for a fundraising book *Cartoons by Claude Marquet*, after *The Worker*'s cartoonist drowned. Marquet's body was never found and Lawson pictured his widow mourning over 'the gave they'll never dig'.[13]

Calling himself 'John Lawrence', he was back in the Mental Hospital in June, labelling it in his letters as 'Brain Infirmary, next the Rat Joint', the 'Royal Horrors Department' and 'Hunt-fleas House'. One of his envelopes was decorated with a drawing of a man dangling from a noose with the caption 'High-strung pote'. Nurses had to forcibly bathe him, yet even in his perilous health he wrote to Robertson telling him that Mrs Byers was 'having a rotten time and is trying obstinately to keep the hole we call "home" and which I never want to see again – mostly on account of her cats ... There are seven or eight ...'[14] His clothes were so tattered, his underwear so putrid that 'the nurses have left me nothing but my skin, a suit of boys flannels, and an old overcoat for outdoor wear ...'[15]

Lawson left the Mental Hospital in July 1920 at the same time that the Commonwealth Government's Literary Fund finally granted him a small pension,[16] a decision that made Ted Brady mock Australia's largesse. 'Lawson has for thirty years been the most popular writer in this country. ... And now he is rewarded with a Federal pension of One Pound per week to save the public scandal apparently of his being found dead on a publisher's doorstep.'[17] Robertson, who continued paying Lawson's private pension, sent a cutting of Brady's article to Thomas Lothian, on whose doorstep Lawson had crashed years before.

When he finally found his way back to Euroka Street, Lawson discovered that Mrs Byers could not pay her 12 shillings and sixpence a week rent and did not have blankets or firewood to stay warm during winter. Lawson asked Robertson for some old timber to burn and some of the green baize, which the publisher used to line his bookshelves, to use as blankets.[18] On his travels to *The Bulletin* office, Lawson befriended Joe Seymour who ran a dry-cleaning business across the road. Lawson would often volunteer to 'mind the rag shop' for him and listen dutifully to Mrs Seymour's admonitions about Lawson's boozing. *The Bulletin* eventually paid Mrs Byers's landlord for three months of back rent as Lawson returned to the Thomas Walker Hospital for another session to dry out.

He was there two weeks when his mother died at Gladesville on 12 August 1920. Lawson left hospital in a hurry to collect some personal belongings in Louisa's possession, and outraged his siblings when he asked for a £5 advance from her estate. Lawson wrote 'To the Memory of Louisa Albury', choosing not to remember any maternal affection but portraying her as a bush girl riding with freedom through the ranges.[19]

Louisa was buried beside her parents at Rookwood Cemetery. She left her estate to Peter, the only one of the family Louisa had not quarrelled with, but after paying off Louisa's debts the four surviving children divided the £400 equally.

LOUISA'S DEATH ONLY WORSENED Lawson's sombre, reflective mood. When Mudgee councillors mentioned erecting a memorial to his work, he suggested instead a suitable headstone over the grave of his long-dead sister whose memory haunted him.[20] He continued to live the desperate life of an addict: cadging, carousing, collapsing, promising to reform. When Grace McManus asked him about coming back for another holiday to Coolac, Lawson gladly accepted a gift of £2 from her. Despite repeated promises, he never made the return journey to repay it. When Mutch rebuffed him again for a loan, Lawson let him have it in 'The Parsin for Edgerkashun'[21] for *The Lone Hand*, now being edited by Walter Jago.[22]

Lawson's work became more infrequent and indifferent, and he admitted to the Commonwealth Literary Fund, which was enquiring about extending his pension in April 1921, that his son was away on the land for months and that he had little contact with his wife and daughter.[23] Two of Lawson's visitors at Euroka Street were Percy Cowan and the Indigenous soldier Douglas Grant, who had been a prisoner of the Germans during the Great War and spent his later life campaigning for Aboriginal freedom.[24] Cowan would play a violin that Lawson had inscribed 'To My mate Perce Cowan and his violin, with gratitude for light in dark hours'.[25] In his lucid moments, Lawson waged a constant and frustratingly ineffective fight through the *North Shore and Manly Times* over the 'vandalism and commercialising' that he saw as the development around the north side of Sydney Harbour.[26]

But Lawson's fighting days were about done. On 14 July 1921, just as Beau Smith began filming *While the Billy Boils* at Windsor, north-west of Sydney,[27] Lawson was admitted to the Coast Hospital at Little Bay. 'Not drink this time,' he told Robertson. 'Loss of use of left leg and arm preceded by great pains in right side … I suppose it was all along of the life I lived …'[28] Lawson had suffered a slight stroke but initially he was so ill that he could not take food, only beer that friends brought him. Soon he was joking, with his sardonic humour, though, that the paralysis was a *'wisitation'* by a 'ghastly spook'. Within days he was well enough to scratch out letters, but he stayed in the hospital for two months. Mrs Byers went to live with a niece at Hunters Hill.

As news of Lawson's collapse travelled around the nation, Tom Mutch patched up their friendship, bringing Lawson pyjamas. Lawson suggested they take another holiday together, this time at Coolac where Lawson said he 'had a house'. Mutch had collected a lot of Lawson's old work from *The Boomerang* and Lawson wanted to sell it to Robertson.[29] He wrote 'A Song of Mutch and Little' and Mutch would use it in his election campaign of 1925.

In hospital, Lawson lost most of his teeth 'except the old pipe fang and had to fight chloroform and three doctors for that'.[30] He had flights of fantasy. He said he had 'broken up the North Shore "Home"' and planned to 'rent a little unfurnished place up the Hornsby line with a view to ultimate purchase' so he could indulge in the exercise of woodwork.[31] He sent Robertson's son Douglas a list of timber sizes he wanted in order to make a table with a drawer and a stool. Writing was hard, he said, and he wanted to rest his brain and strengthen his arms with his favourite hobby, carpentering.[32]

Rod Quinn discovered that Lawson had given away all the gifts of tobacco and cigars to other patients, and he asked Quinn to bring some bananas for them too. Jim Gordon and Robert Cassidy came to visit, and Barta brought her mother to the hospital for a form of reconciliation.

When *The Sun* newspaper ran a sickly sweet article by R.L. Jamieson about the hundreds of letters, cards and bunches of flowers pouring into the hospital for Lawson, from ministers of the Crown down to hardy bushmen and 'little tots with kindly hearts' praying for his recovery, Lawson thought it made him look like some teary old codger. He was well enough to spit vitriol, asking Robertson, 'Did you see that blasted wowser article by young Brother Jamieson? They'll think I got a scare and "found Christ"...'[33] He composed a stinging reply about the article in the mocking tone of a small child, but Robertson said such an act was beneath Lawson, and when Walter Jago told Lawson that Jamieson was just a battling journalist writing for a penny a line, Lawson tore up his rebuke. He knew all about the life of a struggling writer.

Lawson was still angry, though, when John Lockley came to talk business about publishing Lawson's 'The Auld Shop and the New', and, forgetting that he had sold the poem to Lockley, Lawson complained that the publisher was 'a little mad, and he was sick of being bothered by mad people'.[34]

Jack Lang, now the treasurer in the New South Wales Labor Government of new premier John Storey, called in to talk about Lawson getting back together with Bertha and promised to send Lawson and the whole family to Lord Howe Island for Christmas. When Bertha and Barta came to visit Lawson on another occasion, they had just left when the Australian writer Bernard Shaw sat down next to Lawson's bed and delivered a long sermon on the evils of alcohol. Lawson's fury was the signal that he was ready to leave the Coast Hospital, and instead he moved to the Denistone House Convalescent Hospital in Eastwood, walking with a stuttering step as a legacy of the stroke.[35] He wrote one of the few notable poems for the year, 'The Low Lighthouse', about what the stroke suggested for his future.[36]

Ethel Brown invited Lawson to again stay at her boarding house in Ashfield, pointing out that they were both lonely, and he accepted. He now had the promise of royalties from the *Billy Boils* motion picture but his friends in the Labor Party remained concerned by his circumstances, even if they were of his own making. They set forth to help him with State Government funds. Lawson wrote to Simon Hickey, who held the seat of Botany, thanking him for his efforts and telling him he was likely to be crippled 'as far as the left arm and leg is concerned' and that he needed someone with him to get about. He implored Hickey to keep his address secret lest Mrs Byers find out about Mrs Brown.[37]

New premier James Dooley heard how there had been a fund for Lawson in the past and how the money was wasted, and that his case was 'a hopeless one'. However, Hickey asked Parliament on 26 October 1921 if more could be done for Lawson since 'he had fallen upon evil days through ill health'.[38]

Cabinet, which included Jack Lang and Tom Mutch, set aside £100 for Lawson in the Premier's Estimates but it still had to be passed by Parliament. So, Jack Lang advanced him £10 from the public coffers.

At the same time, Billy Hughes's Commonwealth Government had decided to raise Lawson's pension to £3 a week, but when news of a pension from New South Wales was released soon after, it scrapped his money until the £100 from the State had been spent.

Things did not go as Lawson had hoped. He now preferred Mrs Brown's company to Mrs Byers's, but not knowing this, Mutch arranged for Mrs Byers to receive £2 a week of the State money to look after him and advanced her £20 from the fund. When Mutch visited Lawson at Ashfield, he was staggered by Lawson's refusal to cooperate almost as much as by Ethel Brown's demand for £6 for Lawson's unpaid board. A government messenger was quickly sent to Ashfield with the £6 and specific instructions that the money was to be given only to the landlady. However, Lawson intercepted the transfer of funds and there was a scene. Lawson claimed £3 10 shillings of the money for himself, and Mrs Brown, despite her loneliness, gave him his marching orders.

There was another saviour.

Lawson had started writing occasional pieces for the magazine *Aussie* which had been born on the battlefields of France by the small, dapper, quick-moving Lieutenant Phillip Harris as a means of raising morale for the diggers. Harris continued publishing the magazine in Sydney after the war and he became a great mate of and benefactor for Lawson. At his suggestion, Lawson went for a seven-week rest in the cool Blue Mountains air at Waverley House in Katoomba, run by a friend of Joe Seymour's. Lawson spent Christmas with the Seymours there and told his host to bill the State for his recuperation.

He was a hard man to please, though. With his mind disordered more than usual, Lawson told his friend Charlie Webb,[39] of whom he had written twenty years before in the poem 'The Bulletin Hotel',[40] that while he was still very weak and permanently lame,

Lawson waiting for the horse ferry at Dawes Point three weeks before he died. Phillip Harris, the editor of *Aussie*, took the last photographs of him. State Library of NSW, FL214475

he had been 'pestered by Ministers and their jackals and pimps coming to my lodgings behind my back and questioning my landlady about my financial and private affairs and behaviour'. New South Wales's 'mongrel government', he said, had cost him £3 a week from Billy Hughes.[41]

Phil Harris found another landlady for Lawson: young Mrs Gertrude Wheatland, who together with her husband George had a cottage called 'Ballarat' on the corner of Werona Avenue and Great North Road in the suburb of Abbotsford. Lawson contacted

Angus & Robertson to send him more timber, in specific lengths, to make a dresser this time, explaining that carpentry would keep him 'sane and out of Sydney'.⁴² *The Bulletin* published his poem 'The Rhyme Of The Three Greybeards'⁴³ in which he mocked the concern of his friends over his health before the Coolac trip, but prophetically he killed off his alter ego Joe Swallow in the verses with a 'paralytic stroke'. 'Aaron's Pass' a week later dealt with the tragedy of a lost cattle pup as told by a man dying at the Coast Hospital.⁴⁴

BERT STEVENS had been in poor health for years but his death at his Lindfield home on 14 February 1922, at the age of just forty-nine, reminded Lawson of his own frail mortality. He felt enormous guilt, too, over the slurs he had cast on Stevens, who had tried to help him by publishing his work, raising money for him and negotiating some sort of peace with Bertha. Lawson recalled their years of mateship in a sketch for *The Bulletin*.⁴⁵

He also sent the publication two photographs of his children, saying the pictures were 'soiled and knocked about carrying them about the country with me. When my daughter attained her degree and majority last year, as you noted in your page, you could get no late portrait of her. While in hospital, I got her to have one taken for her disreputable old dad, who has so far got over his disgust at having a Bachelor of Arts in the family ...'⁴⁶ Barta's portrait ran in *The Bulletin* on 16 March.

She became a librarian, and recalled that her father tried hard to attend to her needs and 'he was proud of me for graduating. But always his comrade was Jim.' She met Lawson one night 'in Grandma's shop' and he began to ask her about her life and new job. She had been 'deeply conditioned ... in what to say and how to act towards him' and changed the subject.

Dad said nothing. But when I went to work I found a note from him. Such a quiet note, and oh! So deeply hurt. He said, of course he loved me, and of course he knew what his children were doing, 'but never have the slightest fear

Lawson's daughter Barta after graduating with a Bachelor of Arts from Sydney University. State Library of NSW, FL3319453

that I would come to you or give you the faintest cause for embarrassment or worry'. He never would. He never did. In all the times I saw him I had nothing from him but gentleness and love.[47]

Mrs Wheatland, who had been a stranger to Lawson, received £2 a week for his board and keep, as, under the terms laid down by Mutch, he was not to be given money directly. The situation rankled Lawson. So, early in March 1922 Harris found him a low-set, double-fronted cottage two doors down Great North Road called 'Glenormonde'. The rent was modest and Mrs Byers, who had already been given £20 of government money, was persuaded to take the cottage as Lawson's housekeeper and carer.

The Bulletin ran Lawson's humorous recollections of one of his mother's bush seances, but as his body became more and more frail, Mary Gilmore said that Lawson became 'bitter and sad' at his declining status at the publication as 'he was no longer on top of the wave' but rather 'treated with rudeness and contempt, as a nuisance'.[48] In early August, Harris took Lawson, dressed smartly in a suit, tie, hat and coat, across to North Sydney, and took a series of photographs of him in front of houses where Lawson had lived, and of him chatting with small children and yarning with the crew on the horse-ferry.[49] An artist named Reg Russom accompanied them and sketched Lawson, giving prominence to his still luxurious moustache. Stooped and haggard, he now needed help walking, though, and the fear of poverty was ever present. On 22 August 1922 Lawson wrote to Alexander Poynton, the Federal Postmaster-General and one of the men who had overseen his Commonwealth pension. Lawson told him that the £100 from New South Wales was almost exhausted and that as a 'cripple' suffering 'severe headaches' he was desperate. A few days later he gave Harris an outline for the third instalment of a series called 'The Casual Australian'. It would be called 'Deadly in Earnest and Casually Australian' and would involve Lawson making for the Strand in London and getting directions from a big-nosed Cockney called 'The Conk', who kept changing his mind.

On 1 September Lawson was back in the city. He 'looked white and shaken', Joe Seymour recalled.[50] 'He said that he was very tired, but that he had to go across to *The Bulletin* office, and fix up some business there.' Perce Cowan volunteered to see him safely home. Seymour watched Cowan guiding Lawson by the arm 'carefully and lovingly between the trams and through the rushing traffic'.[51] Walter Jago saw Lawson later in the day and recalled that 'his head was turned to the right and his arms [were] twisted about so the left hung where the right should have been and the right hand strained rigidly in a line with the centre of the back'.[52] That night, at the cottage on Great North Road, Lawson took his dinner and a glass of beer in his room where he was resting. He wrote a little on his sketch about 'The Conk', a man whose nose was so prominent 'that it didn't seem to belong to the face so much as the face belonged to it'. Wearily, he told Mrs Byers he would be working all night, but at 9 o'clock he called to her and complained about his headache. Before long he found it hard to speak. She made Lawson as comfortable as she could and left him to rest but when he cried out again soon after, she shuffled across to Mrs Wheatland's and asked her to phone for a doctor. [53]

Mrs Wheatland then accompanied Mrs Byers back to Lawson's bedside. Lawson mumbled something about 'that curtain-rod'[54] and then fell silent apart from the sound of his laboured breathing.

JUST AFTER DAWN ON SATURDAY, 2 September 1922, Dr Adam Newton, whose practice was in the same street, arrived at the cottage and told Mrs Byers that Lawson needed to go to hospital that morning.

The doctor left to return home, but before Mrs Byers could arrange transport for Lawson, his condition worsened and shortly after nine o'clock, Dr Newton was summoned again.

While Mrs Byers was waiting for him to arrive, Lawson staggered out of bed and made an apparent attempt to reach the door, only to collapse in a corner of the room. Beside him were his pencil and paper. Lawson had written about 300 words of his sketch, with The Conk giving him the first set of directions to the Strand.

> 'Yes, I'll show you, Mister. You see them green buses goin'
> along there? – there's one now! You follow them green
> buses and they'll take you right round into Charncery Lane.
> *Don't take no notice of them courts* – follow them green buses.'
> I thanked him and went on, but in a moment or two he was
> at my elbow ...[55]

They were the last words Lawson ever wrote.

Dr Newton arrived for the second time that morning just before 10 o'clock. He found Henry Lawson dead.

Epilogue

I wish for no snivelling about me
(My work was the work of the land)
But I hope that my country will shout me
The price of a decent brass band.
LAWSON PREVIEWING HIS OWN FAREWELL[1]

POLICE ARRIVED at Glenormonde just after noon. George Robertson was informed soon after and sent out Walter Walker and accountant Frank Brodie with £10 to help Mrs Byers. Phil Harris also arrived at the Abbotsford cottage to find the blinds still closed and Lawson dead on the floor under a dirty blanket in a corner of his darkened room. Mrs Byers was 'stupefied by shock'.[2] Robertson was dreadfully upset, given he had been almost a surrogate brother to his wayward writer, but he remembered Lawson's poem 'The Jolly Dead March' from twenty-five years before when Lawson had mused about his send-off being a raucous occasion of stirring songs.

'By Jove, the old chap shall have a State funeral, band and all,' Robertson declared.[3]

Robertson immediately contacted Hugh Wright at the Mitchell Library asking him to press government ministers he knew to accord Lawson a State funeral.

Brodie telephoned Robertson from Abbotsford to say that no arrangements with an undertaker had been made but that there was branch of Wood Coffill's nearby. Robertson told him to arrange with them for the care of Lawson's body, assuring them that Robertson would pay the costs of the funeral if the State did not step in.

When the New South Wales Government offered to pay the expenses but demurred on a State occasion, Harris and Mary Gilmore discussed making a representation to Billy Hughes, and the Australian Journalists Association appealed to him on their behalf.

Hughes, who arrived in Sydney on government business the next morning, told reporters at Central Station that Lawson 'knew intimately the real Australia, and was its greatest minstrel ... Australia's greatest writer has passed away, and Australia will sincerely mourn him. He was part of our national life ... The Commonwealth decrees him a public funeral, and in the name of Australia, I invite all to pay to him their last respects.'[4]

The New South Wales Government was still left with the bill.

Mary Gilmore claimed that Bertha did not want to go to the funeral but that Harris persuaded her, and in the words of Jack Lang 'they buried Harry like a Lord'[5] on Monday, 4 September.

From early morning until noon Lawson lay in state in an open cedar coffin at Wood Coffill's George Street mortuary as hundreds filed past. Buster Illingworth created a death mask.

Shortly after noon the coffin was carried into St Andrew's Cathedral, draped in purple and covered with a bunch of native roses, a cluster of golden wattle, some gum leaves and bush ferns. The funeral commenced at 2.15 p.m. with all 1000 seats filled.

Lawson's wife and children, siblings, aunts, uncles, mates, fellow writers, Billy Hughes and several other government members took the front pews. Wreaths were everywhere including one from Isabel Ramsay, who had moved to Paris.

Archdeacon Gerard D'Arcy-Irvine finished the service by amending some of Lawson's lines to say: 'They will take the golden sliprails down and let poor Corney in.'[6]

The organ played Chopin's 'Funeral March' and the choir sang 'Rock of Ages', as a cortege was formed, headed by the mounted police and a police band, playing the 'Dead March' from *Saul*.

Crowds lined the route as the hearse moved slowly through Kings Cross, Paddington and Bondi Junction on the way to Waverley Cemetery ten kilometres away.

On the way, Tom Mutch and a group of Lawson's friends stopped for a beer near the Darlinghurst Court House with an orphan glass on the bar to remember their mate.

Several hundred people gathered around the grave. As the band played 'Abide With Me', Lawson was gently lowered into the grave that his mother had bought next to the one originally occupied by Henry Kendall.

Lawson's wife and daughter, Mrs Byers and Mary Gilmore cried together. As Mrs Byers wept bitterly, Bertha went over to her and comforted her.[7]

But the old wounds festered.

Four days later, Sydney's *Daily Mail* published a letter from Gilmore paying tribute to Mrs Byers and calling for a government allowance in recognition of her caring for him until his death. Gilmore reminded the public that it was Mrs Byers

Lawson's funeral beside the sea at Waverley Cemetery. State Library of NSW, FL904926

who ministered to Lawson during his darkest days, and not his estranged wife.

Gertrude agreed in another report, saying that Gilmore 'was a lifelong friend' and that Mrs Byers had 'mothered him for twenty years and attended him during his long months of ill-health ... I feel sure that had it not been for her care he would not have been among us for so long.'[8]

Bertha sent Gilmore a stinging letter, warning her that she would let everyone know 'the true facts of your conduct in my home in England and also on the voyage to Australia ...'[9]

Even 24-year-old Jim Lawson joined the fray, and appeared at the Central Police Court after punching John Lockley in the face and smashing his glasses, claiming that Lockley had insulted Bertha in a newspaper article[10] of 'melodramatic tripe',[11] praising the devotion of Mrs Byers. Jim was given a six-month good behaviour bond.

Mrs Byers and Gertrude distributed Lawson's few belongings to friends: a pen to Joe Noonan, his spectacles to Tom Mutch, a tin matchbox to George Robertson, his walking stick, collar stud and necktie to Jim Tyrrell, his pipe to Phil Harris and two packets of tobacco to Rod Quinn.

Bertha, though, claimed Lawson's fame, and for the next thirty-five years represented him at the opening of monuments, memorials, fetes and institutions named in his honour.

In 1924 she and Barta were in Grenfell for the unveiling of an obelisk erected on what was claimed to be Lawson's birthplace.

The cottage Lawson died in was torn down and, with the public fund forgotten, Mrs Byers died at her sister's home in Willoughby in 1930, aged eighty-two.

The following year Bertha and both children were the guests of honour when Governor-General Sir Philip Game unveiled a statue of Lawson in Sydney's Domain.

Ted Brady thundered at the recognition coming for his friend so many years too late, noting that the cost of the monument, £1700, could have sustained Lawson for a decade and kept him out of Darlinghurst Gaol.

'It makes me sick,' Brady wrote, 'this posthumous exaltation of a writer, who was scorned and exploited while living, and whose value was only recognized after he was well underground.'[12]

To coincide with the unveiling of the statue, Barta edited, with Jack Brereton, *Henry Lawson by His Mates*, and began a relationship with one of the contributors, Walter Jago, eventually adopting his surname.

Barta was told after Lawson's funeral that just before he died, he received a garbled message, that he thought was from her, to meet him at a city corner. 'I heard that, exhausted and sick as he was, he went there and stood for long over an hour,' she wrote, 'and would not go away, in hope that I might come ...'[13]

Barta died at the Graythwaite Nursing Home, North Sydney, in 1985.

Jim spent his life as a schoolteacher and died in 1978. Both died childless.

In late 1932 George Robertson fell and struck his head in the bathroom of his flat above his Castlereagh Street headquarters and never properly recovered. He died the next year in a private hospital in Sydney.

As well as her contribution to Barta's book, Bertha published her own memoir in 1943, pointedly called *My Henry Lawson*, showing him more sympathy than she did in the years he was destitute. Her ghost writer was another alcoholic writer Will Lawson[14] (no relation to Henry), whose wife had left him. Bertha became 'all gooey'[15] about Will and they lived out their lives together.

Bertha had found Will literally in a gutter and she achieved what she had failed with her husband – reforming an alcoholic writer. Hazel-eyed, with 'a craggy face, a strong beak of a nose, large ears and thick untidy hair',[16] Will became her 'shield against loneliness in later life',[17] though she was always quick to remind others that she was Mrs *Henry* Lawson, not Mrs *Will* Lawson.

In 1945 Bertha was at the opening of the Henry Lawson Memorial College in Sydney with Premier William McKell, instituting a program at Trades Hall to 'produce more men and women as ... skilled fighters' for the party.[18] Then she took centre stage at the opening of a memorial around a chimney stack at Eurunderee – all that remained of Lawson's bush home.

Though Bertha complained in 1950 that Lawson was being forgotten in Australia and that Russian publishers translating his work gave him more respect than his own people,[19] Lawson has been remembered in festivals and place names around Australia, and a museum at Gulgong. His work has been honoured with postage stamps, and from 1966 until 1993 his face featured on the ten-dollar note, until Banjo Paterson scored another point by usurping him.

Mary Gilmore, whose face also appears on the ten-dollar bill, became a socialist and literary icon and was made Dame Mary Gilmore in 1937. Despite her long association with communism, Gilmore's political leanings did not extend to all her family, one of whom is her great-great-nephew, Liberal Prime Minister Scott Morrison.

Gilmore treasured a lock of Lawson's hair all her life. Her husband and son worked in remote Queensland stations for many years while she remained in Sydney. Will and Billy Gilmore died within months of each other in 1945 and Mary's ashes were buried with them in Cloncurry Cemetery, when she died in 1962 aged ninety-seven.

Perhaps she had borrowed the idea of her last resting place from her long-time rival.

At the foot of Henry Lawson's grave overlooking the sea in Waverley Cemetery another plaque declares 'In Loving Memory of his wife Bertha Marie Louise Lawson Died 19 July 1957, aged 81 years'.

Despite the chaos of their life together – the fights, the jail, the rancour, the hate, the madness and badness between them – Lawson and Bertha were reunited at last.

Andy's Gone With Cattle

Our Andy's gone to battle now
  'Gainst Drought, the red marauder;
Our Andy's gone with cattle now
  Across the Queensland border.

He's left us in dejection now,
  Our thoughts with him are roving;
It's dull on this selection now,
  Since Andy went a-droving.

Who now shall wear the cheerful face
  In times when things are slackest?
And who shall whistle round the place
  When Fortune frowns her blackest?

Oh, who shall cheek the squatter now
  When he comes round us snarling?
His tongue is growing hotter now
  Since Andy crossed the Darling.

The gates are out of order now,
  In storms the 'riders' rattle;
For far across the border now
  Our Andy's gone with cattle.

Poor Aunty's looking thin and white;
  And Uncle's cross with worry;
And poor old Blucher howls all night
  Since Andy left Macquarie.

Oh, may the showers in torrents fall,
  And all the tanks run over;
And may the grass grow green and tall
  In pathways of the drover;

And may good angels send the rain
  On desert stretches sandy;
And when the summer comes again
  God grant 'twill bring us Andy.

                              Henry Lawson, 1888

Bibliography

BOOKS

A Golden Shanty, Australian Stories and Sketches in Prose and Verse, Bulletin, 1890.

Frank Bate, Samuel Bate, *Singular Character*, Brookdale Press, 1987.

John Le Gay Brereton, *Knocking Round*, Angus and Robertson, 1930.

Alison Brooks, *A Shepherd from Kent: The Story of John Albury and His Family, 1838–1988*, A. Brooks, 1988.

Gregory Bryan, *To Hell and High Water*, Big Sky Publishing, 2012.

Leon Cantrell (ed.), *A. G. Stephens: Selected Writings*, Angus & Robertson, 1977.

Harry F. Chaplin, *Henry Lawson*, Wentworth Press, 1974.

Jill Dimond and Peter Kirkpatrick, *Literary Sydney*, University of Queensland Press, 2000.

Kerrie Davies, *A Wife's Heart: The Untold Story of Bertha and Henry Lawson*, University of Queensland Press, 2017.

Arthur Wilberforce Jose, *The Romantic Nineties*, Angus & Robertson, 1933.

Grantlee Kieza, *Banjo*, HarperCollins/ABC Books, 2018.

Olavi Koivukangas and John Stanley Martin, *The Scandinavians in Australia*, AE Press, 1986.

E. H. Lane, *Dawn to Dusk*, Wm. Brooks & Co, 1939.

J. T. Lang, *I Remember*, McNamara's Books, 1956.

Bertha Lawson, *My Henry Lawson*, Frank Johnson, 1943.

Bertha Lawson Jr [Jago] and John Le Gay Brereton (eds), *Henry Lawson by his Mates*, Angus & Robertson, 1931.

Henry Lawson, *Short Stories in Prose and Verse*, Dawn, 1894.

Henry Lawson, *While the Billy Boils*, Angus & Robertson, 1896.

Henry Lawson, *In the Days When the World was Wide and Other Verses*, Angus & Robertson, 1896.

Henry Lawson, *Verses, Popular and Humorous*, Angus & Robertson, 1900.

Henry Lawson, *On the Track*, Angus & Robertson, 1900.

Henry Lawson, *Over the Sliprails*, Angus & Robertson, 1900.

Henry Lawson, *The Country I Come From*, William Blackwood and Sons, 1901.

Henry Lawson, *Joe Wilson and His Mates*, William Blackwood and Sons, 1901.

Henry Lawson, *Children of the Bush*, Methuen & Co., 1902.

Henry Lawson, *When I Was King and Other Verses*, Angus & Robertson, 1905.

Henry Lawson, *The Romance of the Swag*, Angus & Robertson, 1907.

Henry Lawson, *Send Round the Hat*, Angus & Robertson, 1907.

Henry Lawson, *The Skyline Riders and Other Verses*, Fergusson, 1910.

Henry Lawson, *The Rising of the Court and Other Sketches in Prose and Verse*, Angus & Robertson, 1910.

Henry Lawson, *For Australia and Other Poems*, Standard Publishing, 1913.

Henry Lawson, *Triangles of Life and Other Stories*, Standard Publishing, 1913.

Henry Lawson, *My Army, O, My Army! and Other Songs*, Tyrrell's Ltd., 1915.

Henry Lawson, *Song of the Dardanelles and Other Verses*, Harrap, 1916.

Henry Lawson, *Selected Poems of Henry Lawson*, Angus & Robertson, 1918.

Henry Lawson, Leonard Cronin (ed), *A Camp-Fire Yarn: Henry Lawson Complete Works, 1885–1900*, Lansdowne, 1984.

Henry Lawson, Leonard Cronin (ed), *A Fantasy of Man: Henry Lawson Complete Works, 1901–1922*, Lansdowne, 1984.

Henry Lawson, *Selected Stories of Henry Lawson*, Harper Collins, 2017.

Norman Lindsay, *Bohemians of the Bulletin*, Angus & Robertson, 1965.

Bede Nairn, *The 'Big Fella': Jack Lang and the Australian Labor Party 1891–1949*, MUP, 1986.

Lorna Oliff, *Louisa Lawson*, Rigby, 1978.

Ruth Park, *Fishing in the Styx*, Penguin, Melbourne, 1993.

A. B. (Banjo) Paterson, *Singer of the Bush: Complete Works, 1885–1900*, Lansdowne, 1983.

A. B. (Banjo) Paterson, *Song of the Pen: Complete Works 1901–1941*, Lansdowne, 1985.

A. B. (Banjo) Paterson, *Happy Dispatches*, Angus & Robertson, 1934.

Bill Pearson, *Henry Lawson among Maoris*, Australian National University Press, 1968.

Xavier Pons, *Out of Eden: Henry Lawson's life and works. A psychoanalytic view*, Sirius Books, 1984

Denton Prout (real name Charles Walter Phillips), *Henry Lawson: The Grey Dreamer*, Rigby, 1963.

Colin Roderick, *Banjo Paterson: Poet by Accident*, Allen & Unwin, 1993.

Colin Roderick, *Henry Lawson: A Life*, Angus & Robertson, 1991.

Colin Roderick (ed), *Henry Lawson: Autobiographical and Other Writings 1887–1922*, Angus & Robertson, 1972.

Colin Roderick (ed), *Henry Lawson: Letters 1890–1922,* Angus & Robertson, 1970.

Jill Roe, *Stella Miles Franklin: A Biography,* HarperCollins Australia, 2010.

Gavin Souter, *A Peculiar People: William Lane's Australian Utopians in Paraguay,* University of Queensland Press, 1991.

A. G. Stephens, *Victor Daley,* Bulletin Newspaper Co., 1905.

Anthony Trollope, *Australia and New Zealand,* George Robertson, 1876.

James Robert Tyrrell, *Old Books, Old Friends, Old Sydney,* Angus & Robertson, 1952.

W. H. Wilde, *Courage A Grace,* Melbourne University Press, 1988.

FEATURE ARTICLES

John Barnes, 'Son of a Foreign Father, A View of Henry Lawson,' *La Trobe Journal*, No 70, Spring 2002.

John Barnes, 'The Making of a Legend: Henry Lawson at Bourke', *La Trobe Journal,* No. 99, March 2017

Christopher Lee, 'The Status of the Aborigine in the Writing of Henry Lawson: A Reconsideration', *La Trobe Journal,* No 70, Spring 2002.

T. D. Mutch, 'Lawson the Man and His Country', *Smith's Weekly* (Sydney), 16 September 1922.

T. D. Mutch, 'The Early Life of Henry Lawson', *Royal Australian Historical Society Journal,* Vol XVIII, Part VI, 1932.

INTERNET RESOURCES

'19th century school readers: Irish National Readers', fusion.deakin.edu.au

ancestry.com.au

austlit.edu.au

Australian Dictionary of Biography, adb.anu.edu.au

bmlocalstudies.blogspot.com

budgeebudgee.wordpress.com

dictionaryofsydney.org

Elizabeth Huf, 'Great Shearers Strike 1891', qhatlas.com.au.

fusion.deakin.edu.au

'George Cox and Burrundulla', ourfamilypast.com

goldtrails.com.au

grenfell.org.au

grenfellhistory.co.uk

gutenberg.org

Gwenyth Dorothy McLellan, 'Henry Lawson's women: the angel/devil dichotomy, 1991, University of Wollongong Thesis Collection 1954-2016', ro.uow.edu.au/theses/2195.

'Henry Lawson Lighted Lamps for Us in A Vast and Lonely Habitat', meanjin.com.au

'Henry Lawson: A Manly Bard And Poet', pittwateronlinenews.com

'Henry Lawson remembered', canadabayconnections.wordpress.com

Jeff Powell, [Curator, Cobb+Co Museum], 'Henry Lawson's other skill', blog. qm.qld.gov.au

Mark Latham, 'The Forgotten Lang, Australian Society for the Study of Labour History', labourhistory.org.au.

thescottishaustralian.wordpress.com

Wikipedia

Acknowledgements

HENRY LAWSON inspired generations of Australian writers, and it was my great honour to document the life of such an important figure in this country's national identity.

So many people helped me do this.

Thank you to the staff of the National Library of Australia and the state libraries of New South Wales, Victoria, Queensland and South Australia, who are the custodians of so much of Lawson's correspondence, memorabilia and manuscripts.

The Henry Lawson Centre at Gulgong and the Grenfell Museum and Historical Society also provided important insights into Lawson's life and career.

I will always be indebted to the authors and scholars who have previously written about aspects of Lawson's life – Colin Roderick, Denton Prout, Kerrie Davies, Harry Chaplin, John Barnes and Christopher Lee.

Thanks so much to my editors Kevin McDonald and Annabel Adair for shaping and polishing my words.

I am especially grateful to the magnificent team at HarperCollins/ABC Books, who have supported my work for many years. I could not have written this book without the backing of Jude McGee, Lachlan McLaine, Brigitta Doyle, Georgia Williams and Nicolette Houben.

Endnotes

Prologue

1 Miles Franklin, in an address delivered at the Lawson statue, Outer Domain, Sydney, on 5 September 1942. First published in *Meanjin Papers*, no. 12, Christmas 1942.

2 T.D. Mutch in *Henry Lsawson by his Mates*, Angus & Robertson, 1931, p. 152.

3 'Summary: Weather Forecast', *Daily Telegraph* (Sydney), 2 September 1922, p. 1.

4 Thomas Davies Mutch, born 17 October 1885, Lambeth, London; died 4 June 1958, Clovelly, Sydney.

5 T.D. Mutch, 'The Early Life of Henry Lawson', *Royal Australian Historical Society Journal*, Vol XVIII, Part VI, 1932, pp. 276–77.

6 'Dead Poet's Trifles', *Sun* (Sydney), 10 September 1922, p. 2.

Chapter 1

1 Henry Lawson, 'The Wander-Light', *Bulletin*, 10 December 1903, p. 26.

2 'Re the Birthplace of Henry Lawson', *Grenfell Record and Lachlan District Advertiser*, 17 December 1915, p. 6.

3 'Local News', *ibid*, 24 October 1908, p. 2. Lawson later wrote the 'Golden Graveyard' for the *Bulletin*.

4 Lawson (under the name Henry Hertzberg Larsen), 'The Song of Broken English', *Bulletin*, 15 December 1910, p. 30.

5 'Epitome of News', *Mining Record and Grenfell General Advertiser*, 22 June 1867, p. 2.

6 John Granville Grenfell (1826–1866).

7 Between 1867 and 1869 more than 40,000 ounces of gold were produced each year on the Grenfell goldfields (from grenfell.org.au).

8 Louisa Lawson, born 17 February 1848, Guntawang Station near Gulgong, NSW; died 12 August 1920, Gladesville, Sydney.

9 Niels Hertzberg Larsen, aka Peter Lawson, born Tromøy, Arendal, Norway, 12 September 1832; died 31 December 1888, Mount Victoria, Blue Mountains, NSW.

10 Lawson, 'The Song of Broken English'.

11 Lawson, *A fragment of autobiography, Vol. 2*, State Library of NSW, Angus & Robertson manuscripts, A 1887.

12 John Albury, born 15 July 1794, Farleigh, Kent; died 18 June 1868, Oxley Island, NSW. (His parents were Henry Albury, a farrier, and Margaret Miller.) On 8 January 1821 he married Ann Relph (or Ralph) at Aylesford Kent.

13 Mutch, 'The Early Life of Henry Lawson', p. 277.

14   Charlotte, eighteen, Mary Ann, sixteen, John, fifteen, Henry, thirteen, Abel, ten, Margaret, six, Mercy, four, and William, two.

15   State Records Authority of New South Wales (SRA NSW): Entitlement certificates of persons on bounty ships; Series: 5314; Reel: 1296.

16   'Ship News', *Sydney Gazette and NSW Advertiser*, 18 September 1838, p. 2.

17   'Shipping Intelligence', *ibid*, 18 September 1838, p. 2.

18   'Government Gazette', *Colonist* (Sydney), 22 September 1838, p. 3.

19   'Ship News', *Sydney Gazette*, 18 September 1838, p. 2.

20   SRA NSW: Entitlement certificates of persons on bounty ships; Series: 5314; Reel: 1296.

21   'Government Gazette', *Colonist* (Sydney), 22 September 1838, p. 3.

22   Among others, the Waterloo Creek massacre, the Myall Creek massacre, the Gwydir River massacre and slaughters near present-day Moree, and near the confluence of the Murrumbidgee and Murray Rivers.

23   Eg: 'Atrocious Massacre of Thirty Natives Of New South Wales', *Sydney Monitor and Commercial Advertiser*, 30 September 1839, p. 2.

24   Anne Alburey (sic), Liverpool, St Luke's, 9 January 1839–25 March 1866; Anglican Church Diocese of Sydney Archives.

25   *Registers of Coroners' Inquests and Magisterial Inquiries, 1834–1942*, SRA NSW.

26   William Cox had supervised one of the great engineering feats of colonial NSW with a road across the Blue Mountains in 1815.

27   'Poet's Mother – Louisa Lawson', *Bulletin*, 24 October 1896, p. 2.

28   Henry Albury, born 25 July 1825, East Farleigh, Kent; died 17 August 1908, St Leonards, Sydney.

29   The address is now 1270 Richmond Road at Marsden Park.

30   Charles Tompson, born about 1784, Birmingham; died 11 January 1871, Surry Hills, Sydney.

31   'Clydesdale – House, Barn, Cottage and Farm Landscape', NSW State Heritage Register, Office of Environment and Heritage, H00674.

32   Charles Tompson Jr, born 26 June 1807, Sydney; died 5 January 1883, Sydney.

33   Charles Tompson, Jr., *Wild Notes, from the Lyre of a Native Minstrel*, Robert Howe, Govt. Printer, 1826.

34   Harriet Elizabeth Winn, born 26 October 1825; died 1 October 1895, Goulburn, NSW.

35   Now Winbourne Function Centre, 1315 Mulgoa Road, Mulgoa.

36   Joseph Winn (1792–1841), a commercial traveller and Ann (Hannah) Nicols (1792–1841). Though Lawson, in his autobiography, claimed Harriet's father was a clergyman, Louisa Lawson wrote that Joshua 'had died suddenly at a wayside Inn upon a trip'. He was a commercial traveller for a London warehouse that dealt in the silk-mix fabric bombazine.

37   Denton Prout (real name Charles Walter Phillips), *Henry Lawson: The Grey Dreamer*, Rigby, 1963, p. 16.

38   Lawson, *A fragment of autobiography, Vol. 1*, State Library of NSW, Angus & Robertson manuscripts, A 1887.

39   Lawson, *Autobiography, Vol. 1*.

40   Emma Sophia Albury, born 29 November 1845, St Marys, NSW; died 24 April 1934, Mosman, Sydney.

41   'Louisa Lawson and her son', *Bulletin*, 2 September 1920, Red Page.

42   'The Mother Of Henry Lawson', *Geraldton Express*, 6 September 1922, p. 4.

43   Lawson, 'Tales of a Grandfather', *Bulletin*, 21 December 1905, Red Page.

44   Between 1856–71 he appeared in court twice as the plaintiff and twelve times as the defendant.

45   Lawson, 'Tales of a Grandfather'.

46   Prout, *Henry Lawson*, p. 15.

47   'The Mother Of Henry Lawson', *Geraldton Express*, 6 September 1922, p. 4.

48   She was baptised by the Reverend James Gunther, rector of the parish of Saint John the Baptist in Mudgee.

49   'The Mother Of Henry Lawson', *Geraldton Express*, 6 September 1922, p. 4.

50   *Ibid.*

51   *Ibid.*

52   On 12 February 1851, while riding with John Lister, William Tom and James Tom in Lewis Ponds Creek.

53   'The Gold Fever', *Bathurst Free Press*, 17 May 1851, p. 4.

54   Manning Clark, *A History of Australia*, Melbourne University Press, 1993, p. 234.

55   Olavi Koivukangas, John Stanley Martin, *The Scandinavians in Australia*, AE Press, 1986, pp. 37, 146.

56   'Shipping Intelligence', *Argus*, 21 December 1855, p. 4.

57   Henry Lawson, 'A Foreign Father', Lothian Publishing Company Records, State Library of Victoria, MS 6026.

58   *Ibid.*

59   Lawson, *A fragment of autobiography, Vol. 2.*

60   Roderick, *Henry Lawson Autobiographical and Other Writings*, p. 194. Only Lars and Eilert are known to have perished at sea.

61   Wilhelm Heinrich Johann Slee, better known as W.H.J. Slee or John Slee, born 3 May 1836, Rostock, Germany; died 10 April 1907, Turramurra, Sydney.

62   Colin Roderick, *Autobiographical and Other Writings*, p. 194.

63   *Ibid.*

64   Martin Koivukangas, Martin, *The Scandinavians in Australia*, p. 37.

65   Lars Jensen, born 7 January 1721, Schaaland Holt, Norway; married Helje Pedersdatter (born 1746) in 1776 at the Østre Moland Church; died 12 April 1804.

66   Peder Larsen, born 1784, Rødøy, Norway; married Martha Magaretha Holst Diurhuus on 17 December 1804 at Arendal, Norway; died 10 February 1868.

67   Sigvard Brarup Diurhuus, born 29 September 1750, Bergen, Norway; died 7 April 1803, Voie, Østre Moland.

68   Colin Roderick, *Henry Lawson: A Life*, Angus & Robertson, 1991, p. 2.

69   Christiane Jensdatter Hertzberg, born 2 July 1760, Fumås, Norway.

70   Martha Magaretha Holst Diurhuus, born 1786, Tromøy, Norway; died 9 April 1863, Hisøy, Norway.

71   Roderick, *Henry Lawson: A Life*, p. 3.

72   Report of Dean Krogh, 22 August 1818, from Roderick, *Henry Lawson: A Life*, p. 3.

73   *Ibid.*, p. 4.

74   Lars, Sivert, Jens and Eilert.

75   Helene and Pedrine.

76   Roderick, *Henry Lawson: A Life*, p. 4. The passport was issued 23 February 1853, from Statsarkivet I Kristiansand, Passport Register 1853–54.

77   Eighteen-year-old Serine Marie Svensdatter.

78   Niels Christian Borck.

79   Henry Lawson, 'A Foreign Father', State Library of Victoria, MS 6026.

80   Index to Registers of Land Purchases, 1856–7, NSW State Archives, Series 13846, Box No. 8, Roll No. 1725.

81   Phoebe Emily Albury, born 11 January 1850, Bombira, near Mudgee; married Richard John Stear, 8 July 1875 at Gulgong; died 13 February 1926, Cook Road, Centennial Park, Sydney.

82   Elizabeth Albury, born 30 November 1852, Mudgee; died February 1861, Mudgee.

83   Peace Mary Albury, born February 1857, Mudgee; died 24 January 1923, Stanmore, Sydney.

84 'Louisa Lawson and her son', *Bulletin*, 2 September 1920, Red Page.
85 James Webber Allpass, born 1822, Bristol, England; died 1911, Woolwich, Sydney.
86 Lawson, *Autobiography, Vol. 1*.
87 Susannah Gertrude Albury, born 17 December 1854, baptised 14 January 1855 at St John the Baptist's, Mudgee; married Job Levers Falconer in Mudgee 1875; died 9 May 1927 while hanging out the washing while working as the housekeeper for her widowed brother-in-law Richard John Stear at Centennial Park, Sydney; Ann (Annie) Albury, born 17 August 1859, Mudgee; died 27 December 1940, Auburn.
88 Joseph John Henry Albury, born 9 October 1861, Mudgee; died 26 March 1943, Hornsby, Sydney.
89 Louisa Lawson Papers, State Library of NSW, MLMSS 1630.
90 'The Mother Of Henry Lawson', *Geraldton Express*, 6 September 1922, p. 4.
91 Mutch, 'The Early Life of Henry Lawson', p. 279.
92 'Louisa Lawson and her son', *Bulletin*, 2 September 1920, Red Page.
93 Roderick, *Henry Lawson*, p. 2.
94 'Louisa Lawson and her son', *Bulletin*, 2 September 1920, Red Page.
95 Louisa Lawson Papers, State Library of NSW, MLMSS 1630.
96 Mutch, 'Lawson the Man and His Country', from Bertha Lawson, John Le Gay Brereton (eds), *Henry Lawson by his Mates*, Angus & Robertson, 1931, p. 160.
97 'The New Diggings Near Mudgee', *Sydney Morning Herald*, 3 March 1863, p. 5. Quoting the *Mudgee Liberal* of 26 February.
98 Mutch, 'The Early Life of Henry Lawson', p. 280.
99 *Ibid*, p. 282.
100 Frances Albury, born 17 March 1864, Budgee Budgee, New South Wales; died 1950, Melbourne; Ellen Albury, born 28 April 1866, Mudgee; died 1937, Burwood, NSW.
101 Mutch, 'The Early Life of Henry Lawson', p. 286.
102 Louisa Lawson Papers, State Library of NSW, MLMSS 1630.
103 Sometimes written as Wilbertree.
104 Mutch, 'The Early Life of Henry Lawson', p. 286.
105 Roderick, *Lawson Autobiographical and Other Writings*, p. 194.
106 Louisa Lawson Papers, State Library of NSW, MLMSS 1630.
107 William John Stear, son of Louisa's sister Phoebe; from 'Henry Lawson's Birth Place', *Grenfell Record and Lachlan District Advertiser*, 9 January 1947, p. 2.
108 'The Mother Of Henry Lawson', *Geraldton Express*, 6 September 1922, p. 4.
109 Louisa Lawson Papers, State Library of NSW, MLMSS 1630.
110 Mary Luck and Sarah Turner, wife of the officiating minister, J.G. Turner, were the witnesses.
111 NSW Registration of Marriages, 2535/1866.
112 Gertrude O'Connor, 'The Lawson Family', State Library of NSW, A 1898.
113 Cornelius O'Brien (1830–1901).
114 'Discovery of a Rich Quartz Reef', *Burrangong Argus*, 6 October 1866, p. 2.
115 On 15 October 1866. NSW Registration of Marriages, 2553/1866.
116 'Henry Lawson's Birth Place', *Grenfell Record and Lachlan District Advertiser*, 9 January 1947, p. 2.
117 *Ibid*.
118 'Louisa Lawson and her son', *Bulletin*, 2 September 1920, Red Page.
119 'Henry Lawson's Birth Place', *Grenfell Record*, 9 January 1947, p. 2.
120 'Epitome of News', *Mining Record and Grenfell General Advertiser*, 22 June 1867, p. 2.
121 'Public Works for Grenfell', *ibid*.
122 'Advertising', *Mining Record and Grenfell General Advertiser*, 15 June 1867, pp. 1, 3.
123 On 25 June 1867.

124 Robert Burns (25 January 1759–21 July 1796).

125 Bertha Lawson, *My Henry Lawson*, Frank Johnson, 1943, p. 7.

126 'Louisa Lawson and her son', *Bulletin*, 2 September 1920, Red Page.

127 Gertrude O'Connor, Henry Lawson's sister, in *Aussie* (magazine), 15 October 1921.

128 'Sticking-up the Forbes mail', *Mining Record and Grenfell General Advertiser*, 28 September 1867, p. 3.

129 NSW Registration of Births 11928/1867.

130 Emma Brooks (formerly Rotenberg, nee Albury) to J.F. Thomas 1924, State Library of NSW Al 29/Folder 2.

Chapter 2

1 Mutch, 'The Early Life of Henry Lawson', p. 274.

2 *Ibid*, NSW Registration of Births 11928/1867. The draft registration was 24 July 1867.

3 Mutch, 'The Early Life of Henry Lawson'.

4 Tom L. Mills, 'One of Australia's Poets: A Sketch of Henry Lawson', *Otago Witness*, 5 March 1896, p. 48.

5 Lawson, 'The Song of Broken English', *Bulletin*, 15 December 1910, p. 30.

6 'Epitome of News', *Mining Record and Grenfell General Advertiser*, 21 September 1867, p. 2.

7 Lawson, 'Said Grenfell to My Spirit', *A Fantasy of Man: Henry Lawson Complete Works 1901-1922*, Lansdowne, 1984, p. 932.

8 Emma Brooks (formerly Rotenberg) to J.F. Thomas 1924, State Library of NSW, Al 29/Folder 2.

9 To Emma Nelson in Young in 1869.

10 On 1 May 1874.

11 Henry Albury made the claim on 15 July 1869 but never went through with the purchase, instead moving to Wallerawang the next year.

12 Henry Spencer had built a home and established a garden nearby and had on 13 May 1869 applied for forty acres unconditional purchase.

13 Lawson, *Autobiography, Vol. 1*.

14 *Ibid*.

15 *Ibid*.

16 *Ibid*.

17 Charles William Lawson, born 25 June 1869, Eurunderee, NSW; died August 1947.

18 Lawson, *Autobiography, Vol. 1*.

19 Mutch, 'The Early Life of Henry Lawson', p. 291.

20 Lawson, *Autobiography, Vol. 1*.

21 *Ibid*.

22 geomaps.com.au.

23 Anthony Trollope, *Australia and New Zealand*, George Robertson, 1876, p. 187.

24 Lawson, *Autobiography, Vol. 1*.

25 'The Rush', *Australian Star* (Sydney) 14 October 1899, p. 5.

26 'Old Joe Swallow', *Worker* (Sydney), 22 December 1894, p. 5.

27 Record of Joseph Swallow (32-2844), Convict Indents, 1788–1842, State Archives NSW; Series: NRS 12189; Item: [X634]; Microfiche: 701.

28 Libraries Tasmania, Registers of Male Convicts, 1804–1840, CON23/1/3, entry 564.

29 *New South Wales Government Gazette*, 9 January 1833, p. 14.

30 Emma Brooks to J.F. Thomas 1924, State Library of NSW Al 29/Folder 2.

31 'Publicans Licences', *New South Wales Police Gazette*, 31 August 1877, p. 3373.

32 Lawson, *Autobiography, Vol. 1*.

33 *Ibid*.

34 Ernest Peter Albury, born 29 February 1872, Lidsdale near Wallerawang; died 5 June 1942, Cowra. Child No. 11 was Blanch Albury, born 4 January 1869, Wilbetree, NSW; died 1926, Sydney.
35 Lawson, *Autobiography, Vol. 1.*
36 *Ibid.*
37 *Ibid.*
38 *Ibid.*
39 Henry Lawson, 'The Wander-Light', *Bulletin*, 10 December 1903, p. 26.
40 Lawson, *Autobiography, Vol. 1.*
41 *Ibid.*
42 *Ibid.*
43 Peter James Lawson, born 18 September 1873, Eurunderee, NSW; died 14 November 1944, Berala, Sydney.
44 Lawson, *Autobiography, Vol. 1.*
45 *Ibid.*
46 *Ibid.*
47 *Ibid.*
48 Mutch, 'The Early Life of Henry Lawson', p. 296.
49 Lawson v Johnson: Mudgee Court House, January 1875; 'The Attendance of Witnesses', *Sydney Morning Herald*, 28 January 1875, p. 5.
50 'Advertising', *Australian Town and Country Journal* (Sydney), 9 June 1877, p. 5.
51 Lawson, *Autobiography, Vol. 1.*
52 *Ibid.*
53 'Fatal Accident', *Sydney Morning Herald*, 22 June 1874, p. 5.
54 Lawson, 'Shall We Gather at the River?', from *Children of the Bush*, Methuen, 1902.
55 Lawson, *Autobiography, Vol. 1.*
56 Records.nsw.gov.au, NRS 3931.
57 Henry George Hanks (1840–1925), from *Teachers' Rolls, 1869–1908 (1876)*, NRS 4073, State Records Authority of New South Wales, Kingswood.
58 *Ibid.*
59 Lawson, *Autobiography, Vol. 1.*
60 *Ibid.*
61 *Ibid.*
62 John Tierney, born Tipperary, Ireland, 1842; died 20 November 1891, Mudgee.
63 Lawson, *Autobiography, Vol. 1.*
64 Roderick, *Henry Lawson*, p. 21.
65 Lawson, 'The Provisional School', *Bulletin*, 9 May 1896, p. 27.
66 Lawson, *Autobiography, Vol. 1.*
67 *Ibid.*
68 Mutch, 'The Early Life of Henry Lawson', p. 301.
69 Lawson, *Autobiography, Vol. 1.*
70 *Ibid.*
71 Lawson, 'The Master's Mistake', *Bulletin*, 1 February 1896, p. 28.
72 Lawson, *Autobiography, Vol. 1.*
73 *Ibid.*

Chapter 3
1 Lawson, *Autobiography, Vol. 1.*
2 Annette Elizabeth Lawson, born 30 April 1877, Mudgee; died 20 January 1878, Mudgee.
3 Gertrude Eloise Lawson, born 30 April 1877, Mudgee; died 21 May 1945, Balmain, Sydney.

4   Lawson, *Autobiography, Vol. 1*.

5   'Amongst My Own People: The Last Shaft In Log Paddock', *Bulletin*, 3 June 1915, p. 47.

6   Lawson, *Autobiography, Vol. 1*.

7   On 1 February 1879.

8   'Table Legs, Wooden Heads and a Woman's Heart', *Bulletin*, 30 March 1922, p. 47.

9   *Ibid.*

10 Louisa Lawson, 'My Nettie', from *The Lonely Crossing*, Dawn Office, 1905.

11 Mutch, 'The Early Life of Henry Lawson', p. 311.

12 Lawson, *Autobiography, Vol. 1*.

13 Gertrude O'Connor, Henry Lawson's sister in *Aussie* (magazine), 15 October 1921.

14 Lawson, *Autobiography, Vol. 1*.

15 '19th century school readers – Irish National Readers', fusion.deakin.edu.au

16 Mutch, 'The Early Life of Henry Lawson', p. 305.

17 'The Old Bark School', *Bulletin*, 22 May 1897, p. 28.

18 Lawson, *Autobiography Vol. 1*.

19 Mutch, 'The Early Life of Henry Lawson', p. 306.

20 *Ibid.*

21 *Ibid.*

22 Roderick, *Henry Lawson*, p. 21.

23 The school stood for fifty years. It might have been there longer but for the fact it was closed for about four years, and the building became neglected.

24 Lawson, *Autobiography, Vol. 1*.

25 *Ibid.*

26 Mutch, 'The Early Life of Henry Lawson', p. 307.

27 Lawson, *Autobiography, Vol. 1*.

28 Charles Kevin, born 1846, Magherafelt, County Londonderry, Ireland; died 3 October 1922, Chatswood, Sydney. Lawson spelt his name as 'Kevan'.

29 Thomas Henry Kendall, born 18 April 1839, Ulladulla, NSW; died 1 August 1882, Surry Hills, Sydney.

30 Lawson, *Autobiography, Vol. 1*.

31 *Ibid.*

32 'Pursuing Literature in Australia', *Bulletin*, 21 January 1899, Red Page.

33 Henry George, *Progress and Poverty*, Sterling Publishing Company, 1879.

34 Lawson, *Autobiography, Vol. 1*.

35 Quoted by her son, John Tierney, in a letter to J.K. Moir, State Library of Victoria, Box 23/2, Moir Collection.

36 Lawson, *Autobiography, Vol. 1*.

37 'A Foreign Father', Lothian Publishing Company Records, State Library of Victoria, MS 6026.

38 *Ibid.*

39 'A Child in the Dark', *Bulletin*, 13 December 1902, p. 14.

40 Bridget Anastasia Lambert, born 19 July 1872, Gulgong, NSW; died 19 March 1960, Newcastle, NSW; married Jack Donnelly 1904 in Nyngan, NSW.

41 Xavier Pons, *Out of Eden: Henry Lawson's Life and Works, A Psychoanalytic View*, Sirius Books, 1984, p. 24.

42 Gertrude Lawson (O'Connor), Notes upon the personal life of Henry Lawson, State Library of NSW, MLMSS A 1542/1.

43 *Ibid.*, 'The Lawson Family', State Library of NSW, MLMSS A 1898.

44 'Men Who Did Their Work', *A Fantasy of Man*, pp. 980–82.

45 Lawson, *Autobiography, Vol. 2*.

46 'Trouble on the Selection', *Freeman's Journal* (Sydney), 27 December 1890, p. 8.

47 Lawson, *Autobiography, Vol. 1*.

48 'The Song of a Prison', *Bulletin*, 23 December 1909, p. 43.

49 Lawson, *Autobiography, Vol. 1*.

50 '1. The Reason', *Triangles of Life and Other Stories*, Standard Publishing Co, 1913.

51 Lawson, *Autobiography, Vol. 2*.

52 *Ibid.*

53 *Ibid.*

54 'Dr. Stanish [sic]', *Burrangong Argus*, 22 January 1896, p. 3.

55 Lawson, *Autobiography, Vol. 2*.

56 *Ibid.*

57 *Ibid.*

58 *Ibid.*

59 *Ibid, Vol. 1*.

60 'The Way I Treated Father: A Bush Song', *Boomerang*, 29 August 1891, p. 8.

61 Lawson, *Autobiography, Vol. 2*.

62 'A Foreign Father', Lothian Publishing Company Records, State Library of Victoria, MS 6026.

63 *Ibid.*

64 Thomas Frederic De Courcy Browne (1838–9 October 1899), NSW Legislative Assembly Member for Mudgee, and then Wentworth.

65 Mutch, 'The Early Life of Henry Lawson', p. 307.

66 Lawson, *Autobiography, Vol. 1*.

67 *Ibid, Vol. 2*.

68 Charles William Lawson, also known as Charles Lee, Charles Clancy and Mark Allen.

69 *Ibid*, NSW State Archives, Gaol Inmates, Series: NRS1998.

70 'Poet's Mother – Louisa Lawson', *Bulletin*, 24 October 1896, Red Page.

71 State Library of NSW, MLMSS A 1542/1.

72 Lawson, *Autobiography, Vol. 1*.

73 'Faces in the Street', *Bulletin*, 28 July 1888, p. 17.

74 Lawson, *Autobiography, Vol. 2*.

75 'Labour Market', *Sydney Morning Herald*, 11 June 1884, p. 12.

76 Jeff Powell, Curator, Cobb+Co Museum, 'Henry Lawson's other skill', blog.qm.qld.gov.au.

77 Lawson, *Autobiography, Vol. 2*.

78 *Ibid.*

79 *Ibid.*

Chapter 4

1 'Pursuing Literature in Australia', *Bulletin*, 21 January 1899, Red Page.

2 Mary Gilmore to George Robertson 1923, State Library of NSW, MLMSS 3269/Box 736, Folder 4.

3 George Mure Black (15 February 1854–18 July 1936).

4 Georgina Duggan, née Johnson (1850–1924).

5 'Kendall's Grave', *Freeman's Journal*, 15 November 1884, p. 18.

6 Lawson, *Autobiography, Vol. 1*.

7 'A Poet's Mother', *Sun*, 9 May 1915, p. 16.

8 'Unveiling of the Monument to Henry Kendall', *Sydney Morning Herald*, 22 November 1886, p. 3.

9 Henry Lawson, 'Shadows Before', *A Camp-Fire Yarn: Henry Lawson Complete Works 1885-1900*, Lansdowne, 1984, p. 805.

10 Lawson, *Autobiography, Vol. 2*.

11 *Ibid.*

12   *Ibid.*

13   *Ibid.*

14   J.F. Archibald, born 14 January 1856, Kildare, Victoria (now Geelong West); died 10 September 1919, St Vincent's Hospital, Sydney.

15   'The Jubilee Bulletin', *Bulletin*, 28 May 1887, p. 6.

16   J.F. Archibald to Banjo Paterson, 22 August 1886, from Paterson, *Singer of the Bush*, A.B. 'Banjo' Paterson, *Complete Works, 1885–1900*, Lansdowne, 1983, p. xii.

17   'An Australian Poet: "The Banjo" Interviewed', *Table Talk* (Melbourne), 31 January 1896, p. 6.

18   Andrew Barton 'Banjo' Paterson, born 17 February 1864 Narrambla near Orange, NSW; died 5 February 1941 Sydney.

19   '"Banjo" Paterson Tells His Own Story – Giants of the Paddle, Pen, and Pencil', *Sydney Morning Herald*, 11 February 1939, p. 21.

20   Banjo Paterson writing about J.F. Archibald, from 'Great Australian Journalist, J.F. Archibald', *Sydney Sportsman*, 25 January 1922, p. 9.

21   William Henry McNamara (18 March 1857–11 May 1906).

22   William Whitehouse Collins (4 September 1853–12 April 1923).

23   Thomas Walker (5 February 1858–10 May 1932).

24   'Pursuing Literature in Australia', *Bulletin*, 21 January 1899, Red Page.

25   F.B. Smith, 'Walker, Thomas (1858–1932)', *Australian Dictionary of Biography*, MUP, 1976.

26   Alban Joseph Riley (8 June 1844–24 July 1914).

27   'News of the Day', *Sydney Morning Herald*, 4 June 1887, p. 11.

28   'Pursuing Literature in Australia', *Bulletin*, 21 January 1899, Red Page.

29   Lawson, *Autobiography, Vol. 2*.

30   'Australia for the Australians', *Bulletin*, 2 July 1887, p. 4.

31   'Celebration of the Queen's Jubilee', *ibid*, 11 June 1887, p. 8.

32   'The Jubilee Celebration', *ibid*, 16 June 1887, p. 15.

33   'Correspondence', *Bulletin*, 18 June 1887, p. 15.

34   'Pursuing Literature in Australia', *Bulletin*, 21 January 1899, Red Page.

35   'Australia for the Australians', *Bulletin*, 2 July 1887, p. 4.

36   A sailor or militiaman usually from the Indian Subcontinent or Southeast Asia.

37   Lawson, *Autobiography, Vol. 2*.

38   Description by Banjo Paterson writing about J.F. Archibald, from 'Great Australian Journalist, J.F. Archibald', *Sydney Sportsman*, 25 January 1922, p. 9.

39   Lawson, *Autobiography, Vol. 2*.

40   *Ibid.*

41   *Ibid.*

42   *Ibid.*

43   *Ibid.*

44   Roderick, *Henry Lawson*, p. 38.

45   Reference for Henry Lawson from William Kerridge, carriage and buggy manufacturer, 1887, State Library of NSW, MLMSS 3269/Box 736.

46   'Correspondence', *Bulletin*, 23 July 1887, p. 6.

47   *Ibid*, p. 7.

48   Rosa Frankenstein, born London, 1853; died Darling Point, Sydney, 1911.

49   'The Distant Drum', *A Camp-Fire Yarn*, p. 806.

50   *Bulletin*, 30 July 1887, p. 6.

51   Lawson, *Autobiography, Vol. 2*.

52   *Ibid.*

53   *Ibid.*

54   On 15 October 1877.

55   'Australian Loyalty', *A Camp-fire Yarn*, p. 44.
56   'The Republican', *Newcastle Morning Herald and Miners' Advocate*, 17 October 1887, p. 5.
57   Banjo Paterson, 'Great Australian Journalist, J.F. Archibald', *Sydney Sportsman*, 25 January 1922, p. 9.
58   Claude McKay, 'J.F. Archibald was a Living Legend', *Sunday Herald* (Sydney), 23 November 1952, p. 12.
59   John Haynes (1850–1917).
60   Sylvia Lawson, 'Archibald, Jules François (1856–1919)', *Australian Dictionary of Biography*, MUP, 1969.
61   William Henry Traill (7 May 1842–21 May 1902).
62   Roderick, *Autobiographical and Other Writings*, p. 226.
63   'Song of the Republic', *Bulletin*, 1 October 1887, p. 5.

Chapter 5

1   J.F. Archibald, *Bulletin*, 24 December 1887, p. 12.
2   'The Legend of Coo-ee Gully', *Boomerang*, 30 May 1891, p. 10.
3   'Hymn of the Socialists', *Bulletin*, 24 August 1889, p. 20. Reworked as 'Hymn of the Reformers', *Bulletin*, 24 March 1900, p. 3.
4   'Cambaroora Star', *Boomerang*, 19 December 1891, p. 3.
5   'Wreck of the "Derry Castle"', *Bulletin*, 24 December 1887, p. 12.
6   Frederick John Broomfield (1860–1941).
7   Broomfield to George Robertson, 24 March 1924, from Roderick, *Henry Lawson*, pp. 39–40.
8   *Ibid.*
9   Lawson, 'Dind's Hotel', *Bulletin*, 8 December 1923, p. 50.
10   *Ibid.*
11   Andrew Sexton Gray, born 1826, Limerick, Ireland; died 10 July 1907, at his home at 13 Collins Street, Melbourne.
12   'Dr Andrew Sexton Gray – Founder 1863-1907', eyeandear.org.au.
13   Lawson, *Autobiography, Vol 2*.
14   *Ibid.*
15   *Ibid.*
16   *Ibid.*
17   *Ibid.*
18   *Ibid.*
19   *Ibid.*
20   Edward Gault to Dr Darcy Williams, from Ronald F. Lowe, 'Andrew Sexton Gray (1826–1907). A Founder Of Australian Ophthalmology', *Australian and New Zealand Journal of Ophthalmology*, 1985; pp. 421–31.
21   Lawson, *Autobiography, Vol 2*.
22   *Ibid.*
23   *Ibid.*
24   'Golden Gully', *Bulletin*, 24 December 1887, p. 9.
25   Lawson, *Autobiography, Vol 2*.
26   'Pursuing Literature in Australia', *Bulletin*, 21 January 1899, Red Page.
27   'Peter Maginnis, Or Payable Gold', *Freeman's Journal*, 26 December 1891, p. 17. Lawson originally called him 'Peter Mackenzie' in his first attempt at the story, 'Payable Gold' was written for *The Bulletin*, but Archibald rejected it. Lawson believed that the editor thought it "too crudishly simple".
28   'Statue of Robert Burns', *A Camp-Fire Yarn*, p. 40.
29   'Australia's Forgotten Flag', *A Fantasy of Man*, pp. 508–09.
30   'Eureka, A Fragment', *Bulletin*, 2 March 1889, p. 12.

31 'Flag of the Southern Cross', *A Camp-Fire Yarn*, pp. 45–46.
32 'Australia's Forgotten Flag', *A Fantasy of Man*, pp. 508–09.
33 'Pursuing Literature in Australia', *Bulletin*, 21 January 1899, Red Page.
34 John Farrell (18 December 1851–8 January 1904).
35 Lawson, manuscript 1910, from Roderick, *Lawson Autobiographical Writings*, p. 217.
36 Farrell to Lawson, from Roderick, *Henry Lawson*, p. 49.
37 Lawson, *Autobiography, Vol 2*.
38 *Ibid*.
39 Arthur Parker in *Lawson by His Mates*, p. 27.
40 *Ibid*.
41 *Ibid*, p. 22.
42 Gertrude O'Connor (nee Lawson), State Library of NSW, MSS 314/255, A 1898.
43 Quoted by her son, John Tierney in a letter to J.K. Moir, SLV, Box 23/2, Moir Collection.
44 'A May Night on the Mountains', *Australian Town and Country Journal*, 29 June 1889, p. 32.
45 Lawson, *Autobiography, Vol 1*.
46 *Ibid*.
47 'A Christmas in the Far West, or, the Bush Undertaker', *Antipodean*, 1892, pp. 95–102.
48 *Ibid*.
49 *Ibid*.
50 Christopher Lee, 'The Status of the Aborigine in the Writing of Henry Lawson: A Reconsideration', *La Trobe Journal*, No 70, Spring 2002, pp. 76–77.
51 'Leggo Me Ear', *Bulletin*, 28 November 1907, p. 39.
52 Jack Jones in *Lawson by His Mates*, p. 32.
53 Lawson, *Autobiography, Vol. 1*.
54 *Ibid*.
55 *Ibid*.
56 'The Name of the Colony', *Sydney Morning Herald*, 31 December 1887, p. 8.
57 'United Division', *A Camp-Fire Yarn*, pp. 51–52.
58 'Song of the Outcasts', *Bulletin*, 12 May 1888, p. 13.
59 'The Army of the Rear', *The Rising of the Court and Other Sketches in Prose and Verse*, Angus & Robertson, 1910, pp. 122–25.
60 George Black, *Australian Bystander*, 26 October 1922.
61 'A Neglected History", *Republican*, 4 April 1888.
62 From *The Republican*, 29 January 1888.
63 Louisa Lawson, 'About Ourselves', *Dawn*, 15 May 1888.
64 'Poet's Mother – Louisa Lawson', *Bulletin*, 24 October 1896, Red Page.
65 *Ibid*.
66 *Ibid*.
67 *Ibid*.
68 Lawson, *Autobiography, Vol. 2*.
69 *Ibid*.
70 *Henry Lawson by His Mates*, p. 62.
71 Lawson, 'Faces in the Street', *Bulletin*, 28 July 1888, p. 17.
72 'An Australian National Association', *Australian Star* (Sydney), 13 July 1888, p. 8.
73 *Australian Nationalist*, 8 August 1888.
74 'Lachlan Side', *Bulletin*, 17 November 1888, p. 15.
75 'Andy's Gone with Cattle', *Australian Town and Country Journal*, 13 October 1888, p. 757.
76 'Andy's Return', *ibid*, 24 November 1888, p. 1068.
77 'Beaten Back', *Bulletin*, 29 December 1888, p. 8.
78 Lawson, *Autobiography, Vol. 2*.
79 *Lawson by His Mates*, pp. 17, 19.

80   'For Auld Lang Syne', *While the Billy Boils*, Angus & Robertson, 1896, pp. 328–33.
81   'Cherry-Tree Inn', *In the Days When the World Was Wide and Other Verses*, Angus & Robertson, 1900, pp. 135–36.
82   'The Third Murder', *Boomerang*, 13 December 1890, p. 11.
83   'The Hairy Man', *Worker*, 20 December 1902, p. 1.
84   Arthur Parker notes, Lawson's characters and incidents, State Library of NSW, MLMSS 1639/vol. 17 item 1, p. 7.
85   'For Auld Lang Syne', *While the Billy Boils*.
86   *Henry Lawson by His Mates*, p. 21.
87   *Ibid*, p. 20.
88   'General News', *Maitland Mercury and Hunter River General Advertiser*, 7 February 1865, p. 3.
89   George Black, *Australian Bystander*, 26 October 1922.
90   Lawson, *Autobiography, Vol. 2*.
91   Roderick, *Henry Lawson*, p. 33.
92   Lawson, *Autobiography, Vol. 2*.
93   Edward Hume Morgan (1862–1924).
94   Gertrude O'Connor, State Library of NSW, MSS 314/255, A 1898.
95   *Lawson*, 'A Foreign Father', State Library of Victoria, MS 6026.
96   *Ibid*.
97   T.D. Mutch, 'Lawson the Man and His Country', *Smith's Weekly* (Sydney), 16 September 1922, p. 10.

Chapter 6

1   Bertram Stevens, "Henry Lawson", State Library of NSW, Angus & Robertson manuscripts, Volume 218, C 863, p. 6.
2   Probate and Administrations, *Evening News* (Sydney), 19 February 1889, p. 6.
3   'Murder on Victoria Pass, Caroline Collits', bmlocalstudies.blogspot.com.
4   'The Ghost at the Second Bridge', *Freeman's Journal*, 26 December 1891, p. 5.
5   *Freeman's Journal* eventually became the *Catholic Weekly*.
6   Prout, *Henry Lawson*, p. 75.
7   Victor James William Patrick Daley, born Navan, County Armagh, Ireland 1858; died 29 December 1905, Waitara, Sydney.
8   Philip Henry Mitchell (Phil) Mowbray, born 1845, Tullibody, Clackmannanshire, Scotland; died 2 November 1903, Narrandera, NSW.
9   Edward George Dyson, born 4 March 1865, Ballarat, Victoria; died 22 August 1931, Saint Kilda, Melbourne.
10   'To The Irish Delegates', *Freeman's Journal*, 22 June 1889, p. 14.
11   'The Ballad of the Drover', *Town and Country Journal*, 9 March 1889, p. 30.
12   'Cinderella', *ibid*, 10 August 1889, p. 32.
13   'Oh Cupid, Cupid; Get Your Bow!', *ibid*, 30 November 1889, p. 33.
14   'The "Seabolt's" Volunteers', *Illustrated Sydney News*, 31 October 1889, p. 12.
15   'The Mountain Splitter', *Town and Country Journal*, 20 April 1889, p. 33.
16   'Grandfather's Courtship', *Lone Hand*, 1 August 1913, pp. 300–07.
17   *Ibid*.
18   'Bushranging By Escaped Prisoners', *Empire*, 13 April 1868, p. 3.
19   'Ben Duggan' ('Talbragar'), *Bulletin*, 19 December 1891, p. 9.
20   'Arvie Aspinall's Alarm Clock', *Bulletin*, 11 June 1892, p. 11.
21   'A Visit of Condolence', *Bulletin*, 23 April 1892, p. 24.
22   Serialised in two instalments in *The Worker* between 1 June and 15 June 1895.
23   'Two Boys at Grinder Bros', *Over the Sliprails*, Angus & Robertson, 1900, pp. 123–28.
24   On 9 February 1889, in Richmond, Melbourne.

25 'Eureka!', *Bulletin*, 2 March 1889, p. 12.

26 'Blackheath', *Nepean Times* (Penrith, NSW), 30 March 1889, p. 4.

27 *Lawson by His Mates*, pp. 26–27.

28 Arthur Wilberforce Jose, *The Romantic Nineties*, Angus & Robertson, 1933, p. 15.

29 Norman Alfred William Lindsay, born 22 February 1879, Creswick, Victoria; died 21 November 1969, Sydney.

30 Norman Lindsay, *Bohemians of the Bulletin*, Angus & Robertson, 1965, p. 82.

31 Sarah Ann Riley, born 29 May 1863, Indented Head, Victoria; died 31 July 1935, Camberwell, Victoria.

32 From a description by Colonel WDC Williams and Major A.E. Perkins of the Medical Corps in George Burnett Barton, Frank Wilkinson, *The Story of South Africa Vol II*, World Publishing Co, 1902, p. 368.

33 Lindsay, *Bohemians of the Bulletin*, p. 82.

34 A.B. (Banjo) Paterson, 'Singers Among Savages', *Song of the Pen: Complete Works 1901-1941*, Lansdowne, 1985, p. 563.

35 'The Story of Malachi', *Bulletin*, 22 June 1889, p. 20.

36 'The Song of the Waste-Paper Basket', *Bulletin*, 14 September 1889, p. 21.

37 'The Ghost', *Bulletin*, 10 August 1889, p. 20.

38 *Ibid*.

39 Prout, *Henry Lawson*, p. 78.

40 'The Teams', *Town and Country Journal*, 21 December 1889, p. 16.

41 'Brighten's Sister-in-Law', *ibid*, p. 25.

42 'Mount Bukaroo', *ibid*, p. 32.

43 'The Roaring Days', *Bulletin*, 21 December 1889, p. 26.

44 *Ibid*.

45 'The Legend of Mammon Castle', *ibid*, 21 December 1889, p. 26.

46 Paterson, 'Singers Among Savages', p. 563.

47 'Looking Backward', *Sydney Mail*, 28 December 1938, p. 7.

48 Paterson, 'Clancy of the Overflow', *Bulletin*, 21 December 1889, p. 17.

49 *Francis* William Lauderdale *Adams*, born 27 September 1862, Malta; died 4 September 1893, Margate, England.

50 'Property Sales', *Daily Telegraph* (Sydney), 31 December 1889, p. 7.

51 'The 1890s Depression', rba.gov.au.

52 'A Search for the Shelterless', *Bulletin*, 25 January 1890, p. 9.

53 '"Dossing Out" and Camping"', *Worker*, 25 November 1893, p. 3.

54 *Ibid*.

55 *Gaol Description and Entrance Books, 1818–1930*, State Archives NSW, Series: *2134*; Item: *1931*; Roll: *281*.

56 'Forbes Quarter Sessions', *Sydney Morning Herald*, 6 March 1890, p. 8.

57 Mary Jean Cameron, born 6 August 1865, Cotta Walla near Crookwell, NSW; died 3 December 1962, Kings Cross, Sydney. Married William Alexander Gilmore (1866–1945), at Cosme, Paraguay, on 25 May 1897.

58 W.H. Wilde, *Courage A Grace*, Melbourne University Press, 1988.

59 'Our Anniversary', *Dawn*, 1 May 1895, p. 14.

60 *Ibid*.

61 Louisa Lawson, 'The Divorce Extension Bill, Or The Drunkard's Wife', *Dawn*, 5 March 1890, p. 7.

62 John Le Gay Brereton, *Knocking Round*, Angus & Robertson, 1930, p. 5.

63 Alberta de Villiers MacCallum, sister-in-charge when Lawson was an inmate at the Mental Hospital at Darlinghurst, writing to Dame Mary, 16 August 1933, from W.H. Wilde, *Courage A Grace*.

64 Dame Mary Gilmore, *Old Days, Old Ways*, Angus & Robertson, 1934.

65 'Henry Lawson and I', Dame Mary Gilmore Papers, p. 2.

66 *Ibid*, p. 1.

67 Bertha Lawson, *My Henry Lawson*, Frank Johnson, 1943, p. 22.

68 'Henry Lawson and I', Dame Mary Gilmore Papers, p. 4.

69 'The Messageries Maritimes Company's S.S. Australien', *Sydney Morning Herald*, 28 May 1889, p. 4.

70 'The Australien', *ibid*, 14 April 1890, p. 9.

71 'Straight Talk: The Mistakes of Other Colonies', *Albany Observer*, 3 June 1890, p. 3.

72 'A Word to Texas Jack', *Bulletin*, 29 March 1890, p. 15.

73 'The Song of Old Joe Swallow', *Bulletin*, 24 May 1890, p. 13.

74 'The Black Tracker; Or, Why He Lost The Track', *Freeman's Journal*, 14 June 1890, p. 17.

75 'To "Doc" Wylie, An Eccentric Bush Doctor', *ibid*, 19 April 1890, p. 17.

76 'Middleton's Rouseabout', *ibid*, 8 March 1890, p. 14.

77 *Ibid*.

78 'Stand by the Engines', *ibid*, 15 March 1890, p. 17.

79 'Over The Ranges And Into The West', *ibid*, 5 April 1890, p. 17.

80 'To a Pair of Blucher Boots', *ibid*.

81 'The Glass On The Bar', *ibid*, 19 April 1890, p. 17.

82 *A Golden Shanty, Australian Stories and Sketches in Prose and Verse*, Bulletin, 1890.

83 'Ireland Shall Rebel', *Freeman's Journal*, 3 May 1890, p. 17.

84 'The Statue Of Our Queen', *ibid*, 24 May 1890, p. 17.

85 'The Golden Nineties', *Australian Star*, 14 October 1899, pp. 4–5.

86 Gertrude O'Connor to Dame Mary Gilmore, 12 May 1926, State Library of NSW, A 3292, p. 2.

87 Dame May Gilmore to Gertrude O'Connor, 5 June 1926, *ibid*.

88 'The Golden Nineties', *Australian Star*, 14 October 1899, pp. 4–5.

89 Lancelot Lindley-Cowen (1862–1902). The *Observer* ceased publication on 23 March 1891 and Lindley-Cowen became Western Australia's Secretary for Agriculture.

90 'Death of Mr. Lindley Cowen', *Daily News* (Perth), 19 February 1902, p. 3.

91 Lawson to Lancelot Lindley-Cowen, 20 May 1890, State Library of Western Australia, ACC 1158A.

92 'Who's Dot Pulleteen?', *Albany Observer*, 22 May 1890, p. 3.

93 'Straight Talk', *ibid*, 24 May 1890, p. 3.

94 *Ibid*: The Mistakes of Other Colonies', *ibid*, 3 June 1890, p. 3.

95 *Ibid*: Nationality In Colonisation', *ibid*, 21 June 1890, p. 3.

96 *Ibid*: The New Religion', 5 July 1890, p. 3.

97 *Ibid*.

98 *Ibid*.

99 *Argus*, 1 September 1890, p. 4.

100 'Shipping Labour Difficulty', *Launceston Examiner*, 27 September 1890, p. 3.

101 Price to Major General Tulloch, 27 September 1890, quoted in *Argus*, 29 September 1890, p. 5.

102 Dame Mary Gilmore in *Lawson by His Mates*, p. 257.

103 'Exciting Scene At Circular Quay', *Barrier Miner* (Broken Hill), 19 September 1890, p. 2.

104 Emma Brooks to J.F. Thomas 1924, State Library of NSW, A2539.

105 'John Cornstalk', *Freeman's Journal*, 1 November 1890, p. 17.

106 'Lily', *ibid*, 27 December 1890, p. 17.

107 'The Fire at Boss's Farm', *Bulletin*, 6 December 1890, p. 5.

108 Emma Brooks to J.F. Thomas 1924, State Library of NSW, A2539.

Chapter 7

1 'Pursuing Literature in Australia', *Bulletin*, 21 January 1899, Red Page.
2 *Ibid.*
3 John Norton, born 25 January 1858, Brighton, England; died 9 April 1916, Melbourne.
4 'The Pavement Stones: A Song of the Unemployed', *A Camp-Fire Yarn*, pp. 114–15.
5 'The Australian Marseillaise', *Truth* (Sydney), 23 November 1890.
6 *Ibid.*
7 'The Water-Lilie', *Dawn*, 5 December 1890, p. 14.
8 John Le Gay Brereton, born 2 September 1871, Sydney; died 2 February 1933, Tamworth.
9 Brereton, *Knocking Round*, p. 7.
10 *Ibid.*
11 'The Good Old Concertina', *Town and Country Journal*, 17 January 1891, p. 34.
12 'Society', *Bulletin*, 10 January 1891, p. 14.
13 NSW Teachers' Rolls, 1869-1908 for Bridget A Lambert, Teachers' Roll, State Records Authority NSW, Archive Series: NRS 4073; Reel Number: 1993.
14 'The Free-Selector's Daughter: A Song of "Sunny Lachlan Side"', *Boomerang*, 28 March 1891, p. 19.
15 'The Bush Beyond The Range', *Bulletin*, 21 February 1907, p. 14.
16 'The Drover's Sweetheart', *Boomerang*, 20 June 1891, p. 10.
17 'The Sliprails and the Spur', *Bulletin*, 1 April 1899, p. 32.
18 Harry F. Chaplin, *Henry Lawson*, Wentworth Press, 1974, p. 7.
19 'Pursuing Literature in Australia', *Bulletin*, 21 January 1899, p. 2.
20 Gresley Lukin, born 21 November 1840, Launceston; died 12 September 1916, Wellington, New Zealand.
21 'Latest Telegrams', *Telegraph* (Brisbane), 15 June 1886, p. 4.
22 William Lane, born 6 September 1861, Bristol, England; died 26 August 1917, Auckland.
23 'Mail Bag', *Worker*, 29 November 1890, p. 7.
24 'The Third Murder', *Boomerang*, 13 December 1890, p. 11.
25 *Brisbane Courier*, 21 February 1891, p. 4.
26 Ann Nugent, 'The Queensland Shearers Strike in the 1890s', *National Library Magazine*, June 2012, p. 19.
27 'The Shearing Dispute', *Brisbane Courier*, 3 February 1891, p. 5.
28 '200 Men Landed From Victoria. The Scene at the Wharf', *Toowoomba Chronicle and Darling Downs General Advertiser*, 12 February 1891, p. 3.
29 'The Shearing Dispute', *Brisbane Courier*, 11 February 1891, p. 5.
30 John (Julian) Alexander Salmon Stuart, born 18 December 1866, Eagleton, New South Wales; died 3 July 1929, Perth, Western Australia.
31 'The Shearers' Dispute', *Brisbane Courier*, 19 February 1891, p. 5.
32 *Ibid*, 21 February 1891, p. 5.
33 'The Shearers' Dispute', *Queensland Times*, 21 February 1891, p. 5.
34 'The Shearers' Trouble', *Bathurst Free Press*, 23 February 1891, p. 3.
35 'The Queensland Shearers', *Express and Telegraph* (Adelaide), 19 February 1891, p. 3.
36 *Sydney Morning Herald*, 6 May 1891, p 7.
37 Sir George Grey (14 April 1812–19 September 1898).
38 'Sir George Grey: One Man One Vote', *Barrier Miner*, 10 April 1891, p. 2.
39 'The Editorial Mill', *Worker* (Brisbane), 16 May 1891, p. 1.
40 'Original Labour Songs: One-Man-One-Vote', *Worker*, 11 July 1891, p. 4.
41 'Good days, hard days – days to be remembered', *Courier-Mail* (Brisbane), 13 January 1951, p. 2.
42 'Great Floods In The South', *Capricornian* (Rockhampton), 22 March 1890, p. 31.

43 'At The Seat Of War', *Worker*, 21 March 1891, p. 6.

44 Alfred George Stephens, born 28 August 1865, Toowoomba; died 15 April 1933, Darlinghurst, Sydney.

45 Lindsay, *Bohemians of the Bulletin*, p. 29.

46 A.G. Stephens, 'Henry Lawson', *Art in Australia*, Ure Smith, 1922.

47 *Ibid.*

48 'Pursuing Literature in Australia', *Bulletin*, 21 January 1899, p. 2.

49 *Ibid.*

50 'Two Young Girls Drowned At Walloon', *Queensland Times*, 23 March 1891, p. 2.

51 'The Babies of Walloon', *Dawn*, 1 May 1891, p. 18.

52 'The Position At Barcaldine', *Queenslander* (Brisbane), 11 April 1891, p. 706.

53 'Bogg of Geebung', *Boomerang*, 23 May 1891.

54 'Proposed Socialist Settlement', *Ballarat Star*, 2 April 1891, p. 2.

55 George Taylor, William Fothergill, Hugh Octavius Blackwell, Thomas Joseph Ryan, William James Bennett, Alfred John Brown, Isaac Fry, Robert Prince, William Hamilton, Julian Alexander Salmon Stuart, Patrick Joseph Griffin, Henry Charles Smith-Barry, Edward Hartnett Murphy and Alexander Forrester.

56 'Legislative Assembly', *Queenslander*, 11 July 1891, p. 1.

57 'The Situation At Barcaldine', *ibid*, 9 May 1891, p. 898.

58 'Freedom on the Wallaby', *Worker*, 16 May 1891, p. 8.

59 *Ibid.*

60 'Argentine Scheme', *Darling Downs Gazette*, 3 June 1891, p. 4.

61 *Ibid.*

62 'As Ireland Wore The Green', *Worker*, 27 June 1891, p. 3.

63 Frederick Brentnall, born 17 June 1834, Riddings, Derbyshire; died 11 January 1925, Brisbane.

64 'The Vote Of Thanks Debate', *Worker*, 25 July 1891, p. 3.

65 'Patriotic League', *Worker*, 8 August 1891, p. 3.

66 'Spread The Truth!', *Worker*, 22 August 1891, p. 3.

67 'The Way I Treated Father: A Bush Song', *Boomerang*, 29 August 1891, p. 8.

68 'On the Wallaby', *ibid*, 11 July.

69 'Pursuing Literature in Australia', *Bulletin*, 21 January 1899, Red Page.

70 'Lay Your Ears Back and Fight', *Boomerang*, 12 September 1891, p. 8.

71 'The "Boomerang"', *Maryborough Chronicle*, 12 December 1891, p. 6.

72 'New "Boomerang"', *Telegraph* (Brisbane), 3 January 1891, p. 2.

73 'Watching the Crows', *Freeman's Journal*, 28 November 1891, p. 17.

74 'Big Jack Dale', *Boomerang*, 19 December 1891, p. 5.

75 'The Cambaroora Star', *ibid*, p. 3.

76 'Pursuing Literature in Australia', *Bulletin*, 21 January 1899, p. 2.

Chapter 8

1 Lawson, 'Pursuing Literature in Australia', *Bulletin*, 21 January 1899, p. 2.

2 'The Shame of Going Back', *Bulletin*, 10 October 1891, p. 22.

3 'When The Irish Flag Went By', *Freeman's Journal*, 17 October 1891, p. 17.

4 'Eight-Hours' Day', *Daily Telegraph* (Sydney), 5 October 1891, p. 5.

5 'The Old Man's Welcome', 14 November 1891, p. 18.

6 Bernard Espinasse, 'An Australian Poet: "The Banjo" Interviewed', *Table Talk* (Melbourne), 31 January 1896, p. 6.

7 'Events of the Week', *Sydney Mail*, 28 November 1891, p. 1191.

8 Lawson, 'The Captain of the Push: A Sydney Ballad Of The "Gory Bleeders"', *Bulletin*, 26 March 1892, p. 19.

9   *Ibid.*
10   Lawson, 'Constable McCarty's Investigations', *Bulletin*, 30 April 1892, p. 21.
11   Francis (*Frank*) *Mahony* (1862–1916).
12   Bernard Espinasse, '"The Banjo" Interviewed', *Table Talk* (Melbourne), 31 January 1896, p. 6.
13   Brereton, *Knocking Round*, p. 7.
14   Colin Roderick, *Banjo Paterson: Poet by Accident*, Allen & Unwin, 1993, p. 72.
15   Lawson, 'The Helpless Mothers', *Dawn*, 2 November 1891, p. 22; first appeared *Goulburn Evening Penny Post*, 24 October 1891, p. 3.
16   'Pursuing Literature in Australia', *Bulletin*, 21 January 1899, p. 2.
17   'God Save The Queen!', *Truth*, 27 September 1896, p. 4.
18   'The Rebel', *Truth*, 11 October 1891.
19   'The Literary Friend', *Bulletin*, 31 October 1891, p. 23.
20   Charles Edward Pilcher (1844–1916).
21   'The House of Fossils', *Truth*, 28 February 1892.
22   'Wales the First', *Truth*, 6 March 1892.
23   'The English Queen', *Truth*, 22 May 1892.
24   'The Shanty on the Rise', *Bulletin*, 19 December 1891, p. 21.
25   Edwin James Brady, born 7 August 1869, Carcoar, NSW; died 22 July 1952, Pambula, NSW.
26   Edwin J. Brady, 'Vive Anarchy', *Australian Workman*, 27 December 1890, p. 2.
27   *Protestant Standard* (Sydney), 2 January 1892, p. 10.
28   E.J. Brady, 'Henry Lawson', *Bulletin*, 22 January 1925, Red Page.
29   *Ibid.*
30   'Ned's Delicate Ways', *Bulletin*, 18 June 1892, p. 16.
31   'A Song of Southern Writers', *Bulletin*, 28 May 1892, p. 24.
32   *Ibid.*
33   Barcroft Henry Thomas Boake (26 March 1866–2 May 1892).
34   'Suicide of Mr. B. H. Boake', *Wagga Wagga Express*, 17 May 1892, p. 2.
35   'A Song of Southern Writers', *Bulletin*, 28 May 1892, p. 24.
36   'Charlie Lilley', *ibid*, 7 May 1892, p. 23.
37   'Rise Ye! Rise Ye!', *Bulletin*, 9 July 1892, p. 19.
38   'Henry Lawson and I', Dame Mary Gilmore Papers, State Library of NSW, A 3292.
39   'Corny Bill', *Bulletin*, 7 May 1892, p. 24.
40   'A Day on a Selection', *Bulletin*, 28 May 1892, p. 21.
41   Lawson to Lala Fisher, undated, Fisher Library Rare Books and Special Collections, University of Sydney Library.
42   'The Drover's Wife', *ibid*, 23 July 1892, pp. 21–22.

Chapter 9
1   A.B. Paterson, 'In Answer To Various Bards', *Bulletin*, 1 October 1892, p. 2.
2   *Ibid*, 'Clancy of the Overflow', *Bulletin*, 21 December 1889, p. 17.
3   Arthur Wilberforce Jose, born 4 September 1863, Bristol, England; died 22 January 1934, Brisbane.
4   Edward George Dyson, born 4 March 1865, Ballarat, Victoria; died 22 August 1931, St Kilda, Melbourne.
5   William Henry Ogilvie, born 21 August 1869, Kelso, Scotland; died 30 January 1963, Ashkirk, Scotland.
6   Rose Isabella Barton (married name Paterson), born 30 December 1844; died 24 February 1893.
7   Andrew Bogle Paterson, born 1833, Lesmahagow, Lanarkshire, Scotland; died 7 June 1889, Illalong Station, near Binalong, NSW.

8   A.W. Jose, *The Romantic Nineties*, Angus & Robertson, 1933, p. 18.

9   '"Banjo" Paterson Tells His Own Story: Giants of the Paddle, Pen, and Pencil', *Sydney Morning Herald*, 11 February 1939, p. 21.

10 Lawson to Harriet Albury, 4 July 1892, State Library of NSW, QA820/A.

11 Henry Lawson, 'Borderland', *Bulletin*, 9 July 1892, p. 21. Renamed 'Up the Country' in Lawson's *Poetical Works* in 1917.

12 *Ibid.*

13 A.B. Paterson, 'In Defence of the Bush', *Bulletin*, 23 July 1892, p. 17.

14 *Ibid.*

15 Edward Dyson, *The Fact of the Matter* (also known as 'The drovers in reply'), *Bulletin*, 30 July 1892, p. 19.

16 'In Answer to "Banjo" and Otherwise', *Bulletin*, 6 August 1892, p. 5.

17 *Ibid.*

18 H.H.C.C., 'The Overflow of Clancy', *Bulletin*, 20 August 1892, p. 21.

19 Herbert Humphrey Cripps-Clark (1860–1929).

20 Francis Kenna (21 September 1865–23 June 1932).

21 'Grog- An'- Grumble Steeplechase', *Bulletin*, 10 September 1892, p. 20.

22 A.B. Paterson, 'The Ace, from Snowy River (The Open Steeplechase)', *Bulletin*, 19 December 1891, p. 6.

23 *Ibid*, 'In Answer To Various Bards', *Bulletin*, 1 October 1892, p. 2.

24 'The Poets of the Tomb', *Bulletin*, 8 October 1892, p. 20.

25 'A Christmas in the Far West, or, the Bush Undertaker', *Antipodean*, 1892, pp. 95–102.

26 A.B. Paterson, 'In Answer To Various Bards', *Bulletin*, 1 October 1892, p. 2.

27 *Ibid.*

28 'The Poets of the Tomb', *Bulletin*, 8 October 1892, p. 20.

29 A.B. Paterson, 'The Man from Ironbark', *Bulletin*, 17 December 1892, p. 5.

30 'The Man from Waterloo' (With kind regards to 'Banjo'), *Verses, Popular and Humorous*, Angus & Robertson, 1900, pp. 151–54.

31 A.B. Paterson, '"A Voice from the Town"', A sequel to "A Voice from the Bush"', *Bulletin*, 20 October 1894, p. 24.

32 *Ibid.* '"Banjo" Paterson Tells His Own Story – 2. Giants Of The Paddle, Pen, And Pencil', *Sydney Morning Herald*, 11 February 1939, p. 21.

33 *Ibid.*

34 'When Your Pants Begin to Go', *Bulletin*, 17 December 1892, p. 24.

Chapter 10

1   Jim Grahame in *Henry Lawson by his Mates*, p. 211.

2   'Mudgee Matters', *Australian Star*, 1 October 1892, p. 6.

3   'Daring Burglary', *Evening News* (Sydney), 26 August 1892, p. 6.

4   E.J. Brady, 'Henry Lawson', *Bulletin*, 22 January 1925, Red Page.

5   *Ibid.*

6   'A Stranger on the Darling', *Western Herald*, 1 October 1892.

7   'Mary Called Him "Mister"', *Bulletin*, 1 October 1892, p. 20.

8   Jim Grahame, *Camp Mates with Henry Lawson*, ABC Weekly, 4 June 1949, p. 35.

9   'That Pretty Girl in the Army', from *Children of the Bush*, Methuen, 1902, pp. 24–45.

10 John Barnes, 'The Making of a Legend: Henry Lawson at Bourke', *La Trobe Journal*, No. 99, March 2017, p. 43.

11 Lawson to Emma Brooks, 21 September 1892, State Library of NSW, Al 29.

12 'In a Dry Season', *Bulletin*, 5 November 1892, p. 20.

13 'That Pretty Girl in the Army', from *Children of the Bush*, pp. 24–45.

14 Henry Lawson to Edward Garnett, '27th (or 28th)' February 1902, Harry Ransom Humanities Research Centre, University of Texas at Austin.

15 Lawson to Emma Brooks, 21 September 1892, State Library of NSW, Al 29.

16 Prout, *Henry Lawson*, p. 106.

17 'Bourke', *When I Was King and Other Verses*, Angus & Robertson, 1905, pp. 101–05.

18 Lawson to Emma Brooks, 21 September 1892, State Library of NSW, Al 29.

19 'Our Members – Present and Future', *Western Herald*, 28 September 1892.

20 William Walter Davis, born 5 July 1840, Bathurst, NSW; died 14 September 1923, Randwick, Sydney.

21 Lawson, 'That Pretty Girl in the Army'.

22 *Ibid.*

23 'Henry Lawson', *Sydney Morning Herald*, 20 February 1939, p. 7.

24 William Andrew Joseph Wood, born 23 May 1861, Ballan, Victoria; died September 1934, Caazapa, Paraguay.

25 Donald Macdonell, born January 1862, Stuart Mill, Victoria; died 26 October 1911, Melbourne.

26 Hugh Langwell (1860 – 15 May 1933).

27 'Martin Farrell', *Worker*, 18 August 1894, p. 2.

28 'Send Round the Hat', *Children of the Bush*, pp. 1–21.

29 *Ibid*, 'That Pretty Girl in the Army'.

30 *Ibid.*

31 'Lawson's Bourke', *Daily Telegraph* (Sydney), 22 March 1924, p. 14.

32 Referred to as Watty Broadweight or Watty Bothways in Lawson's stories.

33 'That Pretty Girl in the Army'.

34 *Ibid.*

35 'Polo', *Sydney Morning Herald*, 8 October 1892, p. 10 and 24 October 1892, p. 3.

36 'In a Dry Season', *Bulletin*, 5 November 1892, p. 20.

37 *Ibid.*

38 James William Gordon, born 23 October 1874, Creswick, Victoria; died 12 August 1949, Leeton, NSW.

39 Jim Grahame, *Camp Mates with Henry Lawson*, ABC Weekly, 4 June 1949, p. 35.

40 *Ibid.*

41 *Ibid.*

42 James Gordon, Cyril Goode Papers, State Library of Victoria, PA 271/Box 7.

43 *Ibid.*

44 Jim Grahame, *Camp Mates with Henry Lawson*, ABC Weekly, 4 June 1949, p. 35.

45 *Ibid.*

46 Frank Moorhouse, 'Henry Lawson could be a "queer hero for all Australian kids"', *Sydney Morning Herald*, 24 October 2017.

47 James Gordon, Cyril Goode Papers, SLV, PA 271/Box 7.

48 Jim Grahame, *Camp Mates with Henry Lawson*, ABC Weekly, 4 June 1949, p. 35.

49 *Ibid.*

50 Lawson, 'The Union Buries Its Dead: A Bushman's Funeral', *Truth*, 16 April 1893.

51 James Gordon, Cyril Goode Papers, SLV, PA 271/Box 7.

52 Jim Grahame, 'Henry Lawson on the Track', *Bulletin*, 19 February 1925, Red Page.

53 James Gordon, Cyril Goode Papers, SLV, PA 271/Box 7.

54 Jim Grahame in *Henry Lawson by his Mates*, p. 215.

55 Lawson, 'The Ghosts of Many Christmases', *Children of the Bush*, pp. 278–88.

56 Sir Samuel McCaughey, born 1 July 1835, Tullyneuh, Ireland; died 25 July 1919, Yanco, New South Wales.

57 'Some Popular Australian Mistakes', *Bulletin*, 18 November 1893, p. 20.

58 'The Boss's Boots', *Bulletin*, 20 February 1897, p. 3.
59 William Wood to George Reeves, April 1926, from *Henry Lawson by his Mates*, pp. 35–36.
60 *Ibid.*
61 Jim Grahame in *Henry Lawson by his Mates*, p. 213.
62 'The Ghosts of Many Christmases', *Children of the Bush*, Methuen, 1902, pp. 278–88.
63 Henry Lawson, 'Out Back', *Bulletin*, 30 September 1893, p. 19.
64 Lawson to Emma Brooks, 16 January 1893, State Library of NSW, Al 29.
65 *Ibid.*
66 Jim Grahame, 'Mates', *Murrumbidgee Irrigator* (Leeton, NSW), 14 April 1916, p. 5.
67 'The Song of the Darling River', *Bulletin*, 25 March 1899, p. 3.
68 'The Western Stars', *Freeman's Journal*, 23 December 1893, p. 5.
69 'That Pretty Girl in the Army'.
70 'Hungerford', *While the Billy Boils*, Angus & Robertson, 1896.
71 *Ibid.*
72 Henry Lawson to Emma Brooks, 16 January 1893, State Library of NSW, Al 29.
73 *Ibid.*
74 'Hungerford', *While the Billy Boils*.
75 'Baldy Thompson', *Worker*, 13 October 1894, p. 1.
76 Henry Lawson to Emma Brooks, 6 February 1893, State Library of NSW, Al 29.
77 'Banjo Paterson Tells His Own Story – An Execution and Royal Pardon', *Sydney Morning Herald*, 25 February 1939, p. 21.
78 Harry 'Breaker' Harbord Morant, born 9 December 1864, Bridgewater, England; executed by firing squad 27 February 1902, Pretoria, South Africa.
79 'Pursuing Literature in Australia', *Bulletin*, 21 January 1899, p. 2.
80 'In a Wet Season', *Bulletin*, 2 December 1893, p. 20.
81 *Ibid.*
82 'Stragglers', *Bulletin*, 27 May 1893, p. 22.
83 'The Shearing of the Cook's Dog', *Worker*, 17 June 1893.
84 'A Typical Bush-Yarn', *Bulletin*, 11 November 1893, p. 21.
85 'Two Sundowners', *Children of the Bush*, Methuen, 1902, pp. 74–85.
86 'Pursuing Literature in Australia', *Bulletin*, 21 January 1899, Red Page.
87 'The Paroo "River"', *Bulletin*, 12 May 1894, p. 2.
88 'The Bush and the Ideal', *Bulletin*, 27 February 1897, Red Page.
89 'Some Popular Australian Mistakes', *Bulletin*, 18 November 1893, p. 20.
90 Leon Cantrell (ed.), *A. G. Stephens: Selected Writings*, Angus & Robertson, 1977, p. 85.
91 A.G. Stephens, 'Henry Lawson', *Art in Australia*, 1 November 1922.
92 Jim Grahame in *Henry Lawson by his Mates*, p. 211.
93 'To an Old Mate', *In the Days When the World was Wide and Other Verses*, Angus & Robertson, 1896.

Chapter 11
1 'The Emigration to New Zealand', *A Camp-Fire Yarn*, p. 335.
2 'Three or Four Archibalds and the Writer', *A Fantasy of Man*, pp. 986–91.
3 *Ibid.*
4 'Pursuing Literature in Australia', *Bulletin*, 21 January 1899, Red Page.
5 'An Old Mate of Your Father's', *Worker*, 24 June 1893, p. 4.
6 William Henry Thomas McNamara, born 18 March 1857, Taradale, Victoria; died 11 May 1906, Darlinghurst, Sydney.
7 Matilda Emilie Bertha Kalkstein, born 28 September 1853, Posen, Prussia (now Poznań, Poland); died 1 August 1931, North Sydney.

8   'Death Of Mrs. McNamara, "Mother" Of Labor Movement"', *Labor Daily* (Sydney), 1 August 1931, p. 1.

9   Ragnar Redbeard, *Might is Right*, Auditorium Press, 1896.

10   ragnarredbeard.com.

11   'Active Service Brigade', *Queenslander* (Brisbane), 25 November 1893, p. 1012.

12   John Thomas Lang, born 21 December 1876, George Street, Sydney; died 27 September 1975, Auburn, Sydney.

13   J.T. Lang, 'Bookstore Was Labor's Cradle', *Truth* (Sydney), 2 April 1950, p. 21.

14   William Morris (Billy) Hughes, born 25 September 1862, London; died 28 October 1952, Lindfield, Sydney.

15   W.M. Hughes, 'The Rise and the Fall of the "New Order"', *Wingham Chronicle and Manning River Observer* (NSW), 7 May 1920, p. 6.

16   'A Leader Of The Future', *Worker*, 10 June 1893, p. 2.

17   'The Waving of the Red', *ibid*.

18   William Henry Traill, born 7 May 1843, London; died 21 May 1902, Brisbane.

19   'The English Ne'er-do-well', *Truth*, 2 July 1893.

20   'The Other Gum', *A Camp-Fire Yarn*, p. 314.

21   Lawrence (Larry) D. Petrie, aka Larry de Petrie (1859–1901).

22   William Arthur Holman, born 4 August 1871, London; died 5 June 1934, Gordon, Sydney.

23   'The Rise and the Fall of the "New Order"', *Wingham Chronicle*, 7 May 1920, p. 6.

24   'The "New Australia" Movement', *Morning Bulletin* (Rockhampton), 2 June 1893, p. 6.

25   'The New Australians', *Bathurst Free Press*, 18 July 1893, p. 2.

26   'Henry Lawson and I', Dame Mary Gilmore Papers, State Library of NSW, A 3292.

27   Ernest Henry Lane, born 26 December 1868, Bristol, England; died 18 June 1954, Annerley, Brisbane.

28   Gavin Souter, *A Peculiar People: William Lane's Australian Utopians in Paraguay*, University of Queensland Press, 1991, p. 208.

29   Anne Whitehead, *Paradise Mislaid: In Search of the Australian Tribe of Paraguay*, King Tide Publishing, 2018.

30   'The "New Australia" Movement', *Morning Bulletin*, 2 June 1893, p. 6.

31   'The "New Australia" Madness', *Bulletin*, 10 June 1893, p. 6.

32   William Lane, *The Workingman's Paradise*, Edwards, Dunlop and Co, 1892, p. 51.

33   Arthur Edward George Rae, born 14 March 1860, Christchurch, New Zealand; died 25 November 1943, Liverpool, Sydney.

34   'Otherside', *Bulletin*, 23 January 1892, p. 24.

35   *New Australia*, 18 December 1893.

36   'The Rejection', *Bulletin*, 21 October 1893, p. 19.

37   E.H. Lane, *Dawn to Dusk*, Wm. Brooks & Co, 1939.

38   *Ibid*.

39   'The Explosion on the Aramac', *Gympie Times*, 1 August 1893, p. 3.

40   *National Times*, 6–11 May 1974.

41   *Ibid*.

42   Mary Cameron (as M.J.C.), '"I Have to Thank the Crows for the Saving of my Life" – L De Petrie', *Worker*, 9 September 1893, p. 3.

43   *Woman's World*, 1 June 1924.

44   'Henry Lawson and I', Dame Mary Gilmore Papers, State Library of NSW, A 3292.

45   'For Auld Lang Syne', *While the Billy Boils*, pp. 328–33.

46   'Macquarie's Mate', *Worker*, 28 October 1893, p. 3.

47   'The Mystery Of Dave Regan', *Worker*, 4 November 1893, p. 2.

48   'The Man Who Forgot', *Truth*, 6 August 1893.

49   'Pursuing Literature in Australia', *Bulletin*, 21 January 1899, Red Page.

50 'Sweeney', *Bulletin*, 16 December 1893, p. 17.

51 *Ibid.*

52 John Medway Day, born 24 February 1838, Bedford, England; died 8 July 1905, Hobart.

53 'For Auld Lang Syne', *While the Billy Boils*, pp. 328–33.

54 Lawson, 'Coming Across: A Study in the Steerage', *While the Billy Boils*. Reprinted from *The New Zealand Mail*, 15 December and 29 December 1893.

55 *Ibid.*

56 'For'ard', *Worker*, 3 November 1894, p. 2.

57 Tom L. Mills in *Henry Lawson by His Mates*, p. 53.

58 'Pursuing Literature in Australia', *Bulletin*, 21 January 1899, Red Page.

59 'For'ard', *Worker*, 3 November 1894, p. 2.

60 'Pursuing Literature in Australia', *Bulletin*, 21 January 1899, p. 2.

61 *Ibid, Dawn*, 1 January 1894.

62 Thomas Lewis Mills (1865–1955).

63 Tom L. Mills, 'Henry Lawson, Australia's Poet and Storyteller: His Connection With New Zealand', *New Zealand Railways Magazine*, 2 April 1934, p. 37.

64 *Ibid.*

65 *Ibid, Henry Lawson by His Mates*, p. 52.

66 *Ibid*, 'Henry Lawson, *New Zealand Railways Magazine*, 2 April 1934, p. 37.

67 *Ibid, Henry Lawson by His Mates*, p. 53.

68 Lawson, 'In the Days When the World Was Wide', *Bulletin*, 15 December 1894, p. 6.

69 *New Zealand Mail*, 25 January 1894.

70 *Worker*, 1 December 1894, p. 1.

71 'Pursuing Literature in Australia', *Bulletin*, 21 January 1899, Red Page.

72 'The Last Review', *Bulletin*, 29 September 1904, p. 35.

73 'Steelman's Pupil', *Bulletin*, 14 December 1895, p. 19.

74 'Stiffner and Jim', *Worker*, 1 September 1894, p. 1.

75 'The Geological Spieler', *While the Billy Boils*, pp. 305–16.

76 Anthony Cashion in *Henry Lawson by His Mates*, p. 58.

77 'Tui brewery tower', *The Encyclopedia of New Zealand*, teara.govt.nz.

78 *Pahiatua Herald*, 5 March 1894.

79 *Ibid*, 28 March 1894.

80 17 June 1897.

81 'The Latter End of Spring', *Bulletin*, 24 June 1909, p. 3.

82 'Beautiful Maoriland; or, Love And The Union', *Worker*, 25 August 1894, p. 3.

83 'Some Reflections on a Voyage Across Cook's Straits', *Worker*, 12 January 1895, p. 1.

84 Tom L. Mills, 'Henry Lawson', *New Zealand Railways Magazine*, 2 April 1934, p. 37.

85 State Library of NSW, MSS 1890.

86 'Pursuing Literature in Australia', *Bulletin*, 21 January 1899, Red Page.

87 *Ibid.*

88 *Ibid.*

Chapter 12

1 A.G. Stephens, 'Henry Lawson: An Australian Poet', *Bulletin*, 5 January 1895, p. 15.

2 'Society News', *Worker*, 4 Aug 1894, p. 2.

3 'Pursuing Literature in Australia', *Bulletin*, 21 January 1899, Red Page.

4 'To Correspondents', *Worker*, 11 August 1894, p. 2.

5 'Beautiful Maoriland; Or, Love And The Union', *Worker*, 25 August 1894, p. 3.

6 'How the Rodney was Burnt', *Glen Innes Examiner*, 26 October 1894, p. 3.

7 'Burning of the Rodney', *Armidale Express*, 5 March 1895, p. 2.

8 One of the men, Billy McLean, was sentenced to three years' imprisonment in Goulburn gaol but developed tuberculosis from the bullet wound to his lung. He was released from prison but died a few weeks later.

9 'Two Unionists Shot', *Queenslander*, 1 September 1894, p. 425.

10 'Public Meeting at the Protestant Hall', *Worker*, 8 September 1894, p. 3.

11 *Ibid.*

12 Samuel Hoffmeister (1862–1894).

13 Robert 'Bob' Macpherson (1855–1930), John Macpherson (1862–1903), Gideon Macpherson (1848–1930) and Angus Macpherson (1851–1930).

14 'The Shearing Strike', *Morning Bulletin* (Rockhampton), 5 September 1894, p. 5.

15 'Radical Songs', *Worker*, 8 September 1894.

16 Leon Paul Blouet (under the pen-name Max O'Rell), *John Bull & Co*, Warne & Company, 1894.

17 'Max O'Rell', *Worker*, 8 September 1894, p. 2.

18 'Pursuing Literature in Australia', *Bulletin*, 21 January 1899, Red Page.

19 *Ibid.*

20 'The Cant and Dirt of Labor Literature', *Worker*, 6 October 1894, p. 1.

21 'The City and the Bush', *Worker*, 8 December 1894, p. 4.

22 *Ibid.*

23 *Sydney Morning Herald*, 2 June 1894, p. 8.

24 'New Australia', *Age*, 20 December 1894, p. 5.

25 John Le Gay Brereton, born 3 September 1871, Sydney; died 2 February 1933, Tamworth, NSW.

26 Brereton, *Knocking Round*.

27 *Ibid.*

28 *Ibid.*

29 'A Rough Shed', *On The Track*, Angus & Robertson, 1900, pp. 128–36.

30 Brereton, *Knocking Round*.

31 *Ibid.*

32 A.G. Stephens, 'Lawson and Brereton', 28 February 1933, State Library of NSW, MLMSS 426/23.

33 *Ibid.*

34 Brereton, *Knocking Round*.

35 'To The Advanced Idealist', *Elector*, 2 November 1895.

36 *Ibid.*

37 Hilda Spong, born 14 May 1875, London; died 16 May 1955, Ridgefield, Connecticut.

38 Bland Holt (birth name Joseph Thomas Holt), born 24 March 1851, Norwich, England; died 28 June 1942, Kew, Melbourne.

39 'The Spong Benefit', *Daily Telegraph* (Sydney), 15 August 1894, p. 6.

40 Henry Lawson, *Short Stories in Prose and Verse*, L. Lawson, 1894.

41 *Ibid.*, Preface.

42 *Hermes*, 20 November 1894.

43 Brereton in *Henry Lawson by His Mates*, p. 6.

44 A.G. Stephens, 'Henry Lawson: An Australian Poet', *Bulletin*, 5 January 1895, p. 15.

45 *Ibid.*

46 State Library of NSW, MLMSS 184/8.

47 Louisa Lawson to T.D. Mutch, 4 February 1917, State Library of NSW, MLMSS 426/24.

48 George Robertson, born 14 April 1860, Gosfield, near Halstead, Essex, England; died 27 August 1933, Sydney.

49 David Mackenzie Angus, born 12 July 1855, Thurso, Caithness-shire, Scotland; died 21 February 1901, Edinburgh, Scotland.

50 H. Peden Steele, *A Crown of Wattle*, Angus & Robertson, 1888 and Arthur Jose (under pen-name Ishmael Dare), *Sun and Cloud on River and Sea*, Angus & Robertson, 1888.

51 Henry Kendall, *Leaves from Australian Forests*, George Robertson, 1869.

52 Angus & Robertson to Paterson, 3 September 1895, State Library of NSW. Reference code: 1232021.

53 Brereton, *Knocking Round*.

54 Roderic Joseph Quinn (1867–1949).

55 Jack Moses (12 January 1861–10 July 1945).

56 Brereton, *Knocking Round*.

57 Jack Moses in *Henry Lawson by His Mates*, p. 50.

58 Bernard Espinasse, 'An Australian Poet: "The Banjo" Interviewed', *Table Talk* (Melbourne), 31 January 1896, p. 6.

59 James Robert Tyrrell, *Old Books, Old Friends, Old Sydney*, Angus & Robertson, 1952, p. 84.

60 *Ibid*.

61 *Bulletin*, 17 August 1895, p. 8.

62 *Ibid*, 23 November, p. 27.

63 *Ibid*, 31 August 1895, p. 28.

64 'The Star of Australasia', *In the Days When the World Was Wide*, Angus & Robertson, 1896.

65 *Bulletin*, 30 November 1895, Red Page.

66 'Henry Lawson and I', Dame Mary Gilmore Papers, State Library of NSW, A 3292.

67 Bertram Stevens, 'Henry Lawson', State Library of NSW, Angus & Robertson manuscripts, Volume 218, C 863, p. 12.

Chapter 13

1 Bertha Lawson, *My Henry Lawson*, Frank Johnson, 1943, p. 51.

2 Carl Lindquist (born about 1861, Växjö, Sweden; died 22 September 1936, Guildford, Sydney). Bertha Lawson wrote his name as 'Karl [or Carl] Lindgrist' in her recollections and mistakenly wrote that he died while she and Lawson were courting.

3 Bertha Marie Louise Bredt, born 18 July 1876, Bairnsdale, Victoria; died 19 July 1957, Northbridge, Sydney.

4 Ruth Park, *Fishing in the Styx*, Penguin, Melbourne, 1993, p. 194.

5 *Ibid*, p. 193.

6 Bertha Lawson, *Henry Lawson by His Mates*, p. 80.

7 *Ibid*, p. 81.

8 Bertram Stevens, 'Henry Lawson', State Library of NSW, Angus & Robertson manuscripts, Volume 218, C 863, p. 11.

9 The occupation listed on her marriage certificate.

10 'A Case for the Oracle', *Over the Sliprails*, Angus & Robertson, 1900; the original article in *The Bulletin* (30 December 1899) had used the name 'Ruth Wilson' instead of Bertha.

11 Bertha Lawson, *Henry Lawson by His Mates*, p. 81.

12 *Ibid*, *My Henry Lawson*, p. 33.

13 Wilde, *Courage A Grace*.

14 Gavin Souter, *A Peculiar People*, University of Queensland Press, 1991, p. 163.

15 *Ibid*.

16 State Library of NSW, MLMSS 184/8.

17 Ruth Park, manuscript notes of interview with Bertha Lawson 1952, State Library of NSW, MLMSS 8078, Series 3, Box 12.

18 Bertha Lawson, *My Henry Lawson*, p. 35.

19 *Ibid*, *Henry Lawson by His Mates*, p. 83.

20 Hilda Amelia Bredt, born 1878/9, Bairnsdale, Victoria; died 25 May 1964, Sydney.

21 On 14 March 1896.

22 Bertram Stevens: 'Henry Lawson', State Library of NSW, Angus & Robertson manuscripts, Volume 218, C 863, p. 11.

23 Bertha Lawson, *My Henry Lawson*, p. 36.

24 *Ibid*, *Henry Lawson by His Mates*, p. 82.

25 'Henry Lawson and I', Dame Mary Gilmore Papers, State Library of NSW, A 3292.

26 Roderick, *Henry Lawson*, p. 147.

27 Bertha Lawson, *My Henry Lawson*, p. 37.

28 'Recent Publications', *The Evening News*, 15 February 1896, p. 4S.

29 A.G. Stephens, 'Henry Lawson's Poems', *Bulletin*, 15 February 1896, Red Page.

30 'Ballads of Out Back', *Sydney Morning Herald*, 15 February 1896, p. 7.

31 J. Le Gay Brereton, 'A Reflection On Lawson's Poems', *Bulletin*, 18 January 1896, p. 3.

32 Bertha Lawson, *Henry Lawson by His Mates*, p. 84.

33 David McKee Wright, born 6 August 1869, Ballynaskeagh, Ireland; died 5 February 1928, Glenbrook, New South Wales.

34 'The Occasional Dictionary. A Cyclopaedia For Casual Folk', *Triad*, 10 May 1917, p. 67.

35 Bertha Lawson, *Henry Lawson by His Mates*, p. 82.

36 Roderick, *Henry Lawson*, p. 149, quoting a letter from Mills to Walter Ashe Woods, aka Walter Head, March 1896.

37 Lawson, 'After All', *Bulletin*, 28 March 1896, p. 13.

38 Bertha Lawson, *Henry Lawson by His Mates*, p. 82.

39 'An Unfinished Love Story', *Worker*, 21 March 1896, p. 1.

40 Louisa Lawson, 'Don't marry a man to reform him', *Dawn*, 5 November 1889, p. 16.

41 'Marriages, Marriages', *Sydney Morning Herald*, 2 April 1896, p. 9.

42 George Lewis Becke (or Louis Becke), born 18 June 1855, Port Macquarie, New South Wales; died 18 February 1913, Sydney.

43 Lawson to Lala Fisher, undated, Fisher Library Rare Books and Special Collections, University of Sydney Library.

44 Bertha Lawson, *Henry Lawson by His Mates*, p. 85.

45 *New South Wales Marriage Index*, 2223/1896.

46 William Macleod, born 27 October 1850, London; died 24 June 1929, Mosman, Sydney.

47 Bertha Lawson, *My Henry Lawson*, p. 40.

48 Christina Rutherford Moreton Macpherson, born 18 June 1864, Peechelba, Victoria; died 27 March 1936, St Kilda, Victoria.

49 The song was first published in 1818, with words by Scottish poet Robert Tannahill and music by James Barr. Godfrey Parker converted the music into a marching tune in 1894.

50 'Who'll Come a Waltzing Matilda With Me', pandora.nla.gov.au.

51 *Bulletin*, 18 November 1893, p. 20.

52 Bertram Stevens, 'Henry Lawson', State Library of NSW, Angus & Robertson manuscripts, Volume 218, C 863, p. 10.

53 A.B. 'Banjo' Paterson, 'Some Reminiscences of George Robertson, Australian Publisher', *Sydney Mail*, 20 September 1933, p. 8.

54 'Henry Lawson's Poems', *Worker*, 4 July 1896, p. 1.

55 Bertha Lawson, *Henry Lawson by His Mates*, p. 87.

56 *Ibid*.

57 Brereton, *Knocking Round*.

58 William Alexander Gilmore, born 20 March 1866, Strathdownie, Victoria; died 20 February 1945, Cloncurry, Queensland.

59 Wilde, *Courage A Grace*.

60 Mary Cameron to Lawson, 5 August 1896, State Library of NSW, MLMSS 314/vol. 250.

61 Ruth Park, manuscript notes of interview with Bertha Lawson 1952.

62 Bertha Lawson, *Henry Lawson by His Mates*, p. 88.

63 Vance Marshall, *ibid*, p. 285.
64 Bertha Lawson, *ibid*, pp. 89–90.
65 *Ibid*.
66 *Ibid, My Henry Lawson*, p. 41.
67 *Ibid*, p. 42.
68 Lawson, '1. The Reason', *Triangles of Life and Other Stories*, Standard Publishing Co, 1913.

Chapter 14

1   Bertram Stevens, 'Henry Lawson', State Library of NSW, Angus & Robertson manuscripts, Volume 218, C 863, p. 13.
2   'The Golden Nineties', *Australian Star* (Sydney), 30 September 1899, p. 4.
3   *Ibid*.
4   Steele Grey, 'Henry Lawson', *Free Lance*, 25 June 1896, p. 3.
5   *Ibid*, 'Henry Lawson Goes West', *Free Lance*, 9 July 1896, p. 14.
6   'The Golden Nineties', *Australian Star* (Sydney), 4 November 1899, p. 4.
7   'The Donnybrook Gold Find', *Western Mail* (Perth), 11 August 1899, p. 59.
8   ''The Golden Nineties', *Australian Star* (Sydney), 4 November 1899, p. 4.
9   *Ibid*.
10 *Ibid*.
11 Ibid, 30 September 1899, p. 4.
12 Bertha Lawson, *My Henry Lawson*, p. 43.
13 'The Hero of Redclay', *Over the Sliprails*, Angus & Robertson, 1900. The character was Dr Lebinski.
14 'The Golden Nineties', *Australian Star* (Sydney), 18 November 1899, p. 4.
15 *Ibid*, 11 November 1899, p. 4.
16 *Ibid*.
17 *Ibid*, 25 November 1899, p. 4.
18 Almost a half century later in *My Henry Lawson*, Bertha said they spent seven weeks at the Shamrock, but her memory proved false.
19 *Ibid*.
20 *Ibid*.
21 *Ibid*.
22 *West Australian* (Perth), 12 September 1896, p. 9.
23 *Ibid*, 14 November 1896, p. 9.
24 *Ibid*, 3 October 1896, p. 9.
25 *Ibid*.
26 Christopher Lee, 'The Status of the Aborigine in the Writing of Henry Lawson: A Reconsideration', *La Trobe Journal*, No 70 Spring 2002, pp. 77–79.
27 'Black Joe', *The West Australian*, 12 September 1896, p. 9.
28 Alfred Arthur Greenwood Hales, born 21 July 1860, Kent Town, Adelaide; died 29 December 1936, Herne Bay, Kent, England.
29 Arthur Parker in *Henry Lawson by His Mates*, p. 30.
30 'The Golden Nineties', *Australian Star* (Sydney), 23 December 1899, p. 4.
31 David Ferguson, *Review of Reviews*, 20 August 1896.
32 'Current Literature', *Sydney Morning Herald*, 29 August 1896, p. 4.
33 'News and Notes', *West Australian*, 14 September 1896, p. 5.
34 John Tighe Ryan, born 1870, Miltown, Tipperary, Ireland; died 20 September 1922, Sydney.
35 Roderick, *Henry Lawson*, p. 162.
36 Lawson to George Robertson, 3 September 1896, State Library of NSW, MLMSS 314/vol. 45/item 1.

37   'The Golden Nineties', *Australian Star* (Sydney), 25 November 1899, p. 4.

38   Bertha Lawson, *My Henry Lawson*, p. 47.

39   *Ibid, Henry Lawson by His Mates*, p. 93.

40   'The Sanitation Of Perth', *West Australian*, 19 September 1896, p. 12.

41   'Bill Will', *Worker*, 16 December 1907, p. 10.

42   *Ibid.*

43   Henry Hyde Champion, born 22 January 1859, Poona, India; died 30 April 1928, South Yarra, Melbourne.

44   *Champion*, 17 October 1896, p. 1.

45   Bertha Lawson, *My Henry Lawson*, p. 48.

46   *Ibid, Henry Lawson by His Mates*, p. 95.

47   *Ibid, My Henry Lawson*, p. 48.

48   Bertram William Mathyson Francis Stevens, born 8 October 1872, Inverell, New South Wales; died 14 February 1922, Sydney.

49   'My Friend', *Bulletin*, 2 March 1922, Red Page.

50   Bertram Stevens, State Library of NSW, Angus & Robertson manuscripts, Volume 218, C 863, p. 12.

51   *Ibid.*

52   Bertha Lawson, *Henry Lawson by His Mates*, p. 94.

53   *Ibid, My Henry Lawson*, p. 49.

54   Bertram Stevens, State Library of NSW, Angus & Robertson manuscripts, Volume 218, C 863, p. 12.

55   *Ibid.*

56   Prout, *Henry Lawson*, p. 147.

57   'The Uncultured Rhymer to his Cultured Critics', *Bulletin*, 25 December 1897, p. 3.

58   *Ibid.*

59   Lawson to Robertson, January 1897, State Library of NSW, MLMSS 184/8.

60   *Ibid.*

61   *Ibid*, February 1897.

62   Robertson to Lawson, 8 February 1897, ibid.

63   Bertram Stevens, 'Henry Lawson', State Library of NSW, Angus & Robertson manuscripts, Volume 218, C 863, p. 15.

64   *Ibid*, p. 16.

65   *Ibid*, p. 20.

66   Roderick, *Henry Lawson*, p. 171, quoting Hannah's friend Matron Winifred Holford in a letter to Roderick, 29 May 1959.

67   *Ibid.*

Chapter 15

1   'The Writer's Dream', *Bulletin*, 21 May 1898, p. 32.

2   Nelson William Illingworth, born August 1862, Portsmouth, England; died 26 June 1926, Harbord, Sydney.

3   Rose Lindsay, born Rosa Soady, 5 July 1885, Gosford, New South Wales, but known as Rose. Married Norman Lindsay on 14 January 1920; died 23 May 1978, Lane Cove, Sydney.

4   'Rose Lindsay's Memoirs', *Bulletin*, 18 February 1953, p. 34.

5   *Ibid.*

6   Hannah Forrester Thornburn, daughter of John Thornburn and Betsy Forrester; born 1877, Egremont, Cumberland, England; died 1 June 1902, Melbourne. Death registration 6517/1902.

7   Lawson 'Hannah Thomburn' (the name was misspelt by a compositor who mistook Lawson's 'r' and 'n' running together, *For Australia and Other Poems*, Standard Publishing, 1913.

8   Bertram Stevens, 'Henry Lawson', State Library of NSW, Angus & Robertson manuscripts, Volume 218, C 863, p. 20.

9   *Ibid.*

10   *Ibid.*

11   Lawson, 'Hannah Thomburn'.

12   'That Pretty Girl in the Army', from *Children of the Bush*, pp. 24–45.

13   'The Hero of Redclay', *Over the Sliprails*, Angus & Robertson, 1900.

14   'That Pretty Girl in the Army'.

15   Bertha Lawson, *My Henry Lawson*, p. 55.

16   'Pursuing Literature in Australia', *Bulletin*, 21 January 1899, p. 2.

17   *New Zealand Times*, 10 April 1897, p. 3.

18   Bertha mistakenly wrote that it was sold to Gresley Lukin of the *Evening Post* for 3 guineas, but much of her recollection of events in New Zealand were warped by time.

19   New Zealand Department of Education, 97 387/178.

20   *Ibid.*

21   Bertha Lawson, *Henry Lawson by His Mates*, p. 97.

22   *Ibid*, p. 98.

23   *Ibid*, p. 102.

24   *Ibid*, p. 99.

25   *Ibid*, *My Henry Lawson*, p. 62.

26   Roderick, *Lawson and Other Autobiographical Writings*, Angus & Robertson, 1972, p. 220.

27   Bertha Lawson, *Henry Lawson by His Mates*, p. 100.

28   *Ibid*, pp. 102–03.

29   Lawson to Hugh Maccallum, 25 June 1897, State Library of NSW, MLMSS 184/7.

30   'The Ghosts of Many Christmases', *Children of the Bush*, pp. 278–88.

31   *Ibid.*

32   'Lawson's black period', *Sydney Morning Herald*, 26 December 2003.

33   Bertha Lawson, *My Henry Lawson*, p. 62.

34   Lawson to Angus & Robertson, 25 June 1897, State Library of NSW, MLMSS 184/8.

35   'The "Spectator's" Opinion of Henry Lawson', *Australian Town and Country Journal*, 24 July 1897, p. 11.

36   'An Australian Humorist', *Academy*, 17 July 1897.

37   Lawson to Hugh Maccallum, 25 June 1897, State Library of NSW, MLMSS 184/7.

38   *Ibid.*

39   Bertha Lawson, *Henry Lawson by His Mates*, p. 103.

40   Bill Pearson, *Henry Lawson among Maoris*, Australian National University Press, 1968, p. 123.

41   Bertha Lawson, *Henry Lawson by His Mates*, p. 104.

42   *Ibid*, p. 105.

43   Lawson to Hugh Maccallum, 25 June 1897, State Library of NSW, MLMSS 184/7.

44   'A Daughter of Maoriland', *Antipodean*, Christmas No. 3, 1897, pp. 25–34.

45   *Ibid.*

46   *Ibid.*

47   *Ibid.*

48   *Ibid.*

49   'The Writer's Dream', *Bulletin*, 21 May 1898, p. 32.

50   *Ibid.*

51   'The Ports of the Open Sea', *Bulletin*, 4 June 1898, p. 32.

52   'The Jolly Dead March', *Bulletin*, 11 December 1897, p. 39.

53 'The Lights of Cobb and Co.', *ibid*, p. 7.
54 'The Old Mile-Tree', *Bulletin*, 23 November 1911, p. 44.
55 Lawson to Emma Brooks, 19 September 1897, State Library of NSW, MLMSS Al 29.
56 'Personal Items', *Bulletin*, 23 October 1897, p. 13.
57 Bertha Lawson, *My Henry Lawson*, p. 64.
58 Mrs Mary E Moss in Mangamaunu to Lawson, 27 November 1910, State Library of NSW, MLMSS 184/3.
59 Ibid, p. 219.
60 'Local and General', *Evening Post*, 11 November 1897, p. 4.
61 Lawson to Jack Louisson, 3 February 1898, Alexander Turnbull Library, Sydney Bulletin Writers, Q091, Letters 88A.
62 Lawson to Hugh Maccallum, 15 November 1897, State Library of NSW, MLMSS 184/7.
63 *Ibid*, 30 December, *ibid*.
64 'Earthquake of the 8th December 1897', *Transactions And Proceedings Of The Royal Society Of New Zealand, Volume 31*, 1898, p. 583.
65 Bertha Lawson, *My Henry Lawson*, p. 65.
66 *Ibid, Henry Lawson by His Mates*, p. 106.
67 *Ibid, My Henry Lawson*, p. 65.

Chapter 16
1   'Joe Tries His hand at a Sex-Problem Story', *Co-operator*, 24 October 1898.
2   *A Camp-Fire Yarn*, pp. 811–58.
3   Bertha Lawson, *Henry Lawson by His Mates*, p. 106.
4   *A Camp-Fire Yarn*, pp. 811–58.
5   *Ibid*.
6   Bertha Lawson, *My Henry Lawson*, p. 63.
7   Marion Williams produced and directed the Coonamble Theatrical Group's production of *Pinter's Son Jim* at the Combara Hall on 26 and 27 October and 2 and 3 November 1990, State Library of NSW, MLMSS 7482.
8   *Bulletin*, 6 August 1898, p. 26.
9   *Over the Sliprails*, pp. 32–56.
10 *Children of the Bush*, pp. 1–21.
11 *Bulletin*, 4 October 1902, p. 35.
12 *The Rising of the Court and Other Sketches*, Angus & Robertson, 1910, pp. 33–53.
13 Lawson to Brereton, 24 December 1897, from Roderick, *Henry Lawson Letters*, p. 81.
14 'Houses and Land for Sale', *Sydney Morning Herald*, 15 January 1898, p. 3.
15 'Personal', *New Zealand Times*, 12 March 1898, p. 2.
16 *Verses Popular and Humorous*, Angus & Robertson, Sydney, 1900, pp. 10–12.
17 *Bulletin*, 28 January 1899, p. 31.
18 Bertram Stevens, State Library of NSW, Angus & Robertson manuscripts, Volume 218, C 863, p. 17.
19 Bertha erroneously recorded it as £3 10s a week.
20 Bertha Lawson, *My Henry Lawson*, p. 67.
21 Lawson to Angus & Robertson, 4 April [May] 1898, State Library of NSW, MLMSS 184/8
22 *Ibid*.
23 Angus & Robertson to Lawson, 8 May 1898, State Library of NSW, MLMSS 184/8.
24 *Bulletin*, 28 May 1898, p. 32.
25 *Ibid*, 16 July 1898, p. 19.
26 *Ibid*, 6 August 1898, p. 26.
27 E.J. Brady, 'Henry Lawson', State Library of NSW, MLMSS 314/vol. 102/item 2.
28 Bertha Lawson, *Henry Lawson by His Mates*, p. 107.

29 J.T. Lang, 'They Buried Harry Like a Lord', *Truth*, 12 September 1954, p. 25.
30 *Bulletin*, 24 September 1898, p. 31.
31 *Ibid.*
32 *Ibid.*
33 J.T. Lang, *I Remember*, McNamara's Books, 1956.
34 A.G. Stephens, *Victor Daley*, Bulletin Newspaper Co., 1905, p. 21.
35 Bertram Stevens, State Library of NSW, Angus & Robertson manuscripts, Volume 218, C 863, p. 18.
36 *Ibid.*
37 *Bulletin*, 2 March 1922, Red Page.
38 *Ibid.*
39 James Alexander Philp, born Scotland 1860; died 28 June 1935 at his home in Hawthorne Street, South Brisbane.
40 'Obituary: Mr. J. A. Philp', *Courier-Mail*, 1 July 1935, p. 16.
41 George A Taylor, *Those Were the Days*, Tyrrell's, 1918, pp. 10–11.
42 Bertha Lawson, *Henry Lawson by His Mates*, p. 107.
43 E.J. Brady, 'Yes, this was Bohemia', *Herald* (Melbourne), 3 December 1938, p. 38.
44 Brereton, *Knocking Round*.
45 'My Friend', *Bulletin*, 2 March 1922, Red Page.
46 Bertram Stevens, State Library of NSW, Angus & Robertson manuscripts, Volume 218, C 863, p. 19.
47 Bertha Lawson, *Henry Lawson by His Mates*, p. 107.
48 Fred Broomfield, *ibid*, p. 66.
49 Bertha Lawson, *ibid*, p. 108.
50 Recollections of their daughter, Bertha Louisa Lawson [later Mrs Jago], unpublished notes, State Library of of NSW, MLMSS 7692.
51 *Bulletin*, 30 January 1913, p. 47. [Not to be confused with Lawson's 1907 poem of the same name].
52 *Co-operator*, 24 October 1898.
53 *Ibid.*
54 Roderick, *Henry Lawson*, p. 201.
55 Bertha Lawson, *Henry Lawson by His Mates*, p. 108.
56 *Ibid.*
57 Frank Bate, *Samuel Bate, Singular Character*, Brookdale Press, 1987.
58 'Sydney's Temperance Sanatorium For Male Inebriates', *Evening News*, 6 June 1896, p. 5.
59 *Ibid.*
60 *Children of the Bush*, pp. 121–26.
61 *Ibid.*
62 *Ibid.*
63 *Ibid.*

Chapter 17

1 Norman Lindsay, *Bohemians of the Bulletin*, Angus & Robertson, 1965, p. 7.
2 'The Boozers' Home', *Children of the Bush*, pp. 121–26.
3 *Ibid.*
4 Bertram Stevens, State Library of NSW, Angus & Robertson manuscripts, Volume 218, C 863, p. 18.
5 Lawson to Angus & Robertson, 14 January 1899, State Library of NSW, MLMSS 8183/8.
6 *Bulletin*, 11 February 1899, p. 35.
7 'Pursuing Literature in Australia', *Bulletin*, 21 January 1899, Red Page.
8 *Bulletin*, 11 February 1899, Red Page.

9   *Ibid*.
10 A.G. Stephens, 'Lawson and Literature', *Bookfellow*, 18 February 1899.
11 *Ibid*.
12 *A Camp-Fire Yarn*, pp. 861–63.
13 *Bulletin*, 25 March 1899, p. 3.
14 *Ibid*, 1 April 1899, p. 32.
15 *Australian Magazine*, 30 May 1899, p. 156.
16 *Ibid*.
17 Lawson to Mrs H.R. Curlewis (Ethel Turner) 17 April 1899, Ethel Turner Papers, State Library of NSW, MLMSS 667/12.
18 A.B. Paterson, *Old Bush Songs*, Angus & Robertson, 1905. Publication was delayed by Paterson's time as a war correspondent in South Africa.
19 *On the Track*, Angus & Robertson, 1900, pp. 1–17.
20 *Bulletin*, 8 April 1899, Red Page.
21 *Ibid*, 22 July 1899, Red Page.
22 Lawson to Bland Holt, 30 July 1899, State Library of NSW, MLMSS 184/8.
23 William Lygon, 7th Earl Beauchamp (20 February 1872–14 November 1938).
24 Lawson to Bland Holt, 30 July 1899, State Library of NSW, MLMSS 184/8.
25 'Reminiscences of Henry Lawson by Isabel Byers', compiled by Aubrey C. Curtis, State Library of NSW, MLMSS 3694.
26 Lawson to Angus & Robertson, 15 August 1899, State Library of NSW, MLMSS 184/8.
27 Shenstone to Lawson, 16 August 1899, *ibid*.
28 Lawson to George Robertson, 23 August 1899, *ibid*.
29 *Ibid* to Angus & Robertson, 6 September 1899, *ibid*, MLMSS 184/7.
30 'The Golden Nineties', *Australian Star*, 7 October 1899, p. 4.
31 *Ibid*.
32 'Concerning the Awful Contingent', *Bulletin*, 21 October 1899, p. 8.
33 *Ibid*, 10 February 1900, p. 7.
34 'Our Fighters', *Australian Star*, 28 October 1899, p. 4.
35 'Henry Lawson holds forth mainly about "Holman"', *Bulletin*, 28 October 1899, p. 24
36 George Black, 'Lawson Speaks Ill of the Dead', *Worker*, 4 November 1899, p. 1.
37 'The Story of the Oracle', 'No Place for a Woman', 'New Year's Night' and 'Jimmy Grimshaw's Wooing'.
38 Lawson to Angus & Robertson, 11 November 1899, State Library of NSW, MLMSS 184/8.
39 Miles Franklin to Lawson, 19 November 1899, State Library of NSW, MLMSS 364/6.
40 *Ibid*.
41 Lawson to Miles Franklin, 29 December 1899, *ibid*.
42 *Ibid*, [Jan 1900], ibid.
43 Stella Maria Sarah Miles Franklin, born 14 October 1879, Talbingo, New South Wales; died 19 September 1954, Drummoyne, Sydney.
44 Lindsay, *Bohemians of the Bulletin*, p. 44.
45 'New Year's Eve', *Daily Telegraph* (Sydney), 1 January 1900, p. 6.
46 Bertha Lawson, *My Henry Lawson*, p. 72.
47 Lawson to Earl Beauchamp, 19 January 1900, State Library of NSW, MLMSS A3012.
48 Lawson to David Scott Mitchell, *ibid*, SAFE/Al 29/Folder 3 (Safe 1/119).
49 *Ibid*.
50 Lawson to Miles Franklin, 18 January 1900, State Library of NSW, MLMSS 364/6.
51 Lawson to Walter Alan Woods, 31 January 1900, from Roderick, *Letters*, p. 114.
52 Bertram Stevens, State Library of NSW, Angus & Robertson manuscripts, Volume 218, C 863, p. 20.

53   Lawson to Mrs H.R. Curlewis (Ethel Turner) March 1900, State Library of NSW, MLMSS 667/12.

54   Bertha Lawson, *Henry Lawson by His Mates*, p. 109.

55   Lawson, *Autobiography, Vol. 2*.

56   A.B. Paterson, 'At the Front', *Sydney Morning Herald*, 21 April 1900, p. 9.

57   *Ibid, Happy Dispatches*, Angus & Robertson, 1934, Chapter III.

58   Published from 1772 to 1937.

59   A.B. Paterson, *Happy Dispatches*, Chapter II.

60   Bertha Lawson to Miles Franklin, 13 March 1900, State Library of NSW, MLMSS 364/6.

61   Lawson to George Robertson, April 1900, State Library of NSW, MLMSS 184/8.

62   A.G. Stevens, 'Farewell Dreamers', *Bulletin*, 14 April 1900, p. 15.

63   *Ibid.*

64   Fred Broomfield in *Henry Lawson by His Mates*, p. 71.

65   Bertha Lawson, *My Henry Lawson*, p. 74.

66   *Aussie*, 16 September 1922.

67   Lawson to Miles Franklin, 16 April 1900, State Library of NSW, MLMSS 364/6.

68   Miles Franklin to Lawson, 19 April 1900, *ibid*.

69   'New Books', *Town and Country Journal* (Sydney), 7 April 1900.

70   'The Bendigo Jubilee', *Bendigo Independent*, 10 April 1900, p. 2.

71   'Recent Publications', *Evening News* (Sydney), 14 April 1900, p. 4.

72   'On the Track', *Sydney Morning Herald*, 7 April 1900, p. 4.

73   Robert Basil Vincent McKilliam, born 25 June 1861, Aberdeen, Scotland; died 29 June 1934, Sydney.

74   'At Port Natal', *Age* (Melbourne), 9 February 1901, p. 14.

75   Lawson prose writings, State Library of NSW, MLMSS 184/8.

76   'For He Was a Jolly Good Fellow', *A Fantasy of Man*, p. 338.

Chapter 18

1   Edith Dean to J.F. Archibald, 18 October 1900, A.G. Stephens Papers, State Library of NSW, MLMSS 4937/20.

2   *A Fantasy of Man*, p. 926.

3   Sir John Campbell Longstaff, born 10 March 1861, Clunes, Victoria; died 1 October 1941, Melbourne.

4   'The King, The Queen and I', *When I Was King and Other Verses*, Angus & Robertson, 1905, pp. 179–81.

5   *Bulletin*, 8 April 1899, Red Page.

6   Bertha Lawson, *Henry Lawson by His Mates*, p. 111.

7   *Ibid.*

8   *A Fantasy of Man*, p. 926.

9   Lawson to Shenstone, 25 April 1900, State Library of NSW, MLMSS 184/8.

10   'Casually at Sea', *Aussie*, 16 September 1922.

11   'Henry Lawson En Route', *Australian Star*, 10 May 1900, p. 5.

12   Lawson to David Scott Mitchell, State Library of NSW, Al 29.

13   'Henry Lawson En Route', *Australian Star*, 10 May 1900, p. 5.

14   'Casually at Sea', *Aussie*, 16 September 1922.

15   'Still Casually at Sea', *ibid*, 14 October 1922.

16   *Ibid.*

17   'At Port Natal', *Age*, 9 February 1901, p. 14.

18   *Ibid.*

19   *Ibid.*

20   'At Port Natal No. 2', *ibid*, 16 February, p. 13.

21   'Casually at Sea', *Aussie*, 16 September 1922.

22   Lawson to Robertson, August 1900, State Library of NSW, MLMSS 8183/8.

23   'Letters to Jack Cornstalk: I. From an Australian in London', *Triangles of Life and Other Stories*, Standard Publishing Co, 1913.

24   *Ibid.*

25   Bertha Lawson, *Henry Lawson by His Mates*, p. 111.

26   On 9 July 1900. Parliament had passed the Act four days earlier.

27   Born Ella Edith Helen Goldstone in 1865 in Cheltenham, Victoria.

28   George Bernard Shaw, Stanley Weintraub (ed), *The Diaries, 1885-1897,* Pennsylvania State University Press, 1985, p. 919.

29   Bertha Lawson, *Henry Lawson by His Mates*, p. 111.

30   *Ibid*, p. 113.

31   *Ibid*, p. 112.

32   Bertha Lawson to her mother Bertha McNamara, 30 July 1900, State Library of NSW, MLMSS 7692.

33   Arthur Frank Maquarie Mullens (1874–1955).

34   David Storrar Meldrum, born 29 August 1864, Kirkcaldy, Fife, Scotland; died 25 February 1940, Brentford, Middlesex, England.

35   Edward William Garnett, born 5 January 1868, London; died 19 February 1937, Chelsea, London.

36   James Brand Pinker, born 13 October 1863, Paddington, London; died 8 February 1922, Biltmore Hotel, New York.

37   William Blackwood to Lawson, 13 August 1900, State Library of NSW, MLMSS 8183/8.

38   Lawson to Miles Franklin, 6 September 1900, State Library of NSW, MLMSS 364/6.

39   John Barnes, 'Son of a Foreign Father: A View of Henry Lawson', *La Trobe Journal*, No 70 Spring 2002, p. 66.

40   'A Double Buggy at Lahey's Creek: The Writer Wants to Say a Word', *Joe Wilson and His Mates*, William Blackwood, 1901, p. 152.

41   John Barnes, 'Son of a Foreign Father: A View of Henry Lawson', *La Trobe Journal*, No 70 Spring 2002, p. 66.

42   Lawson, *Autobiography, Vol 2.*

43   Bertha Lawson, *My Henry Lawson*, p. 74.

44   *Australian Star*, 2 September 1899, p. 3; *On the Track*, Angus & Robertson, 1900.

45   Bertha Lawson to Bertha McNamara, 11 September 1900, State Library of NSW, MLMSS 7692.

46   Bertram Stevens, State Library of NSW, Angus & Robertson manuscripts, Volume 218, C 863, p. 21.

47   Andrew Roberts, 'The Lunacy Commission, A Study of its Origin, Emergence and Character', section 3.8, 1981, studymore.org.uk.

48   Bertha Lawson, *Henry Lawson by His Mates*, p. 114.

49   Edith Dean to J.F. Archibald, 18 October 1900, State Library of NSW, MLMSS 4937/20.

50   Marie Louise Hamilton Mack, born 10 October 1870, Hobart; died 23 November 1935, Mosman, Sydney.

51   'Bohemia Up To Date', *Freeman's Journal*, 2 February 1901, p. 11.

52   Henry Lawson, 'The Triangles of Life', *Triangles of Life and Other Stories*.

53   Maude Wheeler, 'The Lights of London', *Truth*, 28 April 1901, p. 8.

54   *Bulletin*, 8 December 1900, p. 4.

55   *Maga*, April 1901.

56   *Children of the Bush*, Methuen 1902, pp. 178–91.

57   *Joe Wilson and His Mates*, pp. 285–305.

58   'Lawson's Last Book – A Temporary Adjustment', *Bulletin*, 12 January 1901, Red Page.

59 *Bulletin*, 13 December 1902, p. 14.
60 Lawson to Robertson, 15 May 1901, State Library of NSW, MLMSS 8183/8. (Lawson most likely wrote the letter a day or two earlier before Bertha was committed to Bethlem.)
61 Bethlem Royal Hospital patient admission and casebooks 1683–1932, BAP-109 Series C7 Box 5.
62 *Ibid.*
63 *Ibid.*

Chapter 19

1 Bertha Lawson to Bertha McNamara, dated 18 July 1900 [thought to be 1901], State Library of NSW, MLMSS 7692.
2 'Henry Lawson and I', Dame Mary Gilmore Papers, State Library of NSW, A 3292.
3 Bertha Lawson to Bertha McNamara, 18 July [1901], State Library of NSW, MLMSS 7692.
4 *Triangles of Life and Other Stories.*
5 *Ibid.*
6 *Blackwood's Magazine*, November 1900.
7 Roderick, *Henry Lawson*, p. 231.
8 Arthur Maquarie to Archibald, 29 July 1901, State Library of NSW, SAFE/Al 29.
9 *Bulletin*, 24 May 1902, Red Page.
10 Roderick, *Henry Lawson*, p. 232.
11 *Bulletin*, 11 January 1902, Red Page.
12 Bertha Lawson, *Henry Lawson by His Mates*, p. 114.
13 *When I Was King and Other Verses*, pp. 63–66.
14 Bertha Lawson to Bertha McNamara, 2 November 1901, State Library of NSW, MLMSS 7692.
15 Bertha Lawson, *My Henry Lawson*, p. 74.
16 *Ibid, Henry Lawson by His Mates*, p. 115.
17 Roderick, *Henry Lawson*, p. 237.
18 *Children of the Bush*, pp. 192–201.
19 *Ibid.*
20 Bertha Lawson, *Henry Lawson by His Mates*, pp. 116–17.
21 Lawson to David Scott Mitchell, 11 February 1902, State Library of NSW, SAFE/Al 29.
22 'The History of an Invention', *Dawn*, 1 January 1903, p. 5.
23 Edward Garnett, 'An Appreciation', *Academy and Literature*, 8 March 1902.
24 Randolph Bedford, 'Letters from Exile', *Critic* (Adelaide), 10 October 1903, p. 13.
25 Edward Verrall Lucas, (11/12 June 1868–26 June 1938).
26 'Henry Lawson and I', Dame Mary Gilmore Papers, State Library of NSW, A 3292.
27 *Ibid.*
28 *Ibid.*
29 'Personal Items', *Bulletin*, 26 July 1902, p. 15.
30 'Lawson to the "*Bulletin*"', 28 June 1902, *Bulletin*, Red Page.
31 *Ibid.*
32 'Henry Lawson and I', Dame Mary Gilmore Papers, State Library of NSW, A 3292.
33 'Hannah Thornburn', *For Australia and other Poems.*
34 *Bulletin*, 11 December 1915, p. 32.
35 *Ibid*, 8 December 1904, p. 17.
36 'The Last Review', *Bulletin*, 29 September 1904, p. 35.
37 'The Lily of St Leonards', *ibid*, 4 April 1907, p. 32.

Chapter 20

1   'Henry Lawson and I', Dame Mary Gilmore Papers, State Library of NSW, A 3292.

2   *Ibid.*

3   'On the Karlsruhe and Another Boat", Roderick, *Henry Lawson: Autobiographical and Other Writings*, p. 244.

4   'German Liner Karlsruhe', *Ballarat Star*, 17 July 1902, p. 1.

5   'Henry Lawson and I', Dame Mary Gilmore Papers, State Library of NSW, A 3292. Ruth Park, who was friendly with Bertha in later years, suspected that during their battles, Lawson had goaded Bertha about him and Mary having once been lovers.

6   *Ibid.*

7   Bertha Lawson, *My Henry Lawson*, p. 77.

8   "Henry Lawson and I', Dame Mary Gilmore Papers, State Library of NSW, A 3292.

9   Lawson to Bland Holt, 22 August 1902, Papers of Bland Holt, National Library of Australia, MS 2244, Series 1.

10   'Personal Items', *Bulletin*, 26 July 1902, p. 15.

11   Bertha Lawson, *My Henry Lawson*, pp. 79–80.

12   Roderick, 'Henry Lawson and Hannah Thornburn', *Meanjin Quarterly*, Vol. 27 no. 3 Spring 1968, p. 87.

13   Roderick, *Henry Lawson*, pp. 244–45.

14   *Ibid.*

15   'Ruth', *Bulletin*, 20 December 1902, Red Page.

16   'To Hannah', *Bulletin*, 1 September 1904, p. 3.

17   *Ibid.*

18   'Do They Think that I Do Not Know?', *The Skyline Riders and Other Verses*, Fergusson, 1910, pp. 31–33.

19   'Henry Lawson and I', Dame Mary Gilmore Papers, State Library of NSW, A 3292.

20   *Ibid.*

21   'Back From Utopia', *Argus*, 18 July 1902, p. 6.

22   *Ibid.*

23   Bertha Lawson, *My Henry Lawson*, p. 80.

24   'Grimy Old Babylon', *Daily Telegraph*, 2 August 1902, p. 7.

25   *Bulletin*, 2 August 1902, Red Page.

26   'Grimy Old Babylon', *Daily Telegraph*, 2 August 1902, p. 7.

27   *Ibid.*

28   'The Sweet Uses of London: One View', *Bulletin*, 22 October 1903, Red Page.

29   Possibly the private hospital run by Nurse K. Younger at 5 Wellesley Street, Summer Hill.

30   Lawson to Bland Holt [August 1902], Papers of Bland Holt, National Library of Australia, MS 2244, Series 1.

31   David Ferguson to Walter Alan Woods, 28 October 1902, Roderick, Henry Lawson Letters, p. 444.

32   Thomas Robinson & Son. Ltd., Wood Cutting Machinists & Flower Mill Engineers of 317 and 319 Kent Street, Sydney.

33   Bertha to Lawson, August 1902, Lothian Publishing Company Records 1895-1950, State Library of Victoria, MS 6026, Box XXI A.

34   Lawson to Bland Holt, 12 August 1902, National Library of Australia, MS 2244, Series 1.

35   Ferry advertisements used the slogan in the 1920s.

36   'The Bards Who Lived at Manly', *For Australia*, Standard Publishing Co, 1913.

37   Lawson to A.C. Rowlandson, 19 August 1902, Roderick, *Henry Lawson Letters*, p. 133.

38   'A Stroll to the Strand', *Bulletin*, 19 November 1903, p. 35.

39   'The Lost Souls' Hotel', *Bulletin*, 13 September 1902, pp. 35–36.

40   *Ibid.*

41 Banjo Paterson to Miles Franklin, 31 May 1902, State Library of NSW, MLMSS 364/7.
42 A.B. 'Banjo' Paterson, 'An Execution and a Royal Pardon', *Sydney Morning Herald*, 25 February 1939, p. 21.
43 Jill Roe, *Stella Miles Franklin: A Biography*, HarperCollins Australia, 2010.
44 Henry Lawson to Miles Franklin, 5 September 1902, State Library of NSW, MLMSS 364/6.
45 Lawson to Bland Holt, [undated], Lothian Publishing Company Records, State Library of Victoria, MS 6026, Box XXI A.
46 Mary Gilmore to Walter Alan Woods, 25 September 1902, Roderick, *Henry Lawson Letters*, pp. 443–44.
47 David Ferguson to Walter Alan Woods, 28 October 1902, *ibid*, p. 444.
48 Francis Augustus Bennet, born 1856, Cullen Banffshire, Scotland; died 13 September 1931, at his residence, Dunsinane, Ocean Street, Woollahra.
49 Xavier Pons, *Out of Eden: Henry Lawson's life and works. A psychoanalytic view*, Sirius Books, 1984, p. 116.
50 Lawson to George Robertson, January 1917, State Library of NSW, MLMSS 1875.
51 'Accident To Mr Henry Lawson', *Sydney Morning Herald*, 8 December 1902, p. 6.

Chapter 21
1 *Bulletin*, 10 December 1903, p. 26.
2 *Brisbane Courier* (Quoting *To-day*), 22 May 1903, p. 13.
3 Ernest Charles Buley, born 4 July 1869, Ballarat, Victoria; died 10 April 1933, London.
4 George Reginald Percy Hall, born 1871, Armidale, New South Wales, died 5 October 1966, Ebenezer, New South Wales.
5 'Accident To Mr Henry Lawson', *Sydney Morning Herald*, 8 December 1902, p. 6.
6 *Ballarat Star*, 9 December 1902, p. 2.
7 Bertha to Lawson, 14 December 1902, Lothian Publishing Company Records, State Library of Victoria, MS 6026, Box XXI A.
8 Lawson to Robertson, 17 December 1902, State Library of NSW, MLMSS 184/7.
9 Lawson, 'In Hospital', *Bulletin*, 28 February 1903, p. 29.
10 *Ibid.*
11 *Ballarat Star*, 9 December 1902, p. 2.
12 'Henry Lawson: Found at Bottom of Cliffs', *Australian Star*, 8 December 1902, p. 6.
13 *Bulletin*, 28 February 1903, Red Page, quoting London *Chronicle* of 13 January.
14 'Personal Items', *ibid*, 3 January 1903, p. 15.
15 Lawson to Dr Frederick Watson, 31 March 1916, from Roderick, *Henry Lawson*, p. 252.
16 'Lawson's Fall', from 'Henry and Bertha Lawson: Some Unpublished Letters And Stories', *Latrobe Journal*, No. 28, October 1981, p. 74.
17 'Reminiscences of Henry Lawson by Isabel Byers', by Aubrey C. Curtis, State Library of NSW, MLMSS 3694.
18 *Ibid.*
19 Bertram Stevens, State Library of NSW, Angus & Robertson manuscripts, Volume 218, C 863, p. 21.
20 Bertha to Lawson, late December 1902/early January 1903, Lothian Publishing Company Records, State Library of Victoria, MS 6026, Box XXI A.
21 'Personal Items', *ibid*, 3 January 1903, p. 15.
22 '"Banjo" Paterson Tells His Own Story – 2. Giants Of The Paddle, Pen, And Pencil', *Sydney Morning Herald*, 11 February 1939, p. 21.
23 Lawson, 'The Separation', *When I Was King*, pp. 75–76.
24 'Personal Gossip', *Critic* (Adelaide), 28 February 1903, p. 6.
25 Lindsay, *Bohemians of the Bulletin*, p. 59.

26 Bertha to Lawson, [undated] February 1903, State Library of Victoria, MS 6026, Box XXI A.

27 *Ibid.*

28 Bertram Stevens, State Library of NSW, Angus & Robertson manuscripts, Volume 218, C 863, p. 22.

29 *Ibid.*

30 NRS 13495, Divorce Case Papers #4676 Bertha Lawson, 1903, State Records Authority NSW.

31 Bertha to Lawson, 23 April 1903, State Library of Victoria, MS 6026, Box XXI A.

32 *Ibid.*

33 Lawson to Robertson, 26 April 1903, from Prout, *Henry Lawson*, p. 205.

34 Later Sir Charles Bickerton Blackburn OBE (1874–1972), Chancellor of Sydney University.

35 Roderick, *Henry Lawson*, p. 254.

36 Lawson to Bertha [undated], State Library of NSW, MLMSS 7692.

37 *Ibid*, State Library of Victoria, MS 6026, Box XXI A.

38 NRS 13495, Divorce Case Papers #4676 Bertha Lawson, 1903, State Records Authority NSW.

39 'Personal Gossip', *Critic* (South Australia), 30 May 1903, p. 8.

40 'Divorce Court', *Sydney Morning Herald*, 5 June 1903, p. 8.

41 A.B. 'Banjo' Paterson, *Rio Grande's Last Race and Other Verses*, Angus & Robertson, 1902.

42 *Bulletin*, 19 May 1904, p. 29.

43 'Brother, You'll take My Hand', *A Fantasy of Man*, p. 188.

44 Bertha Lawson, *My Henry Lawson*, p. 80.

45 Bertha to Lawson, 15 June 1903, State Library of Victoria, MS 6026, Box XXI A.

46 *Ibid*, 25 July 1903, *ibid*.

47 *The World's News* (Sydney), 1 August 1903, p. 2.

48 *Bulletin*, 24 September 1903, p. 36.

49 Lawson to George Robertson, January 1917, State Library of NSW, MLMSS 1875.

50 Louisa Lawson, *The Lonely Crossing and Other Poems*, Dawn, 1905.

51 *Bulletin*, 8 October 1903, Red Page.

52 Lawson to Angus & Robertson, 1 October 1903, State Library of NSW, MLMSS 184/7.

53 Isabella [Isabel] Ann Byers (nee Ward), born 6 May 1848, District of Lower Hawkesbury, NSW; married Charles Byers 22 April 1885, Paddington, Sydney; died 11 November 1930, Willoughby, Sydney.

54 Prout, *Henry Lawson*, p. 206.

55 'Reminiscences of Isabel Byers', State Library of NSW, MLMSS 3694.

56 Bertram Stevens, State Library of NSW, Angus & Robertson manuscripts, Volume 218, C 863, p. 21.

57 Kerrie Davies, *A Wife's Heart: The Untold Story of Bertha and Henry Lawson*, University of Queensland Press, 2017.

58 *Bulletin*, 10 December 1903, p. 8.

59 *Ibid*, 12 November 1903, p. 17.

60 James Edmond, born 21 April 1859, Glasgow, Scotland; died 21 March 1933, Sydney.

61 Sylvia Lawson, 'Edmond, James (1859–1933)', *Australian Dictionary of Biography*, Volume 8, (MUP), 1981.

62 *Bulletin*, 7 January 1904, p. 32.

63 *Ibid*, 14 July 1904, p. 36.

64 *Ibid.*

65 *Ibid*, 22 September 1904, p. 36.

66 State Library of NSW, MLMSS 184/7.

67   *Bulletin*, 29 September 1904, p. 35.
68   *Evening News*, 29 April 1905, p. 9.
69   'Progress of the Evening News', *Evening News*, 11 October 1906, p. 6.
70   *When I was King*, Angus & Robertson, 1905.
71   *Ibid.*
72   *Ibid.*
73   *Evening News*, 24 March 1906, p. 9.
74   'Brave Rescue by Henry Lawson', *Advertiser* (Adelaide), 28 December 1904, p. 4.
75   'Personal Items', *Bulletin*, 5 January 1905, p. 15.
76   'Henry Lawson to the Rescue', *Australian Star* (Sydney), 27 December 1904, p. 5.
77   Lawson to Bland Holt, 28 December 1904, Papers of Bland Holt, National Library of Australia , MS 2244, Series 1.
78   'A Wife's Attempted Suicide', *Australian Star*, 4 January 1905, p. 5.

Chapter 22
1   *Bulletin*, 9 March 1905, p. 3.
2   'Reminiscences of Henry Lawson by Isabel Byers', State Library of NSW, MLMSS 3694.
3   Bertha Lawson, *My Henry Lawson*, p. 81.
4   *Ibid.*
5   Bertha Lawson [Jago], unpublished notes, State Library of NSW, MLMSS 7692.
6   Prout, *Henry Lawson*, p. 209.
7   *Bulletin*, 19 January 1905, p. 8.
8   *Ibid.*
9   Admiral Sir Harry Holdsworth Rawson, born 5 November 1843, Upper Islington, Liverpool, England; died 3 November 1910, London.
10   'Robert Burns' Statue', *Daily Telegraph*, 31 January 1905, p. 7.
11   *Bulletin*, 23 February 1905, p. 36.
12   Now called The Art Gallery of New South Wales.
13   'The Soul of a Poet', *Newsletter* (Sydney), 23 December 1905, p. 8.
14   Dr Richard Arthur, born 25 October 1865, Aldershot, England; died 21 May 1932 at his home in Military Road, Mosman.
15   Lawson to Robertson, 15 February 1905; from Prout, *Henry Lawson*, p. 218.
16   *Ibid*, p. 213.
17   James Robert Tyrrell, born 3 July 1875 Darlington, Sydney; died 30 July 1961 Cammeray, Sydney.
18   Edward Vivian (Vance) Palmer, born 28 August 1885, Bundaberg, Queensland; died 15 July 1959, Kew, Melbourne.
19   Prout, *Henry Lawson*, p. 213.
20   *Amateur Gardener*, 15 March 1905.
21   *Ibid*, 16 February 1905.
22   John Gilmore Lockley (1865–1937).
23   Lawson, *The Skyline Riders and Other Verses*, Ferguson, 1910.
24   Lockley, in introduction to *The Skyline Riders and Other Verses*.
25   Prout, *Henry Lawson*, p. 218.
26   'Personal Pars', *Murchison Advocate*, 1 April 1905, p. 2.
27   'Henry Lawson and I', Dame Mary Gilmore Papers, State Library of NSW, A 3292.
28   'Howard's Holocaust', *Truth* (Brisbane), 19 July 1903, p. 2.
29   'Jimmy Governor Executed', *Weekly Times* (Melbourne), 19 January 1901, p. 19.
30   'Criminals and Their Treatment', *Tocsin* (Melbourne), 5 December 1901, p. 2.
31   'Darlinghurst Reception House (1868–1958), State Records Authority NSW, researchdata.edu.au.

32 Lawson to Bland Holt, 4 April 1905, Roderick, *Letters*, p. 147.

33 *Ibid* to David Scott Mitchell, [undated], State Library of NSW, SAFE/Al 29.

34 *Bulletin*, 27 April 1905, p. 3.

35 'The Vanguard', *Bulletin*, 15 June 1905, p. 9.

36 'Australia's Peril: The Warning,' *Worker*, 24 June 1905, p. 4.

37 *Ibid.*

38 Francis Sheriff Isaacs, born 1848 Antigua, West Indies; died 18 March 1929, Leeton, NSW.

39 'Going In', *A Fantasy of Man*, pp. 861–64.

40 'Our Institutions: Darlinghurst Gaol', *Guyra Argus*, 29 July 1909, p. 5.

41 'Going In', *A Fantasy of Man*, pp. 861–64.

42 'Our Institutions: Darlinghurst Gaol', *Guyra Argus*, 29 July 1909, p. 5.

43 'The Rising of the Court', *Bulletin*, 14 November 1907, pp. 39–40.

44 *Bulletin*, 6 December 1906, p. 44.

45 'The Lawsons – Three Generations: Tales of a Grandfather', *Bulletin*, 21 December 1905, Red Page.

46 A.G. Stephens, 'Mother and Son', *Bulletin*, 21 December 1905, Red Page.

47 *Ibid.*

48 *Ibid.*

49 *Newsletter*, 13 January 1906, p. 10.

50 Bertha Lawson [Jago], unpublished notes, State Library of NSW, MLMSS 7692.

51 *Bulletin*, 9 March 1905, p. 3.

Chapter 23

1 'One Hundred and Three', *Bulletin*, 26 November 1908, p. 39.

2 'My Friend', *Bulletin*, 2 March 1922, Red Page.

3 *Truth*, 14 January 1906.

4 *Ibid.*

5 'To Victor Daley', *Bulletin*, 8 February 1906, p. 25.

6 *Catholic Press* (Sydney), 22 February 1906, p. 15.

7 Lawson to Robertson, January 1906, State Library of NSW, MLMSS 184/8.

8 *Ibid* to Francis Sheriff Isaacs, *ibid*, MLDOC 1062.

9 'Personagraphs', *Sun* (Kalgoorlie), 30 July 1905, p. 6.

10 Lawson to Robertson, February 1906, State Library of NSW, MLMSS 184/7.

11 'A Tribute to Victor Daley by his fellow artists', Souvenir Theatre Royal, Matinee, 30 March 1906.

12 Thomas C. Lothian to Harry Chaplin, 12 September, 1961, University of Sydney Library.

13 Lawson to Robertson, undated 1906, State Library of NSW, MLMSS 184/7.

14 Arthur W. Jose, *The Romantic Nineties*, Angus & Robertson, 1933, p. 16.

15 Bertha Lawson [Jago], unpublished notes, State Library of NSW, MLMSS 7692.

16 Lawson to Robertson, undated 1906, State Library of NSW, MLMSS 184/7.

17 *Ibid.*

18 'For England At The Theatre Royal', *Daily Telegraph*, 4 June 1906, p. 7.

19 All four notes – Lawson to Bland Holt, May–June 1906, Papers of Bland Holt, National Library of Australia , MS 2244, Series 1.

20 Holt to Lawson, 30 June 1906, State Library of NSW, SAFE/Al 29.

21 *Bulletin*, 26 July 1906, p. 17.

22 *Ibid*, 25 October 1906, p. 9.

23 *Bulletin*, 11 April 1907, p. 40.

24 *For Australia and Other Poems*, Standard Publishing, 1913.

25 *Bulletin*, 5 July 1906, p. 3.

26 Lawson to Robertson, 24 July 1906, State Library of NSW, MLMSS 184/8.

27   *Ibid*, 27 July 1906, State Library of NSW, MLMSS 184/8.
28   Bertha to Lawson, 6 October 1906, State Library of Victoria, MS 6026.
29   Lawson to Bland Holt, November 1906, Roderick, *Letters*, p. 155.
30   Lawson to Robertson, December 1906, State Library of NSW, MLMSS 184/7.
31   'Lily of St Leonards', *Bulletin*, 4 April 1907, p. 32.
32   Thomas Carlyle Lothian, born 7 May 1880, Newcastle-upon-Tyne, England; died 19 April 1974, Mont Albert, Melbourne.
33   Roderick, *Henry Lawson*, p. 278.
34   'King Billy', Lothian Papers, State Library of Victoria, MS 6026.
35   *Ibid*.
36   *Ibid*.
37   Lawson, '1. The Reason', *Triangles of Life and Other Stories*.
38   Lawson to Robertson, c. April 1907, State Library of NSW, MLMSS 184/7.
39   Roderick, *Henry Lawson*, p. 280.
40   Lothian publishing agreement, State Library of NSW, MLMSS 184/8.
41   Lawson to Robertson, c. May 1907, State Library of NSW, MLMSS 184/7.
42   Lothian to Lawson, 17 May 1907, State Library of NSW, MLMSS 184/7.
43   Lawson to Lothian, 3 December 1907, State Library of Victoria, MS 6026.
44   Lothian to Lawson, 5 December 1907, *ibid*.
45   William Henry Dyson, born 3 September 1880, Alfredton, Victoria; died 21 January 1938, Chelsea, London.
46   Later Sir Frank Ignatius Fox, born 12 August 1874, Adelaide; died 4 March 1960, Chichester, Sussex.
47   Lawson to Fox, 7 November 1907, State Library of NSW, MLMSS 184/8.
48   *Ibid*.
49   Known as 'Charlemont' after 1919.
50   Lawson to Angus & Robertson, 7 April 1908, State Library of NSW, MLMSS 184/7.
51   *Bulletin*, 27 February 1908, p. 40.
52   'The Benign "Bulletin": Litterateur Lawson Lumbered', *Truth*, 1 March 1908, p. 2.
53   Lawson to The Cashier, Bulletin Office, undated, State Library of NSW, MLMSS 184/8.
54   *Bulletin*, 12 March 1908, p. 39.
55   'Life & Letters. Henry Lawson's Early Days', *Lone Hand*, 2 March 1908, pp. 568–76.
56   *A Fantasy of Man*, pp. 888–92.
57   Royal Commission on the administration of the mental hospitals and the Reception House for the insane at Darlinghurst (1913).
58   Bede Nairn, *The 'Big Fella': Jack Lang and the Australian Labor Party 1891-1949*, MUP, 1986, p. 34.
59   The application was made on 11 August 1908 and cancelled three days later.
60   Lawson to Robertson, 27 August 1908, State Library of NSW, MLMSS 184/7.
61   'One Hundred and Three', *Bulletin*, 26 November 1908, p. 39.
62   State Library of NSW, SAFE/Al 29.
63   *Bulletin*, 26 November 1908, p. 39.
64   *Ibid*.

Chapter 24
1   'Reminiscences of Henry Lawson by Isabel Byers', State Library of NSW, MLMSS 3694.
2   'Boxing', *Barrier Miner* (Broken Hill), 11 November 1908, p. 6.
3   Randolph Bedford, 'White v. Black', *Herald* (Melbourne), 26 December 1908, p. 6.
4   *A Fantasy of Man*, p. 897.
5   Lawson to Robertson, undated 1913, State Library of NSW, MLMSS 184/8.
6   Isabel Byers to Robertson, 20 April 1909, State Library of NSW, MLMSS 184/7.

7 'Sticking to Bill', *Fantasy of Man*, pp. 433–34.
8 'Reminiscences of Henry Lawson by Isabel Byers', State Library of NSW, MLMSS 3694.
9 *Ibid.*
10 Arthur Henry Adams, born 6 June 1872, Lawrence, New Zealand; died 4 March 1936, Royal North Shore Hospital, Sydney.
11 Emile Saillens, 'The Discovery Of Australia By France', *Lone Hand*, 1 June 1909, pp. 236–40.
12 *Ibid.*
13 The French volume went unpublished after a dispute between George Robertson and a French editor who tried to supplant Saillens as translator.
14 *The Skyline Riders and Other Verses*, Fergusson, 1910, pp. 39–40.
15 Bland Holt to Isabel Byers, 16 June 1909, State Library of NSW, MLMSS 3694/Box 2/ Folder 2.
16 *Bulletin*, 18 November 1909, p. 43.
17 *Ibid*, 23 December 1909, p. 43.
18 Lawson called him 'Joseph Love' as he was known in gaol as 'Old Joe'.
19 'The Newtown Murder', *Australian Star*, 26 June 1896, p. 6.
20 'The Song of a Prison', *Bulletin*, 23 December 1909, p. 43.
21 'In the Shadow of the Gallows', *Mudgee Guardian*, 18 June 1903, p. 7.
22 Lawson to Robertson, 23 March 1917, State Library of NSW, MLMSS A1876.
23 'Central Criminal Court', *Sydney Morning Herald*, 2 June 1905, p. 3.
24 *Bulletin*, 15 December 1910, p. 34.
25 *Ibid*, 23 December 1909, p. 43.
26 Lawson in Preface to Vance Marshall, *The World of the Living Dead*, W. J. Anderson, 1919.
27 State Library of NSW, MLMSS 184/7.
28 *Ibid.*
29 *A Fantasy of Man*, p. 902.
30 *Ibid*, pp. 904–05.
31 *Ibid*, p. 906.
32 *Bulletin*, 9 December 1909, p. 26.
33 Lawson to Robertson, 26 September 1909, State Library of NSW, MLMSS 184/7.
34 Lawson to Isabel Byers, *ibid*, Roderick, *Letters*, p. 175.
35 'Reminiscences of Henry Lawson by Isabel Byers', State Library of NSW, MLMSS 3694.
36 'Her Vagabond Friend', *A Fantasy of Man*, p. 908.
37 Lawson to Bland Holt, 29 September 1909, National Library of Australia , MS 2244, Series 1.
38 Lawson to Isabel Byers, 7 October 1909 and 13 October 1909, Roderick, Letters, pp. 176–77.
39 Lawson to Bland Holt, 31 October 1909, National Library of Australia , MS 2244, Series 1.
40 'Reminiscences of Henry Lawson by Isabel Byers', State Library of NSW, MLMSS 3694.
41 Lawson to Bland Holt, 31 October 1909, National Library of Australia , MS 2244, Series 1.
42 'Reminiscences of Henry Lawson by Isabel Byers', State Library of NSW, MLMSS 3694.
43 Lawson to Isabel Byers, 7 October 1909, 11 November 1909, Roderick, Letters, p. 179.
44 T.D. Mutch, 'Lawson The Man And His Country', *Smith's Weekly*, 16 September 1922, p. 10.
45 Lawson to Sister A. de V. MacCallum, 7 January 1910, *ibid*, Roderick, Letters, p. 179.
46 *Ibid.*
47 Brereton to Lawson, 2 January 1910, State Library of NSW, MLMSS 184/7.
48 Roderick, *Henry Lawson*, p. 314.

49 Lawson to Robertson, 13 January [1910], State Library of NSW, MLMSS 184/7.
50 Lawson to Bertram Stevens, 25 January 1910, State Library of NSW, SAFE/Al 29.
51 Bertha to Lawson, 29 January 1910, State Library of NSW, MLMSS 3694, Box 1.
52 Bertha Lawson [Jago], unpublished notes, State Library of NSW, MLMSS 7692.
53 *Bulletin*, 27 January 1910, p. 18.
54 Lawson to Robertson, February 1910, State Library of NSW, MLMSS 184/7.
55 *Ibid.*
56 Bertram Stevens, 'Henry Lawson', State Library of NSW, Angus & Robertson manuscripts, Volume 218, C 863, p. 23.
57 *Ibid*, p 24.

Chapter 25
1   *Ibid.*
2   'Poets at Mallacoota', *Register* (Adelaide), 16 March 1910, p. 7.
3   T.D. Mutch, 'Lawson: The Man And His Country', *Smith's Weekly* (Sydney), 16 September 1922, p. 10.
4   Edwin J. Brady, from J.K. Moir Collection (Box 23/5) of the State Library of Victoria, 1938. From *La Trobe Journal*, No. 70, Spring 2002, p. 86.
5   T.D. Mutch, 'Lawson: The Man And His Country'.
6   Lawson to Robertson, 1 March 1910, State Library of NSW, MLMSS 184/7.
7   T.D. Mutch, 'Lawson: The Man And His Country'.
8   Lawson to his son Jim, 22 March 1910, State Library of NSW, 360/1.
9   *Bulletin*, 28 July 1910, p. 3.
10 *Sydney Mail*, 7 December 1910, p. 10.
11 *Ibid*, 20 December 1911, p. 2.
12 *Worker*, 10 December 1910, p. 29.
13 *A Fantasy of Man*, p. 473.
14 Lawson to Margaret Midson, 7 June 1910, State Library of NSW, MLMSS 184/7.
15 *Ibid*, 18 September 1913, Roderick, *Letters*, p. 215.
16 'Herbert Low', *Worker*, 9 June 1910, p. 21.
17 *Bulletin*, 16 June 1910, Red Page.
18 *A Fantasy of Man*, pp. 980–82.
19 Lawson to Robertson, c. August 1910, State Library of NSW, MLMSS 184/7.
20 Lawson to Sister A. de V. MacCallum, 9 October 1910, Roderick, *Letters*, p. 199.
21 'Henry Lawson', *Bulletin*, 1 September 1910, Red Page.
22 John Lockley (as Redgum) 'George Robertson: Henry Lawson's Tribute', *Sydney Morning Herald*, 2 September 1933, p. 9.
23 Lawson to Robertson, c. December 1910, State Library of NSW, MLMSS 184/7.
24 *Ibid* to Mutch, 22 December 1910, State Library of NSW, MLMSS 426/21.
25 Mary Lucy (Lala) Fisher, born 27 January 1872, Rockhampton, Queensland; died 27 February 1929, Gladesville, Sydney.
26 Lala Fisher to A.G. Stephens, 29 January 1916, Fisher Library Rare Books and Special Collections, University of Sydney Library.
27 *Ibid.*
28 'Advertisements', *Lone Hand*, 1 April 1913, p. lii.
29 *Ibid.*
30 Lawson to Lala Fisher, undated, University of Sydney Library.
31 *A Fantasy of Man*, p. 932.
32 *Ibid*, pp. 933–34.
33 *Ibid*, pp. 935–36.
34 Lawson to Robertson, undated 1911, State Library of NSW, MLMSS 184/8.

35 *Ibid*, 22 September 1911, *ibid*.

36 *Ibid*, December 1911, State Library of NSW, MLMSS 184/7.

37 *Bulletin*, 30 May 1912, p. 47.

38 *Ibid*, 20 August 1908, p. 12.

39 *Ibid*, 20 February 1913, p. 15.

40 *Ibid*, 19 September 1912, p. 47.

41 *Westralian Worker* (Perth), 28 November 1919, p. 1.

42 *Bulletin*, 26 December 191, pp. 47–48.

43 *Ibid*, 8 March 1923, pp. 47–48.

44 *Ibid*, 16 January 1913, pp. 43–44.

45 *Ibid*, 8 March 1923, pp. 47–48.

46 *Lone Hand*, 1 August–1 September 1913.

47 *Ibid*, 'Ah Soon: A Chinese-Australian Story', 1 August 1912, pp. 324–28.

48 *Ibid*.

49 *Ibid*.

50 Lawson to Robertson, 12 August 1912, State Library of NSW, MLMSS 184/7.

51 *Ibid*, 20 December 1912, *ibid*.

52 Jim Lawson to Lawson, 22 December 1912, State Library of NSW, MLMSS 3694.

53 Bertha Lawson (Jnr) to Lawson, undated 1912, *ibid*.

54 *Bulletin*, 27 February 1913, p. 16.

55 'George Lewis Becke', *Port Macquarie News*, 3 December 1948, p. 3.

56 Lawson to Robertson, 15 May 1913, State Library of NSW, MLMSS 184/8.

57 Bertha Lawson, *My Henry Lawson*, pp. 82–83.

58 *Ibid*.

59 'A Prodigal Poet', *Truth*, 21 March 1914, p. 5.

60 Lawson to Shenstone, March 1914, State Library of NSW, MLMSS 184/7.

61 'Callaghan's Hotel', *Bulletin*, 28 January 1915, p. 3.

62 Lawson to Mutch, April 1914, State Library of NSW MLMSS 426/21.

63 'Eurunderee' and 'The Flour Bin'.

64 Lawson to Mutch, 22 April 1914, State Library of NSW MLMSS 426/21.

65 Eurunderee Public School Visitors book – entry for visit of Henry Lawson 20 April 1914, including poem composed during visit [4/7550] and School records, NRS 3931, records. nsw.gov.au.

66 'On looking Through an Old Punishment Book', *A Fantasy of Man*, p. 587. First published in Mudgee's *Western Post*.

67 *Australian Worker* (Sydney), 31 December 1924, p. 13.

68 'Literature: Our Lost Field', *Sydney Morning Herald*, 22 October 1927, p. 13.

69 *Ibid*.

70 *Bulletin*, 2 March 1916, p. 48.

71 *Mudgee Guardian and North-Western Representative*, 23 April 1914, p. 27.

72 *Bulletin*, 9 December 1915, pp. 47–48.

73 *Ibid*.

74 Samuel Henry Prior, born 10 January 1869, Brighton, South Australia; died 6 June 1933 at his Mosman home.

75 Lawson to James E Elliott, undated [May–June 1914], State Library of NSW, MLMSS Al 29.

76 Ibid, [June 1914], ibid.

77 T.D. Mutch in *Henry Lawson by His Mates*, p. 162.

78 Nairn, *The Big Fella, Jack Lang and the ALP 1891-1949*, p. 34.

79 *Bulletin*, 17 September 1914, p. 7.

80 *Ibid*, 15 October 1914, p. 13.

81 *Ibid*, p. 3.

82   *Ibid*, 29 October 1914, p. 3.
83   *Ibid*, 19 November 1914, p. 7.
84   Lawson to 'Barta', 11 February 1915, State Library of NSW, MLMSS 184/7.
85   *Bulletin*, 18 February 1915, p. 24.
86   *Ibid*, 18 March 1915, p. 16.
87   Lawson to Robertson, undated 1915, State Library of NSW, MLMSS 184/7.
88   *Bulletin*, 24 June 1915, p. 14.
89   *Ibid*, 26 August 1915, p. 26.
90   *Ibid*, 9 September 1915, p. 14.
91   *Ibid*, 24 February 1916, p. 14.
92   *Lone Hand*, 1 December 1915, p. 33.
93   The others were T.W. Heney, the editor of the *Sydney Morning Herald*, and E.J. Dempsey
      and E.H. Collis from the *Evening News*.
94   Lawson to G.J. Evatt, Secretary, Water Conservation and Irrigation Commission,
      16 December 1915, State Library of NSW, MLMSS 184/7.
95   Lala Fisher to A.G. Stephens, 29 January 1916, University of Sydney Library.

Chapter 26
1   Lawson to Robertson, [January 1917], State Library of NSW, MLMSS A 1875.
2   Lawson to George Evatt, 14 January 1916, from Roderick, *Letters*, p. 232.
3   'About People', *Murrumbidgee Irrigator* (Leeton), 14 January 1916, p. 4.
4   Lawson to George Evatt, 14 January 1916, from Roderick, *Letters*, p. 232.
5   'Guards of the letters page', *Bulletin*, 5 March 1977.
6   'Travellin', *Bulletin*, 30 March 1916, pp. 47–48.
7   'First Impressions of Leeton', *Murrumbidgee Irrigator*, 28 January 1916, p. 2.
8   'Drought and Irrigation', *Ibid*, 4 February 1916, p. 2.
9   'Bonnie of the Area', *Australian Worker* (Sydney), 28 December 1916, p. 15.
10   *Murrumbidgee Irrigator*, 11 February 1916, p. 2.
11   Lawson to Dr Frederick Watson, 31 March 1916, Roderick, *Letters*, p. 236.
12   'Real Estate', *Sunday Times* (Sydney), 2 December 1917, p. 11.
13   'By the banks of the Murrumbidgee', *Bulletin*, 18 May 1916, p. 22.
14   Jim Grahame, 'Henry Lawson', Cyril Goode Papers, State Library of Victoria, PA 291,
      Box 7.
15   Ibid.
16   Grahame in *Henry Lawson by his Mates*, p. 218.
17   *Ibid*, p. 220.
18   *A Fantasy of Man*, pp. 822–83.
19   'By the banks of the Murrumbidgee', *Bulletin*, 18 May 1916, p. 22.
20   *Bulletin*, 24 April 1919, pp. 47–48.
21   *Ibid*, 10 December 1921, p. 13.
22   Lawson to Bertram Stevens, 1 April 1916, Roderick, *Letters*, p. 239.
23   *Bulletin*, 17 February 1916, pp. 6–7.
24   Isabel Ramsay [as Isabelle Ramsay], 'Poet & Peasant', *Sunday Times* (Sydney), 4 June 1916,
      p. 6.
25   *Ibid*.
26   Gordon to T.D. Mutch, 15 December 1931, State Library of NSW, MLMSS 426/24.
27   *Ibid*.
28   Jim Grahame, 'Henry Lawson', Cyril Goode Papers, State Library of Victoria, PA 291,
      Box 7.
29   Lawson to Robertson, [January 1917], State Library of NSW, MLMSS A 1875.
30   Grahame in *Henry Lawson by his Mates*, p. 247.

31 Lawson to Robertson, [January 1917], State Library of NSW, MLMSS A 1875.

32 *Frank Beaumont* (Beau) *Smith,* born 15 August 1885, Hallett, South Australia; died 2 January 1950, Royal North Shore Hospital, Sydney.

33 'While The Billy Boils', *Sunday Times*, 1 October 1916, p. 13.

34 Lawson to Evatt, 8 November 1916, Roderick, *Letters*, p. 253.

35 Lawson to Robertson, 26 March 1917, State Library of NSW, MLMSS A 1876.

36 'To the Electors of Botany', *A Fantasy of Man*, p. 723.

37 Bertha Lawson, *My Henry Lawson*, p. 86.

38 Lawson to Robertson, 7 September 1917, State Library of NSW, MLMSS 184/7.

39 'Reminiscences of Henry Lawson by Isabel Byers', State Library of NSW, MLMSS 3694.

40 *Land*, 3 May 1918, p. 7.

41 *Bulletin*, 5 December 1918, p. 6.

42 *Ibid*, 21 November 1918, p. 16.

43 Lawson to Robertson, 25 November 1918, State Library of NSW, MLMSS A 1877.

44 'Australian Poetry', *Sydney Morning Herald*, 30 November 1918, p. 8.

45 Preface, Marshall, *The World of the Living Dead*.

46 *Bulletin*, 9 December 1922, pp. 20–22.

47 'Foundation stones of cottage where Lawson lived lay hidden in bushland at Como West', theleader.com.au, 21 January 2020.

48 *Bulletin*, 18 September 1919, p. 16.

49 Lawson, 'Three or Four Archibalds and the Writer', *A Fantasy of Man*, pp. 986–99.

Chapter 27

1 *Birth: A Little Journal of Australian Poetry*, March 1922, p. 25.

2 'An Explanation', *Dawn*, 1 July 1905, p. 5.

3 Lawson to Robertson, 5 December 1919, Prout, *Henry Lawson*, pp. 278–79.

4 Bertha Lawson (Jago), unpublished notes, State Library of NSW, MLMSS 7692.

5 *Lone Hand*, 1 September 1916, p. 214.

6 Lawson to Robertson, 23 March 1917, State Library of NSW, MLMSS A 1876.

7 'Pars About People', *Australian Worker*, 1 April 1920, p. 1.

8 Lawson recorded her name as 'O'Sullivan'.

9 Lawson to Gordon, 22 March 1920, State Library of NSW, MLMSS 184/7.

10 Lawson to C.J. Dennis, 18 March 1920, Fisher Library, University of Sydney.

11 Lawson to Robertson, Prout, *Henry Lawson*, p. 281.

12 Charles Lawson, 'The First Poems of Henry Lawson', *Bulletin*, 23 September 1920, Red Page.

13 'In Memory of Claude Marquet', *A Fantasy of Man*, p. 779.

14 Prout, p. 282.

15 Lawson to Walter Walker, 23 June 1920, State Library of NSW, MLMSS 184/7.

16 'Poet's Pension', *Mudgee Guardian,* 26 July 1920, p. 3.

17 *Ross's Monthly* (Melbourne), *2 October 1920.*

18 Lawson to Robertson, 12 July 1920, State Library of NSW, MLMSS 184/7.

19 *Bulletin*, 28 October 1920, p. 28.

20 Lawson to Robertson, 20 September 1920, State Library of NSW, MLMSS 184/8.

21 *Lone Hand*, 1 February 1921, p. 5.

22 Walter Jago (1885–1943).

23 Lawson to Professor Mungo MacCallum, 21 April 1921, State Library of NSW, MLMSS 184/7.

24 Paul Daley, 'When Douglas Grant met Henry Lawson', guardian.com.au, 27 February 2018.

25 J and A Seymour in *Henry Lawson by his Mates*, p. 299.

26 Lawson to Harry Meatheringham, 20 June 1921, State Library of NSW MLMSS, A29/2.

27 'Week to Week', *Windsor and Richmond Gazette*, 15 July 1921, p. 4.
28 Lawson to Robertson, [Received] 18 July 1921, State Library of NSW, MLMSS 184/8.
29 Lawson to Mutch, State Library of NSW, 4 August 1921, MLMSS 426/21.
30 Lawson to Robertson, [Received] 22 August 1921, State Library of NSW, MLMSS 184/7.
31 Ibid.
32 Lawson to Douglas Robertson, 7 August 1921, *ibid*, MLMSS 184/8.
33 *Ibid*, 24 August 1921, Prout, p. 290.
34 Lawson to Robertson, [Received] 25 August 1921, State Library of NSW, MLMSS 184/8.
35 Lawson to Walter Walker, 27 September 1921, State Library of NSW, MLMSS 184/8.
36 *Bulletin*, 17 November 1921, p. 47.
37 Lawson to Simon Hickey, 23 October 1921, Roderick, *Letters*, p. 410.
38 NSW Hansard 26 October 1921.
39 Webb killed himself later that same year with cyanide while prospecting in Western Australia.
40 *Children of the Bush*, pp. 92–93.
41 Lawson to Charlie Webb, 24 January 1922, State Library of NSW, MLMSS 184/7.
42 Lawson to Walter Walker, 14 February 1922, *ibid*, MLMSS 184/8.
43 *Bulletin*, 9 February 1922, p. 20.
44 *Ibid*, 16 February 1922, p. 47.
45 *Ibid*, 2 March 1922, Red Page.
46 Bertha Lawson, *My Henry Lawson*, p. 81.
47 Bertha Lawson (Jago), unpublished notes, State Library of NSW, MLMSS 7692.
48 Mary Gilmore, note accompanying poem 'Ghost Haunted the Street He Goes', 23 February 1952, Lawson Collection (Lawson 164), Rare Books & Special Collections, Fisher Library, University of Sydney.
49 State Library of NSW, PXB 526.
50 J and A Seymour in *Henry Lawson by his Mates*, p. 299.
51 *Ibid*.
52 *Fair Play*, 4 September 1922.
53 'Reminiscences of Isabel Byers', State Library of NSW, MLMSS 3694.
54 'Henry Lawson Dead', Sun (Sydney), 3 September 1922, p. 2.
55 'Deadly in Earnest and Casually Australian', *A Fantasy of Man*, pp. 828–33.

Epilogue

1 'The Jolly Dead March', *Bulletin*, 11 December 1897, p. 39.
2 'Henry Lawson and I', Dame Mary Gilmore Papers, State Library of NSW, A 3292.
3 Roderick, *Henry Lawson*, p. 395.
4 'Mr. Hughes Tribute', *Maitland Daily Mercury*, 4 September 1922, p. 2.
5 *Truth*, 5 September 1954, p. 40.
6 'Australia Mourns', *Sun*, 4 September 1922, p. 7.
7 Zora Cross, 'Recollections of Henry Lawson', Lawson Collection (204), Fisher Library, University of Sydney.
8 'A Poet's Trifles', *Mail* (Adelaide), 9 September 1922, p. 7.
9 Dame Mary Gilmore Papers, State Library of NSW, A 3292.
10 'Lawson's Life', *Sun*, 8 September 1922, p. 9.
11 'Lawson's Son', *Evening News*, 4 December 1922, p. 7.
12 Prout, *Henry Lawson*, p. 297.
13 Bertha Lawson (Jago), unpublished notes, State Library of NSW, MLMSS 7692.
14 Will Lawson, born 2 September 1876, Gateshead, England; died 13 October 1957, Randwick, Sydney.

15 Alice McNamara to Barta, 5 February 1940, State Library of NSW, MLMSS 3888.
16 Elizabeth Webby, 'Lawson, William (Will) (1876–1957)', *Australian Dictionary of Biography*, Volume 10, (MUP), 1986.
17 Bertha Lawson (Jago), unpublished notes, State Library of NSW, MLMSS 7692.
18 Official inauguration of the Henry Lawson Labor College by the Hon. W.J. McKell, M.L.A., Premier of New South Wales, National Library of Australia, Bib ID: 399574
19 'Works of Henry Lawson Published In Russia', *Northern Star* (Lismore), 4 September 1950, p. 5.

Index

The abbreviation HL refers to Henry Lawson.
Some subentries are ordered chronologically, not alphabetically, for ease of use.
Lawson's poems, stories and other works are indexed separately on page 502.

Index of works by Henry Lawson